RED ROCKS COMMUNITY COLLEGE

U18960 009 617 0

D0712221

58957

GN 790 .J6813 1988

Joussaume, Roger.

Dolmens for the dead

ILL #			
882986			
DPL			
3:22·00			

COMMUNITY COLLEGE
OF DENVER
RED ROCKS CAMPUS

Contents

RED ROCKS
COMMUNITY COLLEGE

List of illustrations

Translator's preface

Europe is a rather small continent with a remarkable number of ancient sites, thanks to a long history of human occupation and to favourable conditions for the survival of fragile archaeological remains. There may be a quarter of a million sites in Britain alone. Few are better known than the megalithic monuments which are the subject of this book, ruins of prehistoric structures built of massive untrimmed rocks. Sites like Avebury in southern England or Carnac in western France still startle even the professionals in the scale of their engineering. Even a rather small megalithic monument, like the dolmen at Browneshill in rural Ireland, is a staggering piece of work, with a capstone weighing 100 tonnes that was raised bodily off the ground.

Equal to the remarkable concentration of archaeological sites in Europe is the remarkable concentration of archaeologists in Europe, again thanks to a long history of occupation – by antiquarians and scientific researchers – and to favourable conditions for the survival of the species. The prehistoric remains of old Europe are now divided between the territories of small nation-states; although scientific techniques are much the same, each country has its own style of study. Sometimes, there is simple chauvinism: a recent fat French book on later European prehistory, in a respected series, left out Britain, Spain and Portugal altogether, presumably thinking they did not really belong in European archaeology. And there is every opportunity for mutual misunderstanding between archaeologists who work with contrary ideas expressed in unfamiliar languages about, supposedly, the same subject; but there is also every chance of benefit when the varied approaches actually complement each other.

National schools partly reflect what archaeological material a national territory happens to hold: palaeolithic remains from the glacial era are so frequent in France that working with them is a mandatory part of every archaeologist's training, while sites of that date are a rarity in Britain. They also reflect different aims for archaeology as an academic inquiry, and this is vividly illustrated by the work being done in Britain and in France on the megaliths of

Europe, a very active interest in both countries at the moment. Part of the interest of M. Joussaume's book is that it is not the kind of thing that is being written by active researchers of the British school, whose work has been taking them in different directions.

Megaliths, gaunt and mysterious ruins of a forgotten past, were obvious curiosities for antiquaries to inquire into. As early as the seventeenth century the mounds in Denmark, France, England and Ireland were being explored, and some kind of sense made of the bones and stones found inside them. Old names and folk-tales of their building by races of giants, or of their curative powers, record an even earlier interest. In the first decades of scientific archaeology, after the idea of prehistory in the 1860s had put the antiquarian collections into a new order, the 'megalithic problem' was a central issue.

The megaliths remain a major focus of research. Bruised and battered, broken up for road-metal or bulldozed for vineyards though they have often been, many megaliths have somehow survived, saved 'by their own weight and worthlessness'. In some areas they still amount to the major stock of prehistoric remains of which we know. The Carnac area of southern Brittany, with its astounding collection of mounds and megaliths, has been studied and explored for decades, yet it has been only in the last couple of years that the first useful traces have been found there of one of the settlements where the megalith-builders may have actually lived. The reasons for building the monuments, whatever they may have been, cannot have been directly to do with day-to-day necessities of food or shelter; but they nevertheless provide indirect information about the societies that built them, about tribal or family territories, if their distribution in the landscape is taken as markers of land ownership. And, since the motives for their construction were surely to do with ancient beliefs, religions and values, it will be by the evidence of the megaliths that we will gain some insight into prehistoric minds – if such an insight can ever be gained.

Before the 'radiocarbon revolution' of the 1970s overturned the old order in European prehistory, the outline of the megalithic phenomenon seemed clear enough. The monuments of the north and west, along the 'Atlantic façade' of Europe from Portugal to Denmark, seemed a unitary phenomenon, whose varied designs and forms could be traced back to the western Mediterranean, and from there back again towards the more developed cultures of the 'most ancient east', whose skill and learning had diffused into barbarian Europe. Radiocarbon dating blew away that 'oriental mirage', as M. Joussaume calls it. We now know that megalithic monuments in western Europe are older than their supposed precursors in the east. And in the west there are two distinct areas, a long way apart in Portugal and in Brittany, where megalith-building is very early indeed; and a case has been made for an autonomous development of a megalithic tradition in other parts of Europe.

A strong concern of British archaeology in the last few years has been the making of social inferences, seeing, for example, if megalithic monuments, and the remains found in them, can indicate whether they were built by stratified societies under the command of chiefs and nobles, or by egalitarian societies. A stage further is to attempt a 'cognitive' archaeology, assessing from the physical relics what might have been going on inside prehistoric minds. Of course those megalithic structures which are the subject of this book usually contain human remains, and so they are places of burial – as M. Joussaume forcefully insists. But the dead are placed in tombs by those that survive them, and the monuments can, for that reason, be seen as 'tombs for (the use of) the living'. The Arc de Triomphe on the Champs Elysées contains a body, that of the Unknown Soldier, but that does not mean its *primary* purpose is as a means of getting rid of a dead body, or that a future archaeologist would find its main value to be in showing what twentieth-century burial rites were like.

French archaeology has stuck more closely to the physical evidence of monument and artefact – according to varying points of view either because it is more effective and practical, or because it is more timid and narrow in its interests. (Ironically, it has been *French* structuralists and post-structuralists, especially anthropologists like Claude Lévi-Strauss, who have been a major influence on the British new wave.) The working-out of culture-history sequences, which sometimes seems in Britain to be an irrelevance or an unpleasant necessity, remains a major aim in the French order of things.

For either tradition of work, megaliths are important. The radio-carbon affair has left some major questions in turmoil. There is new and secure evidence that megalith-building has been invented more than once in Europe, to go with the old evidence from distant regions of the world, in the Far East and in the Americas, that the same engineering devices, and even the same burial rites, were developed in places thousands of kilometres and thousands of years apart. So what is now to be made of the similarities in the megalithic structures in different parts of Europe? In the diffusionist way of thinking, they demonstrated actual cultural links joining the areas settled by megalithic colonists. Should we now see them instead as indicators of the same processes of social and economic development, taking place under broadly similar conditions and therefore arriving at broadly similar results? And if a *broad* common process, such as the pressure on land of a growing European population, may have led to *broadly* similar building habits, there are still the very specific similarities, like the 'porthole' entrances cut through megalithic slabs, to be made sense of. This is a question M. Joussaume covers thoroughly, as he explores the world of megalith-building, not just in prehistoric Europe, but in more recent cultural contexts in Asia, Africa and America. Old oral histories from Madagascar, where they were still building megaliths until a century or two ago, also give him a vivid insight into the living place megalithic monuments are known to have held in one human society.

Ideas are translated from one language to another despite words, rather than because of them. In 1949 Glyn Daniel, until his recent death the senior megalithic scholar in Britain, thought the variety of names then used for the different kinds of monuments were 'notoriously confusing'. Almost 40 years and a radiocarbon revolution or two later, the English names are – to be honest – in a mess, whilst the French names are in a different mess of their own. Take 'cromlech', for example, a word which came into the English language from Cornish and perhaps Welsh. In English, a 'cromlech' is a vague word for any megalithic structure whose uprights huddle together to support a roofing-slab or capstone. In French, which got the word from Breton, *un cromlech* is a circle of well-spaced standing stones without a capstone – megalithic and often prehistoric, to be sure, but not at all the same thing as a 'cromlech'.

The word 'dolmen', which gives the title to this book, has an even more confused meaning and history. It has been used by British archaeologists for a little over a century as a general term for megalithic structures of the upright-plus-capstone variety, that is, as a synonym for what had previously been called a 'cromlech'. The word and the meaning came from the French *dolmen* (and the French, remember, called their stone circles *cromlechs* so as to *distinguish* them from *dolmens*). If you look at the history of the French word *dolmen*, it turns out to be a corruption of British origin, a misreading of the Cornish word *tôlven*, which meant not an artificial construction at all, but a boulder left naturally perched on humps of rock. It has not helped that archaeologists, at different times, in different places, and in different languages, have used the word 'dolmen' under a variety of special definitions. In doing so, they have been bedevilled by a habit, reasonable but very confusing, that has run through European megalithic studies. The monuments are compared and contrasted by the variety of their forms, in their plans, designs, and construction methods, that is by *morphological* features. The main aim of doing this, at least before radiocarbon began to provide independent means of dating, was to recognize the relations of the different designs in space and time, and to set out their evolutionary order (under, as we now know, the mistaken belief they all might ultimately derive from east Mediterranean architecture). The morphological features were, and still quite reasonably are, treated as possible *genetic* markers which may show a direct affinity, how one kind of monument relates to another. Monuments of rather similar form may usefully be given different names if perches on branches of the evolutionary tree seem distant from each other; conversely rather varied monuments, morphologically speaking, may be put together if they seem genetically close. So changes in genetic relations upset names, because these are more than morphological terms – and the genetic relations of European megaliths have been changing a lot recently.

With megalithic terminology in some confusion, a laborious naming of parts is essential here. Roger Joussaume has strong ideas on these matters, and in any case there is no more a universally accepted set of names in French than there is in English. With his permission, we have used the set of English names that seems the least confusing, though we doubt if it is absolutely clear. A 'dolmen' is here used in the vague and broad sense of a rough-stone monument, comprising a chamber made of large upright slabs ('orthostats') supporting a capstone ('roofing-slab'), with or without an entrance-passage, and set in a mound of earth or stones; or the equivalent partly or wholly made of dry-stone walling. As Joussaume strongly argues, the dolmens of prehistoric Europe were, above all, places of burial, so we generally refer to them in the translation as 'chamber-tombs', and use the same term for those not in prehistoric Europe which Joussaume considers comparable. European chamber-tombs have usually been divided into two broad classes: 'passage-graves' have a chamber which is quite distinct from the access-passage which leads to it; for the other class of monument, in which there is no sharp distinction between chamber and passage, we use the French name 'allée couverte' in preference to its English form, gallery grave. For regional types we use regional names when passage-grave or allée is inappropriate or not in common use, so there are Steinkisten in Germany and hunebedden in the Netherlands. One of these regional names from France, which cannot fairly be avoided, is the dolmen simple, set in italics because it is not necessarily a 'simple dolmen' in the English sense. The roof of the chamber, and sometimes of the passage, may be made of piled and overlapping layers of stone, a method called 'false corbelling' (false because it does not make a true arch), and the roof so made is a 'false corbel'. The mound in which a chamber-tomb is set we call a mound in general, a cairn when it is specifically made of stones rather than piled earth, and a barrow when that is the local name. Standing stones we call standing stones, except when the French menhir is appropriate. Not megalithic in the narrow sense of 'built of great stones', but in the same tradition are burial places dug in sand or chalk, or carved into more solid rock. Those in northern France and in the Arles region cut in soft materials we call by the French term hypogée, and those in the solid, elsewhere, by the English 'rock-cut tomb'.

C.R.C.   *Cambridge, September 1986*

Introduction

'Please, Sir, draw me a dolmen!'

I often have to give short lectures on prehistory to school groups. I never fail to ask my audience this question: 'What is a dolmen?' Invariably their arms go up, drawing a large shape in the air, and they tell me that it is a big block of stone held up above the ground by other blocks set in the ground ... and this certainly is the popular image of the dolmen. ...

'Please, Sir, draw me a dolmen.'
'Why a dolmen?'
'For my sheep. ...'

It is true that, not so long ago, a number of dolmens were used for more-or-less domestic purposes: barns, haylofts, sheep-folds (for instance La Frébouchère at Le Bernard in the Vendée), even as a dwelling-house (Kergenteuil dolmen at Trégastel in the Côtes-du-Nord), or as a ballroom (Grand Dolmen of Bagneux near Saumur in Maine-et-Loire), to quote but a few examples among the monuments of France.

I should very much like to have been able to draw a dolmen, and that is in part the reason for this book; but it is not an easy thing, and specialists have practically ceased to use the term in scientific publications.

Imagine three experts, from Denmark, France and Korea. To the Dane, a dolmen is a closed chamber, outlined by large stones and covered with a slab. To the Frenchman, the word by itself means nothing. As for the Korean, he considers a dolmen to be a large lump of undressed stone set on the ground above a burial, which may be contained in a pottery urn.

But perhaps there is one single link between all the dolmens in the world – the use of undressed stone in their construction, but not just any old stones, they must be large stones (*megaliths*). Here the argument fails again, for there are monuments called 'megalithic' in whose construction there is not one large stone. It makes no sense at all.

In fact, there can be no precise and general definition of the word 'dolmen', for it is a popular term ('*stone table*') which has no meaning except in current usage. It could suggest the internal skeleton of a more complex monument whose bones are made of large blocks of undressed stone. Very often nowadays, the mound which covered the megalithic chamber has disappeared through weathering or human activity, and only a few shapeless slabs remain in heath or thicket, haunted by fairies or other supernatural beings.

Anyway, these questions of terminology are not enormously important. It is in no way confusing to keep the name of 'dolmen' for the pile of shapeless stones in the popular imagination. But it should be pointed out that in that sense the dolmen forms only part of a monument, which can have non-megalithic forms but which is generally termed 'megalithic chamber-tomb' by specialists, because these monuments are tombs.

Of course, that is not always what you read in works intended for 'the general public'. Thus F. Niel, in *Connaissance des mégalithes*, which came out in 1976 (this was the second edition of a book first published in 1970 under the title of *La Civilisation des mégalithes*) denies the funerary character of dolmens, based on the fact that in certain areas these monuments were found to contain no human remains. This is partially true for areas where the acidity of the soil has destroyed skeletons, but in limestone areas all the dolmens excavated to date have contained human skeletal remains, sometimes in large quantities. This phenomenon is general for all dolmen-type monuments throughout the world and here, surely, is their first point in common. Those dolmens which no longer contain bodies for reasons of soil chemistry always yield archaeological remains identical to those found in other monuments of the same type. To say, as Niel maintains, that 'not a single object has been found in the dolmens of Korea' is a mistake, and his claim that the *allées couvertes* of the Paris Basin were used as family vaults at a period well after their construction is altogether without foundation. As for the belief that putting only the bones of the deceased in the grave is offering an insult, evidence from Madagascar provides proof that exactly the opposite could have been intended.

So dolmens are tombs, which might imply that the monument should hold a hermetically sealed chamber. However, and we shall see this more precisely later on, these funerary monuments were collective graves in which the bony remains of several bodies were found, which suggests a need for repeated access to the burial space. The users had therefore to maintain a means of access to a chamber which varied in form (circular, polygonal, or rectangular) according to area and period. Several means were envisaged: a movable slab on one of the sides, an easily-removed dry-stone wall, a perforated slab closed by a door of wood or stone; but most often a passage of varying length with some system of closure at one end gives access to the chamber through a mound of earth or stone. We are dealing here with a 'passage-grave', a very widespread type. The most widely accepted definition is that of Dr Jean Arnal: 'The dolmen is an open sepulchral chamber, usually megalithic, covered by a mound and intended to house several burials.'

Each word of this definition is important, because only those monuments which correspond to it exactly can be considered as dolmens. Thus, we have an open structure, or more precisely, one which may be opened at any time. The qualification 'usually mega-lithic' allows the inclusion of monuments formally comparable to megalithic dolmens, but in which the parts built in dry-stone can be a major element; even the roof, instead of being formed from one or several slabs of stone, can be built up in corbelling by piling up small stones overlapping each other (Figure 15). The chamber is 'covered by a mound', fairly high and broad, but necessary to seal the space hermetically, which can take different forms and be bounded either by a facing-wall or 'kerb', or by slabs of stone placed upright. Finally, the chamber is 'intended to house several burials', which rules out rude-stone monuments whose chamber has only one occupant. We would in such a case talk of a megalithic coffer or cist, in so far as the cover of the cist is a single large slab of stone.

I have made a drawing of a theoretical reconstruction of a megalithic passage-grave inside its mound (Figure 1). The chamber here is four-sided and bounded by pillars or orthostats, one of which forms the end-wall. It often happens that the pillars are not touching; in such cases small dry-stone walls effect the closure of the chamber; and that is not, as Niel observes severely of prehistorians, 'a gratuitous affirmation constructed in the comfort of an office, where one is more likely to trap flies than truths'. Examples are very numerous, but we should especially take note of monuments in a good state of preservation. The chamber is covered over by a slab of stone, the 'capstone'; this is still sometimes called a 'table', a souvenir of the period of Celt enthusiasts who imagined Gaulish Druids immolating their human victims on this 'sacrificial table'. The chamber can have a more complex plan, as we shall see in the following pages.

In front of the chamber is an access-passage which is both lower and narrower than the chamber itself. There can be an antechamber between chamber and passage, as is frequently the case in the chamber-tombs of Languedoc particularly. The passage is usually lined with upright slabs, but it can be made of alternating upright slabs and walling, or indeed of dry-stone walling alone. It is usually roofed by juxtaposed slabs of stone. Its floor, like that of the chamber, can be

Figure 1   The different elements of a chamber-tomb under its mound.

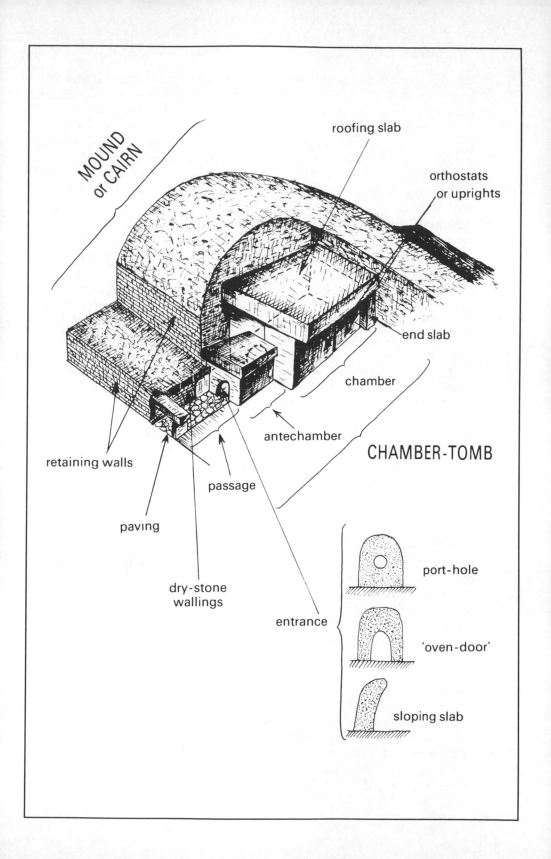

MOUND or CAIRN

roofing slab

orthostats or uprights

end slab

chamber

antechamber

CHAMBER-TOMB

retaining walls

passage

paving

dry-stone wallings

entrance

port-hole

'oven-door'

sloping slab

paved. Certain fittings may be met with where the passage enters the chamber, such as 'porthole' slabs, 'oven-door' slabs or cut-away slabs, which also make an 'oven-door' shape when erected edge to edge.

The dolmen is buried under a mound, which is often also called a 'tumulus' or 'barrow'; it may be called a 'cairn' when it is made solely of small stones. The mound can be round, oval, rectangular or trapezoidal in shape. It can have 'antennae' or 'horns' – sorts of protrusions on either side of the entrance. In external appearance it most often appears as a hump covered with grass, but it usually had a well-built perimeter wall which was slightly higher than the passage. Sometimes several concentric ring-walls are found within the mass of the mound, which could originally have looked like a tower in storeys topped by a dome.

So the dolmen of our old history-books is a long way from the realities brought to light by archaeological research in the field. There are still distinctions, sometimes subtle ones, to be made between different types of dolmens, but we shall discover these as we go along. Perhaps it would be as well to remember, for now, that in western Europe there exist two broad architectural types: passage-graves, in which the chamber is distinct from the passage, and gallery-graves or *allées couvertes*, in which the passage is not differentiated.

Megaliths and charlatans

Since time immemorial megalithic monuments have fascinated people and excited their imaginations. Countless legends surround standing stones, and a whole literature has evolved around dolmens, menhirs and other mounds. It is out of the question to list here all that human wit has managed to devise in the way of theories on the subject, but a few deserve repeating. Among these, the position adopted by Marc Dem (1977) would be a fine example of the exploitation of human gullibility, if only we were taken in by it.

First, you must be convinced that 7000 years ago, when megaliths were being built, 'prehistoric populations were hallucinated creatures, always on the look-out for a leg of aurochs, a rock-shelter, a fire; these men, fashioners of flint axes, sewn into the skins of the beasts they hunted, these victims of cold and storm, this precarious humanity clung to the earth's surface against all odds, rather hindered than helped by the gift of intelligence'. We are almost with Dem in agreement over the period of construction of the first dolmens of western Europe, a little after 5000 BC; but the climatic conditions were far from those of an icy waste, and Dem's bison-hunters, who by the way were not as clumsy as he would have us believe (think of the drawings and paintings at Lascaux, for example), were actually cattle - and sheep-breeders who grew cereals around their farms. They lived in houses of wood covered with puddled clay, with thatched roofs, or built of dry-stone, grouped into large or small villages; and although, indeed, they used no metal, their material equipment in stone, bone, wood and earthenware was already very diverse. They knew how to make clothes, and sailing far from land held no terrors for them. As to fire, they had already known how to produce that for tens of thousands of years.

But our sensational author knows nothing of all this. The men who lived at the time of the megaliths were 'primitive beings', the 'dunces of prehistory'. How did anyone manage to get together enough of these cretins to move a 30-ton rock? We don't know if megalithic man was more or less strong physically than the average modern man, but what we do know is that he was identical in size to us, and that nowadays 170 persons were enough to shift and raise a block of 32 tonnes, a replica of the capstone of one of the dolmens at Bougon (Deux-Sèvres), during an experiment in 1979.

But to construct his theory Dem requires prehistoric men to be imbeciles and the climate to be desert and glacial. There is also the small problem of human remains found in the dolmens, of which some are dated to the fifth millennium BC by radiocarbon. These must have arrived there as a secondary deposit; it is a question of re-use. No, we can't have bones in megalithic monuments with Dem's explanation.

So who did build them all, from northern climes to Africa, from Ireland to Japan? Dem's theory is that it was spacemen, who visited earth in order to mine our uranium supplies. Standing stones and mounds served as beacons on the road: they were just crude signposts, visible from afar as there were no trees on this frozen earth. As for dolmens, they were workmen's huts, or even radiation shelters or 'motels' on the uranium road. The Earth, then, was an inter-galactic service-station, marked out by mounds and standing stones. The large barrows at Carnac offered shelter to aliens, which explains why they are devoid of human remains; superhuman qualities are required to enter a mound without an entrance. As for those little boxes scattered about inside the tumulus with human bones inside, we should take a closer look at those: some of them must contain the remains of some of the people from inside the space-ships.

Dem also theorises: 'Before they were road-signs for mine-workers and metal-porters, between the shore and the seams of grey gold, megaliths, some of them at least, were designed to guide astronauts in their approach manoeuvres.' Now you know the purpose of the Carnac alignments. And then 'the great menhirs form very spaced-out alignments. They carried beacon-lights marking out express routes' – 'airways' of course.

There are many areas in the world where megaliths exist, and they correspond to sites where uranium is found. Where no megaliths exist, no one has yet found the grey gold. There is, conversely, no uranium in Denmark, but there are thousands of megaliths. There is, however, uranium 300 km (186 miles) away; at that period Denmark was probably a dormitory for workers. No doubt it's the same with Roknia in Algeria, but no one has found the mine to this day.

'In eastern Africa, we find two important groups of megaliths: Tambacounda, in Senegal, and Niafunke, in the Sudan, about 200 km south-west of Timbuctoo. It is a curious fact that a line joining these two sites, if prolonged, ends up at Arlit', an important seam of uranium in Niger. After reading 'Mali' for 'Sudan' (the name changed in 1958) and drawing the said line, we find that indeed it passes through the limit of the prehistoric dormitories of Arlit, about 300 km (186 miles) south of the seam.

The aliens did not exploit the United States, Canada, Australia, or South Africa – that is, the richest countries (which is why they still are). In fact, on arrival, not knowing quite where to start, they disembarked in the middle of the dry land, not far from the gulf of Morbihan, and worked eastwards. Only one eccentric went off to Argentina and another fool to Colombia (omitted by Dem).

Finally, they became bored with the earth-dwellers, who showed signs of wanting to become intelligent, broke up most of the monuments they had erected and never came back.

Now, it amuses me to see Obélix carrying his *menhir* about wherever he goes, even though I know that this type of monument had ceased to be made about 1500 to 2000 years before the adventures of these brave Gauls. Astérix was designed to make people laugh, and if Dem's opus had been written with the same aim, I would have been among the first to applaud, because it certainly made me laugh. Unfortunately, that was not the case, and it is very sad. 'The author does not merely form a hypothesis, he verifies it by patient and prodigious research in the field all over the world', we are told. I feel we are being made fun of, and taken for the imbeciles so well described by the author.

Megaliths, time and space

Although it is easy for our Cartesian minds to comprehend that we are now at the end of the second millennium AD, and although we are in nineteen-hundred-and-something, questions of dating appear more complicated when the events took place before the zero year of our calendar. For example, 2500 BC is a date from the middle of the third millennium before the Christian era, 2900 BC is a date from the beginning of the same third millennium BC, and of course 2300 is from the third quarter. It's simple enough, but we are not used to these kinds of mental gymnastics;

0 to 1000 is first millennium BC;

1000 to 2000 is second millennium BC;
2000 to 3000 is third millennium BC;
3000 to 4000 is fourth millennium BC;
4000 to 5000 is fifth millennium BC.

Talking of dates, we must make one thing quite clear. About 30 years ago long lists of dates were established by means of radiocarbon dating; some time later, we realised that they were not accurately measuring calendar years, and in recent times, we have learnt how to correct the discrepancy. Generally speaking, it is these 'calibrated' or 'corrected' dates, translated into 'real' calendar years, which will be given here, and we shall see how much they upset long-held ideas about the influence of the great civilisations on the 'primitive peoples' in the areas surrounding them, in the 'fertile crescent' of the Near East in particular.

Let us set down a few major dates for western Europe, the area where megaliths seem longest established and most abundant:

In the Iberian peninsula, agriculture appears around 5500 BC, the first dolmens around 4400 BC, and copper around 3400 BC, in the south.

In south-western France, agriculture appears a little before 5000 BC, the first dolmens around 4600 BC, and copper about 2700 BC.

In England, agriculture appears about 4300 BC, the first long mounds about 3700 BC, and copper about 2500 BC.

In Denmark, agriculture appears around 4200 BC, and the first dolmens about 3600 BC.

For comparison, note that the pyramids of Egypt date from the beginning of the third millennium BC, and the *tholoi* (tombs) of Mycenae from the second millennium BC.

A distribution map of the megalithic monuments known as 'chamber-tombs' (Figure 2) shows a strong concentration of the architectural type in the western part of Europe, from Scandinavia to the southern tip of the Iberian peninsula, taking in the British Isles and France. This being so, it seems sensible to chart our journey through this huge area following a north-south sequence in a geographical order which is independent of chronology. From there we will progress to the Mediterranean islands and to the Italian peninsula, then into Africa (essentially North Africa and Ethiopia, but also the Central African Republic), to the Arabian peninsula (as yet still largely unexplored) and Madagascar, where we will find some latter-day examples of megalith-building. We shall reach the Near East and the ancient Transjordanian monuments, then the Caucasus and its pierced dolmens, before reaching India and the numerous funerary monuments of the Deccan. Then we shall find megaliths in the Far East

(Manchuria, Korea and Japan), and a great leap across the Pacific will bring us to South America and the monuments of Colombia.

Figure 2   Distribution map of chamber-tombs in Europe, North Africa, and the Near East. Chamber-tombs occur in the hatched areas.

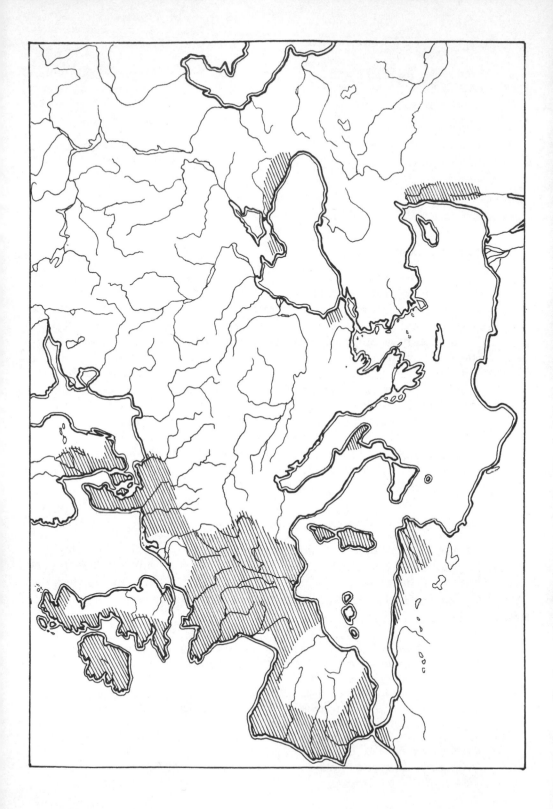

1. Northern Europe

Long mounds

We shall begin our journey through the world of 'dolmens' in northern Europe, where monuments occur in large numbers from Poland to the Low Countries, taking in north Germany and Denmark. But here the first problem arises: there exist in these areas monuments which are formally comparable to the others, but which did not contain as part of their construction, that is, in primary position, a chamber-tomb of any kind. We must pause for a word about them, as these non-megalithic monuments are very often early in date; sometimes they are older than the megalithic monuments of the region. Besides, they often have one or several chamber-tombs in the bulk of their mounds in a secondary context, that is, placed into the monument at a later date.

The phenomenon of non-megalithic mounds extends into the British Isles and Atlantic France, where it will therefore also be dealt with in this chapter.

Long mounds in Poland and northern Europe

At the third Atlantic Conference on megalith-building, in 1969, Konrad Jazdzewski set out his ideas on the relations between the Kujavian barrows of Poland and megalithic tombs in northern Germany, Denmark and western European countries.

Figure 3   Megalithic monuments in Poland, north Germany, and Scandinavia. 1. Distribution map of chamber-tombs with polygonal chambers (1), and of those with quadrangular chambers (2). (After E. Aner, 1963, and L. Kaelas, 1981)
2. Group of long mounds at Sarnavo, Poland. (After K. Jazdzewski, 1973)
3. (a) Plan of the mortuary house at Tustrup, Denmark, and (b) reconstruction of its original form. (After P. Kjaerum, 1955 and 1967)
4. Chamber-tomb at Kruckow, East Germany, in its elongated trapezoidal mound. (After E. Schuldt, 1972)
5. Chamber-tomb of the hunebed *type at Thuine, north Germany. (After E. Sprockhoff, 1938)*

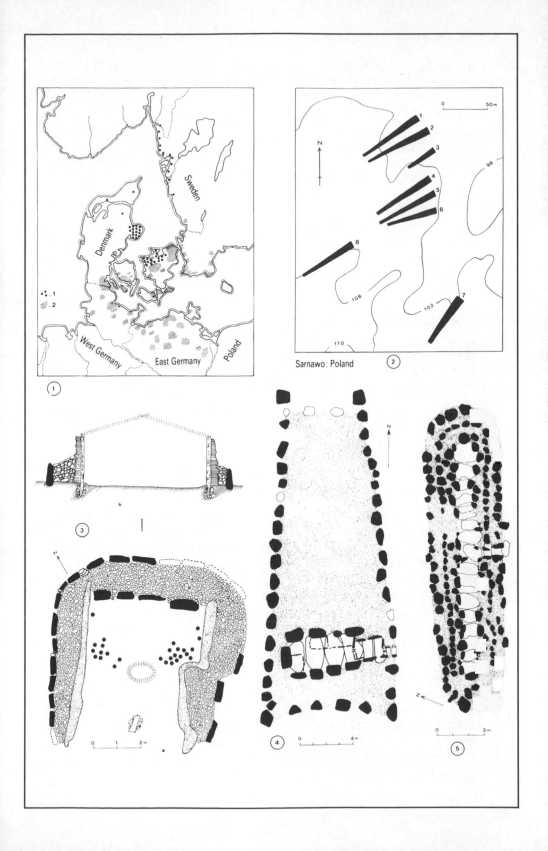

Sarnawo: Poland

The Kujavian mounds (Figure 3:2) form a group of monuments, trapezoid or practically triangular in shape, which were built in Poland, essentially in Kujavia, an area between the lower Vistula and the middle Warta. These mounds are wider and higher at the front end, towards the east, and are surrounded by large erratic blocks which can be man-high. Their bulk is made up of earth taken from ditches along their long sides. They are from 15 m (49 ft) to 150 m (492 ft) long. Their original height is estimated at 3 m (10 ft) or 4 m (13 ft) at the eastern end, and 1 m (3 ft) or 1.5 m (5 ft) at the other, almost-pointed end.

Usually the Kujavian mound was made for a single person, whose body was buried, uncremated, extended on its back in a grave dug in the front part of the monument. This grave, sometimes surrounded and covered over with stones, occasionally contained the remains of several individuals, and we note particularly the case of two men with trepanned skulls from mound V at Wietrzychowice in the Kolo district. A single mound might contain several superimposed individual burials of the Bell-beaker culture. The grave goods are crude (unornamented collared flasks, cups, two-handled amphorae or small big-bellied ones, sometimes large flint blades with retouched edges, long scrapers on flint blades, boars' tusks, yellow amber beads, and trapezoidal flint arrowheads), but for the most part there is nothing. The scattered sherds collected in the front part are perhaps the result of ritual breakage. The existence of hearths and kitchen debris probably indicates funeral feasts. In certain monuments these hearth-layers contained not only animal bones, but also calcined human bones; thus at Sarnowo the calcined bones of five to nine individuals lay in a grave bare of goods, situated near the lower-lying burials.

Detailed excavations have shown that wood was routinely used with stone and earth in the construction of long mounds. At Gaj I, in Kolo district, the remains of a wooden chamber were disclosed at the wider end. This rectangular enclosure, 4 m by 4.5 m (13 ft by 15 ft), had a floor of beaten clay in the middle of which was a hole about 1 m (3 ft) wide and deep. From the bottom of this hole, charcoal, fragments of daub and pottery fragments of Bell-beaker type were excavated. This room, perhaps a religious place above the sepulchre, appeared to have been deliberately burnt. Other individual burials were placed in holes covered by rough stones.

From the pottery and from the radiocarbon dates obtained, the building of the first Kujavian mounds can be dated to the turn of the fifth and fourth millennia BC. Occasionally they were reutilised later to house a megalithic monument of the dolmen type, but often a necropolis of flat tombs of similar date is found close to them. We can therefore ponder about social differences between the users of these small tombs, whose tradition is the older, and the users of the imposing mounds of earth and stone.

According to certain scholars such as Gordon Childe, the builders of the Kujavian mounds of the Bell-beaker culture were imitating the plan of the large dwellings of a group from the Lengyel culture; this idea was taken up by Stuart Piggott, who indicates the possibility of borrowings from other Danubian cultural groups. But with Jazdzewski, we must be surprised that this kind of mound has not been built elsewhere by other Danubian people, and indeed the folk who built them in Kujavia did not live in elongated trapezoid houses at all, but in almost-square ones. This idea of a 'house of the dead' to mirror those of the living, tempting though it is, is therefore not borne out in Poland.

Long mounds without megalithic chambers from the neolithic period are known from Poland through north Germany, Denmark and southern England and into western France, but they display some morphological and chronological differences.

In north Germany (Mecklenburg) and Denmark (Jutland), the Bell-beaker mounds are usually a more definitely trapezoidal shape than those on the other side of the Oder, which tend to be more rectangular. Trapezoidal mounds are still numerous, but rectangular monuments predominate, often in groups and sometimes mixed in with dolmenic complexes. It is practically impossible to tell the difference from external appearances between long mounds with and without a chamber-tomb in those areas where the mounds are surrounded by blocks of stone and dry-stone walling, as they are in England and also in Brittany.

In 1979 Roenne published the results of the excavation of one of the most-studied long mounds in Denmark, Bygholm Nørremark in Jutland. This 60 m (197 ft) long trapezoidal mound belongs to the early Danish Neolithic, which begins with the emergence of agriculture about 4200 BC. In its first phase, the trapezoidal floor was bounded by a trench which held the base of a wooden palisade. Two complexes were shown by traces left on the ground. To the east, a first complex comprised two wooden houses. The first was empty, the second contained the burial in a wooden coffin of a 13 or 14-year-old adolescent, who appeared to have been killed by an arrow. The arrowhead was found at the level of the breast. An amber bead was probably fastened to the dead person's belt and, judging by the size of the funerary structure, he must have belonged to a high-ranking family. Further to the west was found another burial, a grave in which lay four adults, two with heads to the west and two to the east, with no accompanying goods or pottery. No wooden structure surmounted this burial, but a small house had been built not far from there, probably a ritual structure related to the burial, as in the first complex. Things probably remained like this for some time; then the structures fell into disrepair. A mound of earth covered over the whole assembly and was surrounded by large stones. Later, the tumulus was extended to a length of 80 m (262 ft) and a megalithic grave was built into the bulk of it. The discovery on the ground of traces of division of the mound by wooden palisades has led in latter days to a modification of ideas about the large structures at Barkaer, till then interpreted as two large dwellings each comprising several rooms. Thus one of these structures was 80 m (262 ft) long by 6 m (20 ft) wide on average, and was considered to be composed of 26 rooms each about 3 m (10 ft) long. Perhaps they were in reality just two long mounds, compartmented in the style of Bygholm Nørremark.

So we see what complexity a long mound can hide. At the same time it must be admitted that few excavations of large monuments have so far been carried out to this level of scholarship; hence there is very limited information, indeed practically nothing, on matters relating to France. However, it appears, through Danish excavations in particular, that these large mound structures seem to have been built for a single person, as in Poland. The egalitarian character of neolithic society posited by some scholars cannot be applied quite so categorically to the early Neolithic of northern Europe.

Long barrows in Great Britain

Long mounds of earth without megalithic chambers have been known for a very long time in Great Britain. Two hundred and thirty 'earthen long-barrows' have been recorded in the area of the neolithic Windmill Hill culture, most of them in Wessex. They fall into five major groups, and Colin Renfrew has shown a correlation between the long barrows and sites with interrupted surrounding ditches, 'causewayed enclosures'. There would therefore be five territories, each supporting one group of long mounds and a causewayed camp, with its ring of parallel interrupted ditches: the Dorset group and Maiden Castle camp; the Cranborne Chase group and Hambledon Hill camp; the eastern Salisbury Plain group and Whitesheet Hill camp; the western Salisbury Plain group and Robin Hood's Ball camp; and lastly the north Wiltshire group with the camps at Windmill Hill and Knap Hill.

The long barrows are generally oriented east-west and measure from 30 m (98 ft) to 120 m (394 ft) long, with one giant at Maiden Castle 550 m (1800 ft) long. They are mostly built on high sites on chalk land. Two basic forms are recognised: one has parallel sides and a constant height from one end to the other; the other is trapezoidal in plan, with the eastern end higher and wider, reminiscent of the Polish monuments. Like these too, the long barrows of southern England were constructed from ditch-quarries dug parallel to the long sides of the monument; this characteristic is also found in the long mounds of central western France. In some cases the ditch-quarries follow the shape of the ends of the mound, leaving only a narrow passage.

Usually tombs were situated under the higher and wider eastern end, but at South Street and Beckhampton in the north Wiltshire group no inhumations were found, and English archaeologists think that these mounds could have been cenotaphs and never held any burials.

As a general rule, the long barrows house several burials: six on average, and more than 50 in the mound at Fussell's Lodge (Figure 9:1). The bodies are placed directly on the ground, and more rarely in pits, but often they are incomplete or disarticulated, which leads us to suppose that they have been stripped of flesh before being put into the mound. Perhaps the body was exposed in the open; later the bones were collected and deposited in a 'room of the dead'. The construction of a mound would be justified when a sufficient number of bodies lay in the 'house of the dead'. Modern excavations of long barrows have proved the existence of such a wooden mortuary enclosure where bones were stored. The erection of a mound over the 'house of the dead' thus corresponds to a final phase in the funerary rites of neolithic man in these parts.

The complexity of structure of the long barrows has been revealed by such excavations as Nutbane in Hampshire, Wayland's Smithy in Oxfordshire, or Fussell's Lodge in Wiltshire. At Wayland's Smithy, a primary oval mound was enclosed by a long mound, associated with a dolmen situated at its eastern end. The dolmen is in a secondary context in a long trapezoidal mound, which covers an earlier structure (Figure 9:4).

At Hambledon Hill, Dorset, Roger Mercer has in recent years been able to study a particularly important group of structures comprising an enclosure with interrupted ditches, two or three in places (this 'causewayed enclosure' is oval in plan and measures 340 m (1115 ft) by 270 m (886 ft); an exterior ditch (the 'cross dyke'); and a long barrow between the causewayed enclosure and the cross dyke.

At the bottom of the ditches of the causewayed enclosure were found large quantities of organic material, made up of animal and human bone-remains, skulls among them. These deposits seem to have been intentional. Two graves, dug into the bottom of the ditch, yielded entire skeletons accompanied by offerings and covered by a small cairn. The remains of 65 individuals were recovered in this way along a stretch of ditch representing 20 per cent of the whole, which led Mercer to estimate 325 persons in all in the ditches of the enclosure. However, even if the two bodies found in pits in the bottom of the ditch were put there deliberately, it seems that the scattered bone fragments fell in, for the most part. According to Mercer, the inside of the enclosure would have been a funerary area where the bodies were exposed. The retrieved bones would then be deposited in the ditches, and some in the barrow, thus perhaps indicating a kind of social differentiation.

In Denmark, enclosed sites, such as Sarup, are dated to the end of the fourth millennium and seem to have a ritual purpose in their first phase of use. They are contemporary with the great building period of megalithic monuments. These chamber-tombs, 108 in number, have been attributed to the Sarup complex and can be grouped into 16 territories. In a second phase, at the turn of the fourth and third millennia BC, a change seems to occur in the function of the Sarup enclosure, which takes on a domestic usage.

Causewayed enclosures of interrupted ditches are known in central western France, where they are a little later than the English ones. And less work has been done on them. But the Champ-Durand site at Nieul-sur-l'Autize with its triple ditch, which we have been studying for a dozen years or so, seems also to have had a funerary rôle, to judge by the entire bodies as well as scattered fragments of human bone which have been discovered in the ditches. Maybe the interior surface served as an area for the exposure of skeletons, as at Hambledon Hill. But here it seems that the stripped bones were put into the banks of earth and stones which bordered the ditches and it was not until later, when these masses crumbled, that the skeletal remains ended up in the ditch.

In fact, nothing at Champ-Durand proves that the internal surface had a funerary purpose; however, some kilometres away, J.-P. Pautreau found two burials inside the multiple-ditched enclosure of Montigné at Coulon (Deux-Sèvres), which indicated the existence of primary burials within such a site.

The funerary role of causewayed enclosures is thus certain in central western France, but it was perhaps not their only purpose. Each enclosure can be considered as the centre of a territory, a place for meetings, markets, and religious goings-on, for a population living round about, who came there to bring their dead or a few parts of the skeletons, as a secondary deposit in the banks of earth and stones which lined the ditches. But we cannot prove the existence of long mounds contemporary with the enclosures in central western France, although traces recorded by Marsac using aerial photography could correspond to the ditches surrounding such structures.

In Wessex, the five identified groupings are seen to represent tribal entities controlled by an aristocracy who were buried in long barrows. The main centre of each region would have been the causewayed enclosure, which had a social, religious and economic purpose. The farmers would have lived in small social units in isolated farms.

In England, some dates for long barrows indicate usage from the beginning of the fourth millennium BC. So they are earlier than the phase of megalithic-chamber-building considered by English arch-aeologists to be a stone realisation of the wooden 'house of the dead'. The dolmen-type monuments of southern England would have been the result of local development without outside influence. According to Renfrew, this region was one of the creative centres of dolmens in megalith-building. This would deny any influence from the megalith-builders of Armorica, which were, however, largely earlier in date.

Long mounds in Atlantic France

A few long mounds are known in the north of France, such as Wimereux and Fontbourdaine (Pas-de-Calais), which seem to have produced traces of cremations, as in the hundred or so trapezoidal long barrows of the north-east of England, where the bone remains were stripped of flesh before cremation.

Besides these, Sigfried de Laet notes two unexplored mounds at Ottenbourg and Grès-Doiceau in Brabant, Belgium.

La Commune-Sèche mound at Colombiers-sur-Seulles (Calvados) is 65 m (203 ft) long and shaped like an elongated trapezoid. A small circular chamber was found at the eastern end in 1829, and recent excavations have revealed another chamber with a short passage in the central part. This could be a secondary intrusion into a pre-existing long mound.

Long mounds also occur in Brittany, such as Bretineau, or Broga at Guérande (Loire-Atlantique) which is 70 m (230 ft) long, 12 m (39 ft) wide at the north-east end and 8 m (26 ft) wide at the south-east. The monument, built of packed earth, is bounded by a kerb of granite blocks, up to 2.3 m ($7\frac{1}{2}$ ft) high, set close to each other.

In the Carnac area, there are many mounds whose trapezoid shape has been stressed many times; thus Mané-Ty-Ec measured 50 m (164 ft) long by 10 m (33 ft) and 14 m (46 ft) wide at the ends.

The Bilgroix mound at Arzon (Morbihan), recently discovered, and excavated by C. T. Le Roux and his team, measures 120 m long with an average width of 16 m ($52\frac{1}{2}$ ft) and a height of 2 m ($6\frac{1}{2}$ ft).

This tradition of mounds recurs in Ille-et-Vilaine with La Croix-Saint-Pierre at Saint-Just, and in the Côtes-du-Nord with Notre-Dame-de-Lorette at Quillio, but these are rectangular structures bounded by large blocks, some 20 m ($65\frac{1}{2}$ ft) long and 5 m ($16\frac{1}{4}$ ft) to 7 m (23 ft) wide, oriented east-west.

Long mounds used to be numerous in central western France. Many have disappeared under the bulldozer, to make way for cereal cultivation of the rich plains. At La Grosse-Motte at Bouhet (Charente-Maritime), a few post-holes under a trapezoidal mound 60 m (197 ft) long could have belonged to a wooden 'house of the dead'.

At Bougon (Deux-Sèvres), J.-P. Mohen and his team studied two long mounds. Mound B contained two small stone chests, and a secondary intrusion of two passage-graves with four-sided chambers; the ends of the 80 m (262 ft) long trapezoidal mound had been cut off by the construction of one passage-grave with a round chamber and another with a four-sided chamber. The dating obtained for the circular chamber implies that the long mound had been erected during the first half of the fifth millennium BC, but it is not known what was underneath it.

Intensive research in recent years in the forest of Benon (Charente-Maritime) has led to the discovery of about 15 mounds scattered between various cemeteries. Many of them are long mounds whose study has only just begun. They are on the first ridge of high ground overlooking the Poitevin Marais to the north. Moindreaux mound, the sole survivor of a group of three, is 85 m (279 ft) long; its eastern face measures 16 m (52½ ft) wide and its western 10 m (33 ft). As with most of the long mounds in the area, it is higher at the east than the west. One of the Champ-Châlon mounds, also oriented east-west, is 40 m (131 ft) long by 10 m (33 ft) and 5 m (16½ ft) wide at its ends. It was bounded by a wall of dry-stone and had been built from quarry-ditches dug 3 m (10 ft) outside the long sides.

Some monuments, such as Prissé-la-Charrière (Deux-Sèvres) and the Tombe de La Demoiselle at Le Thou (Charente-Maritime), are over 100 m (328 ft) long. La Demoiselle is of earth and has an average width of 9 m (29 ft). At its centre was a small stone coffin containing a fragment of human skull.

But there are even more imposing mounds in central western France. The most spectacular form the group at Tusson (Charente) where there are three gigantic mounds formerly surrounded by 20 or so smaller ones, now destroyed. Le Gros Dognon is 150 m (492 ft) long by 45 m (148 ft) wide and 10 m (33 ft) high; Le Petit Dognon, 85 m (279 ft) by 30 m (98 ft) by 3 or 4 m (10 or 13 ft); and Le Vieux Breuil, 50 m (164 ft) by 28 m (92 ft) by 3 or 4 m (10 or 13 ft). Not far from this group, Mound IV at Luxé, which also seems to have been surrounded by other mounds, is 100 m (328 ft) by 30 m (98 ft) by 10 m (33 ft). Only their huge bulk has saved them from destruction, like the mound at Ligné, also known as Le Gros Dognon, which stood a few years ago in a group of mounds which were getting in the way of cultivation and were destroyed. How many cemeteries have disappeared in this way? We should count these casualties in the middle west of France in hundreds, because the monuments were built for the most part not with big stones but with simple dry-stone walling. This is obviously a question of terrain; you don't build in chalk, where the rock breaks into little square blocks, in the same way as you would in granite.

Among the large monuments of central-western France, La Motte-des-Justices at Thouars (Deux-Sèvres) should also be listed. This one has a rectangular plan 174 m (570 ft) by 16 m (52½ ft) to 18 m (59 ft), and is 1.5 m (5 ft) high to the south-east, with a regular slope down to the north-west. But what does it hide? In the same *département* is La Motte-de-Puitaillé at Assais, 140 m (459 ft) by 55 m (180 ft), made up of three small mounds of which the highest, to the east, measures almost

13 m (43 ft), and the lowest, to the west, perhaps 12 m (39 ft). The group seems to be ringed by a single wall. Here, as with all the giants of the middle west, we do not know what is inside. Of course, comparisons may be made with the 'Carnac' mounds in Brittany, like Le Moustoir (90 m [295 ft] by 40 m [131 ft] by 8 m [26 ft]), Saint-Michel (125 m [410 ft] by 60 m [197 ft] by 10 m [33 ft]), and Le Mané-Lud at Locmariaquer, comparable in its rectangular form and dimensions to Saint-Michel. At Arzon, by contrast, the Tumiac mound is circular, 200 m (656 ft) round with a height of 15 m (49 ft). We know that these Breton monuments contained rich goods in a chest placed centrally or at either end: a great ceremonial axe with precious stones, beads and pendants in profusion, a collar of green serpentine (Mané-er-Hroeck). They were built in the French middle Neolithic, that is, at the same time as some of the passage-graves, and could indicate social differentiation at any given time.

To the south of the middle west, in Aquitaine, we currently know of two non-megalithic mounds. The Bernet mound at Saint-Sauveur (Gironde), made of sand and bounded by a dry-stone wall, is 26 m (85 ft) by 14 m (46 ft) by 1 m (3 ft) high. As is often the case, a chamber-tomb occupied one end and seemed to be secondary in the structure. At the centre of the mound was a stone box containing one skeleton accompanied by two pots of the middle neolithic type. Between this chest and the northern end, the excavators exposed a series of post-holes, which could once more be interpreted as the traces of a wooden 'house of the dead'.

So was there, along the Atlantic edge of France, a funerary architecture of long mounds, before the construction of passage-graves? It is still difficult to reply to this question, but some evidence tends towards this assumption, at least regarding the middle west and Aquitaine.

In the Lot and Aveyron, 50 or so long mounds have been counted. Most often the mound these days displays an oval shape, but as few excavations have been undertaken, we cannot pronounce upon the original architecture of these monuments of which some, such as Capdenaguet mound (Aveyron), take the form of an elongated trapezoid. This monument is oriented east-west, and is 48 m (157 ft) long. Its eastern face is perhaps 12 m (39 ft) wide, its western face 4 m (13 ft). As is often the case in this area, it contains a small chamber-tomb at its eastern end, but we cannot tell whether it is primary to the mound or intrusive. It is thus not possible to establish a link between these long structures and the long mounds of the middle west.

Since leaving Poland, we have traced long mounds through northern Germany, Denmark and England to reach western France. This apparent unity could be completely fictitious, and some authors have noted the morphological differences which exist between the practically triangular mounds of Poland, the Danish ones which are mostly rectangular, and the trapezoidal mounds of Great Britain and western France. However, we notice that the 'triangular' mounds in Poland are in fact trapezoidal; that there are trapezoidal mounds as well as rectangular ones in north Germany and Denmark; that both architectural types occur in England also; and, although trapezoidal mounds predominate in Atlantic France, rectangular ones are also found there. We should also note that wooden structures have been recognised inside the mounds, in France as well as in England, Denmark and Poland, all similarly situated at one end of the monument. The little that we know about the French monuments seems to indicate that they covered one individual burial, as in Poland and, sometimes, in Denmark, but in very different forms; while in England we are dealing with collective burials, apparently belonging to a single family group.

The earliest dates come from the French monuments, and these are of the fifth millennium BC – that is, before megalithic structures. The English and Nordic monuments seem to be of much the same period, and are dated from the beginning of the fourth millennium BC. If there is a link between these monuments, therefore, we must seek their origins in Atlantic France, which has the oldest chamber-tombs in Europe.

But after what we have said about the differences between these architectural types, should we really be looking for links and therefore a common origin for this group? Personally, I think we should, but that is only an idea, not proven up to now – no more than the reverse idea, which is currently enjoying better favour among specialists.

Ending this section, we note that long mounds belong to the northern world: not one is known in the Iberian peninsula, which is, however, very rich in chamber-tombs, nor in the Midi of Mediterranean France, where dolmens are equally numerous. Yet the custom of establishing a funerary structure at the larger end of an elongated trapezoidal surface occurs in the Franche-Comté and as far as the Valais in Switzerland, but not until a final phase of the Neolithic.

Chamber-tombs in the Nordic countries

In Denmark, the first megalithic burials are in long mounds, *langdysse*.

Figure 4   Megalithic monuments in Mecklenburg, northern East Germany. (After E. Schuldt, 1972)
1. Plan of the chamber-tomb at Gnervitz, Rostock, with the distribution of finds in its compartmented chamber.
2. Plan of the chamber-tomb at Kruckow, Demmin.
3. Plan of the chamber-tomb at Liepen, Rostock, with the deposits of bones in its internal cells.

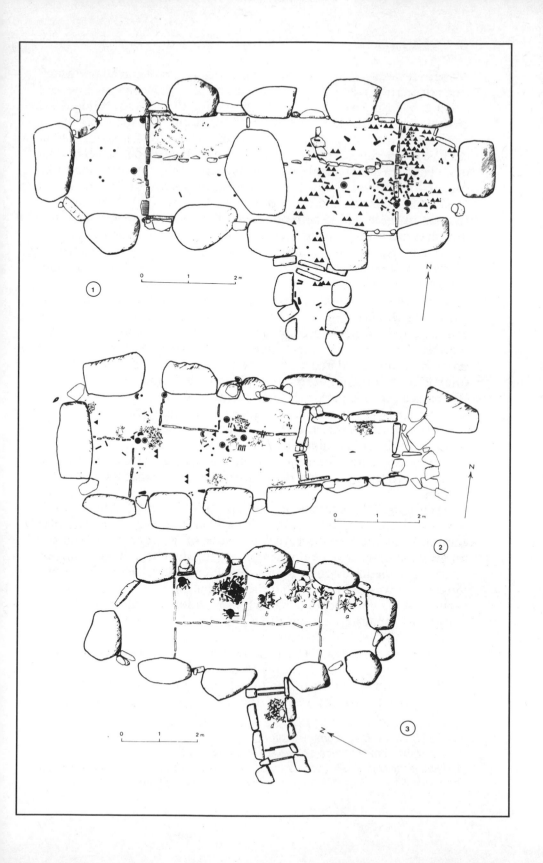

1

0   1   2 m

N

2

0   1   2 m

N

3

0   1   2 m

Z

These are chests made of upright stones, often covered by a large block (the northern '*Urdolmens*'). There may be several in the same mound (Figure 5:5 and 6). Thus in Moen island, the long mound called Groenjaegers Hoej (the 'Green Hunter's Mountain') is oriented east-west, and forms a rectangular platform 102 m (335 ft) long by 10 m (33 ft) wide, bounded by 134 upright stones, which reach the height of a man, between which small walls of dry-stone were built to retain the soil of the mound. To the west a large block of stone conceals a megalithic chamber, and two more, unroofed, are to be found more to the east in the bulk of the monument. There are some much shorter long mounds than this, but there are longer ones also, such as the one on Funen island, near Lindeskov village, which measures 166 m (545 ft), is surrounded by 126 upright stones, and contains a small megalithic chamber.

Such mounds occur in northern Germany but also in Lower Saxony, where the 'Fiancés' of Visbek some 50 km (31 miles) south-west of Bremen form a fairly impressive group with the monuments surrounding them. 'La Fiancée' is four-sided (80 m [262 ft] by 7 m [23 ft] at its narrowest end), bordered by upright stones of decreasing height from one end to the other of the mound, which hides a chamber at its centre. 'Le Fiancé', for his part, measures 108 m (354 ft) by 10 m (33 ft); he is oriented east-west and while the blocks which circumscribe him reach 2.4 m (8 ft) at the eastern end, they are only 1.4 m (4½ ft) high to the west. He harbours a central chamber roofed by five large slabs. Among the dozen or so megalithic monuments of this region, several could be compared to the Dutch *hunebedden* which we shall discuss in the next section.

So the megalithic chamber makes its appearance in a long mound, of which we have seen there exist a fair number, not megalithic, in which careful excavations have revealed traces of wooden structures no longer existing today. The origin of rectangular megalithic chambers has been much discussed by Danish and German archaeologists. For a long time it was considered that they were a 'surface' version, inside a mound, of the underground chests for individual burials of the Beaker culture. But that implies that these first megalithic constructions held only one body, which, according to Kaelas, does not seem certain.

While agriculture is attested in Denmark from 4200 BC, the first megalithic tombs, small rectangular dolmens, make their appearance in Zealand in the middle of the fourth millennium. From there, they slowly moved into the rest of the country, where different types

---

Figure 5   Megalithic monuments in Denmark. (After P. V. Glob, 1967)
1–4. Varieties of passage-grave: 1 Mols; 2 Slots Bjerby; 3 Stenstrup; 4 Alsberg.
5–6. Megalithic chambers in long mounds: 5 Sǿnderholm; 6 Gunderslevholm.

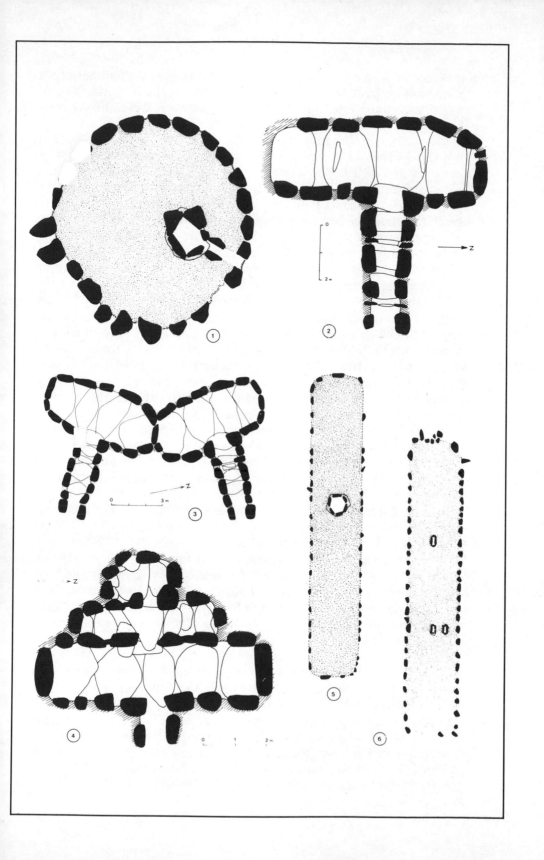

evolved. It would seem that the majority of simple chamber-tombs were built in the course of a few centuries during the second half of the fourth millennium BC, but the first passage-graves were already being built, and non-megalithic tombs also persisted.

Passage-graves are numerous in Denmark, but their construction is not very varied: chamber-tombs with polygonal chambers and short passages are built inside a circular mound bounded by large blocks, such as the chamber-tomb of Mejls in south-west Jutland, or Knebel (Figure 5:1). It seems that this is the earliest type of passage-grave. Next, the chamber becomes elongated, and is set perpendicular to the passage (Figure 5:2). Sometimes chambers are contiguous (Figure 5:3) or form complex groups (Figure 5:4). They can be included in mounds of different shapes, even long trapezoidal or rectangular mounds in the northern megalithic area (Figure 3:4).

Grønhoej ('Green Mound') passage-grave at Horsens, in east Jutland, has a sub-circular chamber scarcely 3 m (10 ft) in diameter, approached by a corridor which measures less than 1 m (3 ft) wide by almost 4 m (13 ft) long. The entrance of the passage into the chamber is marked by a narrowing. During the excavations of 1940, two levels of burial were found in the chamber, accompanied by a few archaeological remains, such as pottery and a flint axe. But the most important discovery was made in front of the passage and on either side of the entrance to it. Here were found more than 7000 sherds from pots which had originally been placed on the walls and the blocks of stone of the mound's perimeter, on either side of the entrance. Thus offerings were made to the dead; a true ritual occurred at these monuments. Identical practices have been recognised in front of the entrance of passage-graves of different types, and took place also around the chamber-tombs of western France, of which the earliest are older than the Danish ones by more than a thousand years.

It is not unrealistic to look towards Brittany, and to envisage an Armorican origin for the northern passage-graves, going as much on the structure as on the funerary customs that are met with in both regions, even if simple chamber-tombs inside long mounds could have begun in northern Europe – a proposition which has not been proved absolutely.

There are fashions in archaeology as well as in *haute couture*. For a few years now, the reigning one as regards chamber-tombs has been a people's capacity for personal invention; and some scholars, such as Colin Renfrew, do not hesitate to see as many creative centres of megalith-building as there are areas of megaliths. This is a radical reaction to those ideas defended by our predecessors, for whom everything came from the East. In fact, as far as megaliths are concerned, there may well have been several creative centres around the world, but each of these may have diffused (or not) in different directions and even made contact with another creative centre. We shall return to this subject.

One of the characteristics of the large northern passage-graves is the division of the chamber into compartments (Figure 4), which seems to be a fairly general phenomenon, found again in the passage-graves of Atlantic France. Studies done in Mecklenburg show that division of the chambers into compartments is not specific to any one type of chamber-tomb, but does not occur in the *Urdolmens*. This division of the internal space within megalithic burial chambers of the Beaker culture does not follow the same plan from one monument to another. Thus Kaelas reports that in Denmark, Schleswig-Holstein and Lower Saxony we are dealing with simple transverse divisions into two or three parts. Each compartment serves to house skeletal remains which, according to Schuldt, would be placed there in a secondary situation, after first having been stripped of flesh. However, observations made at other sites indicate that the body might be deposited entire, in a flexed position, inside the megalithic monument. Perhaps the two customs were practised simultaneously.

The site at Tustrup in the Djursland peninsula in Denmark is of enormous scientific interest because of the interpretations which have been put upon it. It is composed of three chamber-tombs and a horseshoe-shaped structure which, when it was discovered by Poul Kjaerum in 1954, was the first known in a Beaker cultural context. The first chamber-tomb has a polygonal chamber, whose roofing slab may be the single block which lies a few metres away. The second monument, to the south, is a large chamber-tomb with a four-sided chamber 10 m (33 ft) long, with an approach passage on the long east side. Another small rectangular chamber parallel to the first is joined to the long west side by means of a very small passage. The whole is inside a circular mound. The third monument is again a passage-grave with a polygonal chamber, but the mound is outlined by a line of large slabs. These chamber-tombs together form an isosceles triangle, about 70 m (230 ft) along the base and 40 m (131 ft) along the sides.

Slightly to the north of the long base of the triangle formed by the dolmens was found the 'house of the dead' (Figure 3:3). This was a horseshoe-shaped building with stone walls defining a square internal surface, about 5 m ($16\frac{1}{2}$ ft) a side, open to the north-east. The thickness of the walls varied from 50 cm (20 in) to 1.5 m (5 ft); they were bounded by upright stones. The internal divisions of the building would have been made of wooden posts fixed into a trench. The roof was supported by a central post fixed into an oval hole filled with sand, as were the foundation trenches of the wooden walls. The house had been burnt. Twenty-eight pots and spoons typical of the middle neolithic Ib phase in Denmark were recovered in two groups on either side of the central hole.

According to Kjaerum, the pottery found at Tustrup is of the earliest and commonest type from the first passage-graves in Denmark and southern Sweden, and is contemporary with the introduction of this type of tomb into the whole of Scandinavia. In spite of their architectural differences, the three chamber-tombs have been dated, by the material discovered in them, to the same period as the 'house of the dead' which they surround. The remains of some 100 pots were found, essentially on either side of the entrances to the three tombs. The leader of the excavation concluded that examination of the cemetery at Tustrup shows that a single community erected different types of chamber-tombs at one and the same time, and practised the same ritual in tombs of varying types. As for the open four-sided building, should we see that as a 'house of the dead' or a sort of sanctuary connected with the megalithic burials?

Some years later a second 'house' comparable with that of Tustrup was found at Ferslev. The internal surface measured 5 m by 6 m ($16\frac{1}{2}$ by 20 ft), but inside the chamber was a square area bordered with stones, on which were seven complete pots. Twenty-eight others were found between the small enclosure and the wall of the building. All belong to the Danish middle neolithic III phase, while sherds from 25 pots decorated in an earlier style were found in front of the western end of the house, which had therefore been used twice. Kjaerum's hypothesis about this internal cell is that it served as a funerary compartment comparable with those in the passage-graves. So it would be a true 'house of the dead', like those found in the long mounds such as Bygholm Noerremark, which we have already discussed. This arrangement would be a kind of prolongation at the turn of the fourth and third millennia BC of the earlier, non-megalithic mounds. There would have been two parts: one funerary, with relatively few archaeological remains; the other, an area for offerings, where again pots were placed, as was the custom at that period, in front of and on the stones to either side of the entrance to the passage-grave, which generally contains only a few ceramic remains. Thus outside a single megalith in Scania were found more than 50,000 sherds belonging to a thousand or so pots. The 'house of the dead' at Ferslev therefore had a space devoted to offerings; while at Tustrup the house was burnt after a single ceremony, here it had been cleared and a second ceremony had taken place before the destruction by fire.

Yet the interpretation of the Tustrup and Ferslev structures as 'houses of the dead' was called into question some years later by C. J. Becker, who discovered two new structures in 1967–8, and then four others a little later on. The first was at Herrup, comparable to the two already described, but without the use of large stones. It contained 27 pots and spoons disposed in two major groups towards the back of the building, together with 13 arrowheads in a small space. The inside of the house, whose walls were fixed into small trenches, measured 6 m by 6 m (20 ft by 20 ft) and had a forecourt half that size. The other four houses were found within a distance of 1800 m (5900 ft) around Herrup. They are of similar type, but smaller than the first. At Foulum, 40 km (25 miles) to the east of Herrup, another house was brought to light, identical in plan to that at Herrup but of slightly smaller dimensions. Becker notes that these houses were used during period Ib, that is, exactly at the time the first passage-graves were being built in Denmark. Only the second phase at Ferslev belongs to a later period; at Herrup the pottery is earlier, from before the passage-graves. So the links between chamber-tomb and house seem less clear, and so do those indicating a funerary character for these buildings, which could now be considered as little sanctuaries or temples. The debate remains open, but let us notice that Jensen in 1982 opted for a 'house of the dead', a simple extension of the wooden structures of the first farming communities.

I have gone on at length about the problem of the 'houses of the dead' in Denmark for several reasons. The first is that they show the necessity of always excavating very widely around a megalithic monument, on a surface area where there may well be found wooden structures which leave no visible trace on the surface of the ground. The second reason is to insist on the importance of these wooden structures, used at the same time as megalithic chamber-tombs with the same end in view, or even more probably a complementary one. Such a study has never been made around the megalithic monuments of Atlantic France.

Hunebedden in Holland

In the north of Holland, the province of the Drenthe is in part made up of the remnants of the frontal moraine of the Scandinavian glacier, the Hondsrug ('Dog's Back') which, from Groningen to Emmen, was dotted with erratic rocks just right for building the megalithic monuments known as hunebedden (hunebed in the singular). Fifty-two megaliths are in existence of which only one, Noorlaren, is in the province of Groningen; at least 32 other hunebedden have now disappeared.

A hunebed has a chamber whose length varies from 3 m (10 ft) to 20 m (66 ft), with a small access passage, usually situated on the south side (Figure 6:2 and 3). So, typologically speaking, it is a 'passage-grave with side-entrance' in the French classification, and some monuments in the Mayenne, such as Petit-Vieux-Sou at Brecé, recently excavated by R. Bouillon, would fit neatly among the Dutch hunebed-den. They are enclosed in an earthen mound, more or less oval in shape, bordered by a row of large blocks. Often the chamber is made up of juxtaposed trilithons, that is, two upright stones supporting a horizontal lintel – hence the definition of the monuments in the Michelin guide: 'a covered way formed in some sort from a line of "several dolmens"'. To the author of this definition, each trilithon is a dolmen, which corresponds to the popular image, but cannot be accepted in a general definition; in fact it is the *hunebed* as a whole which is a dolmen.

A typology of *hunebedden* in Holland was established in 1925 by A. E. van Giffen, comprising *Portaalgraf*, *Ganggraf*, *Langgraf*, and *Trapgraf*. The difference between the two first types, the grouping into which nearly all the monuments fall, is slight, except as regards the small entrance passage, which in the first group is unroofed. Twenty-three *hunebedden*, among them the two small chamber-tombs included in one long mound, D 43 (Figure 6:4), form the first grouping. Fourteen monuments belong to the second type, including Havelte (Figure 6:3) and Schoonord (Figure 6:2), called 'Papeloze Kerk' (the 'Church without a Priest'). Surrounded by large trees, this *hunebed* has been restored in an interesting way, since only half is covered by an earthen mound to the upper level of the roof, large blocks of more or less rounded stone supported by the orthostats. The other half is uncovered, revealing some of the chamber's pillars and the kerb of erratic blocks.

Only one *Langgraf* is known in Holland, which is long mound D 43, Schimmeres at Emmen, which we have already mentioned as containing two *Portaalgraf*-type chamber-tombs. It is an impressive monument, a trapezoidal mound 40 m (131 ft) long which recalls a good number of long mounds in Germany or Scandinavia, even England and Brittany. It is perceptibly oriented north-south with the larger end to the north, and its appearance now, after restoration, is of a platform of earth circled by upright stones, leaving open spaces which have been filled in by small dry-stone walls. To the north is a small chamber-tomb, a rectangular chamber with a short unroofed passage which does not follow the chamber's axis. Towards the centre of the mound there is a second chamber, a little longer than the first. The plans made during the 1913 excavations and the restorations show no passage connecting the chambers with the outside of the mound.

The last type, *Trapgraf*, is represented by monument D 13, which has

Figure 6   Megalithic monuments in Holland and West Germany.
1. Map of the major areas for megaliths: in Holland, 1 Groningen; in West Germany, 2 Hildesheim, 3 Paderborn, 4 Kassel, 5 Marburg.
2. Hunebed at Schoonord, D 49. (After A. E. Van Giffen)
3. Hunebed at Havelte, D 53. (After A. E. Van Giffen)
4. Monument at Emmen, D 43. (After A. E. Van Giffen)
5. Steinkist at Altendorf. (After O. Uenze and W. Lange)
6. Steinkist at Hiddingsen. (After O. Uenze and W. Lange)
7. Steinkist at Fritzlar. (After J. Boehlau)

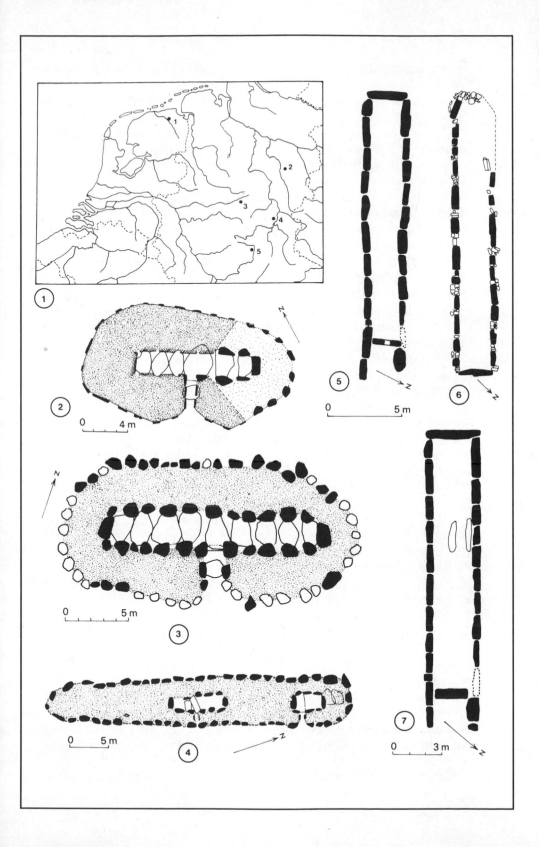

a short rectangular chamber and a very small approach passage which opens at the eastern end of the long south side.

The Dutch *hunebedden*, collective burials, have produced a large amount of archaeological material, coming from the chambers as much as from outside the entrance. These offerings to the dead bear witness to the ceremonies which took place around the monument. The builders of these chamber-tombs belong to the Funnel-neck Beaker culture which spread through northern Europe.

Chamber-tombs of the *hunebed* type can be found on the other side of the Ems in Lower Saxony as far as the Elbe and even beyond in the western Mecklenburg group, as defined by Schuldt. A glance at the plan of the megalithic monument of Gnewitz, Rostock (Figure 4:1), for example, shows that it is morphologically very close to the Dutch chamber-tombs, or the one at Thuine, Lingen (Figure 3:5), which, it is true, lies not far from the other bank of the river Ems. Similar plans are known in Denmark, but the passage is often very much longer. So this is a fairly common kind of structure in northern Europe, and we might be amazed to find very similar ones in Brittany where, however, the distribution of this type of chamber-tomb with a side-entrance centres on the north of the peninsula. We can envisage contacts between the two areas, perhaps by sea, which would also explain the Breton 'collared flasks', bad copies of examples spread throughout the area of the Funnel-neck Beaker culture. Nordic inspiration for this pottery would also indicate a northern origin for the idea of megalithic burials with side-entrances in Brittany, where they appear late in the Neolithic at the beginning of the third millennium BC.

We will describe these in a little more detail in the section on this type of monument in Brittany, and will see that a local origin, stemming from other chamber-tombs of the region, is preferred by Breton scholars. We would therefore have to find an independent origin for every megalithic centre, and similarly for the necked bottle. Why should we reject at any price the possibility of inter-influence, especially when we know that flint objects imported from the centre of France have been found in Holland?

Steinkisten in eastern Germany

In south-east Westphalia, south of Paderborn, and in northern Hesse, essentially west of Kassel, are long stone chests whose affinities with the *allées couvertes* of the Paris basin have been stressed for a long time. A pathway from one area to another via the *allées couvertes* of Wéris in Belgium is altogether plausible. But in which direction? That is another question. This megalithic group of Hesse-Westphalia extends into middle Germany.

Three architectural types have been identified in this region. The first was a very long four-sided chamber whose side-walls, as well as the ends, are formed of upright slabs and small dry-stone walls (Figure 6:6) (*'einteilige Galeriegräber'*). They are generally buried in the earth, and some have even been hewn into the rock. Access to the chamber had to be from above, by lifting up a portion of the wooden or stone roof. The second type seems to have evolved out of the first, by the addition of an antechamber to one of the ends (Figure 6:5 and 7). The transition from antechamber to chamber is made via a porthole cut into a slab (the *'Seelenloch'* of German terminology), or made from two juxtaposed slabs with a notch at the adjoining edges. This is the type most comparable to the *allées couvertes* of the Paris Basin, and should be called *Steinkiste*. The third type is also formed of a long more or less megalithic *allée*, but access to the chamber is by a short passage set into one of the long sides. In the French classification, this would be a chamber-tomb with side-entrance, a type which relates closely to the Dutch *hunebed*.

When the *Steinkiste* was built above the ground, it was covered by a long mound bordered by large blocks of stone, as is shown by the monument at Etteln. When the monument is buried in the ground, the stone tables or roofing slabs could be at ground level, but, as with the *allées couvertes* of the Paris Basin, the roof was sometimes made of wooden beams on which rested a higher or lower mound made of earth and stones. The floor of the chamber and antechamber may be completely or partially paved with slabs and sometimes the chambers are divided into compartments.

The normal length of *Steinkisten* is between 10 m and 20 m (33 ft and 66 ft), but there are smaller ones, such as Lohra and Niederzeuzhein (6–7 m [20–23 ft]). The longest are in Westphalia, where six are longer than 20 m (66 ft), and Atteln II and Beckum-Wintergalen are almost 30 m (98 ft) long. These are collective graves which contained skeletal fragments from between 20 and 250 persons, laid in the chamber at several levels, separated by layers of earth or stones, a technique recurring in the Paris basin *allées couvertes*, but also in central western France and even further afield. The body was laid in the chamber, in an extended or flexed position. When the chamber had filled up with skeletons, the grave-diggers proceeded to arrange the bones in groups, with all the skulls laid next to one another. Thus space was created for newcomers. When the level had reached saturation point, it was closed off with a layer of earth or stones, which then became the ground surface for a new level of skeletal remains. Cremation, known at Lohra, seems to have been practised only rarely.

Among the archaeological material collected from the *Steinkisten*, Muller-Wille notes Beaker pottery, and remarks that generally the pottery found in these monuments does not form a unity; there is no clear link to one identified culture. The lithic and bone material is in common with several neolithic cultures, with transverse arrowheads comparable to those found in the Seine-Oise-Marne culture of the Paris basin, but also found in the Beaker culture of northern Europe. A pointed arrowhead with a straight, concave or convex base seems more specific to the *Steinkisten* of eastern Germany. We may add to this several small objects in Baltic amber, and, occasionally, in copper.

Muller-Wille has listed the monuments in middle Germany which are related to the ones in Hesse-Westphalia. The monument at Gotha, destroyed today, was 10 m (33 ft) long; it seems to have had an antechamber and would have contained the skeletal remains of around 100 entire individuals. It was set into the ground. Those monuments, now all destroyed, which were built above the ground are the 'chambers of middle Germany'. The chambers, mostly about 5 m (16½ ft) long, were covered by a mound and oriented east-west. They sometimes had an antechamber, a porthole-slab, even internal compartments, and they were collective tombs in which 10 to 15 individuals had been deposited. We must also mention the 'cists' with access ramps, chambers averaging 4 m (13 ft) long under mounds, the side-walls of which extended on each side of the entrance, forming a sort of antechamber. They can contain up to five skeletons and so should not be called 'cists', a term reserved in French nomenclature for individual burials. Lastly there are chambers with side-walls built of dry-stone which seem to have developed out of the *Steinkisten*. They are found in Harz and Thuringen and are set into, or built on, the ground surface. They are 3 m (10 ft) to 6 m (20 ft) long and must have been closed with a wooden roof and covered over by a mound.

Allées couvertes in Belgium

Three megalithic burials are known today in Belgium, and S. de Laet mentions traces of three others. They are all in the province of Namur and Luxembourg (Figure 7:1). Two of these monuments are at Wéris, a little more than a kilometre apart. They belong to the *allée couverte* family in that their chambers form an elongated rectangle. The smaller, called the 'Little dolmen' ['Le petit dolmen'] (Figure 7:4) is an *allée couverte* of the Paris Basin type, buried in the ground up to the level of the roofing slabs which, like the orthostats, are of a pudding-stone brought from at least 3 km (2 miles) away. The whole structure approaches 10 m (33 ft) in overall length. The chamber is 4.6 m (15 ft) long and 1.2 m (4 ft) wide. It is approached via an antechamber, and the passage from one to the other is through a porthole-slab, of the kind we often see in the Paris Basin *allées couvertes*. When it was discovered in 1888, human and some animal bones were collected, as well as arrowheads, scrapers of flint, polished-stone axes, and sherds of crude pottery which are probably attributable to the Seine-Oise-Marne culture. The second *allée couverte*, called the 'Great dolmen' ['Le grand dolman'] (Figure 7:3) is longer by 1 m (3 ft), but its features are identical, with a porthole-slab at the point of entry from the antechamber to the chamber. But this monument was built at ground level and seems to have been covered by a mound. The third monument was discovered in 1976, near the Lamsoul farm at Jemelle. Of this there remain only seven uprights and one roofing slab. Perhaps it had also been an *allée couverte*.

Three megalithic tombs were destroyed in the nineteenth century, one at Velaine, called 'La Pierre du Diable' ('The Devil's Rock'), and two at Hargimont. According to de Laet, one of the tombs at Hargimont, 15 m (49 ft) long and 1.25 m (4 ft) wide, may have held 200 skeletons. Since it had no antechamber and no porthole-slab, it would have been morphologically closer to the *einteilige Galeriegräber* of eastern Germany (Figure 6:6) than to the Paris basin *allées couvertes*. He considers that, apart from the long undivided chambers (*einteilige Galeriegräber* in German terminology) which are themselves an adaptation to a funerary purpose of the elongated rectangular long-houses of the *Linearbandkeramik* culture, the Paris Basin monuments have their origins in Hesse-Westphalia. It is a tempting hypothesis, more especially as the *allées couvertes* of Westphalia and Hesse, whose structure is identical to that of the Paris Basin monuments, do seem to be earlier. In such a case we would have to envisage this architecture extending into Brittany. Of course, not everyone agrees, and the known dates are too imprecise to determine the direction of flow, if it exists.

In the Wéris region several authors have pointed out the alignment made over about 5 km (3 miles) by the standing stone of Tour, the 3 m (10 ft) high standing stone and *allée couverte* at Wéris, another standing stone 3.6 m (12 ft) high, then the second Wéris *allée couverte*, and lastly the Bouhaimont group of three standing stones at Oppagne (Figure 7:2).

During the 1963 excavations of the *Linearbandkeramik* village at Stein. P. J. R. Modderman revealed a paved surface 5.5 m (18 ft) long by 1.75 m (6 ft) wide (Figure 7:5); its narrower, eastern end seems to correspond to an antechamber separated from the chamber by a threshold made of larger stones. The other end is set slightly lower, with larger stones forming a second threshold between what could be seen as the principal funerary chamber and the end-chamber. On each side of this second threshold is a hole which must have held a solid wooden post. Two identical holes, also facing one another, are towards the east of the structure. The whole could be seen as the inner end of an *allée couverte* whose side-walls were of wood, the four holes corresponding to the wooden posts which would have supported some kind of roof. Thus we would have a wooden replica of a megalithic monument of the *allée couverte* type. This is enormously interesting, as it gives rise to the idea that certain peoples could have identical funerary customs to those of the populations erecting megaliths, but using wooden monuments. The remains collected during this excavation consist of two piles of incinerated bone (but unburnt bones could have disappeared), 96 transverse flint arrowheads, 11 bone arrowheads, and some pottery fragments. One of these, according to de Laet, comes close to pottery belonging to the culture which built the *allées couvertes* of western Germany (the '*Galeriegrab-Kultur*'), as does the bottle with a collar in the form of a six-pointed star which lay on the threshold separating the two chambers. A radiocarbon date of 2830 ± 60 b.c., when corrected, places the monument in the middle of the fourth millennium BC.

Figure 7   Megalithic monuments in Belgium.
1. Distribution map of: (1) chamber-tombs; (2) standing stones; (3) burial caves. (After S. de Laet, 1981)
2. The 'Champ Sacré' at Wéris: an alignment of standing stones and allées couvertes over a distance of 5 km (3 miles): (1) chamber-tombs: (2) standing stones. (After S. de Laet, 1982)
3. Allée couverte at Wéris: the 'petit dolmen'. (After A. De Loë, 1928)
4. Alée couverte at Wéris: the 'grand dolmen'. (After A. De Loë, 1928)
5. Plan of the inner section of the funerary monument at Stein. The dotted areas show the placing of sturdy posts which must have held up the roof. (After P. J. R. Modderman, 1964)

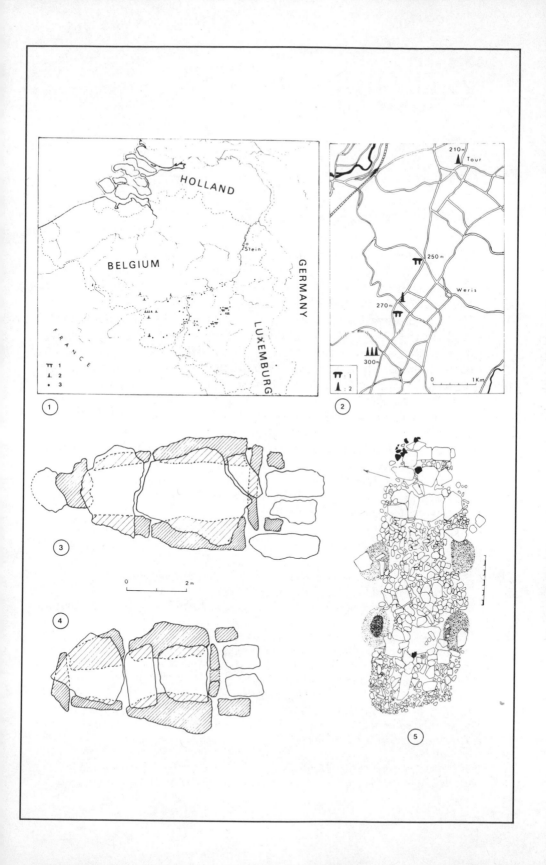

2. The British Isles

Megalithic monuments of the chamber-tomb kind are very numerous in England, Wales, Ireland, and Scotland. In Ireland alone, around 1200 megalithic tombs have been listed, and they fall into four principal categories: 330 *court-tombs*, 160 *portal-tombs*, 400 *wedge-tombs*, 150 *passage-graves*, and a few unclassifiable monuments. Add to these the *Severn-Cotswold tombs* of south-west England, and we have all the architectural forms of the British Isles. So, rather than treating the question by areas, from north to south, it is more sensible to describe each group and to show its variants and its geographical distribution.

As regards the origins of megalith-building in the British Isles, two major and opposing schools of thought raise their voices. Sometimes the balance of judgement falls in favour of diffusionism from Brittany and Scandinavia; sometimes autonomy is preferred, with two creative centres, one in Ireland for the court-tombs, which are said to be the earliest of the region's megaliths, the other in south-west England for the Severn-Cotswold monuments.

Figure 8   Megalithic monuments in Ireland, Scotland and Wales.
1. Court-tomb at Creevykeel, Co. Sligo, Ireland.
2. Court-tomb at Ballymarlagh, Co. Antrim, Ireland. (After J. X. W. P. Corcoran)
3. Double court-tomb at Audleystown, Co. Down, Ireland.
4. Double court-tomb at Cohaw, Co. Cavan, Ireland.
5. Portal tomb at Dyffryn Ardudwy, Gwynedd, Wales. (After F. Lynch)
6. Mid Gleniron I, Wigtownshire, Scotland. (After J. X. W. P. Corcoran)
7. Mid Gleniron II, Wigtownshire, Scotland. (After J. X. W. P. Corcoran)
8. March Cairn, Shetland, Scotland, a square mound. (After A. S. Henshall)
9. Horned cairn at Garrywhin, Caithness, Scotland. (After A. S. Henshall)
10. Horned cairn at Tulloch of Assery, Caithness, Scotland. (After A. S. Henshall)
11. Passage-grave, Maes Howe, Orkney, Scotland. (After A. Gible, 1861)
12. Wedge tomb, Island, Co. Cork, Ireland. (After M. J. O'Kelly)

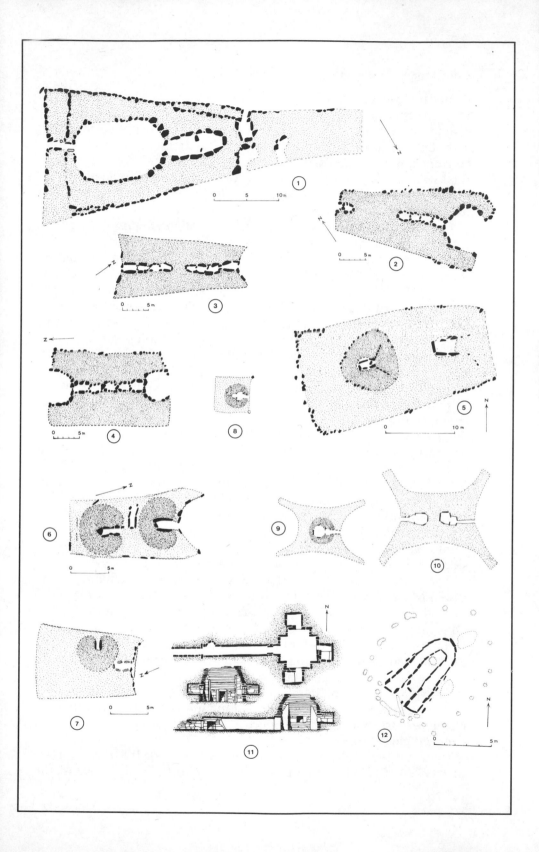

Court-tombs in Ireland and Scotland

Court-tombs were for a long time known as *court-cairns* inasmuch as they are usually made up of a courtyard, in a stone cairn, on to which give one or several chambers. Two major groups have been recognised. The first occupies the northern half of Ireland, with a strong concentration to the west in the counties of Mayo, Sligo and Donegal; this is the *Carlingford* group. The second grouping is in Scotland, on the other side of the Irish Sea; this *Clyde* group includes about 80 monuments of the type.

The Irish monument of Creevykeel, Co. Sligo (Figure 8:1), dominates the port of Mullaghmore from a height of 30 m (98 ft). The cairn, which is perceptibly oriented east–west, is in the form of an elongated trapezoid, about 55 m (180 ft) long by 25 m (82 ft) wide on the eastern face and 12 m (39 ft) on the west. The monument was excavated in 1935 by the Harvard Archaeological Expedition. The cairn is bordered by a line of large stone blocks, in which is a narrow opening to a passage in the centre of the eastern façade. The 5 m ($16\frac{1}{2}$ ft) long corridor gives access to an oval court, about 15 m (49 ft) by 9 m ($29\frac{1}{2}$ ft) and open to the sky, which is bordered by large stones. To the west of the court, facing the passage, stand eight larger stones; the centre two serve as supports for a lintel and thus mark the entrance to the chamber. The chamber itself is a long oval shape, 9 m ($29\frac{1}{2}$ ft) by 3 m (10 ft); it is divided into two parts by two slabs whose spacing allows passage from one part to another. The excavation discovered neolithic pottery, more or less decorated, flint arrowheads and scrapers, also some polished-stone axes which are now in the National Museum of Ireland. Five small piles of burnt bone found in the chamber are the remains of five cremated individuals whose ashes were deposited there. Behind the chamber which gives on to the court of the court-tomb, three more small chambers were revealed. Two of these open on to the long north side, the third and best preserved on to the south side.

The central court of a court-tomb can serve several chambers. At Malin More, Co. Donegal, the oval court in an elongated trapezoidal mound is approached through the centre of the eastern façade. Opposite this entrance, that is, on the other side of the court which was certainly a place of ritual, open two parallel rectangular chambers, each divided in two, while on either side of the entrance passage to the court two other lesser chambers were constructed.

Ballyglass cairn, Co. Mayo, has a different design. Here access to the court is by a short passage from the long north-east side and the two chambers are diametrically opposed. The constructed material is rounded glacial rocks.

In the examples already quoted, the court is inside the mound, more or less centred within it and usually closer to the widest face of the elongated trapezoidal tumulus (although it may also be oval or rectangular). But sometimes, as with the Ballymarlagh court-tomb, Co. Antrim, the court is no more than a more or less circular scoop at the widest end of the mound. At Ballymarlagh, this court, bounded by large stones, closes into a kind of pincer shape, at the end of which the megalithic chamber is formed by a long corridor divided into four parts by three partitions. At the other end of the monument a small chamber opens on to the smaller straight façade (Figure 8:2).

Behy court-tomb, Co. Mayo, is identical with Ballymarlagh in having a pincer-shaped court, but differs in having a 'transepted' chamber, a feature much more widespread in the passage-graves of the Boyne Valley culture, which are dealt with later on. Perhaps we should see in this monument a link between the two architectural types.

Sometimes there is a court at each end of the trapezoidal tumulus, as at Audleystown (Figure 8:3), Co. Down, or Cohaw (Figure 8:4), Co. Cavan; but in the latter case the two long sides of the tumulus are parallel and the two chambers join up, forming a group of five cells.

In general, the dividing walls of the court-tomb are megalithic – made up of large rocks; sometimes they are also built in dry-stone. The roof is normally made up of several large slabs corbelled over the chamber, which was most often used as a depository for several incinerated bodies. The quantity of funerary deposits is normally small, but the remains of more than 30 individuals were found at Audleystown. Although the rite of cremation is by far the most widespread, it is by no means unique; unburnt bones have been found in some court-tombs. The pottery most commonly met with in this type of tomb is a carinated pot with a rounded base.

The Clyde group from south-east Scotland is comparable with the Carlingford group, but has some interesting variations. In its final form, the Clyde kind of monument comprises an elongated trapezoidal tumulus with a semi-circular court in its wider end. A rectangular chamber opens out of the end of this court.

However, Corcoran's painstaking excavations at Mid Gleniron have shown that these monuments could result from a progressive growth. The mound of Mid Gleniron I shows three phases of construction (Figure 8:6). In a first stage a rectangular megalithic chamber was buried under a circular mound. Some metres in front of the entrance to this first monument a second, identical in form, was built in a second stage. Finally a third megalithic chamber was built between the two circular mounds, perpendicular to the axis of the earlier chambers, and the whole thing was buried under an elongated trapezoidal mound with a semi-circular court to the north-east. We will find similar evolutions in the megalith-building of Atlantic France. Mid Gleniron II is made up of a first rectangular chamber in a circular mound. The monument was taken into a trapezoidal mound with a court whose slight curvature is marked by upright slabs and dry-stone walls. A rectangular chamber opens off the centre of this court, which here is at the narrowest part of the cairn.

Hiding behind the name of court-tomb or court-cairn we actually find a fair number of different monuments. Many people, Colin Renfrew among them, suppose these to be the earliest megalithic architecture in Ireland, from the beginning of the fourth millennium BC, with a local origin independent of any other Atlantic megalith-building. Some researchers, such as M. J. O'Kelly, put court-tombs in a second phase of Irish megalith-building, after the passage-graves, whose radiocarbon dates do indeed give reason to believe that the first monuments of a passage-grave type are earlier than was usually imagined. The cruciform plan of monuments such as Behy would originate in the passage-graves of Co. Sligo, themselves of a design brought from France some time before. Ruaidhrí De Valera happily put court-tombs into the earliest phase of Irish megalith-building; believing the few transepted monuments of north-west Ireland to be the oldest, he sought their origins around the Loire estuary, in France.

So we have a diffusionist theory in two variants, each finding an origin in France, as well as an autonomous theory to explain the existence of court-tombs. I do not personally believe that a definitive answer can yet be given; although theories can and should be put forward, we should consider them only as theories, without according them the standing of proofs. According to our own mental make-up, we will have more or less sympathy with one diffusionist theory or the other, but no one at present is in a position scientifically to prove any of the alternatives. To refute diffusionism in the light of our knowledge of stock-rearing and agriculture in western Europe (even if some attempts at it did take place here and there, independently and in restricted areas) would be ridiculous, where one would in particular have to recognise the spontaneous appearance of the sheep; conversely, to make everything come from the East, that is, to deny any creative ability in European peoples, is an attitude also totally without foundation.

Portal-tombs in Ireland, Wales, and England

Portal-type tombs are numerous in north-west Ireland, in this respect echoing the distribution of court-tombs; but there is another major group in the south-east, which follows through into the Isle of Anglesey, Wales and as far as Cornwall. The monuments are distinguished by the massive form of the megalithic components of the chamber which, itself, is of fairly small dimensions, 2–3 m ($6\frac{1}{2}$–10 ft) long by 1–2 m (3–$6\frac{1}{2}$ ft) wide. The chamber is bounded by dry-stone walls and large orthostats (most often only three) which support a single, often enormous, slab. The one at Browneshill, Co. Carlow, is of granite, weighs 100 tonnes and would have required the joint efforts of 700 to 800 people to bring it there. Often the roofing-slab of a portal-tomb is sloped down towards the back.

There are about 200 portal-tombs in Ireland and England. Pentre Ifan near Nevern, on the Pembrokeshire coast in Dyfed, is one of the best-known Welsh megalithic monuments. The 5 m (16½ ft) long roofing-slab is supported by upright stones, 2.5 m (8 ft) above the floor of the chamber, which is at the southern end of a 40 m (131 ft) long cairn. A semi-circular façade, as in the Irish court-tombs, is marked by two upright stones on either side of the portal. A shouldered pot, a triangular arrow and a flint point were discovered during Grimes' excavations in 1949.

Still in Wales, at Dyffryn Ardudwy, Gwynedd (Figure 8:5), Terence Powell excavated a four-sided mound 27 m (88 ft) long, slightly narrower to the east than the west, and containing two portal-tombs. The first has a four-sided chamber with a portal composed of two upright slabs leaving an entrance; as with the majority of monuments of this type, the entrance is closed by another slab. The chamber is covered by a single slab, and the sides of the portal extend on either side into a horn of small upright stones. The whole is enclosed in an oval mound. In a second phase another portal-tomb was built to the east, in front of the first; it shares the same characteristics but is set in a trapezoidal mound which took in the first monument. So here we find general architectural characteristics – a long trapezoidal mound, orientation to the east, semi-circular façade forming a court and different stages of building – which suggest links with the Irish and Scottish court-tombs; and many scholars agree in thinking that the portal-tomb, chronologically slightly later, derives from the court-tomb. It would have begun in Ireland, more precisely in Ulster, and thence spread east and west in the island and across to Wales and Cornwall. But M. J. O'Kelly thinks it not at all obvious that one type derives from the other, and the origin of portal-tombs could equally be sought in Cornwall.

Wedge-tombs in Ireland

'Corner-tombs' essentially occupy the western half of Ireland. For a long time these wedge-tombs were known as 'wedge-shaped gallery-graves'; there are about 400 of them in Ireland. They come in the form of an *allée couverte* about 6–8 m (20–26 ft) long, bounded by stone uprights and covered by several stone slabs. But in fact the entrance is usually wider and higher than the narrow, low interior; hence the appearance of a corner which gives them their other name.

The wedge-tomb at Island (Figure 8:12), Co. Cork, conforms to this definition. It is enclosed by a mound which perceptibly echoes the shape of the chamber and has a kerb, less than 2 m (6½ ft) from the chamber, of upright stones. This form has often been set beside the Armorican *allées couvertes* of Brittany, from which they perhaps derive. A series of holes around the monument marks the position of wooden posts which surrounded the building. Similarly positioned wooden posts occur around the court-tomb of Shanballyedmond, Co. Tipperary, and there are strong architectural resemblances between the Shanballyedmond court-tomb and the Island wedge-tomb. At Shan-ballyedmond, the court is in the shape of a fairly narrow funnel, not semi-circular, and it gives access to a long chamber divided into two parts, as is the rule in court-tombs. The mound, edged by a line of upright slabs, is not as large as those normally seen on court-tombs, but follows the form of the chamber and its court in a horse-shoe shape. Taking these two monuments as a starting-point we might be tempted to see a possible link between court-tombs and wedge-tombs. But to archaeologists like O'Kelly, finding an origin for the wedge-tombs in the Breton *allées couvertes* has always been rather far-fetched.

From material recovered in the wedge-tombs, it appears that their construction began in the last stages of the neolithic in the British Isles, and went on into the early Bronze Age. Inhumation seems to be the burial rite most often practised there.

It should be noted that, like the portal-tombs of the late Neolithic, wedge-tombs are usually found on the sides of hills and on low ground, perhaps indicating a more intensive occupation of the terrain than at the time of the court-tombs and passage-graves, which are situated on the high ground in areas of easier agricultural exploitation. Other types of burial were practised in the late Neolithic in Ireland, in particular the individual burial of adult males, in megalithic chests under circular mounds.

Severn-Cotswold tombs in western mainland Britain

The monuments we have been concerned with up to now are in the west of the British Isles, essentially Ireland, with forays into Scotland, Wales and Cornwall depending on the architectural form. Those we shall look at now are centred on south-west England, in the counties of Somerset, Wiltshire, and Gloucestershire. These long barrows, which contain one or several megalithic chambers, are later in date than the earthen long barrows discussed in the preceding chapter; some scholars consider them to have evolved out of these, with the wooden 'house of the dead' replaced by a megalithic passage-grave. Although this hypothesis is tenable for certain megalithic chambers situated at the widest end of the long barrow, it is more difficult to maintain for tombs set laterally in the mound, nor is it easy to find a local origin for megalith-building in this area.

In the south of England 180 mounds with megalithic chambers have been listed, and three basic types distinguished: barrow with simple terminal chamber; barrow with transepted terminal chamber; and barrow with lateral chambers; a fourth group takes in all the hybrid and variant monuments. In a general way, the Severn-Cotswold mounds with megalithic chambers present an external aspect fairly like that of the earthen long barrows: an elongated trapezoidal mound, bordered by quarry-ditches, built of stone or earth and usually oriented east–west. It is wider and higher at the eastern end than the western, and has an inward-curving section forming a court in front of the chamber-entrance. Usually the mound is edged by a dry-stone wall with, sometimes, a few upright slabs.

We will describe a few typical sites in more detail.

To the south of Ashbury, Oxfordshire, is Wayland's Smithy, which was excavated in 1962–3 under the direction of Professor Richard Atkinson (Figure 9:4). Two periods of building were revealed: in fact, there are two monuments here, one on top of the other. The first mound was oval, wider at the south than the north, with a concave portion forming a court at the south-east end. It was bordered by a row of stones and covered a wooden 'house of the dead', on whose floor of stone slabs lay the skeletal remains of 14 people. Some of the bodies were disarticulated and seem to have been the result of previous decarnation; others must have been placed entire into the grave. When it was decided to finish with the chamber, it was surrounded by stones and covered by chalk taken out of two ditches, dug on either side of the long mound. A line of stones was set up to mark the outer limit of the monument. This first mound disappeared totally during a second phase, in the course of which a trapezoidal mound, 55 m (180 ft) long by 15 m (49 ft) wide at the south end and only 6 m (20 ft) at the north, was built. It is in the shape of a regular four-sided figure and is edged with upright stones. The south façade has four uprights (of a probable original six) about 3 m (10 ft) high, alternating with small sections of dry-stone walling. At the centre of this façade, which because it is straight does not define a forecourt, is the entrance to the tomb, a passage almost 7 m (23 ft) long with two lateral cells forming transepts. It is megalithic in construction, but the interstices between the upright slabs are closed by dry-stone walling. In the western chamber were found the skeletal remains of eight persons, including a child. The bulk of the mound was built out of material taken from the two quarry-ditches dug parallel to it on the long sides, up to 1.8 m (6 ft) deep and 4.6 m (15 ft) wide. This collection is particularly important because it shows that the megalithic structure is later in date than the mound covering a wooden structure.

To the south of the impressive archaeological group formed by Avebury, Windmill Hill and Silbury Hill, West Kennet tumulus in Wiltshire is among the best-known monuments in Great Britain. The largest of the Severn-Cotswold barrows, it is 101 m (331 ft) long by 2.5 m (8 ft) high at the highest, widest eastern end. It is built of chalk taken from ditches, parallel to the long sides, which averaged 3 m (10 ft) deep and 6 m (20 ft) wide (in modern times they have been filled in). A line of stones, now gone, originally surrounded the monument. There is a megalithic structure at the eastern end, which was partially excavated at the end of the seventeenth century by Dr Troope of Marlborough. He used the human bones he exhumed to make a medicine, like the Chinese who made a nostrum of powdered 'dragon's teeth' – among them those of *Pithecanthropus* – found in deposits of fossil bones. Of course, this specialised use of prehistoric remains is no help to archaeologists, and we will never know just how many skeletons there really were in West Kennet. The megalithic façade is concave, defining a small forecourt, in the centre of which is the entrance to a passage. The passage serves one end-chamber and four side-chambers, symmetrically placed on either side of the passage-way (Figure 9:6). The construction uses large upright blocks, allowing a man to walk upright along the entire length, and the gaps between the slabs are, as usual, filled in with dry-stone walling.

Another excavation took place in 1859, when John Thurnam explored one of the western chambers and a 5 m (16½ ft) length of passage. In the chamber he recovered the skeletal remains of five adults and a child, as well as some pottery. But the monument was not completely excavated until Stuart Piggott and Richard Atkinson's work in 1955–6.

The chambers are roofed by large stones, false-corbelled, with a capstone weighing several tonnes about 2.3 m (7½ ft) above floor-level. Each chamber contained human bones. The north-eastern one yielded the more-or-less complete remains of two women, and one man, who had a flaked arrowhead embedded in one cervical vertebra, the

---

Figure 9 Megalithic monuments and long barrows in England and Wales.
1. Fussell's Lodge long barrow, Wiltshire. (After P. Ashbee)
2. Ashbee's reconstruction drawing of the Fussell's Lodge monument.
3. Randwick, Gloucestershire, trapezoidal long barrow with small end-chamber. (After O. G. S. Crawford, 1925)
4. Wayland's Smithy chambered long barrow, Oxfordshire. (After R. J. C. Atkinson, 1965)
5. Notgrove long barrow, Gloucestershire, with transepted end-chamber. (After E. M. Clifford, 1936)
6. Megalithic chamber in West Kennet long barrow, Wiltshire. (After S. Piggott, 1963)
7. Ty Isaf, Powys. (After W. F. Grimes, 1939)

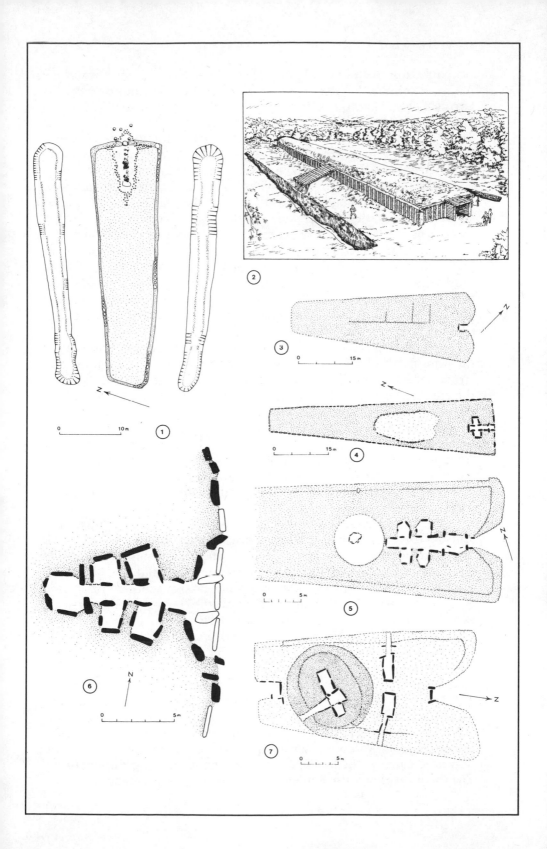

probable cause of his death. In the south-eastern chamber were one
man, one woman and the remains of five children and four babies. The
two side-chambers to north-west and south-west are smaller than the
two others; the south-western contained nine adults, one adolescent
and three children; the north-eastern the disarticulated remains of a
dozen adults. Thus we have a total of 46 individuals inhumed, without
knowing how many disappeared into Dr Troope's medicaments.

The fact that both complete bodies and disarticulated remains were
found in the monument could indicate that the grave was not opened
for each new death, but that some of the dead were buried in another
place. The vault could only be entered on certain occasions, when a
more important person died, or perhaps when there was no more room
in the primary grave. Perhaps not all the bones were taken to the
megalithic vault. It could be that the 'causewayed camps', such as
Windmill Hill, with their multiple enclosures, played a role in a
funerary ritual which is not altogether easy to comprehend in modern
times.

The cessation of use of the funerary chambers was marked by
throwing earth, chalk and stones on to the bones, and we can think of a
structure that was completed, at the scale of the monument itself, by
the erection of the huge slabs, 3.7 m (12 ft) high at the centre, which
closed off the forecourt at this time.

The elongated trapezoidal barrow at Notgrove (Figure 9:5),
Gloucestershire, shows several affinities with West Kennet, especially
since it includes a grave with double transepts at the eastern end, very
like West Kennet's. However, there are also some differences. The
entrance gives access to a fairly wide antechamber at the far end of
which opens the passage which serves the four side-chambers. Also, the
monument is surrounded by a double wall and not by upright stones,
and the forecourt forms a kind of deep funnel. But above all, as at
Wayland's Smithy, the mound conceals an earlier monument, a *cella*
bordered by upright slabs and set in a well-built mound.

There has been long discussion among British scholars about the
origin of the transepted tombs of the Severn-Cotswold long barrows,
especially as this type of structure is to be found in some cairns of the
Irish court-tombs and in passage-graves in Anglesey, Ireland, and the
Orkney Islands. According to some, the megalithic chamber is simply a
stone version of the wooden 'house of the dead'.

The four-sided megalithic chamber would have appeared first.
Taking this first form, a simple cube, as the departure point, we can
make up a linear assemblage of cubes (juxtaposed cubes in a straight
line), an agglomeration of cubes (cubes grouped together), or a
dispersed group of cubes (several unlinked groups of cubes), and we
only need cubes in the first instance to have the idea of grouping them.
The theory is that with a single four-sided chamber as a base unit we

can make up a segmented passage (a linear assembly), a transepted monument (group assembly), a mound with several chambers (dispersed assembly), and that this idea can arise almost anywhere and often independently. This 'modular' system of Kinnes, applied to the British Isles, allows the classification of court-tombs into the first group, the transepted graves of the Severn-Cotswold mounds and some court-tombs into the second group, and the Severn-Cotswold mounds with lateral graves, Bargrennan, and the Clyde cairns in the third.

So we need not look elsewhere for possible links to transepted monuments in Britain – not even to Brittany where they are early and numerous. But this is still a theoretical model which needs to be substantiated; and for the present the diffusionist theory, taking the idea from Brittany, where the theoretical model could also apply, through the Channel Islands and the Irish Sea, has its ardent defenders, and we can still allow the elongated trapezoidal mound its origin in northern Europe.

Ty Isaf (Figure 9:7), Powys, belongs to the type of monument with side-chambers. It is in the shape of a large elongated trapezoid, oriented north-south, wider to the north than the south and bounded by a dry-stone wall. To the north, two 'horns' curve inwards to a funnel-shaped court in which is a false entrance; this is made of two slabs at the sides, which would be the beginning of the passage, and an upright slab between them, which would block the access to it. In fact, there is no passage behind this pseudo-entrance. On the other hand, at the other end of the monument is a small megalithic chamber. Two passages open symmetrically in the long sides of the mound, their sides essentially of dry-stone, and give access to two long four-sided megalithic chambers. What we have just described in fact corresponds to a second phase of building, which is visible at the present time. In reality, there is an earlier monument completely hidden by the new structure. In earlier times, a chamber-tomb had been made, with a dry-stone-walled passage leading to a trapezoidal megalithic chamber. On either long side of the chamber is another, smaller chamber. Thus the group is cruciform in plan, the western transept being longer than the eastern. This chamber-tomb is surrounded by an oval mound with a double line of well-built dry-stone walling.

Despite its obvious differences, the Ty Isaf group should be compared with Champ-Châlon mound B (Figure 17:3) at Benon (Charente-Maritime), France, where we have a first, q-shaped passage-grave in a circular mound with concentric facing walls, inside a second trapezoidal mound which masks it completely and which contains a second passage-grave, also q-shaped, parallel to the first. Here, too, we must doubtless assume coincidence!

On the Cotswold hills, not far to the east of Cheltenham, at Hazleton, Alan Saville had in 1979–82 the opportunity of conducting a complete excavation of one of two long mounds which were being regularly ploughed over and were in danger of disappearing sooner or later. This was the first modern excavation of a monument of the Severn-Cotswold group, and the information obtained from this exhaustive study is particularly important.

The mound belongs to the native type of long barrow with lateral chamber. It forms a trapezium, 52 m (170 ft) long, whose concave western façade is wider than the eastern face. The concavity forms a court, in which passages often have their entrance; that is not the case here, for the façade is blind, without even the representation of an entrance which we sometimes find. In the court at Hazleton the sole evidence for any rites is a carbonised area in which some animal-bone remains have been preserved. The monument was built of material from the digging of two wide ditches at intervals on the long sides, and not from two long narrow ditches parallel to the mound, as is more usual in this group. About in the middle of the long sides are the entrances to the passages, which lead to off-set four-sided chambers, forming a p-shape in plan. The northern passage is almost 6 m (20 ft) long. Lined at first by dry-stone walls, it continues through a double row of upright slabs. The chamber itself is lined by orthostats. We have little idea about the roof, which disappeared long ago, but the floor of the chamber was strewn with human bones in great disorder, as is usual in monuments of this type. While this one was still in use, and it had become necessary to place mortuary deposits in the passage because the chamber was full, one of the orthostats fell, blocking the passage. Inhumations then took place in front of this fallen slab, and two more bodies were placed there. That closest to the entrance was in a perfect state, holding a stone hammer in the left hand, while a large splinter of flint was found in the right shoulder. Its placing had disturbed the previous burial of an individual lying in a flexed position, whose original positioning could still be clearly seen.

The other chamber-tomb to the south had a shorter passage, which also formed a p-shape in plan with its four-sided chamber. The whole was lined with upright slabs apart from the first metre of the passage, built of dry-stone walling. Two slabs in the centre of the orthostat section of the passage narrowed it, and there was a threshold between chamber and passage. The chamber and the whole of the megalithic passage were full of disarticulated human bones, among which some organisation of the skulls and long bones could be seen. There was no last complete skeleton which could have occupied the entrance to the passage, and we can question the contemporaneity of the two last bodies in the other passage with the principal period of utilisation of the graves. However, according to Saville, all the bodies would have been put in whole and would have been displaced later on with the introduction of further burials. From the preliminary observations of

Dr Juliet Rogers of Bristol University, based on the 9000 bone fragments and 33 skulls recovered, there were perceptibly as many men as women in the monument, indicating no sexual discrimination.

Evidence from the ground on which the monument is built indicates mesolithic occupation, but a few pottery fragments and at least one arrowpoint indicate the passage of a neolithic population.

The monument is built along a perfectly straight central axis, by the addition of four-sided cells made of dry-stone walling and filled in with rubble and earth, the chamber-tombs occupying the position, so to speak, of a cell on either side. After the construction of the cells, some lateral walls were added to regularise the shape of the mound, and one additional compartment was added to each corner of the western façade to form the horns of the court. According to Saville, the order of construction was as follows: first the establishment of cells on the northern side, then building of the two passage-graves, erection of the southern side-cells and finally building of an external retaining wall which surrounds the whole structure.

It is striking to find an identical mode of construction in mound C of Champ-Châlon at Benon (Charente-Maritime), France, which has a central backbone forming a double-pitched roof from which cells built of dry-stone project out either side. Here the passage-grave was added to the larger end of the mound in its own circular cairn, related to the cell-system; then the whole was surrounded by a fine retaining wall in dry-stone giving the group the elongated trapezoid shape.

Passage-graves in Ireland and Wales

In Ireland, chamber-tombs with passages are known as passage-graves. There are around 150 of them, concentrated in the northern half of the country, with a few examples in the south-east. An important group developed on Anglesey, and some monuments were built here and there on the Welsh coast (Figure 10:1).

The most impressive Irish passage-graves are grouped in a band across the country from Dublin/Drogheda on the east coast to Sligo in the north-west, taking in four great cemeteries, the Boyne valley and Loughcrew in Co. Meath, and Carrowkeel and Carrowmore in Co. Sligo. The existence of these vast cemeteries is a characteristic of the architectural type, which occupies the high ground, like the court-tombs.

One of the best-known groups in Irish megalith-building is that of the Boyne valley, not far from the Irish Sea. It is situated in a bend of the River Boyne and comprises three very large mounds, each surrounded by a greater or lesser number of smaller mounds. From east to west the large mounds are Dowth, 84 m (276 ft) in diameter and containing two passage-graves; then Newgrange, less than 2 km

($1\frac{1}{4}$ miles) away, containing one passage-grave; and finally Knowth, 1500 m (4920 ft) beyond Newgrange, containing two.

Following the excavations directed by Professor Michael O'Kelly and the subsequent recent restoration, Newgrange, which had several moments of glory in Irish history, has become one of the highspots of the world of megalith-building. Imagine an oval mound, more than 93 m (305 ft) in diameter and almost 12 m (39 ft) high, retained by a wall whose base is made up of 97 slabs placed on edge, some of them decorated. The monument used to be circled by a ring of upright monoliths, of which 12 now remain (Figure 10:5), but there is no evidence for contemporaneity of the mound and stone circle in the first phase of use. Access to the cruciform chamber of the passage-grave is by a 19 m (62 ft) long passage, lined with upright stones supporting the roofing slabs. The roof of the main chamber is false-corbelled, rising almost 6 m (20 ft) above the floor, while the three side-chambers are roofed by slabs at a lower height.

In the north and south side-chambers were discovered three large stone basins, hemispherical in shape, whose cupped surface served as a repository for carbonised bone. One of the features of Newgrange to which we shall return, apart from the decoration, is its orientation towards the winter solstice sunrise, 21 December, and especially the arrangement of a window above the passage allowing the sun's rays to penetrate the depths of the chamber on this special day of the year. Many chamber-tombs are oriented in this manner towards a solstitial sunrise, for example, Gavrinis (Morbihan), France, with which Newgrange has other points in common, both in decoration and in date, towards the end of the fourth millennium BC. However, as regards Gavrinis, Breton scholars only reluctantly accept this relatively late date. But in fact, even if we know pretty well when an architectural type appeared (and that not always), we know little about the period of building, and we should take into account that some architectural

---

Figure 10   Megalithic monuments in Ireland and Wales.
1. Distribution map of passage-graves of the Boyne valley group in Ireland and in Wales. (After M. Herrity)
2. Passage-grave at Fourknocks, Co. Meath, Ireland. (After M. Herity)
3. Plan of Carrowkeel chamber-tomb F, Co. Sligo, Ireland. (After M. Herity)
4. Plan of Carrowkeel chamber-tomb G, Co. Sligo, Ireland. (After M. Herity)
5. Passage-grave at Newgrange, Co. Meath, Ireland, under its mound. (After M. J. O'Kelly)
6. (a) Plan and (b) section of passage-grave, Bryn-Celli-Ddu, Anglesey, Wales. (After T. G. E. Powell)
7. Engraved decoration on the upright slab behind the chamber at Bryn-Celli-Ddu. In the centre is the upper edge of the stone, with its north and south faces drawn on each side. The pecking continues from one side of the slab over the top and onto the other side. (After W. F. Grimes)

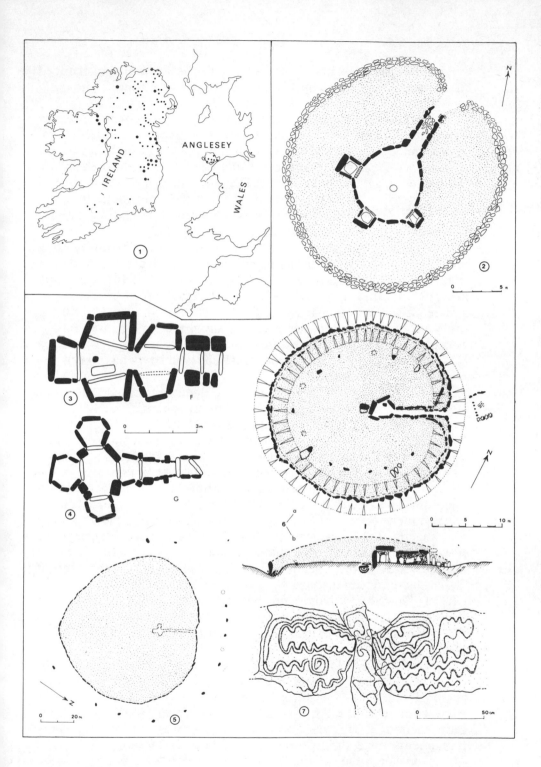

①

②

③ F

④ G

⑤

⑥ a b I

⑦

types continued to be built in one area while the 'fashion' had changed in another. Thus one cannot judge the age of a monument with early characteristics simply by looking at its plan.

The mound at Newgrange follows, in plan, the shape of a dished ovoid; its geometry has been studied by Professor Alexander Thom. From numerous observations, especially of upright stone circles in the British Isles, he has determined the unit of measurement used by the builders of megalithic monuments. The 'megalithic yard', according to Thom, measures 0.829 m (2 ft $8\frac{1}{2}$ in), and the 'megalithic fathom' 2.073 m, or $2\frac{1}{2}$ megalithic yards. We will not go into detail here about these relatively complex measurements, but will only say that the idea has been evolving in some scientific minds that our megalith-building ancestors used a unit of measurement in their constructions, and even that they had fairly advanced notions of arithmetic. It is generally accepted that they knew the Pythagorean triangle, the one where 'the square on the hypotenuse is equal to the sum of the squares on the other two sides'. So this theorem was already being chanted on the benches of schools of architecture in the fourth millennium BC in areas of Atlantic Europe. Poor Pythagoras! He could not have been the originator of 'his' own theorem.

Thom's calculations, based on solid documentation and major statistical work, follow those of a good many others; as early as 1740 William Stukeley arrived at a value of 0.53 m ($20\frac{7}{8}$ in) for the cubit used by the builders of Stonehenge. Gérardin in 1976 arrived at something very similar when he put his megalithic cubit at 0.54 m ($21\frac{1}{4}$ in), taking into account that it could have varied slightly over time, a little as the Egyptian cubit fluctuated through the centuries by several per cent. So Gérardin estimated that the megalithic cubit measured 0.540 m ($21\frac{1}{4}$ in) when Stonehenge was first built, 0.550 m ($21\frac{11}{16}$ in) during the secondary rearrangement of the same monument, and 0.548 m ($21\frac{9}{16}$ in) in its third phase. He further estimated that a numbering system was absolutely necessary, and in the case of Stonehenge this must have been a mixed system using decimal (base 10) and base 6, with the use of base 7 deriving from the Pythagorean triangle (3, 4, 5). He concludes that in the case of Gavrinis the unit of measurement would have been 0.55 m ($21\frac{11}{16}$ in) and the numbering system was base 12 (with base 7 used there also).

A non-specialist can no more evaluate the mathematical calculations made by different scholars than he can the astronomical theories promulgated about megalithic monuments. However, I must make some comment. First must come the duration of the megalithic phenomenon, 2000 years, and its extent over western Europe. Many monuments have disappeared, others have been reorganised, still others have been built to the detriment of earlier monuments. Relative analysis seems impossible, for example, of the '*Grand Menhir brisé*'

Er-Grah, La Table des Marchands and Gavrinis, when we know that the roofs of La Table des Marchands and Gavrinis are made from two fragments of a large slab not unlike Er-Grah. It seems that there is a chance that the builders of La Table des Marchands and Gavrinis were at the bottom of the destruction of the *grand menhir* of Er-Grah. It is plausible that each monument had a unit of measurement used in its construction, and that this unit was used by a whole local population over a period of time – but it is not proved. What is almost certain is that, instead of scoffing at individual attempts at understanding, it would be much more useful if prehistorians, mathematicians and astronomers worked for a common cause. First let the prehistorian do a faultless excavation and extract a correct dating from the monuments; let mathematicians and astronomers make precise observations and accurate calculations – and we will have grounds for serious discussion!

But let us leave these considerations and return to the cemetery of the Boyne valley. The third impressive mound, the furthest west, is Knowth, which rises in the centre of a group of 17 smaller mounds. Of these, nine are passage-graves, rectangular or trapezoid in shape, where the chamber and the passage are only slightly differentiated; four (one of them doubtful) are passage-graves, cruciform in plan, of the same type as Newgrange; and the northern grave at Dowth, and the others are not determined.

The Knowth mound was excavated from 1960 onwards by George Eogan; it is oval in shape, with an east-west diameter of 80 m (262 ft) and a north-south diameter of 90 m (295 ft). It lies partly over one of the small satellite mounds, seeming to show that the large monuments are later than the small passage-graves in their circular mounds. This observation seems to be confirmed by the radiocarbon datings obtained at Newgrange, 2465 ± 40 and 2550 ± 45 b.c. uncorrected, and indicating a calendar date around the end of the fourth millennium BC, while small chamber-tombs such as no. 7 at Carrowmore, Co. Sligo (3290 ± 80 b.c. uncorrected), a single passage-grave, and no. 27, cruciform in plan with a little-differentiated passage ($3090 \pm$ b.c. uncorrected) indicate a construction from the beginning of the fourth millennium BC. Knowth encloses two passage-graves, set back to back and separated by only 3 m (10 ft). The western one resembles a Breton angled chamber-tomb such as Les Pierres Plates at Locmariaquer, or Luffang; it is 34 m (111 ft) long. Knowth East is a cruciform-plan passage-grave, 40 m (131 ft) long and comparable with Newgrange. The passages of the two monuments are megalithic, with juxtaposed roofing-slabs, and their height rises from the entrance towards the chamber. The western chamber-tomb is entirely megalithic while the chamber has a false-corbelled roof. Both, as at Newgrange, contained a large stone basin. In the right-hand cell of Knowth East was found a basin with exceptional decoration; the one found in the angled passage-grave, at the point where the monument changes direction, seems not to be in its original position.

Of the kerb-stones of the mound, many are decorated, as are the orthostats of the two chambers and several of the roofing stones. The recumbent stone in front of the entrance to the western burial-chamber has a motif of engraved concentric rectangles, which are repeated on the entrance-stone of the chamber and on a slab at the far end of it.

The mound is made up of successive layers of different materials. The structure appears uniform and to have been built in a single campaign. The two passage-graves, so different in shape and structure, would have been contemporaneous.

The megalithic cemetery of the Boyne valley contains about 30 mounds, divided into three groups each dominated by a super-monument.

About 60 km (37 miles) further west, the cemetery of Loughcrew, on the highest hills of Co. Meath, also has about 30 monuments. Then the Carrowkeel group of 14 monuments dominates the town of Sligo in the west. In the Carrowmore group, only 34 monuments remain of the 100 or so which were there. To these should be added several groups of two to five monuments, as well as individual passage-graves. But we cannot describe all these sites here, and some plans are given in Figure 10.

As in Brittany, a single mound can contain several chamber-tombs, and the plans of the Irish monuments show certain affinities with those of western France. But in Ireland cremation of the bodies was common practice, although unburnt bones have been discovered in a few passage-graves. It is difficult to assess the number of individuals in each grave, and indications vary from four or five cremated individuals and some unburnt bones at Newgrange, to 24 at Fourknocks, and 100 or more at Tara. These are always collective graves, but they were used over a long period and we cannot know whether the collective aspect of the tomb is primary or secondary. Do the great passage-graves signify a more hierarchical structure in late neolithic society, after an egalitarian period when more numerous monuments belonged to all? This is a theory defended by English prehistorians, and we will return to it.

Archaeological material accompanying the dead in their last resting-place is rare, mostly limited to ornaments worn by the deceased at the time of cremation. The funerary pottery is in the style known as Carrowkeel, richly decorated and round-based. Occupation sites yielding identical pottery also contain transverse arrowheads which, according to Michael Herity and George Eogan, originated in Brittany; these would confirm these authors' supposition of relations between Brittany and Ireland at the period.

In fact, the question of origin of the Boyne-valley type of passage-grave is very controversial. Some see it as originating in the west of France, whence it would cross to the Irish Sea via the Channel Islands. Simple forms would have appeared first in the east of the island, and would perhaps have affected the earliest megalith-building in Ireland. Others would like to see a northern origin, entering through the west of the country, and the large monuments of the Newgrange type would form a final phase of the architectural type. Only the practice of cremation would be purely Irish, and this funerary custom should probably be researched among earlier local populations. Thus the passage-grave would be the local interpretation of an Atlantic idea.

Anglesey passage-graves: ideological conflict and a strange soup

In the Isle of Anglesey in Wales, the passage-grave of Bryn-Celli-Ddu is particularly important as much for its architecture as for its history (Figure 10:6). According to Frances Lynch, it is probably one of the latest megalithic burial-places built in Anglesey; despite its formal resemblance to the Breton passage-graves, which may be very early in the megalithic chronology, this chamber-tomb must have been built in the late neolithic. It is superimposed upon another religious monument, a 'henge', of an architectural type which first appeared in southern England towards the end of the middle Neolithic.

Even if most people have heard of a henge, and the most famous of them, Stonehenge, it is still perhaps useful to say a little more about them. The first henges are larger or smaller circular areas, bounded by a ditch bordered by an exterior bank. On the inner side of the ditch, stones were sometimes set up in a circle. Without doubt the most impressive of these groups is Avebury, to the north of West Kennet long barrow in England. In the earliest phase of use of the henges, just when the causewayed enclosures with their rings of multiple interrupted ditches were going into decline, a single interruption to the ditch gave access to the internal surface, thought to be a sanctuary open to the sky. These monuments seem to have a local origin, not related to continental Europe, and were used until the Bronze Age, when they generally have two opposed entrances and circles of upright stones. Henges are numerous in the north and south of England, less so in Scotland and rare in Wales and Ireland. Durrington Walls, not far from Stonehenge, is one of the largest, 500 m (1640 ft) in diameter and with two diametrically opposed entrances. Woodhenge, which practically touches it, is among the smallest and had the special feature of a wooden roof.

But back to Bryn-Celli-Ddu, which was excavated by W. J. Kemp in 1928. The prevailing explanation for the superimposition of a passage-grave on a henge is the ideological confrontation of two peoples of which one, conservative in character, destroyed the just-introduced symbol of the new ideology. At Bryn-Celli-Ddu, the henge was made up of a circular space a little over 20 m (66 ft) in diameter, bordered by a ditch and probably by a bank, the earth from which could have been used secondarily to cover over the chamber-tomb. It seems that the entrance to the henge was in the same position as the present entrance to the passage-grave. The excavation revealed the position of a circle of 14 originally upright stones not far from the ditch. At the foot of certain of these stones there were sometimes found a few carbonised fragments of human bone; the cremated body of a girl, 8–10 years old, was discovered at the foot of one stone, and another, perhaps 15 years old, had been placed in the same way next to an upright block.

All the upright stones were deliberately knocked down by the passage-grave builders before being covered over by the cairn. This was a voluntary act of destruction which seems to bear witness to a conflict between two religious tendencies. It often happens that monuments are superimposed upon others, and we have seen numerous examples. Sometimes there is even a re-use of the stones from an older structure in a new one, and we shall see some flagrant examples of this, notably in Brittany; at Bryn-Celli-Ddu, Lynch insists on the fact that six stones were shattered, and one burnt, while three more were broken *in situ* by other falling blocks, and finally five were completely removed.

At the centre of the henge, at the crossing-point of lines drawn between two diametrically opposed upright stones, a pit was dug by the builders of the passage-grave. What did they have to destroy at this precise point? A fire had been lit in this pit, where a small human bone from the inner ear was found at the bottom. Lynch remarks in relation to this, but without drawing any conclusions, that inner-ear bones were found in Bronze Age mounds in Anglesey. What mysterious ritual surrounds these deposits?

The hole was closed by a flat stone, close to which was discovered another slab decorated in a style also found in the Gulf of Morbihan, France (Figure 10:7).

The passage-grave is a classic tomb, with a megalithic passage and a polygonal chamber, enclosed by a circular mound with a double retaining wall. One upright stone in the chamber seems to be a stele like those found at Carrowkeel, Co. Sligo, Ireland, and at Clettraval in the Scottish Hebrides, but also like some in the Iberian peninsula and in several monuments in western France. Human bone remains, both carbonised and not, were found during the 1928 excavations on the floor of the chamber and of the passage. The passage is partly open to the sky and partly roofed with large slabs: this section leads to the chamber. A small stone bench on the north side of the passage should be noted, and two upright stones in niches just next to the portal, to the south. These little stelae have sometimes been compared with stones found in front of certain monuments at Los Millares in Spain, but why not also with those found in chamber-tombs in northern Africa or even Ethiopia.

The mound is bordered by stones, set upright in the ditch, some of which had already fallen when the passage-grave was built. The space between adjacent stones is filled by dry-stone walling. A short way into the cairn is a second line of stones, invisible because they are hidden by the cairn, except near the entrance where they are higher and join up with the portal to the passage. Some traces of ritual ceremonies were brought to light in front of the entrance. On the other side of the ditch, an enclosure marked on three sides by small upright stones and a palisade surrounded the skeleton of a bovid. It is difficult to decide what connection there is between this deposit and the passage-grave.

Also in Anglesey, the chambered barrow of Barclodiad-y-Gawres was excavated in 1952–3 by Terence Powell and Glyn Daniel. It comprises a long passage which ends in a central chamber, off which lead three side-cells, one of them having a small annexe chamber. It therefore belongs to the Boyne valley type. It is a megalithic construction, covered by a circular mound of earth and stone. The central chamber was roofed by false-corbelling; the side chambers had much cruder false-corbelling, with only a few large slabs.

As in all monuments of this type, cremation was the funerary rite, and some burnt human bone remains were found in the side chambers. But there were no human burials in the central chamber, which seems to have been a ceremonial place, judging by the remains found in a fireplace at the centre of it. Fishbones identifiable as those of wrasse, eel and whiting were there, but also bones of frog, toad, snake, mouse, shrew and hare. The mind leaps to magical practices: what a soup!

Another, not the least interesting feature of this monument, is the richness of engraved decoration of some of the uprights, comparable to that of the passage-graves of the Boyne valley group, with, in particular, a most pleasing series of spirals.

Megalithic art in the British Isles

We owe to Elizabeth Shee Twohig a brilliant study of megalithic art in Europe. This art occurred only in passage-graves in the Iberian peninsula (42 sites), western France (39 sites), and Great Britain (six sites), and in the French *allées couvertes*, in Brittany (seven sites) and in the Paris Basin (eight sites), to which may be added 11 *hypogées*, underground chambers, from the eastern Paris Basin. Megalithic art can be engraved or painted, but it is probable that in most cases the painting has disappeared in the course of the millennia. In our time, only the monuments in the Iberian peninsula, particularly those in central Portugal, still display painted works of art, while painted traces have been found in the Paris Basin *hypogées*.

In the British Isles, decorative art is associated solely with passage-graves. It comprises engraved or pecked slabs placed as kerb-stones around the mound, in the passage (on side orthostats and roofing-slabs) or in the chamber. It is abundant in the eastern Irish monuments (Loughcrew, Boyne valley, Fourknocks) as well as Anglesey, but absent from the western Irish monuments.

Two styles have been recognised, and termed 'Fourknocks' and 'Loughcrew'. The Fourknocks style is the more elaborate; it is a formal style where the motifs form a coherent design, arranged to create compositions. Often the decoration takes up the whole surface of the stone, or is in a well-defined panel. We note a preference for lozenges, zigzags and spirals (Figure 11). The Loughcrew style, which is much less organised, is made up mostly of concentric circles, circular dots, U-shapes and wavy lines. The decorations concealed on the backs of the stones, invisible once the building was complete, belong to this style. Maybe these hidden decorations are the result of re-use of slabs belonging to an early monument, as seems to be the case in the monument at Gavrinis in France, for example. The Fourknocks style would then appear to be later than the Loughcrew style.

Twohig establishes a classification of the decorative motifs into 11 groups: circles, circles with a central dot, U-shapes, spirals, radiating lines, parallel lines, parallel lines cut by a vertical line, wavy lines, zigzags, lozenges and triangles, and dots. But some compositions made up of abstract motifs may appear anthropomorphic.

Passage-graves in Scotland and the Orkney islands

The Orkney archipelago to the north of Scotland is well known to archaeologists for its exceptional monuments, such as the stone circles of the Ring of Brodgar and the Stones of Stenness, the village of Skara Brae, or the magnificent funerary chambers of Maes Howe and Quanterness, all on Mainland, the largest of the Orkney islands.

It was during a violent storm in 1850 that the village of Skara Brae, buried until then under dunes at the head of an inlet, was swept clean of the sand which covered it. It consisted of a dozen houses, and its singularity lay in its being entirely constructed of small stone slabs. There is no wood on these islands, but they do have the advantage of possessing outcrops of easily-shaped flaking sandstone. This explains why the megalith monuments of Orkney are among the most beautiful architectural structures of this period in Europe. Each house consists of a single room with rounded corners, averaging 6 m by 7 m (20 ft by 23 ft). Their furnishings have been recovered because, like the walls and a part of the roof, they are made from slabs of stone; tables, chests,

Figure 11   Carved kerb-stones from the Newgrange passage-grave, Ireland.

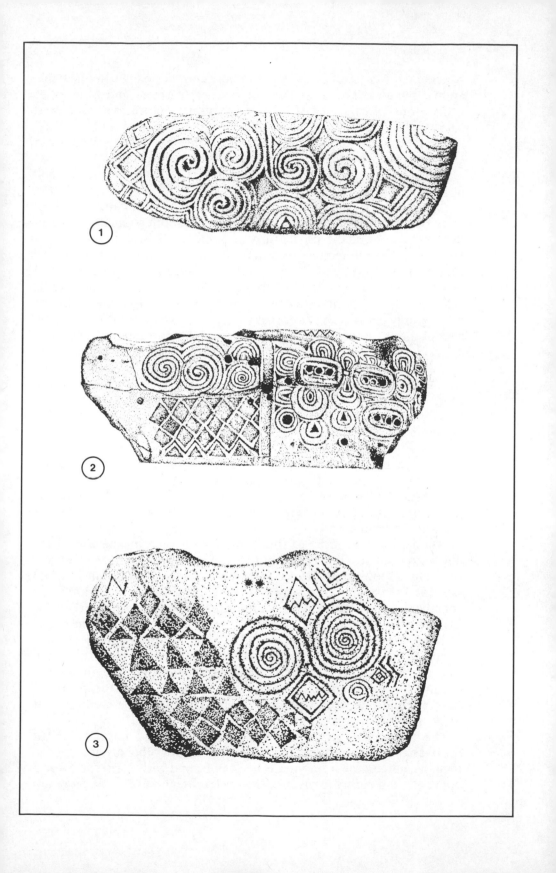

benches, storage cupboards have thus been revealed. In the hearths, animal remains show that these were sheep-farmers and hunters of walrus; but the existence of collective buildings indicates a structured society whose members, or at least some of them, may have been buried in the megalithic tomb of Maes Howe, some 15 km ($9\frac{1}{4}$ miles) away (Figure 8:11). The village underwent some modification in the course of its occupation, which spreads over half a millennium (3000–2500 BC).

The megalithic burial-chambers of Orkney, on Mainland as well as the 13 on the island of Rousay to its north, are built of small slabs and not large blocks, so the appellation 'megalithic' might seem inaccurate. However, the architecture is comparable, in form and in function, to that of other European chamber-tombs where the building material has dictated the design. It is just the same with the false-corbelled vaults called '*tholoi*', inasmuch as they are built of small stone slabs set horizontally one on top of another and slightly overlapping to form the roof of the chamber. This is the roofing principle adopted for the four-sided chamber with re-entrant corners at Maes Howe, probably the most handsome chamber-tomb in Atlantic megalith-building. To the west opens a long passage in two sections of unequal height. Off the other three sides of the chamber open three small lateral cells, also four-sided but at a higher level than the floor of the principal chamber. The monument is dated to 2800 BC, or relatively late in the chronology of western European megaliths.

Like the majority of Orcadian megaliths, Quanterness is in a good state of preservation. It was recently excavated by Colin Renfrew (1979). One passage serves a four-sided principal chamber, around which are set six small chambers, also rectangular. The whole is contained within a circular cairn with four lines of internal walling in dry-stone. But according to Renfrew's reconstruction, the walls were never exposed to view and this was not a stepped monument, as is generally supposed in France. The walls served only as an internal skeleton for the cairn. So why were they erected with such care? The chambers are all built on the same level and covered by corbelling, finished off with larger stones. The working of the stone, both here and at Maes Howe, is admirably regular, and one is surprised at such architectural quality in a people who were ignorant of the use of metal. In fact, the monument was built at the end of the fourth millennium BC. During Renfrew's investigations, only 80 per cent of the principal chamber and one lateral chamber were excavated. The study he has made of this is of great interest.

The human skeletal remains were very fragmented and scattered at the back of the monument; they were mixed with other archaeological remains, among them fragments of 34 pots, and with domestic-animal bones corresponding to seven sheep, 18 lambs, and five cattle, bones of deer and wild mammals, bones of 35 different kinds of birds, and the bones of seven types of fish. We can imagine offerings made to the dead for the Great Journey, or the remains of funeral feasts placed in the chamber.

A study by J. Chesterman of the 1260 human bone fragments recovered indicates at least 157 individuals buried in this part of the main chamber and the small chamber. The extent of fragmentation of the bones shows that they are there in a secondary context, buried after decarnation in another place. There must have been the remains of about 400 individuals placed in the whole of the monument. Division by sex shows near-equal numbers of male and female, but children were not placed in this collective grave, which must have been in use for over 500 years or so by a human group numbering not more than 20 persons at any one time, according to Renfrew's calculations.

During this first period of megalith-building on Mainland in Orkney, the scattered funerary monuments are of comparable size. They belong to small human groups of about 20 people, living by stock-raising and cultivation around 'their' chamber-tomb. Thus no spatial hierarchy appears among the monuments, and Renfrew suggests a relatively egalitarian society, with elaborate funerary rites, secondary burials and offerings to the dead.

Several centuries later, the construction of grandiose monuments such as the megalithic tomb of Maes Howe and the Ring of Brodgar indicates a society turning towards a more centralised, more hierarchical organisation. So Renfrew's idea is that Atlantic megalith-building is not originally the result of hierarchical societies, but rather the opposite, of small egalitarian groups. This supposition seems to apply very aptly to the 13 dry-stone monuments on Rousay, each at the centre of a territory where 25 to 50 people lived. Here the paucity of human bone remains found in each chamber would be due to its regular emptying to make way for fresh burials. Each human group could correspond to a large family autonomously managing the resources of its territory. This is marked by the funerary monument, the only really important building the group had, living as they did in fragile houses, leaving little trace over many moves, every 10 or 15 years, as the exhausted soil was left to lie fallow. More than just a collective grave, the megalith became the territorial marker of the group, hence its monumental character, by no means obligatory for a purely funerary purpose; it is a 'grave for the [use of the] living', as Andrew Fleming has it.

In the Isle of Arran, to the west of Scotland, Renfrew has attempted the same approach towards the 18 tombs contained in mounds which can reach up to 40 m (131 ft) long. To define the territories corresponding to each monument, he uses Thiessen polygons, a method of division used by geographers, in which lines are drawn connecting points halfway between the monuments. He maintains that each tomb corresponds to an agricultural area of the island on which the itinerant farming already discussed was easily practicable. Thus the English scholar's thesis of an egalitarian society at the beginnings of megalith-building seems amply confirmed in these regions. But I am not certain that it can be generalised across the Atlantic world, especially in northern Europe, where we have seen that in Denmark and Poland the long mounds of the earliest period sometimes hold a single corpse, which could be that of a high-ranking personage in a hierarchical society. The interest in Renfrew's theory lies in its offering a new conceptual model; but this model, like all models, requires validation.

Several groups of passage-graves have been identified by Audrey Henshall in Scotland. The O.C.H. group (Orkney, Cromarty, Hebrides), the Bargrennan group of circular cairns, and the Clava group, representing about 50 sites, can be added to the Maes Howe group in Orkney which we have described in more detail. The Clava type of monuments are passage-graves with round chambers, practically the only ones in the British Isles, but according to Henshall they derive from unroofed circular monuments and thus are unrelated morphogenetically to other passage-graves. As with the Clyde group of court-tombs, the majority of Scottish passage-graves were originally buried in a circular mound; but while the Clyde tombs were covered over by trapezoidal mounds, the passage-graves were enclosed by structures of diverse shape: four-sided (Figure 8:8) or with horns (Figure 8:9 and 10). The earliest monuments seem to be those of the Clyde and Bargrennan groups, from the beginning of the fourth millennium BC. The O.C.H. type of passage-grave seem to have appeared in the west of Scotland shortly after the first Clyde monuments, towards the middle of the fourth millennium BC. The Maes Howe type of monument is from the beginning of the third millennium BC.

Figure 12   Megalithic monuments in Jersey, Guernsey, the Scilly Isles, and Cornwall.
1. *La Pouquelaye de Faldouet, Jersey. (After J. Hawkes)*
2. *La Hougue Bie, Jersey. (After Rybot)*
3. *Ville-es-Nouaux, Jersey. (After J. Hawkes)*
4. *Ville-es-Nouaux, Jersey. (After J. Hawkes)*
5. *Le Mont-de-la-Ville, Jersey. (After J. Hawkes)*
6. *Le Mont Ubé, Jersey. (After J. Hawkes)*
7. *Le Déhus, Guernsey. (After V. C. C. Collum)*
8. *Les Fouillages, Guernsey. (After I. Kinnes)*
9. *Innisidgen, St Mary's, Isles of Scilly. (After G. Bonsor)*
10. *Porth Hellick Down, St Mary's, Isles of Scilly. (After G. Bonsor)*
11. *Tregiffian, Cornwall. (After A. M. ApSimon)*

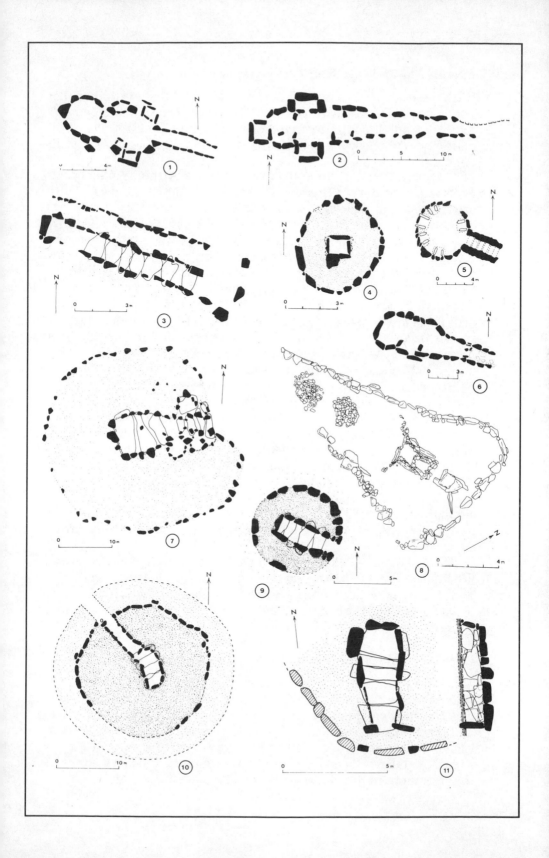

Chamber-tombs in the Scilly Isles and Cornwall

We have mentioned the megalithic monuments of Cornwall when they relate to a type recognised elsewhere in Great Britain or Ireland. We must also call attention to a type of architecture more specific to the region, morphologically close to the traditional passage-grave in its circular mound.

A typical example, recently excavated by Arthur ApSimon, is Tregiffian at St Buryan (Figure 12:11), right at the end of the Cornish promontory and a kilometre from the sea. Near the barrow are several other mounds, some standing-stones and the circle of upright stones called the Merry Maidens. Tregiffian comprises a chamber and passage, little differentiated from each other, of a type proper to the Scilly Isles and the Land's End peninsula, the south-western tip of Cornwall. The chamber, 5 m (16½ ft) long by 2 m (6½ ft) wide, is 90 cm (35 in) high beneath a ceiling consisting of five slabs. Two large orthostats mark either side of the entrance. The one on the southern side is decorated with deep cup-marks. Two pits in the chamber contained cremations of the early Bronze Age. The people of this period did indeed often re-utilise the funerary monuments of their predecessors, to such an extent that for a while this type of chamber-tomb, the *entrance-grave*, was attributed to them. Researchers now incline towards placing the construction of these monuments in the English middle Neolithic, that is, the second half of the third millennium BC. In its present state, the Tregiffian chamber-tomb is enclosed, in an off-centre position, within a polygonal mound. ApSimon has shown that this enclosure was late, and should be seen in relation to the Bronze Age pits. Excavation has revealed an underlying circular enclosure, 17 m (56 ft) in diameter, made up of large stone blocks. The chamber-tomb is perfectly at the centre of this earlier enclosure.

The Scilly Isles, 40 km (25 miles) west of Cornwall, contain several little-differentiated passage-graves in circular mounds generally bounded by large kerb-stones. Sometimes there are two circular lines of walling around the chamber, and some chamber-tombs have a more defined passage (Figure 12:9 and 10).

Chamber-tombs in the Channel Islands, Guernsey and Jersey

Megalithic chamber-tombs, relatively numerous in the Channel Islands, are an extension into the islands of the monuments of Brittany and Normandy. Although the level of the sea was lower in the fourth and third millennia BC than now, Guernsey and Jersey were already islands and about 40 km (25 miles) separated Guernsey from the French mainland. Knowledge of navigation in the English Channel is thus certain from the end of the fifth millennium BC.

A site recently excavated by Ian Kinnes in the island of Guernsey is of great interest for the study of the Neolithic and of megalith-building in this area. It is Les Fouillages, a monument in the north of the island, which Kinnes studied between 1979 and 1981 (Figure 12:8). He thinks that only 12 now remain of the 70 megalithic monuments whose traces have been found in Guernsey. This implies that there would have been one monument to each square kilometre, but since they are not all from the same period the territories they could mark are probably in reality much larger.

When it was opened in 1977, the monument was in the form of an oval mound, 35 m (115 ft) long. It had been built on a site containing geometric microliths, which proves that a mesolithic population from who knows where, or when, had occupied the area. The original mound was shaped like an isosceles triangle, with sides 20 m (66 ft) long on a base of 10 m (33 ft), bounded by large stone blocks. Within this surface, four stone structures were exposed. From west to east they were: first, a circular paved area 1.6 m (5 ft 3 in) in diameter; then a sub-rectangular cairn containing a cist; a small anthropomorphic *menhir* alongside a double chamber, unroofed, 2.6 m (8½ ft) long by 1.7 m (5½ ft) wide, made of upright slabs and dry-stone walling; and lastly, more to the east, a small chamber built of slabs and covered by three stones which opened on to a very small forecourt.

This complex monument which, according to Kinnes, was built in a single campaign, was the work of a population using a ceramic belonging to the large *Linearbandkeramik* group, which spread from central Europe as far as the Paris Basin, and brought with them a knowledge of farming. Seven decorated pots had been deposited at the base of the mound, in the unroofed chamber and on the paved area to the west. Also, a large number of sherds of Linearbandkeramik pottery were collected in the body of the mound. This collection, comparable to those from the occupation sites of Pinacle and Mont Orgeuil, can be dated to the end of the fifth millennium BC, if we judge by the radiocarbon dates obtained from Les Fouillages. Pottery from the same ceramic family had been discovered around and beneath La Hoguette chambered mound in Calvados, France, where the chambers are round and have corbelled roofs. The users of later *Linearband-keramik* pottery thus seem to have built megalithic monuments in Normandy and in the Channel Islands. But is this not more likely to be an autochthonous population, receiving multiple influences from different directions: a process of 'neolithicisation' from the Paris Basin, long triangular mounds from northern Europe, and megalith-building from Brittany? At least, this is as it appears, for it is a little difficult to maintain that, faced with the sea, a population wanting to assure its identity and its cohesion should have spontaneously started to build chamber-tombs in Guernsey when they were capable of crossing an arm of the sea 40 km (25 miles) to 50 km (31 miles) wide. . . . They could have rowed further!

At the end of the first phase of use, the unroofed chamber of Les Fouillages was filled with earth and stones, and the other chamber with sand. As so often with megalithic monuments, we have here a structure which has been deliberately put out of use. Some centuries later a new arrangement was made to the east. In a final fourth phase, a votive deposit was inserted, of eight barbed-and-tanged arrowheads of an advanced type; four of them were made of flint from Grand-Pressigny (Indre-et-Loire), France. It was during this Bell-beaker period, in the second half of the third millennium BC, that the whole was covered by an oval mound 35 m (115 ft) long.

Among the other monuments on Guernsey, we must mention Le Déhus (Figure 12:7), a passage-grave open to the east in a roughly circular mound, 19 m (62 ft) in diameter and bordered by large blocks of stone. It is entirely megalithic and has a plan in the shape of a bottle. Four cells are set, two by two, off either side of the passage. The interior surface of the central roofing slab in the chamber is engraved with a human representation, whose face and two hands are well defined. It seems that this work, partly hidden, was prior to the use of the slab in the structure. Perhaps this is a re-used slab, comparable to La Grand-Mère of Chimquière which was remodelled later, or Le Catel, very characteristic with its two breasts and collar; identical forms are known in Brittany.

The monument was excavated by Lukis in 1837, then by Collum in 1932. The skeletal remains of at least five individuals were collected, and among them were found a copper dagger from the Bell-beaker period as well as two Beakers and the fragments of several others. Beaker-period re-use is general in the Channel Islands. Close to 40 pots and the sherds of about 100 more (now in the Lukis Museum at St Peter Port) were found in La Varde passage-grave, which also yielded a conical V-button. (V-buttons are small bone objects which can take different forms according to area but which are all characterised by a base perforated by two oblique holes which join up, forming a V to take a shank.)

The other Guernsey passage-graves are Le Creux des Faies, La Roque qui Sonne, and Le Trépied.

On Jersey the most imposing monument, La Hougue Bie, is a mound 57 m (187 ft) in diameter and 12 m (39 ft) high, surmounted by two medieval chapels. This same desire for Christianisation is found at Saint-Michel mound at Carnac (Morbihan), France, where the mound is also topped by a chapel.

The chamber-tomb at La Hougue Bie (Figure 12:2) is entirely megalithic, with the spaces filled by dry-stone walling. It comprises a 12 m (39 ft) long passage, open to the east, giving on to a chamber of the same length. Two lateral cells form transepts to the chamber, which has one other, terminal cell; this cruciform plan is widespread from Brittany to Orkney, via England and Ireland. On the eastern orthostat of the northern side-chamber are engraved a score or so cup-marks, most of them hidden by a dry-stone wall, which perhaps implies a re-use of this slab in the construction of the monument. Four small upright stones, perhaps 30 cm (12 in) in height, were discovered, three of them at the end of the principal chamber and the fourth in the western cell. Such *betyls* (sacred stones) are known in the megalithic cemetery of Los Millares in southern Spain.

The excavations of La Hougue Bie yielded the remains of eight burials; most important was the finding of a particular type of pot, consisting of a small cup mounted on a ring-shaped support, which used to be called a '*vase-support*' and is considered to be a perfume-burner. The form, which is very specific to the west of France in the middle Neolithic, is often found in megalithic monuments, from the Channel Islands down to the southern Charentes. Some examples, generally four-cornered, are known in the Paris Basin; a small number of others have reached the Mediterranean, which some scholars would like to be their provenance, a claim which is by no means proved – the 'eastern mirage' again. Nineteen of the cups with feet, mostly richly decorated, were found at La Hougue Bie.

La Pouquelaye de Faldouet (Figure 12:1) stands up on a hill. The passage opening to the east gives on to a chamber made in two horseshoe-shaped lobes joined at the base. Three side-cells open on to the first part of the chamber, and small compartments have been marked out. Two footed cups were recovered.

Le Mont Ubé (Figure 12:6) has a chamber morphologically similar to that of Le Déhus in Guernsey, but without the side-cell on to the passage.

Le Mont-de-la-Ville (Figure 12:5), discovered in 1785, was given as a mark of gratitude to the Governor of Jersey, who had it erected on his estate at Park Place, Henley, after a journey across the Channel and up the Thames. It was a passage-grave with a round chamber, comparable to La Sergenté chamber-tomb in the same island, and to La Hogue and La Hoguette at Fontenay-le-Marmion in Calvados, France, to take but a few examples.

Two *allées couvertes* deserve mention on Jersey. Le Couperon has a passage 8.2 m (27 ft) long by 1 m (3 ft) wide, surrounded by a rectangle of upright stones; one slab at the end has a semi-circular notch, which probably represents half of the circular perforation commonly met with in the *allées couvertes* of the Paris Basin and as far as Westphalia. In the municipal garden of the village of Ville-es-Nouax, near St Helier, is a second *allée couverte* (Figure 12:3), 10.2 m (33½ ft) long by 1.2 m (4 ft) wide, which must also have had a four-sided surround of upright stones. Not far away survives a megalithic cist at the centre of a circular mound, 6 m (20 ft) in diameter, bordered by large blocks of stone (Figure 12:4).

3. Western France – cradle of Atlantic megalith-building?

Chamber-tombs and the sea

On a bright summer's day, a boat trip in the Gulf of Morbihan is an attractive pastime, as much for the magnificent countryside for the nature-lover as for the number and quality of prehistoric remains: the tombs and *menhirs* (standing-stones) of Île-aux-Moines; Gavrinis, known all over the world for its art, where recent work has restored a good measure of its original majestic aspect; Île Longue, with its long passage and chamber covered by a roof made of overlapping stones in a kind of false corbelling. You will find *cromlechs*, circles of upright stones, on the small island of Er-Lannic, and you will be surprised to see that one of them is under water. So the level of the sea must have been lower when this megalithic structure was first built.

In fact, fluctuations in sea-level were very numerous during the quaternary era, which contained at least four long periods of glaciation. After the latest of these, the Wurm glaciation, the water level of the sea was a good 100 m (328 ft) lower than nowadays, exposing vast tracts of land now submerged. The warming-up period which followed this Ice Age, beginning perhaps 12,000 years ago, melted the ice-sheets. The sea gradually rose to its present level. Unfortunately this rise was not regular, and the curve representing its progress shows several oscillations, especially numerous in the last 5000 years BC. These movements have diverse more or less complex causes, and are slightly different from one area to another.

However, it is true to say that at the time of construction of the megalithic monuments of the Atlantic coastline the general level of the ocean was several metres lower than it is today. And the filling-up of the marshes of the Atlantic coast with sea- and river-mud was not finished; it must be borne in mind that these areas were more or less covered by water, sometimes allowing access deep into the land-mass.

The lower sea-level explains why nowadays some monuments are standing in the water; but at the same time the incomplete infilling of the present-day marshes allowed the occupation of their banks by those neolithic peoples, builders of chamber-tombs, whose links with the sea were strong, especially during the earliest phase.

Mounds without chambers

Having already dealt with this question in the presentation of the northern long mounds, I will just recall here the existence of these monuments in the west of France, adding a few considerations peculiar to this region.

Along the 'Atlantic façade' of France were erected some large mounds which, when we know what is inside them, contain a chamber disproportionately small in relation to the sometimes considerable mass which surmounts them. No passage gives access to these chambers, which must, therefore, have been used only on a single occasion, perhaps the death of a high-ranking personage. So these are not, properly speaking, chamber-tombs by the definition we are using.

The best-known of these form the group of Breton mounds called 'Carnacian', at least some of which seem to have been raised in the course of the fifth millennium BC; examples are Le Moustoir and Saint-Michel at Carnac, Mané-Lud and Mané-er-Hroeck at Locmariaquer. Several of them have been opened during the last century but none has been excavated completely. In the mound of Mané-Lud (80 m [262 ft] long by 50 m [164 ft] wide and 5.5 m [18 ft] high), the central tomb is covered by a cairn; to the east, horses' skulls rested on a line of blocks. At the other end of the mound a passage-grave, famous for its rich mural decorations, seems to be in a secondary context. Archaeologists have been surprised by the over-large capstone and have put forward the hypothesis that this is a very large standing-stone being re-utilised. In an earlier phase, this stele might therefore have stood at one end of the mound, which is oriented east-west. This same hypothesis has been advanced for the capstone of Mané-Rutual, which would first have been a large upright stele decorated with a 'shield-idol'.

At Er-Grah-en-Locmariaquer are the worn-down remains of a very long mound, which also contained a cist. The enormous *menhir* there (*'Le Grand Menhir brisé'*), broken into four pieces measuring altogether some 20 m (66 ft) in length and weighing 350 tonnes, must also have been set upright at one end of the mound which here is oriented north-south. It therefore seems that there is a relationship between the *menhir*, which carries one engraving, and the long mound.

We find an identical relationship in the mound of Le Manio, which is not very long and contains a large number of small cists; here also a menhir stands at the eastern end. Sinuous, snake-like engravings can be seen at the base of this stele. We should note that the Le Manio alignment passes over the mound.

The oval mound at Mané-er-Hroeck reaches 10 m (33 ft) in height; it is 100 m (328 ft) long by 60 m (197 ft) wide and contains a small tomb at its centre. Artefacts of the highest quality were recovered here: polished axes of fibrolite and jadeite, an annular disk also of jadeite, beads and pendants of variscite. A decorated stele, broken into several pieces, was found among the stones which were used to block up the chamber. Its discard indicates a lack of interest in the stele on the part of the builders of the giant mound.

We can accept that builders of passage-graves broke up and re-used stelae which no longer mattered to them, although certain engraved symbols appear identical on both. But to find some stelae apparently linked to giant mounds, and others in pieces within the bulk of the mound, is difficult to understand, unless the mounds are not all of the same period, which seems probable.

Another group of giant mounds is known in central western France; unhappily, their internal structure has been little studied. Many of them are in the form of an elongated trapezoid, but while some are more than 100 m (328 ft) long, others are much smaller. They are often oriented east-west and are higher at the wider, eastern, end.

At Tusson, in Charente, there is a group of mounds: three are giants (Le Vieux Breuil, Le Petit Dognon, and Le Gros Dognon, which is 150 m [492 ft] long), surrounded by a score of smaller ones, which have recently been destroyed.

Another example, La Motte-de-Puitaillé at Assais (Deux-Sèvres), reaches a length of 140 m (459 ft) at its maximum; its mound is made up of three interpenetrating parts, surrounded by a wall, and 12 m (39 ft) in height.

In Aquitaine, the much smaller mound of Bernet-Saint-Sauveur harboured a small chest containing a skeleton. This monument, like La Grosse-Motte at Bouhet (Charente-Maritime), shows that wooden structures sometimes entered into the construction of these mounds, which should be looked at much more carefully.

In the Calvados *département* in Normandy, the mound of La Commune-Sèche at Colombiers-sur Seulles is dated to the beginning of the fourth millennium BC.

A chamber at the end of a passage

One does not need to be an informed expert to see the difference between a Louis XV armchair and a Parker Knoll chair. Period and region have always left their mark on human artefacts. It was thus with the chamber-tombs in their earthen mounds (or *cairns*, when built of stones) which evolved over time and altered according to area.

The architectural study of megalithic monuments does allow determination of period of construction and stylistic regions. The simplest element of a dolmen is the funerary chamber, alone at the end of the passage. But this grave may be unique within the mound, or, alternatively, there may be several inside the same stone envelope, built one next to another along a single straight façade, or radiating all round the monument. Sometimes you have to walk down a low, narrow passage, dark and damp, for more than 10 m (33 ft) before reaching the chamber, which can be round or polygonal, or even rectangular, and off-set to right or left. Elsewhere, barely 2 m (6½ ft) will lead you into the chamber, which can be vast.

While some chamber-tombs are made of enormous stone slabs, others are made of much smaller elements and here dry-stone construction plays a large part.

This first group of French passage-graves with a single chamber must therefore be subdivided, and a few characteristic examples will help to demonstrate these differences.

Cairns with multiple passage-graves

The cairn of Barnenez (Figure 13:2), at Plouézoc'h (Finistère), was built near the Morlaix estuary, towards the middle of the fifth millennium BC. In fact, there were two monuments on this site: the more northerly, which occupied the higher ground, has completely disappeared. The other, grander one was built lower down, about 100 m (328 ft) from the first. After being eaten into for quarry-stone – causing some trouble for the contractor – it was methodically excavated by P.-R. Giot and his team over 15 years starting in 1955. Their work revealed well-built retaining walls in dry-stone, arranged in tiers, which supported the structure of the cairn and its 11 passage-graves. The cairn, oriented north-east to south-west, is an elongated trapezoid in shape, and over 70 m (230 ft) long. It is made up of two parts, easily seen by the stones of which it is built which differ in type and (distinctly) in colour – greenish dolerite to the east, and pale granite to the west.

The monument was built in two phases, with 200 to 300 years elapsing between them. The primary cairn, to the east, contains five chamber-tombs (G, G′, H, I, J); the secondary cairn, to the west, has six (A, B, C, D, E, F). Passages 5–12 m (16½–39 ft) long give access to circular or polygonal chambers situated within the body of the cairn. But it is possible that two graves, G and G′, which are constructed entirely of dry-stone, belong to an even earlier phase when their passages were much shorter and narrower. There is an upright slab in

---

Figure 13   Passage-graves in Brittany.
1. Passage-grave of Île Longue, Larmor-Baden (Morbihan). (After L. Bonneau and Z. Le Rouzic)
2. The mound at Barnenez, Plouézoc'h (Finistère). (After P.-R. Giot and Y. Lecerf)
3. Passage-graves under mounds at Min Goh Ru, Larcuste, Colpo (Morbihan). (After J. L'Helgouach and J. Lecornec)

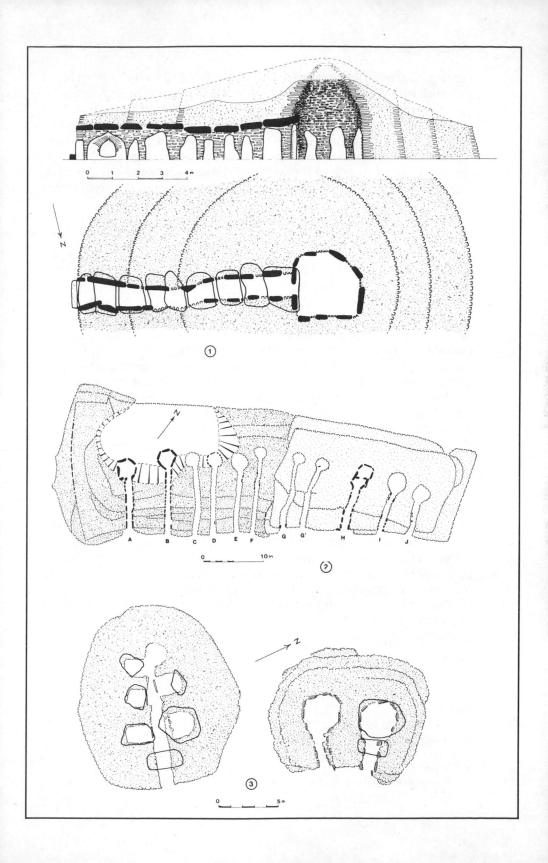

①

0 1 2 3 4m

②

A B C D E F G G' H I J

0 10m

③

0 5m

the small chamber G′, to the left as you go in, which recalls the stelae of the chambers of cairn III on the island of Ile Gaignoc, at Landeda also in Finistère. One of the four cairns on the top of Ile Gaignoc, although now partly destroyed, was also of elongated trapezoid form, built in two phases; it contained at least six passage-graves all built in dry-stone. It was oriented south-east to north-west (thus at almost 90 degrees to Barnenez) and the wider of the short sides was to the east. Five of its graves open towards the eastern section and the sixth opens opposite, to the west.

At Barnenez the four passage-graves G, G′, I, and J share the feature of being built almost entirely of dry-stone, with only a few upright slabs in the passage. The roof of the chamber is a sort of false-corbelled dome of overlapping stones. This is the origin of the Greek name *tholos* sometimes applied to this type of architecture (a long way from the popular image of a dolmen!).

Grave H of this group occupies a special, central position among the four others; megaliths were used in its construction. Moreover, its chamber is much larger and is divided into two parts by two upright slabs, one on either side. While the antechamber is corbelled, the back chamber has a roof made of a classic large slab. If, for one reason or another (the stone-quarry is a good example of the kind of reason which might be involved) the body of the cairn were to disappear, there would remain of this monument a megalithic skeleton conforming to the traditional idea of a dolmen. This is also the case with, among others, Mané-Rutual at Locmariaquer, which is comparable in plan to grave H at Barnenez.

This differentiation between grave H and the other monuments in this early cairn invites comment. Why is this central chamber-tomb much more megalithic? Why does it have a double chamber? And why does it display such advanced mural decoration – wavy lines, axes and curves? There is no easy answer. But we can imagine its being a burial-place for a princely family or that it was a sanctuary. The acid soils of Brittany destroy bone, and we shall never know what purpose chamber-tomb H was destined for; the idea of a sanctuary remains the most attractive.

We should also note the existence of small stelae in the entrance to

Figure 14   Megalithic monuments in western France.
1. Cairn de la Hogue, Fontenay-le-Marmion (Calvados). (After L. Coutil)
2. Cairn de la Hoguette, Fontenay-le-Marmion (Calvados). (After R. Caillaud and E. Lagnel)
3. Montiou, Sainte-Soline (Deux-Sèvres). (After G. Germond and R. Joussaume)
4. Kervélen, La Forêt-Fouesnant (Finistère). (After C.-T. Le Roux and J. L'Helgouach)
5. Gavrinis passage-grave, Larmor-Baden (Morbihan). (After Z. Le Rouzic)

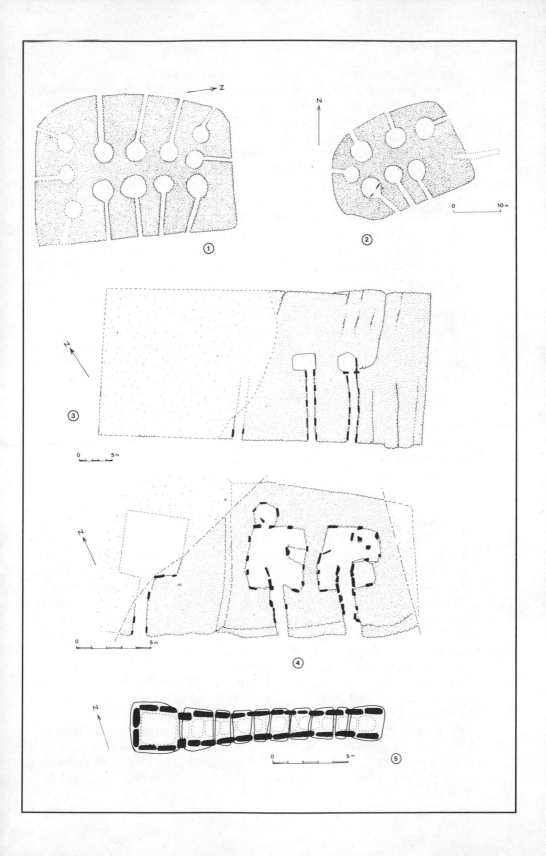

passage H. And, curiously, two more small stelae were found in front of the threshold at the entrance to grave F, which has a very long passage, and is the monument which became the central chamber-tomb of the structure in a second phase.

The secondary cairn displays more numerous megalithic elements, especially in chamber-tombs A and B; the narrow access from passage to chamber in A was further restricted by means of a perforated slab. Did this aperture have a utilitarian purpose, connected with the opening of the chamber, or a more metaphysical one?

At Barnenez, the chamber-tombs at the extremities have decorated slabs: seven pecked U-shapes on the first right-hand passage upright of chamber-tomb A, and a 'shield-idol' on the first roofing-slab in the passage of chamber-tomb J. We shall return to this megalithic art in a subsequent chapter.

Barnenez is the most famous example of a quadrangular cairn containing several single passage-graves. There are others in Armorica, such as La Ville-Pichard at Pléneuf (Côtes-du-Nord), or Gaignoc, which we have already mentioned. But they are also found in many other areas, in Normandy as well as in Poitou, the centre-west of France.

We shall be attacked by purists if we treat the cairns of La Hogue and La Hoguette at Fontenay-le-Marmion (Calvados) (Figure 14:1 and 2) as megalithic monuments, and the champions of chamber-tombs built from large stone slabs would be aroused at the idea that such monuments *could* be classed as chamber-tombs. But the matter is not so simple, and deserves a closer look. Everyone agrees on calling megalithic structure H at Barnenez a chamber-tomb, if its covering of stones is removed. Its enveloping mound does not remove its features as a chamber-tomb or megalithic monument, even with the use of stone corbelling for the roof of the antechamber and some dry-stone walling in the passage. If Barnenez H is a chamber-tomb, we cannot see why G and G', built almost exclusively in dry-stone, but identical in plan, are not chamber-tombs also; they have no megalithic elements, that is all. Of course we might designate monuments built in dry-stone 'domed tombs' and reserve the term 'passage-grave' for slab-built monuments, as Verron advocates. But we would quickly run into trouble with questions of definition, as with Barnenez H, for example.

So we must resign ourselves; those dry-stone cairns of La Hogue and La Hoguette, containing circular burial chambers, built of false-corbelled stone and linked to the outside world by an access passage, really are chamber-tombs; but then those Mycenean *tholoi* must be chamber-tombs too! And what can we say about monuments identical in shape but made out of wood? We shall return to this later.

The mounds of La Hogue and La Hoguette, like all the monuments of this type recorded in Basse-Normandie (Vierville in Manche;

Colombiers-sur-Seulles, Fontenay-le-Marmion, Condé-sur-Ifs, Ernes in Calvados; Habloville in the Orne), were built on high points (or very close to them) – a feature which links them with the Armorican and Charentes-Poitou passage-graves.

If we prefer the term 'mound' to 'cairn' for the Normandy monuments, it is because some of them are not made only of stone; earth occasionally enters into their construction.

La Hogue and La Hoguette stand 600 m (1968 ft) apart; they are almost 12 km (7½ miles) from Caen in the commune of Fontenay-le-Marmion (Calvados). La Hogue, which was excavated at the beginning of the nineteenth century, is vaguely rectangular, with more or less rounded corners. It is 43 m (141 ft) long by 31 m (102 ft) wide, with a well-built wall around its perimeter. Several stepped levels allowed the summit to be reached, some 8–10 m (26–33 ft) above the ground. It enclosed 12 radiating circular funerary chambers, so there is no standard orientation of the access-passages. The dry-stone passages, up to 10 m (33 ft) in length, were covered by slabs, and their floors seem to have been paved. When excavation of La Hoguette began in 1964, the cairn was barely distinguishable from the ground surface, so low was it. A wall surrounds the vaguely four-sided monument, oriented north-east to south-west, which contains seven circular chambers; each has its own passage to the outside. They radiate in the same way as at La Hogue. The mass of the cairn is about 30 m (98 ft) long by 20 m (66 ft) wide. Most often the floors of the chambers were paved with larger or smaller stones, on which the bodies were placed. Chamber VI at La Hoguette was divided in two by two upright slabs with a space a metre wide between them continuing the alignment of the passage. Only the rear part of the chamber contained human remains.

Other cases of internal organisation of the chambers are known. Chamber N at La Hogue had a compartment made of upright slabs, occupying nearly a third of the chamber, the paved, part, which was rich in human bone. But the most mysterious arrangement remains that of Chamber M at La Hogue, excavated in 1829. The excavators found a slab of chalk resting on two vertical slabs, making the shape of an altar which conforms precisely to the popular definition of a dolmen. There were other blocks set vertically round the edge of the chamber, it seems (none of this is very clear); but perhaps this too was only a means of compartmenting the chamber.

The Normandy monuments have the advantage over the Breton ones of having preserved a great number of the human bones placed in the burial chambers, something which the acid Armorican soil has not permitted.

Let us turn now to the great cairns of Charentes-Poitou. It is time to point out that we are not following current administrative divisions in our presentation. Although we have attached the *département* of Loire-

Atlantique to Armorica (which the Bretons anyway consider to be the case historically), the *département* of the Vendée forms an integral part of Poitou, the west-central area of France – and especially its southern part, for the prehistoric period we are studying. Large cairns were numerous in this area, but most have been destroyed, leaving no trace. In 1863 the mound of Peu-Pierroux in the Île de Ré was destroyed to make way for a road. It was 60 m (197 ft) long and contained several round chambers with access passages, some built of dry-stone with corbel-vaulted roofs, others entirely megalithic.

Le Montiou mound (Figure 14:3), at Sainte-Soline (Deux-Sèvres), is another example of a great cairn which contained several passage-graves. Noted in 1889, Le Montiou was still at that time fairly massive, and three '*allées*' had been recognised. Unhappily, this monument, situated about 2 km (1¼ miles) from the small market-town of Sainte-Soline, on the left of the Vanzay road, was partly destroyed around 1920, to obtain stones from it. How many prehistoric cairns have been treated thus? There are numerous oral and written accounts of *chirons* (piles of stones) cleared to recoup the stone or simply because they got in the farmers' way! There may well have been bones which fell into dust, sometimes even a few larger slabs, but all were destroyed, unless those slabs too heavy or too difficult to break up were left on the ground – the dolmenic skeleton of a former grandeur.

At Le Montiou, the monument was so reduced that the small hillock which it represented was easily driven over by present-day agricultural machines. So the corn grew happily – or fairly happily, for the earth was still a bit stony – until the day when a slab from a passage was exposed. Excavations began in 1975. They focused upon a cairn about 50 m (164 ft) long by 23–24 m (75½ ft) wide, a four-sided shape oriented north-west to south-east, in which three tomb entrances – of the five it must have contained before its partial destruction – open to the south-west. Two chambers and their passages could be studied in their entirety. The first was polygonal, and lined by upright slabs, well-squared, set edge-to-edge and smoothed. They were up to 2.2 m (7 ft) high and must have supported a huge megalithic roofing slab which has disappeared. Access was by an 11 m (36 ft) long passage, lined by upright slabs alternating with dry-stone walls and supporting a ceiling made of contiguous slabs placed about 1.3 m (4½ ft) above the floor, which was partly paved, as was the chamber. Human bones accompanied by pottery sherds and mixed flints lay in the tumbled chamber. Some bodies had also been placed in the passage, closed at the entrance by a plug of stones. Where the passage joined the chamber, an ogival opening had been carved in a fine limestone slab, bearing witness to the builders' mastery of the art of stone-working. The first right-hand side-pillar, on entering the chamber, is in a human shape, which seems deliberate; one can imagine painting having been on the perfectly finished surface of this monolith, comparable to the stelae found in Breton monuments such as Gaignoc III. Unfortunately, nothing remains of these hypothetical painted decorations, which are known to survive on some chamber-tombs in Portugal.

The second chamber-tomb is comparable to the first in its architecture, except that the chamber is quadrangular and on a different axis from its passage.

As with all the chamber-tombs of the Atlantic coast, the passage is lower than the ceiling of the chamber, where generally one can stand upright. There is certainly a symbolism there which escapes us. We wonder also about the length of these passages. A chamber which has a roof of false-corbelled dry-stone requires an enormous mass of stones to maintain the balance, and from this point of view the chamber-tomb of Les Cous at Bazoges-en-Pareds (Vendée) is an architectural success.

Les Cous (Figure 15) consists of a single, practically circular chamber, about 4.5 m (15 ft) in diameter, approached by a passage 5 m (15½ ft) long opening to the east. This passage was about 1 m (3 ft) wide and must have been roofed by slabs about 1.2 m (4 ft) above the ground. Its walls are made of upright slabs, alternating more or less regularly with dry-stone walls. The chamber, also paved, is lined with upright stones set flat against a dry-stone wall. So these internal slabs form a wall-facing, and are but little use in holding up the roof. In fact, the roof was raised in false-corbelling on a mass of stones forming a ring 2.5 m (8 ft) wide around the chamber. The whole was solidly held together by a second ring of stones about 1.2 m (4 ft) high and also 2.5 m (8 ft) wide. To the west, where the slope of the land is steepest, a small buttress was added to reinforce this weaker section. At Les Cous, the length of the passage seems, at 5 m (15½ ft), to be the minimum necessary for the structure of the monument. But as soon as the roof of a single monument in its mound becomes megalithic, the passage, as a means of access to the chamber, has no more *raison d'être*. And in monuments with false-corbel-roofed chambers, there is no need for the passage to be 10 m (33 ft) long. So the passage, in these graves, is not just a means of access to the chamber. Low and out of proportion to architectural requirements, it is the narrow passage between the world of the dead and that of the living. It would be difficult to say more.

Single chamber-tombs within mounds

The single chamber-tomb within a mound is fairly widespread on the Atlantic coast, but often several are found grouped together into cemeteries.

Let us return to Brittany to look at the plan of the Île Longue chamber-tomb at Larmor-Baden in the Morbihan (Figure 13:1). In its initial splendour it must have appeared as a circular tower of three stages, which could have been 6 or 7 m (20 or 23 ft) high by 25 m (82 ft) in diameter. A long, curving passage, lined with upright slabs alternating with dry-stone walls, led to a polygonal chamber with a false-corbelled roof. This plan is exactly comparable with that of dolmen I of Le Montiou mound at Sainte-Soline. There is even a narrowing by means of two slabs at the point where the passage enters the tomb, which is a replica, in a different material, of the 'portal' of Le Montiou.

It will be noticed that, at Les Cous, the cairn is built around the chamber as a function of the dome which covers it, and the passage is of a length required by the structure. This is not the case at Île Longue, where the great length of the passage was intentional, and the architect placed the chamber off-centre in the monument, so as not to add to the volume of the cairn. Such a plan must be the result of mature reflection. Let us note also in connection with Île Longue that the second upright slab on the left of the passage displays the characteristic 'shield-idol' shape, and bears, engraved on its surface, the same sign that is found on the slab facing it on the other side of the passage, as well as on the underside of the second and the fifth capstones of the passage. Another symbol, an arc or sickle perhaps, occupies the upper surface (where it is not visible because hidden by the mound) of the seventh capstone of the passage, according to the plan by Le Rouzic. This could be a slab re-used in the monument.

Another single chamber in its cairn, Gavrinis (Figure 14:5), on the island of the same name in the Gulf of Morbihan, is certainly one of the best in this genre. Entirely megalithic, it is located in the middle of an enormous cairn, several metres high. Current excavations are exposing all the revetting walls. A long passage, paved with large slabs, leads to a four-sided chamber. But what characterises Gavrinis is the exuberant carved decoration of the orthostats, which makes this an exceptional monument, a true sanctuary whose exact significance escapes us, although repeated here are numerous symbols known from other passage-graves. Its capstone, according to C. T. Le Roux, who is studying the monument, was once part of the capstone of La Table des Marchands passage-grave at Locmariaquer, which Jean L'Helgouach considers originally to have been a large engraved stele carrying representations of bovids.

Figure 16 illustrates the mounds of Bougon in the *département* of Deux-Sèvres. On 2 April 1840 Arnauld, Baugier and Sauzé explored one of the *chirons* (mound A) of the site at Bougon. Arnauld recounts:

The second day, after slowly alternating hopes and fears, the workers

---

Figure 15   Schematic reconstruction of the passage-grave, with corbelled passage, of Les Cous at Bazoges-en-Pareds (Vendée), France. (R. Joussaume)

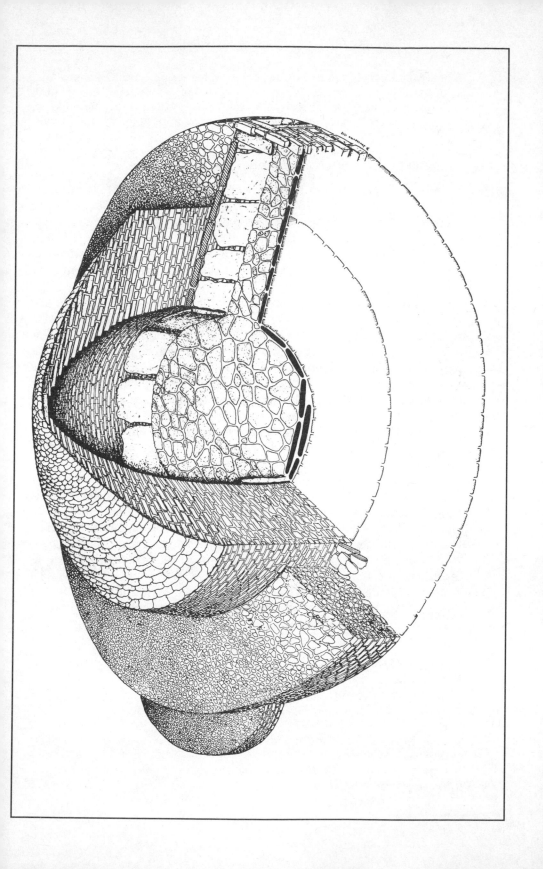

penetrated a layer of piled-up rubble in which we perceived an enormous, long, thick stone. Suddenly, the ground caved in; we searched, we dug again; an opening was made, we slid inside. Everywhere were bones, bodies, and pots, some broken, others intact; there were upright pillars, overturned pillars, dry-stone walls, some crumbling, ruined by weather and time; underfoot, human clay, above our heads, an enormous block of stone. Gigantic structure! How many centuries have flowed over her!

Objects of more-or-less random exploration until 1875, the mounds of Bougon became the property of the *département* in 1879 and were not excavated again for close on 100 years. Scientific work recommenced in 1968, first under the direction of C. Burnez, then of J.-P. Mohen after 1972. The results obtained since that time are of great importance for the understanding of the whole megalithic phenomenon along the Atlantic façade.

Mound A is a vast circular cairn more than 40 m (131 ft) in diameter, which contains a passage-grave with a rectangular chamber. Access is by a passage more than 8 m (26 ft) long. The chamber is almost 7 m (23 ft) by 4 m (13 ft) and is lined with alternating upright slabs and dry-stone walls, which support an enormous capstone. The height under the ceiling is around 2.2 m (7 ft). In the chamber, which is divided into two parts by two pillars, the excavators of a century ago discovered around 200 skeletons. There were three layers of skeletal remains separated by paving. The archaeological remains recovered from this chamber belong to two periods, respectively of the fourth and third millennia BC.

Mound B is 35 m (115 ft) long by barely 12 m (39 ft) wide; in plan it appears as a kind of elongated trapezoid, oriented east-west. It is bounded by a low wall. Excavation has revealed two small stone cists which could relate to the primary function of the mound, and two small chamber-tombs with four-sided chambers and passages opening to the south, which could be a secondary intrusion into the cairn. A stone 'horn' antenna links this mound to mound A. When was it built, and to what end? A depression in the ground to the north, the length of the mound, indicates the position of the quarry from which stones were taken to build the monument.

Figure 16   Megalithic cemetery at Bougon (Deux-Sèvres), France. (After J.-P. Mohen)
1. 'Angoumoisin' chamber-tomb A.
2. Mound E with its two mortuary chambers.
3. Plan of the cemetery group.
4. Chamber-tomb FO, with a circular chamber, at the narrow end of the trapezoidal long mound F.
5. Chamber-tomb F2, of the 'Angoumoisin' type, at the other end of the trapezoidal long mound F.

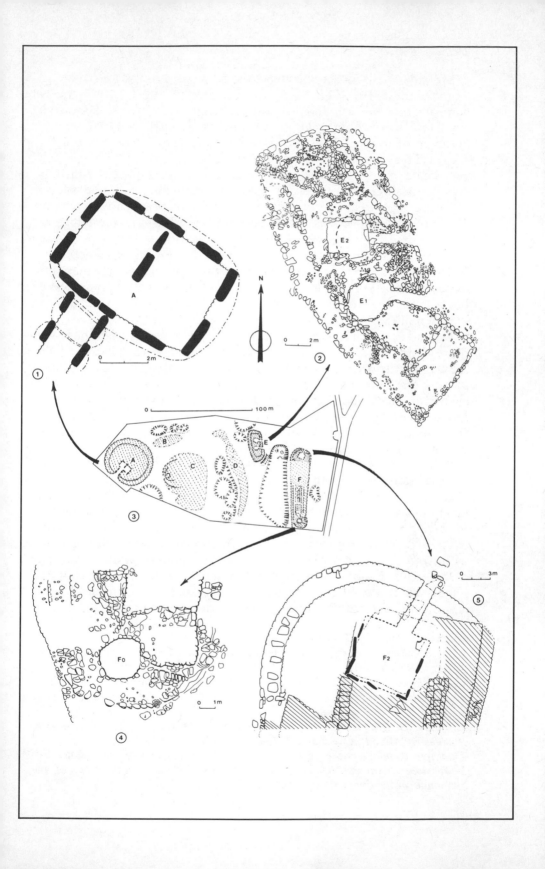

N

① ② ③ ④ ⑤

0   2m

0   2m

0   100 m

0   1m

0   3m

A

E2

E1

B

A

C

D

E

F

F0

F2

Mound C is the most imposing of the Bougon tumuli, 57 m (187 ft) in diameter and 4 m (13 ft) high at the present time. It is vaguely hemispherical in form and was eaten into by a quarry. To the west, a small four-sided chamber-tomb was discovered in 1845. The chamber, made up of four monolithic side-walls, measures 2 m ($6\frac{1}{2}$ ft) long by 1.45 m (5 ft) wide, with a ceiling height of under 1 m (3 ft), making it a very small dolmen. The well-squared and closely juxtaposed orthostats support a single capstone. The passage debouches into the south-western corner of the chamber; that is, it opens practically due west. Three protruding 'hooks' were noted on the northern side-pillar. In this 'q'-shaped dolmen were found four skeletons, which appeared to have been seated along the wall and attached to the three brackets. Recent excavations in the other part of the mound have revealed the existence of a tall quadrangular wall and of diametrically-opposed burials at the foot of this structure.

Mound D seems not to be a prehistoric monument.

Mound E, which was partly excavated in 1840, seems, after the much more complete recent excavations, to have a plan shaped like part of a crown, slightly wider to the north than to the south. It measures almost 25 m (82 ft) long and contains two passage-graves which originally each contained a round chamber. But chamber E2 was squared-off in a second phase, demonstrating at once the chronological precedence of the round chambers over the square, a general phenomenon in megalithic monuments of the Atlantic façade.

This evolution from round to rectangular is clearly seen in a recently-studied monument in the Benon forest in Charente-Maritime, at a place called Champ-Châlon (Figure 17:3). Mound B, at the centre of a group of five mounds set along the line of the ridge dominating the Marais Poitevin, is made up of two dolmens. The first four-sided chamber, off-set from its passage, is enclosed in a circular mound with two concentric circles of walling. The chamber originally had a corbel-vaulted roof. In passing, we should note this type of roof on a four-sided chamber, which is a fairly unusual combination. To the east of this first chamber-tomb, prehistoric men built another whose

---

Figure 17   Megalithic monuments in western France.
1. Les Mousseaux, Pornic (Loire-Atlantique), with transepted chamber-tombs. (After J. L'Helgouach)
2. La Pierre Levée, Nieul-sur-l'Autize (Vendée): a chamber-tomb with a square, compartmented chamber and passage in an elongated trapezoidal mound. (After R. Joussaume)
3. Mound B, Champ-Chalon, Benon (Charente-Maritime), with two square chambers. (After R. Cadot and R. Joussaume)
4. 'Angevin' chamber-tomb, La Bajoulière, Saint-Rémy-la-Varenne (Maine-et-Loire) and its mound. The structure is surrounded by a platform with two 'antennae' projecting in front. (After M. Gruet)

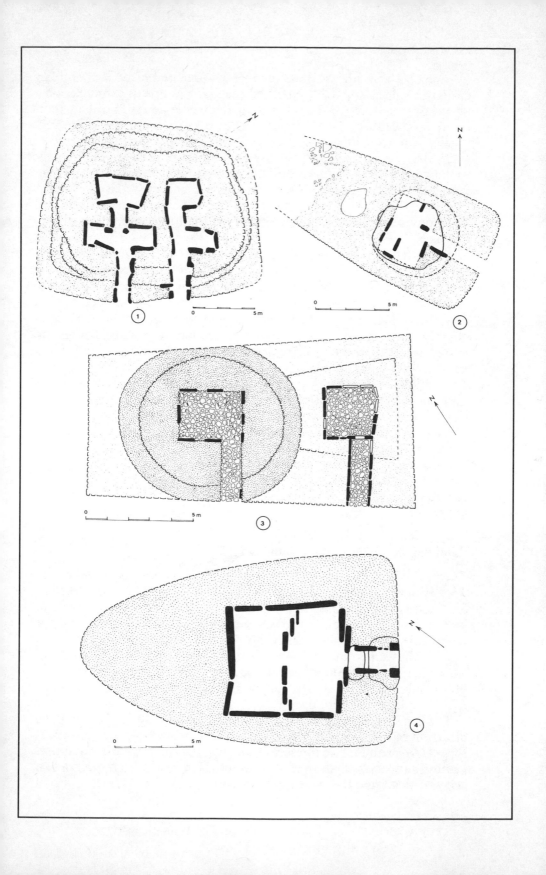

N

5 m
0

N

5 m
0

1

2

5 m
0

3

N

5 m
0

4

'q'-shaped plan is identical to the first; it is enclosed in a quadrangular cairn which has completely engulfed the first monument, which was by no means necessary to the balance of the whole design. It seems that there was a deliberate wish to obscure the round structure by replacing it with an elongated trapezoidal cairn, oriented east-west. It is somewhat surprising that the second chamber-tomb does not open on to the short east side of the mound, but is exactly parallel to the first. In fact, the passages were closed off at their ends by a wall exactly following the line of the perimeter-wall. So the external appearance of the monument was here more important than the orientation of the passages.

Mound F at Bougon is again an elongated trapezoidal mound, oriented north-south and 80 m (262 ft) long. Its history is fairly complex, as there are three components parts: a chamber-tomb with a round chamber to the south; a chamber-tomb with a rectangular chamber to the north; and a long mound in between. The small round-chambered monument, roofed with corbelling, is enclosed together with its access passage in a circular mound, itself overlapping with the southern extremity of a long cairn without our being able to say with any confidence which of the two monuments is the earlier. Do we have here, as at Champ-Châlon, a trapezoidal cairn which takes in a pre-existing round-chambered tomb? Or was the chamber-tomb set into an earlier mound? The rôle of the long mound, of which many unexcavated examples remain to the south of the Marais Poitevin, is still unclear. As for the chamber-tomb with the four-sided chamber at the northern end, its walls of upright stones support an enormous capstone. It is built within a double kerb mound built up against the long cairn.

'How did they build all these dolmens?'

The problem of how the capstones of megalithic monuments were put up has always excited interest, especially since petrographic studies have shown that the slabs had occasionally to be brought from several kilometres away. And what sensational means authors have found for their transport, bringing in antigravity or extraterrestrials or who knows what supernatural forces. It had to be demonstrated once and for all that such huge stones could be moved by simple means and by a group of persons of a size compatible with what we know of the demography of the period.

The experiment took place at Bougon, on 28 July 1979, under the direction of J.-P. Mohen and his colleagues. The whole operation was filmed. At Exoudun, on the actual site where the capstone of chamber-tomb F2 (which weighs about 32 tonnes) may have been quarried, a copy of this same slab was made in concrete. In two days, a rope of linen cords was in place around the block, with four pulling-ropes, each 100 m (328 ft) long. The method of traction used requires a flat underside to the block. If this were not the case, as occurs in some chamber-tombs, the block would have to be attached to a sledge and slid along a roadway, a method which was used by the Egyptians. At Bougon, it was decided to move the block over oak rollers along rails made of squared trunks of oak. Two hundred people provided the necessary force, 170 pulling and 30 working levers to push the slab. In one morning it was shifted about 40 m (131 ft), which led Mohen to say that it would therefore require a month and a half to get the block from Exoudun to Bougon, about 4 km ($2\frac{1}{2}$ miles) away, taking into account a few detours to avoid the steeper slopes.

The 200 people required for the operation represent an overall population for the group responsible of upwards of 1000 individuals, maybe more; and perhaps twice that number would be needed to transport the capstone of Bougon dolmen A. It does not seem possible to envisage one single village containing 2000 or 3000 inhabitants, at this period. It is much more likely that such imposing monuments were the work of a population scattered among several villages within the tribal territory around the structure, a place of veneration for a whole people.

But the experiment did not stop there. It was not enough to demonstrate the possibility of transport by human traction; the slab had also be lifted up to the top of the pillars which were to support it. To achieve this, three 10 m (33 ft) long oak levers were used; slid under one of the sides of the slab, they were pulled down simultaneously. This raised one side of the block about 50 cm (20 in). Chocks were placed to keep the block at this level. The operation was repeated on the other side, rasing the whole of the block to 50 cm (20 in) above the ground. This series of movements repeated alternately on either side of the block, together with the use of scaffolding, allowed the block to be raised to the desired height. It then had only to be shifted across onto uprights previously set in place and held up by the cairn.

The experiment was crowned with success. It was accompanied by related work, such as the felling of oaks 30 cm (12 in) in diameter with polished-stone axes, the making of ropes from vegetable fibres, and the extraction of stone from the quarry close by the chamber-tomb, using antler-picks.

Transepted passage-graves

On either side of the mouth of the Loire a group of megalithic monuments possessing particular architectural features was built. These transepted passage-graves are a regional development of the passage-grave.

Les Mousseaux cairn (Figure 17:1) at Pornic (Loire-Atlantique) is one of the most spectacular examples; it has recently been restored.

On either side of the estuary at the head of which Pornic is built, the heights of Gourmalon to the south and of Les Mousseaux to the north peak at more than 35 m (115 ft) and dominate the sea for some distance. They are the site of numerous chamber-tombs, often now in a parlous state. On the slope near the highest point of Les Mousseaux, there were three mounds; one, Les Trois Squelettes, which contained several chamber-tombs, was excavated at the end of the nineteenth century. The second mound is still a huge cairn 70 m (230 ft) long by 30 m (98 ft) wide, but the buildings on top of it prevent any investigation. The owners are perhaps unaware that they sleep, eat and amuse themselves above a 6000-year-old cemetery.

The third mound, the one which particularly interests us here, is well-known locally by the name of Pierres Druidiques. It must be said that until very recently it was still believed by some, without any proof, that it was the Gauls who were the builders of the dolmens, which were none other than altars on which Druids sacrificed their victims. But it was not until 2000 years after the last Chamber-tomb was built in the Atlantic west that the first Gauls appeared. The burial-places had developed from the collective tombs of the megalithic epoch into individual graves, and cremation was in use even before the arrival of the Gauls. But some ideas die hard, and in our own day bands of jolly Druids, dressed all in white and sometimes festooned in university diplomas, come each year on the same date to address I know not what god in the megalithic circle of Stonehenge in England. It is true that others go into a trance as soon as they touch the stone of a dolmen, which is obviously positioned at the intersection of telluric currents . . . . What a storehouse of energy a site like Roknia in north Africa must be, where several thousand dolmens stand side by side!

Les Mousseaux cairn (another name for the druidic stones) is of a short trapezoid shape with its main façade, 18 m (59 ft) long, towards the south-east; from it open the passages of the two chamber-tombs. The two sides of the cairn to north and south converge towards the fourth side, 14 m (46 ft) long, which is parallel to the first. The four corners of the cairn seem to have been rounded off. At least two other lines of walls distinctly parallel to the outer wall, were clearly seen within the cairn. The two passage-graves are entirely megalithic. The southernmost monument comprises a central passage which ends in the middle of a four-sided chamber. On the way are two side-cells facing one another and giving a transepted appearance to the whole. The north chamber-tomb should be considered as a transepted one which is missing half the chamber and the side-cell on the same side. Jean L'Helgouach, director of the excavation and restoration in 1975–6, discovered 'a line of cup-marks very close together and faithfully following the outside edge of the first slab to the right of the entrance to the north dolmen'. This is the only 'parietal art' recognised on these megalithic monuments.

The chamber-tombs had long since been emptied of their archaeological content but, on the façade of the monument at the level of the entrances, a fair number of potsherds were found during the recent excavations. They allowed the reconstruction of several ceramic forms belonging to an Atlantic Neolithic subjected to later Mediterranean influences. The excavations also revealed that pottery had fallen to the foot of the wall near the entrances – the remains of offerings made to the dead. All modern investigations, at Bougon, Sainte-Soline, Dissignac, Colpo, and Les Cous, to name but a few, have led to the discovery of such remains similarly lying in front of the façades and fully confirming the idea that offerings were placed on the perimeter walls, especially near the entrances.

Other monuments architecturally fairly similar to Les Mousseaux have recently been studied in Brittany at Colpo and Crugellic.

Colpo is about 20 km (12½ miles) north of Vannes (Morbihan) on the Lanvaux heathland. The site of Min-Goh-Ru (Figure 13:3), near Larcuste, at the centre of a major group of prehistoric remains, seems to have comprised three mounds, of which one has now disappeared; it may have contained a passage-grave with a circular chamber. The other two were the object of recent excavation by L'Helgouach and Lecornec in 1968–72, published in 1976.

Cairn I contains two chamber-tombs with oval chambers linked to the outside by a short passage. In the second cairn, oval in shape, one passage serves six chambers; the first two are set opposite one another, on either side of the passage; the second pair are again practically face-to-face; the last two seem like a large double chamber. This is a plan fairly close to the typical transepted passage-grave. It will be noted at Colpo that the façades where the passages open follow the same line, indicating a measure of contemporaneity between the two monuments, one following the other in the same tradition. Everything points to the transepted chamber-tomb having been built after the mount with two simple passage-graves; it is confirmed in various places along the Atlantic coast that this type of plan is the earlier.

The chamber-tomb of Crugellic at Ploemeur (Morbihan) is a monument with a double transept and a terminal chamber, enclosed in a short trapezoidal mound rather like Les Mousseaux at Pornic. The passage opens on the long edge of the trapezium, and the surprise is the position of the chamber-tomb within the mound. Ordinarily, with passage-graves, the bulk of the mound is conceived as a function of the chamber (or chambers) which it covers; its volume is necessary for the balance of the whole design. It was entirely unnecessary, at Crugellic, to build such a grand cairn for the chamber-tomb inside. Therefore the cairn, by its shape, its terraced walls and its bulk, has an intrinsic significance of its own. C. T. Le Roux and Y. Lecerf, directors of the recent excavation at Crugellic, have noted the very worn engravings of 'shield-idols' on two slabs of the chamber-tomb. These designs seem mid-way between those on simple passage-graves and those in angled chamber-tombs. Crugellic has been re-used many times, but, as at Colpo, we find vestiges of middle neolithic occupation. A radiocarbon date obtained from chamber-tomb II at Colpo indicates construction towards the end of the fifth millennium BC for this monument with side-chambers.

Passage-graves with compartmented chambers

Passage-graves with compartmented chambers exist in Brittany and as far away as Poitou. Mané-Groh at Erdevan (Morbihan) is a very megalithic monument whose four-sided chamber is divided into compartments by upright stones which supported a roof made up of several slabs. The passage, lined with orthostats, opens to the east, and the whole is enclosed in a long mound.

The cairn of Forêt-Fouesnant (Figure 14:4) in Finistère comprised two structures, unfortunately damaged. To the east, two compartmented chambers seem to belong to a second phase of construction. The walls are of alternating upright slabs and dry-stone walling. At one side of the end of chamber-tomb B a small cell was built, as we find in other chamber-tombs (Locqueltas at Locoal-Mendon (Morbihan), La Boixe B at Luxé (Charente), etc.). These chambers seem to have had corbel-vaulted roofs, which, while not very common in quadrangular chambers, exist in Charente-Maritime in the chamber-tombs of mound B at Champ-Châlon and probably in those of Fouqueure mound in Charente.

At La Pierre-Levée (Figure 17:2), in the *commune* of Nieul-sur-l'Autize (Vendée), the chamber-tomb with its compartmented, four-sided chamber is roofed by a single slab and is enclosed by an elongated trapezoidal mound.

Angled passage-graves

We keep the name of angled passage-grave for that type of passage-

---

Figure 18   Megalithic monuments in western France.
1. 'Angevin' chamber-tomb, La Roche aux Fées, Essé (Ille-et-Vilaine). (After J. L'Helgouach, P.-L. Gouletquer and Y. Onnée, 1965)
2. Buttressed allée couverte, Lesconil, Poullan (Finistère). (After J. L'Helgouach, 1965)
3. Angled passage-grave, Les Pierres Plates, Locmariquer (Morbihan). (After Beauprée)

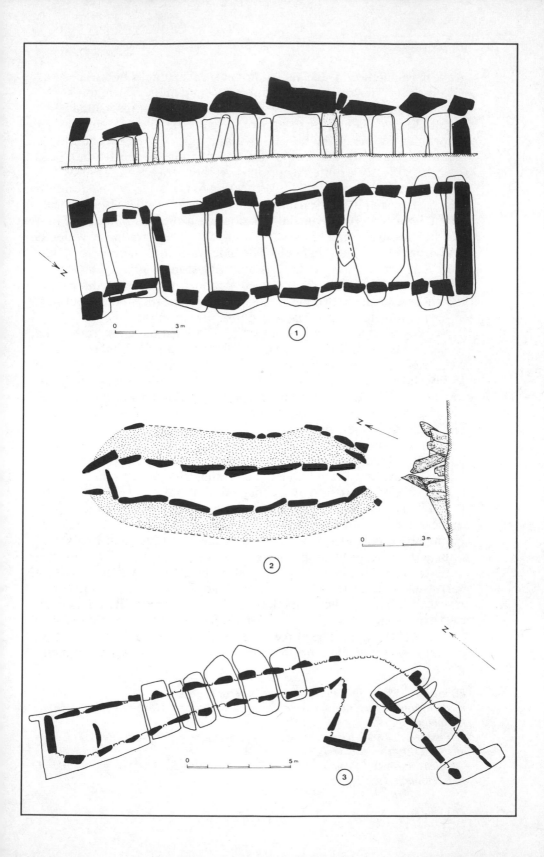

1

2

3

grave in which the passage and chamber form an angle, not necessarily a right-angle. This group of monuments, found in the Morbihan and at the mouth of the Loire, is not very numerous, but it is spectacular.

Les Pierres Plates passage-grave (Figure 18:3) at Locmariaquer (Morbihan) is one of the best-known and most-visited Breton monuments, along with the Table des Marchands, Mané-Rutual, and Gavrinis. It really is quite exceptional. At the entrance we see first of all a *menhir*, re-erected during the restoration of the site. Then we follow a passage for 6 m (20 ft), bearing north. At this point there is a side-cell, about 3 m deep (10 ft), on the left side; then there is a left turn into another passage, some 15 m (49 ft) long, which gets gradually wider as it approaches a small end-cell. The side-walls are made of smooth-faced slabs, alternating with well-built dry-stone walling. Thirteen of these uprights bear deeply engraved symbols: the first on the left on entering the passage, two in the side-chamber, the rest in the other part of the monument, which is enclosed in a huge mound.

Another fine monument of this type, the angled passage-grave of Le Rocher at Le Bono (Morbihan), stands within a sub-circular mound, 28 m (92 ft) in diameter by 4 m (13 ft) high with a fine kerb. The two sections which comprise the passage-grave are at 90 degrees and, as at Les Pierres Plates, we note a progressive widening of the chamber towards the end. The engraved symbols are comparable to those of Les Pierres Plates but less numerous.

The Goërem megalithic monument (Figure 19:1) at Gâvres (Morbihan) was discovered in 1963 during works on the dune for a housing estate. Excavations were made under Jean L'Helgouach's direction. A layer of blackish earth, oval in shape and about 27 m (89 ft) long by 18 m (59 ft) wide, covered a cairn which clearly followed the square shape of the monument underneath it. The passage, 9 m (29$\frac{1}{2}$ ft) long by 1.2 m (4 ft) wide and 1.6 m (5 ft) in average height, is lined by upright slabs and dry-stone walling. Two engravings were found. The entrance to the chamber was closed by a movable upright slab, which blocked a narrowed space at the end of the passage. Four compartments were revealed in the chamber, which extends along 17 m (56 ft) on an east-west axis, from 1.45 m (5 ft) to 1.70 m (5$\frac{1}{2}$ ft) wide, and from 1.25 m (4 ft) to 1.5 m (5 ft) high. The three first compartments are separated by partial dividers, while a double slab closes off the last compartment,

---

Figure 19   Megalithic monuments in western France.
1. Right-angled passage-grave, Goërem, Gâvres (Morbihan). (After J. L'Helgouach, 1971)
2. Passage-grave with side-entrance, Crec'h-Quillé, Saint-Quey-Perros (Côtes-du-Nord). (After J. L'Helgouach, 1967)
3. Allée couverte, Prajou-Menhir, Trébeurden (Côtes-du-Nord). (After J. L'Helgouach, 1967)

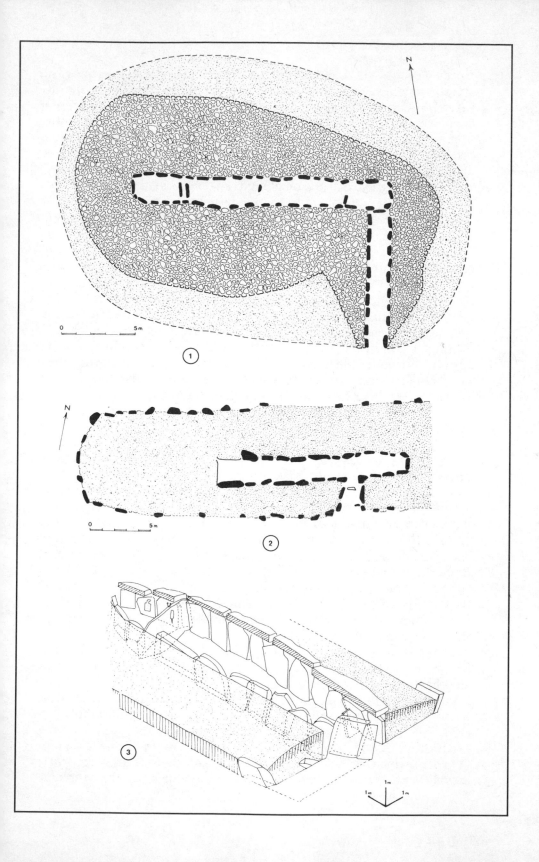

which must have had a greater significance, and a special function. The number of engravings found at Le Goërem places the monument just after Les Pierres Plates, which has the same features. At Le Goërem there are two opposed engravings in the passage at the entrance, one engraving in the first compartment facing the passage, three in the second, two in the third, and none in the fourth; but at Les Pierres Plates the end-cell is decorated. We can wonder if this end-cell was originally the grave of a person of high rank, venerated in other parts of the monument. Charcoal from the terminal chamber is dated to 2480 ± 140 b.c., which, when calibrated, fixes the date of construction of the monument at the very beginning of the third millennium BC.

Brontosauruses of megalith-building: the 'Angevin' type of passage-grave

The 'Angevin' type of megalithic monument, whose distribution is centred on Saumur and Anjou, continues to be the object of numerous debates between specialists, as too few excavations allowing certain dating have been undertaken. Distinguished by Glyn Daniel as long ago as 1941 under the name of 'gallery graves of the Loire type', they were more precisely defined by Michel Gruet in 1956, then listed in his *Inventaire des mégalithes du Maine-et-Loire* (1967).

'Angevin' chamber-tombs are among the most imposing and the most megalithic monuments in France. They have a four-sided chamber which can be square or rectangular. The characteristic feature of the type is the passage, normally confined to three slabs: two side-pillars support a lintel, set lower than the roof of the chamber. This trilithon-porch is narrower than the width of the chamber, and is set along the same axis. In well-preserved monuments, such as La Pidoucière at Corzé (Maine-et-Loire), one slab serves to close the entrance of the porch and another closes the porch off from the chamber. Some 'Angevin' monuments reach gigantic proportions. Bagneux, near Saumur, which stands in the courtyard of a café, was used as a dance-hall. Its interior dimensions are: 4.25 m (14 ft) wide at the entrance, 5.4 m (18 ft) at the far end, 17.3 m (58 ft) long (its surface area is about 85 m² (102 sq yd) – many modern apartments of two or three rooms have less floor-space!).

In Ille-et-Vilaine, La Roche aux Fées at Essé, south-east of Rennes (Figure 18:1), has equally impressive dimensions: 19.5 m (64 ft) overall length, 6 m (20 ft) wide and 4 m (13 ft) high, with a ceiling height of 2.1 m (7 ft). Its plan is interesting because the chamber is preceded by a narrower, lower antechamber and by a trilithon-porch, the whole 4 m (13 ft) in length. An identical arrangement was discovered in the excavation of the 'Angevin' dolmen of La Pierre Folle at Thiré (Vendée) which yielded traces of paving and division into compartments. The skeletal remains of about 40 individuals were recovered at

Thiré, which was reused several times. From the earliest remains discovered, the 'Angevin' chamber-tomb of Thiré must be dated to the late Neolithic, so it would have been contemporaneous with the *allées couvertes* and some advanced types of Breton chamber-tombs.

The 'Angevin' passage-graves, like the *allées couvertes* indeed, are never grouped together under a single mound, nor as a cemetery. High places were not sought for their construction. In these features they diverge from the general run of passage-graves.

La Bajoulière passage-grave at Saint-Rémy-la-Varenne (Maine-et-Loire) (Figure 17:4) has a square chamber, 7 m by 7 m (23 ft by 23 ft), covered by a single slab, now broken. Recent excavations by Gruet and Passini have revealed the existence of a mound of elongated trapezoid shape, with a finely-built kerb, with two horns in front, not unlike some of the forms found in the British Isles. The chamber, as in many of the 'Angevin' chamber-tombs, is divided up by upright slabs.

A distribution map of this architectural type shows that it is centred on the middle Loire valley, pushing up into Brittany and climbing towards the Paris Basin; it reaches the Atlantic coast in the Vendée and the northern edge of the Massif Central, which it skirts slightly to the east. It probably results from a local development of the passage-grave with four-sided chamber; this development may have begun in the middle Neolithic, though that is not proved, but the Angevin passage-grave was certainly in existence during the late Neolithic. Its funerary rôle has been satisfactorily demonstrated at Thiré, but we may question whether it was always built to this end. Let us recall that the construction of monuments such as Bagneux, where we know that the slabs came from several kilometres distant, required enormous man-power, which must have been raised from many villages throughout a whole territory. What metaphysical necessity pushed these men to such technical prowess? Of course these are not the great Egyptian pyramids – which must have been built around the same time – but they are still not a bad effort for these 'savages', who often get such a poor press in our history books. Imagine the chamber-tombs of Bagneux, La Roche aux Fées, or Gennes (La Pagerie and La Madeleine), each enclosed in a vast mound; it must have been quite a sight!

Lateral entrance passage-graves

These monuments, fairly widespread in Brittany and extending into the *départements* of Manche and Mayenne, have a long chamber entered via a passage perpendicular to the long, south side.

The Kerlescan chamber-tomb at Carnac (Morbihan) is a megalithic *allée* 17 m (56 ft) long by 2 m (6½ ft) wide, divided into two distinctly equal parts by two juxtaposed cut-away slabs, leaving an oval opening in the middle. The *allée* is oriented east-west. Almost in the centre of the south side of the eastern part, so about quarter of the way along the monument, two more notched slabs give access to the interior of the chamber. The chamber-tomb with side-entrance, so defined, is enclosed in a rectangular mound, about 40 m (131 ft) long by 8 m (26 ft) wide, which is bounded by upright slabs.

Crec'h Quillé chamber-tomb (Figure 19:2), in Saint-Quay-Perros (Côtes-du-Nord), was discovered in 1955 and excavated by Jean L'Helgouach in 1963–4. A mound, 30 m (98 ft) long by 11 m (36 ft) wide as it now remains, was built of earth, retained by a surround of upright slabs and dry-stone walls. One taller stone marked the eastern end. As at Kerlescan, and generally for this architectural type, access to the chamber is through a short passage from the long south side and towards the eastern end. Here, the transition from passage to chamber is a narrowing between two uprights. This narrowing between passage and chamber, marked by cut-away slabs, carved doorways, uprights, circular or square openings, is repeated throughout the megalithic phenomenon of the Atlantic European coast – and also in the Mediterranean, Palestinian, Caucasian, and Indian megaliths. Yet we have not been able to establish the slightest connection between all these forms, apart from the fact that a funerary chamber, whatever its form, must be closed. At Crec'h Quillé, the chamber extends for about 15 m (49 ft). It is a little wider at the western end than the east. There was much archaeological material of the late Neolithic in this chamber; beneath its entrance doorway, the excavators discovered a sort of small chest containing five pots and a pendant, an offering made to the dead. In fact, this offering was at the foot of a stele facing the access passage on the north side of the chamber, on which is sculpted a 'pair of breasts' in the round, and a horseshoe-shaped necklace joining the two.

The passage-graves with side-entrance can be compared with similar monuments in Holland, the *hunebedden*, and in north Germany, both in the megalithic structure and in the mound around it. It should also be noted that the collared flasks discovered in the Breton monuments, although here considered to be technically the most poorly made ceramic products of the late Neolithic of the Paris Basin and the Atlantic façade, are not without affinities with some Nordic pottery of the Funnel-beaker culture. The question is whether there was interaction between the two regions, by sea for example. L'Helgouach thinks that the Armorican chamber-tomb with side-entrance had a local origin and is definitely different from the Dutch *hunebed*, for which a Danish origin can be envisaged. All the same, these coincidences are surprising.

Chamber-tombs which aren't passage-graves: the *allées couvertes*

One of the masters of French Atlantic megalithic studies, Jean L'Helgouach, has defined the *allée couverte* as 'a monument with parallel rectilinear side-walls supporting a roof of slabs at a constant height over the entire length of the monument. The *allée couverte* has an axial entrance and is enclosed within a long mound.'

But why it is not a dolmen, I fail to understand. There is no valid reason for not calling these monuments dolmens. Admittedly there is no differentiated passage and they are therefore not passage-graves; they are *allées couvertes*. They come in different kinds, and there are many of them distributed all over Armorica. They derive from earlier designs such as the 'V'-shaped monuments of the Mané-Kerioned type at Carnac, and are contemporary with the passage-graves with side-entrance, with which they have many affinities. And only a very fine typologist can grasp the architectural difference between the 'V'-shaped grave of Liscuis I at Laniscat (Côtes-du-Nord) and the neighbouring *allées couvertes*.

The megalithic group at Liscuis comprises three monuments set on a hill overlooking the confluence of the Daoulas and the Blavet. Liscuis I was excavated in 1973–4 by C. T. Le Roux. It has a narrow vestibule giving on to a long chamber via a triangular opening left by an upright slab at the end of the antechamber. The two sides of the chamber are practically parallel, apart from at the entrance, where the chamber is a little narrower and lower (1.5 m [5 ft] as compared with 1.8 m [6 ft] at the end), which puts the monument among the class of 'V'-shaped chamber-tombs. Behind the end-slab, two horns delimit a space not closed off from the outside and which appears not to have been roofed. The whole is enclosed in a pear-shaped cairn. Liscuis II, excavated in 1974–5, is an Armorican *allée couverte*, 15 m (49 ft) long and oriented north-south, with the entrance to the north. It has three parts: a vestibule, a paved chamber swelling out in the middle, and a terminal cell. The monument is enclosed in a vaguely oval mound. Liscuis III is highly comparable in plan to Liscuis II. The transition from antechamber to chamber is in both cases through a scooped slab, leaving a triangular opening which could have been closed off after use by a slab of schist.

The *allée couverte* of Prajou-Menhir (Figure 19:3) at Trébeurden (Côtes-du-Nord) has many similarities with Liscuis III: a flaring vestibule, a triangular passage leading to the chamber, an unclosed terminal cell. This is a plan widespread among Armorican *allées couvertes*.

At Tressé (Ille-et-Vilaine), the Le Tronchet forest *allée couverte*, known as La Maison de Feins, is peculiar in having a terminal cell bounded by two lateral slabs; it seems, therefore, to have been neither closed nor roofed.

These last two monuments have in common a most interesting mural decoration of the end-cells, of which we will speak in more detail in the section on symbolic representations.

Among the *allées couvertes* we should note a type which is special in that the lateral orthostats are set obliquely in the ground and meet at the top, forming the buttressed *allées couvertes* group, such as Lesconil at Poullan (Finistère) (Figure 18:2).

Finally, let us note that the Armorican type of *allée couverte* rarely appears south of the Loire; in that area are mostly found *dolmens simples*.

Dolmens simples are monuments of modest size, megalithic but also using dry-stone, a sort of cupboard with an opening in one of the sides. In fact, they are difficult to identify, since any decayed monument which has lost its passage corresponds to this definition. So it seems impossible to class a monument reliably as a *dolmen simple*, unless a careful excavation has been made. In most cases, this has not occurred. However, *dolmens simples* seem to exist in Haut-Poitou, Berry, and Limousin, and thus join up with a huge group further south, in an area north of Toulouse, Quercy, around Montauban and Cahors. They come late in the chronology and are the equivalent of the sunken-graves of the middle Loire, the Armorican *allées couvertes*, and the Poitou *tombelles*. The latter are not, properly speaking, megalithic monuments. They are small mounds, in which dry-stone construction plays a large part, enclosing a fairly spacious chamber which is completely closed off. They are fairly numerous in Poitou.

An exceptional monument: La Pierre Virante in the Vendée

The megalithic monument of La Pierre Virante (Figure 20), at Xanton-Chassenon (Vendée), which we studied during the years 1970–71, is probably one of the most curious monuments excavated in recent times. A distinctly pyramidal stone block, 2.8 m (9 ft) long, 2.5 m (8 ft) wide and 1.2 m (4 ft) high, is supported about 50 cm (20 in) above a paved area at three points, made by stacking two or three stones to form small pillars. It is situated inside and at the southern tip of an area shaped like an isosceles triangle, with a base 7 m (23 ft) long and a height of 6 m (20 ft). To the north, this triangular area is bounded by a platform built of dry-stone, with a straight edge. The two other sides of the triangle are made up of rows of tumbled stones, in which cylindrical holes mark the settings for wooden posts which perhaps supported a roof. On the west side of the monument a small paved chamber was bounded by small uprights which must have supported a capstone. It contained human skeletal remains in fairly large numbers. The southern part of this chamber was in great disorder, and only a few

Figure 20   A megalithic monument in western France: suggested reconstruction of Pierre Virante monument, Xanton-Chassenon (Vendée). (After R. Joussaume)

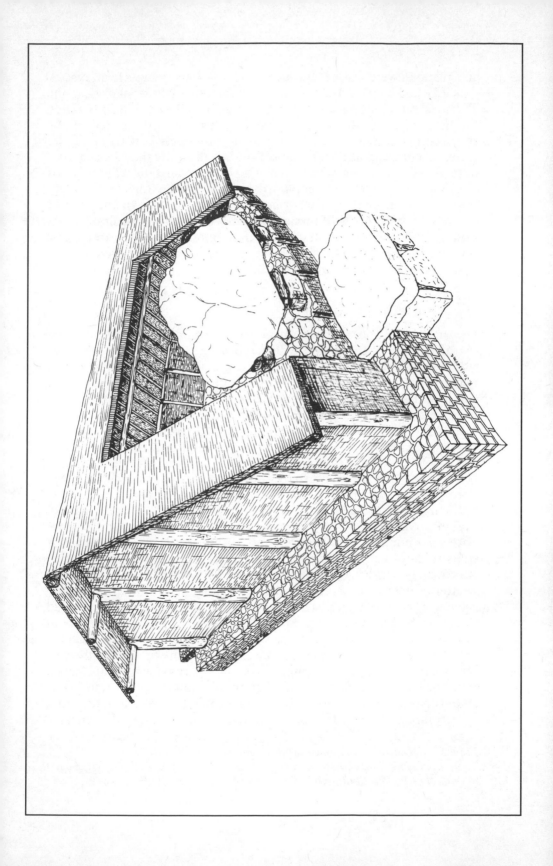

articulations were visible. But to the north, despite superficial disturbance caused by ploughing, several bodies were distinguishable: a pile
of bones representing at least four individuals. Observations made
during excavation showed that the dead had been deposited in the
grave with the limbs flexed. The skulls were found in front of the
vertebral columns, as if they had rolled. So it appears that these bodies
were placed in a sitting position, leaning back against the wall, perhaps
even tied. They were accompanied by rich archaeological material,
especially the trappings of war (daggers and arrowheads), and at least
one wore a collar made of numerous beads of perforated animal teeth,
stone, amber and copper. It appears that, in order to install these four
persons, the people of the time cleared the surface of the paved floor,
pushing the other bones to the south.

Megalithic art in western France

The orthostats, and occasionally also the megalithic ceilings, of some
passage-graves of the Atlantic façade bear engravings and sculptures
whose significance for the most part escapes us. The Morbihan area is
by far the richest in engraved symbols, but they have also been found
on the north coast of Brittany and in the south as far as Charente, in the
'Angoumoisin' type of passage-grave in the area around Angoulême.

In Armorica, the most frequently found symbols consist of a
'U'-shape with upward pointing arms, of varying width and curved
inwards at the ends (Barnenez, Colpo, Mané-Kérioned, Mané-Lud,
Petit Mont). Crooks, with a shaft whose upper end is turned over more-
or-less sharply, are found from northern Brittany down to Charente,
particularly in dolmen A of La Boixe at Cellette, where a carved
example reaches 1.15 m (3¾ ft) high. Axes, with and without hafts, are
also very numerous in western megalithic territory; more or less
stylised, they may have a ring at the base of the haft. Overlapping arcs,
curved lines, and broken lines are also widespread on orthostats of the
Breton dolmens. At Barnenez and Gavrinis, a straight, thick stem,
curved at the ends which are linked by a fine line, could be interpreted
as an arch. Engraved cup-marks, or rings of dots, are found in
monuments of differing architectural styles. A circle surrounded by
rays (Mané-Lud, La Table des Marchands) seems to be a representation of the sun, as does the punched circle with rays round it at Tachen
Paul. In Charente, there is a similar representation on the portal of
chamber-tomb B at La Boixe, but this is probably of recent date (and it
is accompanied, besides, by a hafted axe). Among recognisable

Figure 21   Distribution of megalithic monuments in Brittany.
1. Map showing coastal distribution of passage-graves. (After J. L'Helgouach)
2. Map showing distribution of allées couvertes. *(After J. L'Helgouach)*

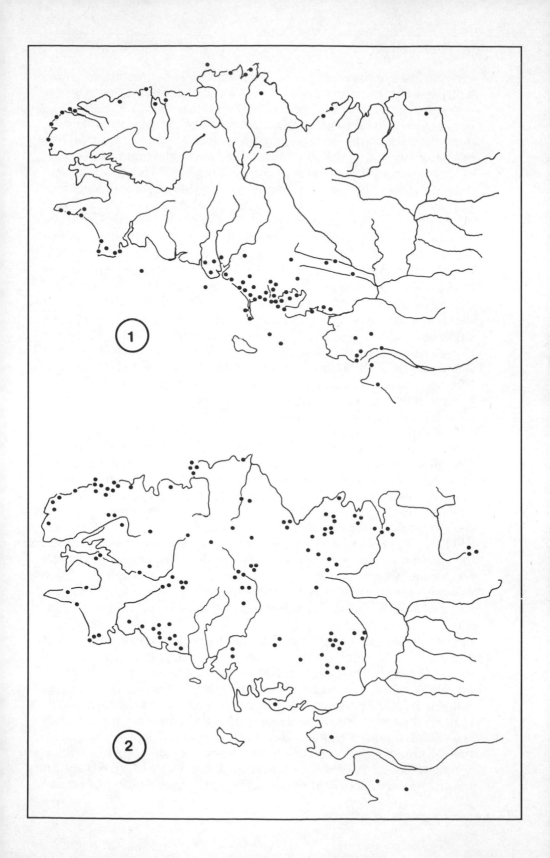

symbols, we can cite snakes (which show up well at Gavrinis) and some which have been interpreted as boats, a kind of broad 'U', one of whose upward stems is higher than the other and turns back on itself, while perpendicular lines, hooked lines and even a shield occupy the central part, the deck of the ship. The last-mentioned symbol, the shield or buckler, is without doubt the most important in the mural decoration of the western French megalithic monuments. The most perfect example is probably that on one of the uprights of the passage of Île Longue (Figure 22:5) at Larmor-Baden (Morbihan). It is a rectangular shape with two slight shoulders and a knob-shaped protrusion at the top. On either side, towards the middle, are two hoops, like handles: engraved parallel curved lines seem to stand for hair, so specialists interpret this as the Goddess of the Dead. In varying guises this figure is found in all forms of megaliths, from passage-graves to *allée couvertes*, but the figure does not exist in Poitou-Charente, where the friability of the limestone may have caused the disappearance of numerous engravings, while sculptures in low relief remain. We should also consider the possibility of painted decoration in these megaliths, as in Portugal. In Petit Mont chamber-tomb at Arzon (Morbihan), a 'buckler' shape is placed above a boat. On this same slab, which has a profusion of crooks and wavy lines, was carved a pair of human feet, as viewed from the sole, whose meaning escapes us.

Megalithic art shows little development in more recent monuments such as the angled passage-graves. The example at Les Pierres Plates at Locmariaquer is the most striking. Here the 'shield-idol' takes different forms; although some of them retain the knob, its position is, by contrast, usually taken by an indentation. Moreover, its internal surface is divided in two by a vertical line, and fairly numerous dots occupy the field of the surfaces thus defined.

There appears to be no general rule, in passage-graves, as to the distribution of the engravings, which can be sited on the orthostats (occasionally on the back of them) or on the ceiling. Some privileged positions can be demonstrated, at the entrance to the passage (as in the end monuments A and J at either end of Barnenez, or the fine 'shield-idol' on the second upright on the left of the passage of Île Longue) or in the axis of the passage on the septal slab (La Grosse Perotte at Fontenille [Charente]). Jean L'Helgouach noticed that the engraved passage-grave in Dissignac mound, which covers two monuments, is oriented towards the winter solstice sunrise. Furthermore, it must be noted that not all passage-graves are decorated. So it is not impossible that monuments with wall-decorations were funerary monuments reserved for a hierarchical class, or perhaps, more probably, sanctuaries. One cannot escape this last hypothesis on entering Gavrinis at L'Armor-Baden (Morbihan), where all the slabs which make up this passage-grave are covered by an exuberant ornamentation of incised lines, including axes, snakes, and 'shield-idols'. One cannot but be struck by the 'buckler'-shaped slab of the chamber of La Table des Marchands at Locmariaquer (Morbihan), with its two panels, comprising four rows of crooks pointing left and right, in the middle of which the sun blazes out.

Regarding these last two monuments, Gavrinis and La Table de Marchands, a recent discovery deserves special mention. C. T. Le Roux, during the restorations at Gavrinis, noticed engravings on the upper, concealed surface of the capstone of the chamber. In particular there were representations of two bovids with very long horns. However, part of the sculpture was missing; and this missing part was found under the capstone of La Table des Marchands. Thus these two enormous blocks belonged to a single stele which had broken into at least three pieces, and which must have been 14 m (46 ft) high. The megalith-builders of La Table des Marchands, Gavrinis, Mané-Rutual and, probably, Mané-Lud, took down and broke up huge *menhirs* to use the pieces in their own structures. In this way, any ritual connected with these imposing megalithic manifestations was totally devalued. There was a period, earlier than that of the large passage-graves, during which enormous monoliths were erected in this region, perhaps in relation to certain large mounds nearby. So L'Helgouach's idea is amply confirmed that the great *menhir* of Er-Grah had been deliberately broken up and that the capstone of Mané-Rutual, among others, is without any doubt a broken *menhir*. The recent notion of re-utilisation of engraved stones in new buildings of passage-grave type should affect the attitudes of scholars towards the decoration of these monuments, especially the decorated backs of some orthostats. It should also mean rejecting any mathematical or astronomical studies which group together large stelae of the Er-Grah type with dolmens such as Gavrinis, Mané-Rutual and La Table des Marchands, since we now know that the latter were built at the expense of the former. Finally, we can now affirm that the great fallen *menhir* of Er-Grah has been on the ground since the neolithic period and before the building of La Table des Marchands; it could not possibly have been seen upright in Gaulish Iron Age times.

The Barnenez mound, as we have said, has two parts, of which the earlier contains five passage-graves. The central monument of this first structure, chamber-tomb H, is the most megalithic. It has the largest chamber, made of two sections; it is the most decorated (axes, bows, 'U'-signs, wavy lines); and in front of its entrance three small stelae were found. All these signs confer a particular character upon chamber-tomb H, which seems to have played an important rôle: the burial of a chief, or a sanctuary linked to the group, we cannot say which. How sad it is that bones do not survive in the acid soils of Armorica. The Gulf of Morbihan, the richest megalithic centre in the world, has yielded practically no human bone – a fact which has led to a rejection of the hypothesis of funerary monuments for chamber-tombs in general. We know now that passage-graves of the same kind built in Normandy or Poitou on limestone rock *all* yielded human bone.

Engravings and sculptures in the *allée couverte* of Prajou-Menhir at Trébeurden (Côtes-du-Nord) (Figure 22:20–33) are of prime importance in illustrating mural art of the late Neolithic in Brittany. All the engravings are situated in the terminal cell of the *allée couverte*. First we note a double 'pair of breasts' cut in relief within a pecked oval cartouche, another 'pair of breasts' above a 'necklace', but also four-sided 'shield-idols' with a terminal beak or axe and surrounded by a line of dots, and lastly 'spearheads' with rounded tips, for which comparisons have been attempted with Cyriot daggers (which is all the easier now that a few examples in copper have been found in western France). Representations of 'pairs of breasts' are fairly widespread in the Armorican *allées couvertes*, in particular in the terminal cell of Bois-du-Mesnil, at Tressé (Ille-et-Vilaine), where a necklace appears under the right-hand pair (the larger) in each group depicted.

In Men Gouarec *allée couverte*, at Plaudren (Morbihan), two breasts are depicted on the outside of the end slab, and were therefore not visible, as they were covered by the mound. There is a link between the outside and inside of this monument which is hard to explain; but it is found again with the 'windows' (perforations in a slab) of the 'Angoumoisin' dolmens and certain openings in *allées couvertes* of the

---

Figure 22   Carvings on megalithic monuments in western France and the Channel Islands.
1. Passage-grave, Mané-Kerioned (Morbihan). (After Z. Le Rouzic)
2. Passage-grave, Kervéresse, Locmariaquer (Morbihan). (After Z. Le Rouzic)
3. Mound, Mané-er-H'roëck (Morbihan). (After Z. Le Rouzic)
5–7. Passage-grave, Île Longue, Larmor-Baden (Morbihan). (After Z. Le Rouzic)
8. Passage-grave, Gavrinis (Morbihan). (After Z. Le Rouzic)
9. Passage-grave, Penhape, Île-aux-Moines (Morbihan). (After Z. Le Rouzic)
10. Passage-grave, Gavrinis (Morbihan). (After Z. Le Rouzic)
11. Passage-grave, Ardillières (Charente-Maritime). (After C. Burnez)
12. Passage-grave, La Grosse Perotte, Luxé (Charente). (After C. Burnez)
13–18. Angled passage-grave, Les Pierres Plates, Locmariaquer (Morbihan). (After Z. Le Rouzic)
19. Angled passage-grave, Lufang, Crach (Morbihan).
20–23. Allée couverte, Prajou-Menhir, Trébeurden (Côtes-du-Nord). (After J. L'Helgouach)
24. Passage-grave with side-entrance, Crec'h-Quillé, Saint-Quay-Perros (Côtes-du-Nord). (After J. L'Helgouach)
25. Statue-menhir, Câtel, Guernsey. (After drawing by B. Wailes, 1958)

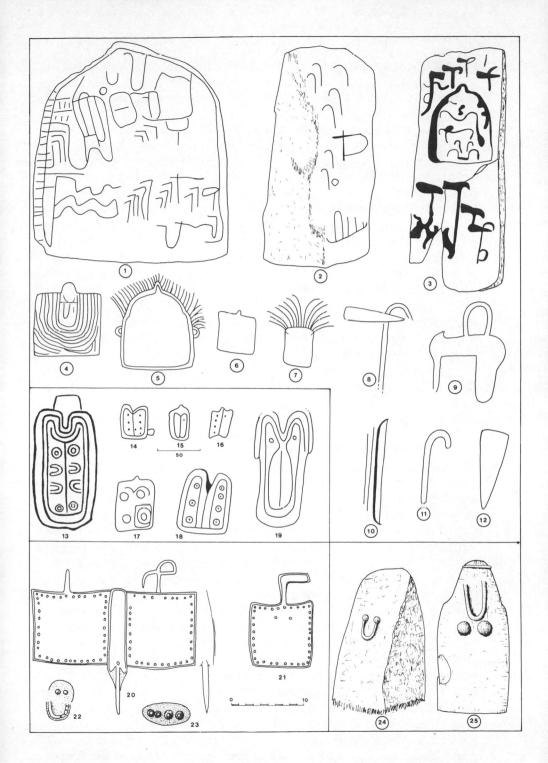

Paris Basin (La Chaussée-Tirancourt, for example). This could also be a case of slabs being taken for re-use from a monument where these features were clearly visible, but which lost their importance in the new structure.

It does not appear that the 'hooks' found carved in relief in some 'Angoumoisin' chamber-tombs of Poitou and the Charente (La Grosse-Perotte, LaMotte de la Garde, Bougon) have any links with the 'breasts' of the Breton *allées couvertes*. Here, in fact, the 'Angoumoisin' passage-graves were built in the middle Neolithic; although the people of the local Chalcolithic built monuments which could be likened to passage-graves, the people of the Peu-Richardien culture of the intervening late neolithic period do not seem to have been drawn to this funerary fashion. Things are different in the Paris Basin, where megalith-building was unknown until the late neolithic adoption of the *allée couverte* form, certainly deriving from Armorica (although this view is not the opinion of all scholars). The same symbolism is found there, with 'pairs of breasts' in this case above the necklaces, but there are also hafted axes and even, in the *allée couverte* of Marly-le-Roi (Figure 24:10), the quadrilateral figure emphasised with dots, very similar to those of Prajou-Menhir (Figure 22:20). In the Paris Basin the decorations are most often in the antechamber; the engravings are generally situated in the terminal cell of the Breton *allées*. But this difference does not seem to be of prime importance and we should rather look at the collective similarity of these representations. If, as we think, the 'shield-idol' ('Goddess of the Dead') of Prajou-Menhir does represent a progression from the 'shield-idol' of the Île Longue type of passage-grave, we can allow that the Armorican *allée couverte* is itself a development of local megalith-building, and that it is the origin of megalith-building in the Paris Basin. Similarly, the existence (or non-existence) of crooks and hafted axes in Poitou Charente shows the link which exists between megalith-building in this area and the passage-graves of Armorica. It should also be noted that certain architectural types, such as transepted passage-graves, or 'Angevin' passage-graves, do not seem to have engravings.

By contrast, engravings do exist in passage-graves with side-entrances, and more especially in the monument of Crec'h-Quillé in Saint-Quay-Perros (Côtes-du-Nord) (Figure 22:24). The pillar in the chamber set facing the entrance to the passage is a real stele on which can be seen a pair of breasts in relief above a collar. The architectural link which could be established with the *allées couvertes* is amply confirmed. We have there not just an engraving but a stele which should be compared with the statue-menhir of Trévoux (Finistère), or with the one in the passage-grave of Kermené-en-Guidel (Morbihan), and with the statue-menhirs of Câtel in Guernsey. Stelae, decorated or not, could not have been rare in passage-graves. We know of the ones in the passage-graves on Gaignoc, placed in the chamber, on the left of the entrance; several small ones at the entrance to chamber I of Le Montiou mound at Sainte-Soline (Deux-Sèvres) – a perfectly smoothed slab with a head which stands out from two cut-away shoulders; probably also the upright stone in the chamber of the 'Angevin' passage-grave of La Frébouchère, at Le Bernard (Vendée), to quote only a few examples.

Small stelae, similar to those of Barnenez, are known in Spain in the megalithic cemetery of Los Millares, but also in association with the north African chamber-tombs and even in the Harar in Ethiopia. Yet 15 centuries separate Barnenez from Los Millares, and 30 centuries rolled by between the construction of the first Breton dolmens and those of Ethiopia.

Engraved symbols, in particular crooks, but also axes and serpents, appear on some *menhirs* in Brittany. In Portugal, the standing-stone of Abelhoa (Reguengos de Monsaraz) has an engraved decoration characterised by a radiating solar disc and wavy lines, at the centre of which a crook can be clearly seen. In the Portuguese chamber-tombs of Alto Alentejo, more especially, crook-shaped plaques of schist have been collected, decorated with incised geometric motifs (Figure 49:1 and 2), which can be set alongside the mural representations of megalithic monuments of Atlantic France.

Funerary customs

While unable to say definitively that the principle aim of the construction of chamber-tombs really was the preservation of the deceased, we can affirm that each time we excavate one that stands on limestone soil we find the remains of human skeletons. Examples in Charente-Poitou and Normandy are numerous. However, the situation is not always clear, either because the excavation was not undertaken with sufficient care (without precise plotting of all the bone fragments), or because the chamber-tomb has suffered much despoliation since the day it was closed up. Is it not surprising to read, in a book dedicated to megaliths, the following? 'At Buzeins (Aveyron), the floor of the dolmen was strewn with bone fragments. Stepping on to such soil gave rise to painful feelings ...' – and contributed to the crushing of the bones! If that author visits all megalithic monuments in the same way, it will indeed be difficult to work out whether the bodies were placed there entire or not – and the majority of unwitting visitors do exactly the same.

Nor is it possible for us always to give any great credit to earlier excavations, in contrast to Niel – that man who walks on a bed of bones and wonders that the bones are broken – who says: 'We accord the same value, at least as regards the quantity and quality of the recovered objects, to the findings of early excavations as to those published more recently.' I will take a few personal examples in proof of this. The original excavation of La Pierre-Levée chamber-tomb at Nieul-sur-l'Autize (Vendée) was effected in two days, 17 and 21 April 1890, with pick and shovel, by labourers working for L. Brochet: 'This chamber contained human bones, boars' tusks, *one* flint scraper, some pieces of iron, fragments of pots from the Gaulish and Gallo-Roman periods, pieces of edged tiles, a hollow tile of the same date, almost intact, positioned in the centre of the dolmen, one key with spiral.' In 1972, and again in 1973, we spent 70 days on a re-excavation of this monument, with the help of some ten people. First of all, we uncovered the plan and the limits of the mound; but as far as archaeological material goes, the results are surprising. Brochet notes the discovery of only a single flint: we found 1215; and, we might add, three thin leaves of gold rolled up spirally, a copper knife, a bone tube with incised decoration, two bone V-buttons, *dentalium* shells, two antler-picks, one boar's tusk, fragments from a dozen undecorated pots, and from 18 more decorated pots of Bell-beaker type, not counting more recent sherds from the Bronze Age and some from the Gallo-Roman period. Trusting the early reports would have been foolhardy indeed.

The passage-grave of Les Cous at Bazoges-en-Pareds (Vendée) was excavated in five days in 1913 and 1914, on behalf of Messrs. Baudouin and Rousseau, by labourers using forks. The human bone recovered allowed Baudouin to recognise the remains of 120 people in the chamber and those of 15 others in the passage, accompanied by a few flints and potsherds ... We also re-excavated this in 1974–5, working for 10 weeks with a team of some ten people. Here, too, we were able to establish the plan of the monument as a whole, but also, we recovered seven arrowheads and about 30 flint flakes, 113 limestone beads, eight *dentalium* shells, one perforated carnivore canine, two fragments of boar's tusk blades, one fragment of a schist pendant, two bone awls, and the remains of 15 or so pots found especially either side of the monument entrance. Add to that some bone remains of around 15 people. Again this proves that we should not trust those early reports.

No more should we trust fairly recent excavations which are only partial: the chamber may have been completely excavated, but without studying the mound and its immediate surroundings. It is almost a certainty that current excavators will one day be criticised for not studying the site over an even broader area.

Under these conditions it is difficult to form a precise idea of funerary customs associated with the chamber-tombs, and it will require many years of research to have a more exact answer to the question. However, a first approach shows a fundamental difference between the earliest monuments of the passage-grave type, and more recent ones such as *allées couvertes*, sunken graves, *dolmens simples*, etc. In the early monuments, the number of skeletons recognised is always low, a dozen on average in the chambers of mounds like La Hogue, La Hoguette, Vierville, Condé-sur-Ifs and Ernes in Normandy. Identical numbers (occasionally fewer) have been found in Poitou at Bougon F0, Saint-Soline, Champ-Châlon (B and C). One remark regarding Champ-Châlon, however: while mound C is a monument with a round chamber and a passage (like the chamber of Bougon F0 and those of the Normandy mounds we have just discussed), mound B comprises two four-sided chambers ('Angoumoisin' passage-graves). The round or four-sided shape of the chamber does not seem to have had much effect on the use of the monument, even if one can demonstrate that in general the four-sided chamber is later than the round.

With a few exceptions, the first impression of the arrangement of the human bones in the chambers is one of disorder. On looking closer, we notice that the bodies have been laid on their sides in a flexed position, and an observation by Jean Dastugue, made at the time of the excavations at La Hoguette, underlines the prime importance of this position: the two heels (*calcaneum*) of a dead, pregnant woman had been perforated to allow passage of a cord which kept the body in a folded position. We can consider that some disturbance of the bones is due to lack of space, and that skeletons had to be pushed aside to leave room for newcomers, but that is not very probably in the early phase when bodies were not very numerous on the floor of the chamber. It now seems possible that in passage-graves only a small number of individuals were placed on their sides in a flexed position. Unfortunately it is not as simple as that, for it appears that the life of a chamber-tomb does not come to an end when a dozen corpses fill up both it and sometimes also the passage.

Thus in chamber-tomb A of La Hogue mound, the bones were found pell-mell. There were eight mandibles, but not one skull. There could have been much later disturbance, or these are burials which have been moved. What is surprising is that at La Hoguette, a few hundred metres away, the bodies are complete, while at La Hogue, the bones are scattered. The two monuments could be seen as complementary, so that when a chamber at La Hoguette was full, the bones were gathered together and placed in a chamber at La Hogue, while some of the bones taken out – the skulls, for example – were brought back to the settlement sites. The observations which have been made are too few to allow us to confirm this ritual, but it would explain the abundance of skeletal remains in Les Cous passage-grave at Bazoges-en-Pareds (Vendée). The remains of between 150 and 160 individuals were recovered from the chamber and passage of this monument. These were not complete skeletons, but bundles of bones belonging to several individuals placed in small piles and protected by small slabs. The group formed a cone in the centre of the chamber. A second passage-grave used to exist right next to Les Cous; nothing remains of it, which is a shame, as it might perhaps have furnished the explanation we were looking for.

We gather from these few remarks that in the earliest phase of megalith-building – the passage-grave phase – a small number of individuals was buried in the chamber-tombs, in a flexed position and laid on one side. When the chamber was full, it was hermetically sealed, and another came into use; or, more probably, it was emptied and the bones recovered were placed in another grave or elsewhere. This idea leads us to believe that the burial-space, the work of the community, served the entire community – men, women and children. Thus in all the chambers at La Hoguette were counted 18 men, 19 women, and 18 children.

The ceremonies must have taken place right in front of the entrance to the monument, and the 15 pots crushed into the ground on either side of the passage-entrance of Les Cous are proof of offerings that were set on the walls of the mound. Similar observations could be made at Bougon, Sainte-Soline, Champ-Châlon, Dissignac, Pornic, and so on. The evidence is invariable. At one time it was said that these finds resulted from the emptying and sweeping-out of the chambers, but this explanation did not take into account the fact that finds at the entrances are almost exclusively of pottery, while beads, awls, and flint come from the chambers; nor does it take into account the fact that these pots are discovered broken *in situ*, at the exact places where they are found, and that could not be the result of sweeping-out.

Was the whole community allowed to put its dead into the chamber-tomb? This is not certain. We have said that it required 200 people to move the capstone of monument F1 at Bougon and probably twice that number to move the one from mound A in the same cemetery, which indicates a population of 1000 to 3000 or 4000 individuals. It seems unthinkable that a single passage-grave could receive all the dead from such a human group. So, either other tombs were in use at the same time, or these large monuments were reserved for a family holding a particular position. And we may consider that the agricultural and pastoral society responsible for these structures was relatively hierarchical. How can we imagine uniting 200 or 300 people from different villages to work together, without envisaging a ruling authority, a spiritual or temporal power, for whom perhaps the monument was finally destined? Obviously we can only make assumptions in this area; also what is true of Bougon need not be so at Fontenay-le-Marmion where the mounds of La Hogue and La Hoguette seen to have been built at one and the same time, and, if this hypothesis is accepted, had several chambers in use simultaneously. The character of collective tomb is more clearly seen in this last case.

We have also noted the case of Barnenez where grave H (at the centre of the four others) stands out among the first group, with its megalithic aspect, its double chamber, and its engraved decoration. Is this the tomb of a ruling family, while the populace or those of lower rank occupied the neighbouring chambers; or is it perhaps a sanctuary common to the four other burial chambers? It is very difficult to say, and both ideas can be envisaged. Not all chamber-tombs were necessarily for the same purpose: collective tombs serving a whole population; collective tombs for a high-ranking family; sanctuaries; collective tombs reserved for a single family (each family having its own chamber in La Hoguette mound).

It should be recalled here that, in general, passage-graves are set on high points, or not far from summits, and the grandiose character of their architecture with their many-walled mounds made them visible from afar. More than just a funerary chamber, more than a sanctuary, they are the symbol of a territory, a place of veneration and sacrifice in which each element of the human group may find the identity of the whole.

Over time, customs change somewhat; passage-graves develop and diversify to take off in new forms, such as the lateral-entrance passage-graves, the 'Angevin' chamber-tombs which are never built in groups and which, most of the time, are placed low down in the landscape, and *allées couvertes* whose chambers get longer and which are also found singly in their mounds, and topographically anywhere.

While classic passage-graves occupy a very definite sea-board position, especially in the first phase, 'Angevin' passage-graves and lateral-entrance passage-graves have, like *allées couvertes*, a wider distribution towards the interior of the country.

Unhappily we know nothing of the funerary customs of the men of the Armorican *allées couvertes*, as the acidity of the soil has caused the disappearance of the bones. We know very little either of the occupants of the 'Angevin' passage-graves, except at La Pierre Folle, at Thiré, in Vendée, where our own excavations have uncovered numerous human remains, the earliest attributable to the late Neolithic. As with the passage-graves, the material filling of Armorican *allées couvertes* can be studied only by comparison with other regions, and more particularly with the Paris Basin, where this type of architecture is fairly similar. In particular it should be noted that there was found in the Breton *allées couvertes* a large number of complete pots, which puts them in a fundamentally different position to the chambers of passage-graves, always poor in ceramics.

Sunken tombs, *tombelles* and the re-use of many chamber-tombs in the late Neolithic show that the number of burials in a single monument becomes very large; it is not rare to hear of the remains of several hundred individuals in these late monuments.

Reports generally speak of wild disorder in the grave; and argue that these must have been true ossuaries, which could only result from a two-phase burial rite. A first burial would have taken place and, after decarnation, the gathered-up bones would have been placed in the monument. If this way of explaining matters seems apt in some cases, more often it is not correct. Modern detailed studies of these 'pseudo-ossuaries' show that in fact the burials are nearly always of individuals laid on their side, as in the preceding phase. However – and this is perhaps linked with a large population explosion in the late Neolithic – funerary chambers went on to serve as depositories for numerous bodies. The bones were tidied into bundles as the need for space for a fresh arrival was felt. When a layer was completely filled with bones, that level was closed off, and a new layer of slabs was generally laid for the reception of new bodies. Several levels were superimposed in this way until the monument was completely full. In several cases the last layer of bones was itself sealed by a pile of stones or earth. But often it seems that the monument was abandoned before it reached full capacity and the upper layer is thus undisturbed by any closure procedure. This would explain the occasional complete skeletons found among disturbed bones in the final layer of burial. That is the case, for example, at Bougon A (Deux-Sèvres); in the re-use layer, dated to the late Neolithic, the discovery of several bodies accompanied by complete pots aroused the enthusiasm of excavators in the last century. It is the same with the side-chamber of La Pierre Virante, where, beside 40 bodies with bones mixed together, lay four complete bodies in flexed positions on their sides. Many other examples could be given.

So, funerary customs seem to be fairly complex during the whole period of megalith-building on the Atlantic façade of France, but this impression is largely because too few precise observations have come out of the excavation of the majority of megalithic monuments. In the present state of our knowledge, and in a somewhat schematic way, we gather that passage-graves from an early phase served as collective graves for a dozen or so people, placed on paving, the body in a flexed position. The monuments are set high up in the landscape and often grouped into cemeteries, and play a primordial rôle in marking territorial identity. Later on, the passage-grave stands alone; it has a large chamber and contains numerous buried bodies placed in identical positions to the preceding phase. The location of the monument in the landscape seems to have lost its importance; perhaps this is linked with the development of large enclosures of ditches with causeways which became the centre of the tribal territory at that time.

Who built the Atlantic chamber-tombs?

Study of the pottery collected in the different types of megalithic monuments permits the attribution of chamber-tombs to cultural groups (Figure 23). The early phase of passage-graves with round and polygonal chambers, which begins about 4600 BC, is characterised by a round-based pottery, fine and of good quality, with minimal decoration. There are several regional variations – the Carn group, Bougon group, Les Cous group, and so on. The second phase of Atlantic megalith-building, from about 4000 BC, sees the monuments diversifying according to area, with transepted passage-graves, 'Angoumoisin' passage-graves, and passage-graves with compartmented chambers. The pottery changes, and we see the appearance of new shapes and decorations which seem linked to Mediterranean influences in the Chasséen culture, albeit rather limited ones. While local groups establish themselves in the south of Armorica (Castellic, Groh-Collé, Kerugou, Conguel) and others in Poitou (Peu-Richard, Artenac), the influence of the powerful Seine-Oise-Marne culture of the Paris basin was felt more deeply in the north of the Atlantic region; there were important exchanges between the two regions, both in pottery styles and in megalithic architecture (the *allée couverte*) and mural art.

To pinpoint these ideas more precisely, it must be remembered that in Poitou the early Neolithic, corresponding to the first farmers, begins towards 5300 BC. The first passage-graves were built towards 4600 BC; the Atlantic Chasséen culture comes in at about 4000 BC; the Peu-Richardiens, builders of large causewayed enclosures, are known from 3600 BC; the Artenaciens, who used a few small copper objects of Mediterranean origin, establish themselves towards 3000 BC; and around 2700 BC the first Bell-beakers appear. These are all agricultural and pastoral populations, cultivating various cereals, raising cattle, sheep, goats and pigs, and hunting the deer and boar which lived in the forests in great numbers.

Figure 23   Pottery of different neolithic cultures in Brittany, 4500–2000 BC.
(After J. L'Helgouach and G. Bailloud)
1. Carn group.
2. Atlantic Chasséen.
3. Castellic group.
4. Groh-Collé group.
5. Kerugou group.
6. Conguel group.

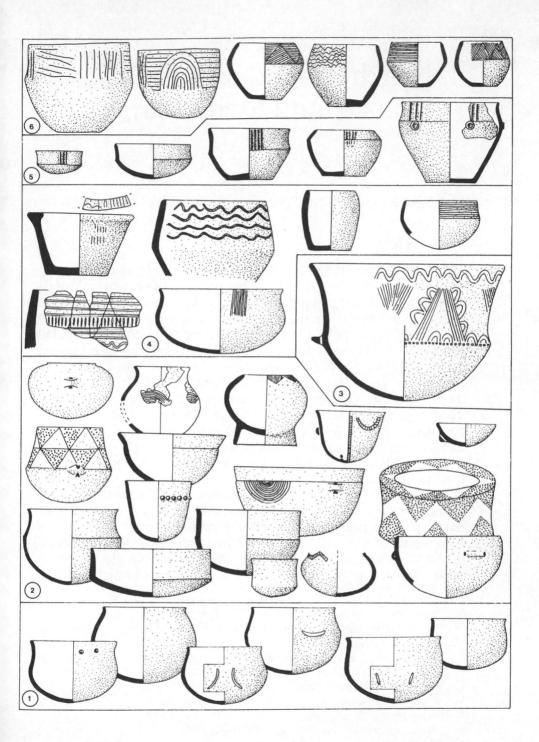

4. Northern and eastern France, and Switzerland

Megaliths in the Paris basin

The megalithic architectural type most specific to this region is the *allée couverte*. It is normally made of two parallel rows of upright orthostats, supporting a roof of juxtaposed slabs. The long, narrow chamber can be up to 20 m (65½ ft) in length. Its floor is sometimes paved, and in some cases the sides of the chamber are made of dry-stone walling (Figure 24:1). In front of the chamber is an antechamber, between 1.5 m (5 ft) and 2.5 m (8 ft) long, and of a width perceptibly the same as that of the chamber; its megalithic construction often has mural decorations (the 'Goddess of the Dead', 'pairs of breasts', hafted axes). There is generally no burial in it, nor was there ever, but it contained collective offerings. Access from antechamber to chamber is through a narrow gap, which can take different forms. The most common is a transverse slab, perforated in its lower third by a hole which is more or less circular or quadrangular with rounded corners. On the antechamber side a rabbet around the 'man-hole' indicates that a close-fitting seal was used there (a stone plug, or a wooden door), which was held in place by pegs, probably wooden, engaging in lateral holes.

In the megalithic *allée couverte* of the Vivez factory in Argenteuil (Val-d'Oise), which is around 20 m (65¼ ft) long and has dry-stone side-walls, a terminal chamber has been observed, access to which is below a

---

Figure 24 Allées couvertes *in the Paris basin, France.*
1. Allée couverte, *Bois Cotourier, Guéry-en-Vexin (Val-d'Oise). (After J. Degros and J. Tarrête)*
2. Allée couverte, *La Justice, Nervil-la-Fôret (Val-d'Oise).*
3. Allée couverte, *La Chaussée-Tirancourt (Somme). (After C. Masset)*
4. Pottery from allée couverte, *Les Mureaux (Val-d'Oise).*
5–6. Pottery from allée couverte, *Argenteuil (Val-d'Oise).*
7. Pottery from allée couverte, *L'Abbaye du Val (Val-d'Oise).*
8–9. Pottery from the hypogée, *Le Petit Morin (Marne).*
10. Engravings in the antechamber of allée couverte, *Marly-le-Roi (Yvelines).*
11. Engravings on the western upright in the antechamber of allée couverte, *Guéry-en-Vexin (Val-d'Oise).*

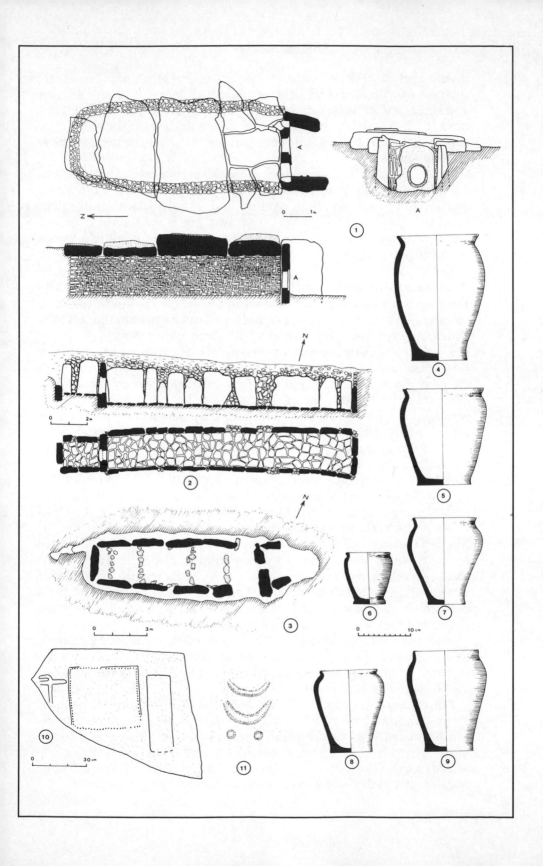

0   1m

Z ←

A

0   2m

N ↑

0   3m

N ↑

①

②

③

④

⑤

⑥   ⑦

0   10 cm

⑩

0   30 cm

⑪

⑧   ⑨

raised upright slab set clear of the ground. Here again there are similarities with Armorica. The whole of this *allée couverte*, chamber and antechamber, was completely buried; that is to say, it was built in a ditch, such that the roofing slabs were just at the level of the ground, or slightly below it. It does not seem that a mound was necessary above such buildings.

In the south of the Paris Basin, in the *départements* of Eure-et-Loir, Loir-et-Cher, and Indre-et-Loire, *allées couvertes* were built above ground and protected by an oval mound, as in Brittany. It does not seem that any particular orientation was preferred for these monuments, which are set for the most part on the side of a hill in a trench perpendicular to the slope.

In the Marne, essentially, we find another type of collective burial from the late Neolithic, which does not belong formally with megalith-building but which is a local adaptation of it: the chalk-cut tomb, or *hypogée*. This is an artificial cave, hollowed out by man in the soft sub-soil. *Hypogées* are often made up of three parts: a *passage* 4–9 m (13–29½ ft) long slopes more-or-less steeply down to an *antechamber* (also called an antegrotto, since it precedes a grotto rather than a built chamber), which is connected to a four-sided *chamber* by a man-hole comparable to those in the *allées couvertes*. The chamber is generally rectangular with rounded corners and may be divided into two by lateral pillars. Small benches exist on either side of the access-hole of the chamber entrance, and sometimes a niche has been hollowed out in the wall to the left of this entrance (Figure 25:1). Another point of comparison with the *allées couvertes* is in the decoration of the antegrotto with the carved motifs of the goddess and the hafted axe.

In the *département* of the Oise, prehistoric men of the Seine-Oise-Marne culture, the builders of the *allées couvertes* and excavators of the Marne chalk *hypogées*, also constructed *hypogées* by making a trench in sand, which was retained by two solid banks. The walls of the chamber, which recalls the *allées couvertes* in its length, are made of upright slabs or dry-stone walling. The floor is often flagged and there is an entrance. Some of these sites, such as Val-de-Nasles at Parmain (Seine-et-Oise), even have a megalithic entrance.

A group of *dolmens simples*, with one side open, seems in the Aube to have replaced the *hypogées* and other collective tombs, but their cultural attribution is difficult to determine. Many other *dolmens simples* stand in the Paris Basin.

Still during this phase of the late Neolithic–Chalcolithic in the Paris Basin – another type of funerary monument, closer to a true chamber-tomb and called a 'sunken tomb', was widely used. This was a tomb, more or less oval in shape, dug under a slab, which was very often already in this position on the ground. The walls are of dry-stone, or occasionally of dry-stone alternating with small upright slabs.

These are the kinds of monuments we find connected with megalith-building in the Paris Basin during the late Neolithic. But we should not imagine that these are the only funerary customs of the populations of the Seine-Oise-Marne culture. Some individual burials are known. Natural cavities, which are very rare, were used, as well as some adapted natural rock-shelters. Finally, multiple inhumations in the ground itself pose the problem of monuments, possibly of the *allée couverte* type, that were built entirely of wood.

It is noteworthy that while the Marne *hypogées* are grouped into cemeteries, sometimes large ones (up to 37 at Razet, Coizard), the *allées couvertes* stand alone, as do the pit-burials. However, researchers have noted that, in a general way, *allées* are much larger than *hypogées*, and that the number of skeletons in *hypogées* is always much lower than that in the *allées couvertes*. The discovery of chambers containing primary burials in the *allée couverte* of La Chaussée-Tirancourt (Somme) shows that such a monument is a true cemetery on its own account, and Gérard Bailloud (1964) has established that the territory of a cemetery of *hypogées* or of one *allée couverte* corresponds more or less to that of a present *commune*. So the differences between *allées couvertes*, burials under slabs and *hypogées* perhaps correspond more to geographical location than to a particular whim of local populations.

These last 20 years have seen some well-conducted excavations which have considerably advanced our knowledge of funerary customs connected with the collective burial of people of the Seine-Oise-Marne culture. We shall summarise the main results of these excavations and attempt to draw from them some general ideas, while remaining aware that the examples given are much too few, and that we shall have to wait a number of years yet before we arrive at a relatively precise view of the funerary customs of the peoples who lived in the third millennium BC.

The *allée couverte* of La Chaussée-Tirancourt

Claude Masset and Jean Leclerc have given us one of the most spectacular and complete accounts of a French megalithic monument. Publication of the results is not yet complete, but the notes which have appeared show all the importance of a careful excavation conducted by a perceptive team. Many old theories have been called into question. As far as funerary customs are concerned, it is as if no *allée couverte* had been excavated before this one. And how many thousands of skeletons had already been taken out of the large graves? The archaeologist of years gone by was happy to empty a monument over a few days, using unskilled workers, in order to retrieve objects out of the middle of the disorder he saw in the so-called ossuary.

At La Chaussée-Tirancourt in the *département* of the Somme (Figure 24:3) it will have taken nearly 10 years of excavation and as many years of complementary work to understand the history of a monument discovered by accident in 1967. Maybe 4800 years ago, in a trench 15 m (49 ft) long and 3.5 m (11½ ft) wide that was dug 1.7 m (5½ ft) into the limestone, men built a monument made of two parallel rows of upright orthostats, blocked at each end by slabs; the eastern one, following the classic plan of the *allées couvertes*, gave access through a small hole into the antechamber. As no roof survives today, it is very difficult to determine what it was made of; probably it was in perishable materials – wood with earth and straw above. The burial space thus defined, of dimensions 11 m (36 ft) by 3 m (10 ft) was divided into five cells by lines of stone slabs on the floor joining up with orthostats set opposite one another.

A first series of burials was made during the early phase. Some time later, nothing was left of them but a few bones, and these were soon covered by a thin layer of sediments. The first orthostat on the north side of the entrance was removed, perhaps along with its opposite number, which was missing at least by the next phase. About 60 bodies were then put successively into the monument, with the arrival of new bodies necessitating the shifting of the bones of those already there. Then a period of inactivity continued for a fair length of time, at the end of which it was decided to bring the grave into use again. In order to do this, a layer of sediments about 15 cm (6 in) thick was spread over the burial level; it is definitely at that time that the right-hand side-entrance was made by the removal of an orthostat. It was then much easier to get into the chamber, especially as a ramp was made at this point. The earlier entrance, a sort of partly obscured man-hole, in part covered, was re-fitted above this. The layer of sediments also filled up, to a level of about 50 cm (20 in), the empty space left behind the orthostats and the wall of the trench in which the monument had been built.

The authors of this study think there would have been a circulation area all around the monument in this narrow corridor between the orthostats and the limestone wall; a special link was made between the inside of the chamber and a subterranean blind space (called a *'muche'*), hollowed out behind the terminal slab, through a little opening made between this same end slab and the last orthostat on the south side. The circulation area had partly filled up during this phase of the monument's history, but the *muche* was still functional, although we do not know precisely what its function was. On the new flat surface of the sepulchral chamber more than 300 bodies were deposited in several primary burial compartments (called *'cases'*). These were quandrangular spaces inside which the bodies were piled as necessary. The space between the *cases* held several disconnected bones, probably coming from the *cases* themselves, and thus became an ossuary. When a *case* reached the end of its time of use, the upper part was disturbed by the bringing-in of other bones which lay around it.

The time came when the collective grave was full and had to be definitively closed. Each *case* was covered with loam, which obliterated the entire monument, including the peripheral passages and the *muche*. Then came the destruction of the upper part of the *allée couverte* by a fire which destroyed the roof and the upper part of each orthostat. This happened about 2100 BC. The carbonised debris and stone flakes were spread out and covered with alluvium, which until 1967 held secret from all eyes the location of this tomb, while generations of farmers tilled the soil above.

The meticulous excavations at La Chausée-Tirancourt have allowed us to understand how this *allée couverte* was used. We should note how few archaeological remains were found among the very numerous bone fragments: two bone awls, a shaped adze with traces of polishing, two copper beads made from a leaf of rolled metal. They are insignificant. However, in the antechamber, which contained no bone remains, a small pot was found belonging indubitably to the Seine-Oise-Marne culture, with three axe-sleeves with transverse perforation of which one is polished, a perforated shell, and an axe-shaped pendant of green rock. We must consider these objects from the antechamber as representing collective funerary material, which obviated the need for funerary material particular to each new burial.

Collective burials at Marolles-sur-Seine

After its structures had been recorded by aerial photography in 1960, the site of La Gours-aux-Lions at Marolles-sur-Seine (Seine-et-Marne) was worked for gravel extraction. Two collective burials were revealed. Although there is nothing truly megalithic about them, study of them threw much light on the burial rites represented in the *allées couvertes*. The first grave was a rectangular trench, 8.4 m (27½ ft) long by 3.6 m (12 ft) wide and oriented east-west. It was a buried *allée couverte* whose walls were in dry-stone. The floor was originally paved, and the monument must have had a roof which was in part megalithic. What is surprising here is a fairly generalised practice of cremation of the deceased, a custom which, although appearing in several other monuments of this type, is not a usual feature. Besides that, the archaeological material recovered was fairly rich (including a copper bead, a bone awl, and flint daggers), but most remarkable were two series of holes, on either side of the trench, extending westwards and outlining a trapezoidal area almost 40 m (131 ft) long, oriented east-west. We must imagine a wooden structure over the entrenched *allée couverte*, which would have been under its eastern end.

The second grave was made up of an oval trench, inside which was built a four-sided compartment, or *case*, for the dead. The whole was roofed with some perishable material, and must have functioned like a wooden chamber-tomb, comparable to each of the *cases* in the *allée couverte* of La Chaussée-Tirancourt. But here the *case* was inside and at the edge of a circular enclosure open to the south and defined by a wooden palisade. The authors of the study, C. Masset, and D. and C. Mordant, put forward the idea of a cult area linked with the collective grave; and here there might be a link with Xanton-Chassenon in Poitou.

The corpses of at least 54 people were placed here in the small space of grave II at Marolles-sur-Seine, and the excavators noted that removal of the skulls and the long bones had begun. Without being able to establish a certain connection between these facts, we should note that human skulls and isolated bones are often found in the ditches of the great camps of the late Neolithic; they appear, at least as far as the sites of west-central France are concerned, to have been put in niches made in the sides of the defensive walls.

The two collective burials of La Gours-aux-Lions seem contemporaneous, and pose, by the differences in custom and funerary furnishings, the question of social differentiation at this period.

Hypogée II of Les Mournouards at Mesnil-sur-Oger

Discovered in 1958, *hypogée* II of Les Mournouards (Figure 25) at Mesnil-sur-Oger (Marne) is an artificial cave hollowed out of the chalk. (Numerous similar sites in the region were the object of excavation at the end of the last century.) It has a sloping access-passage which leads to a small room, the 'antegretto'. We pass from this antechamber to a wider chamber, which is divided into two by lateral pillars, through a sort of tunnel (Figure 25:1 and 2).

Figure 25   Hypogée *II at Les Mournouards, Mesnil-sur-Oger (Marne), France. (After A. Leroi-Gourhan, G. Bailloud, M. Brézillon, and C. Monmignaut, 1962)*
1. *Plan of the* hypogée.
2. *Section of the* hypogée.
3. *Transverse arrowheads.*
4. *Antler sheath for polished-stone axe.*
5. *Polished-stone axe.*
6. *Flint blades.*
7. *Bone chisel and awl.*
8. *Hafted tool.*
9. *Curved pendant.*
10. *Pendant.*
11. *Shells with twin perforations.*
12. *Haft for a tool.*
13. *Teeth perforated at their roots.*

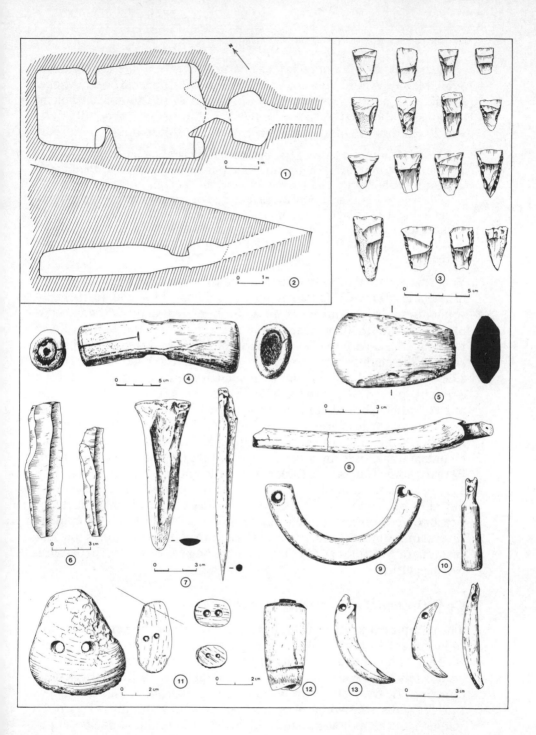

The results of the exemplary excavation of this *hypogée* were made available by André Leroi-Gourhan, Gérard Bailloud, and Michel Brézillon in a 1962 CNRS publication, *Gallia-Préhistoire*. The skeletal remains of about 60 bodies were recovered in the chamber, 40 adults and 20 children. In his demographic study, Brézillon notes:

> The mortality curve shows a population in which infant mortality is high. It establishes, moreover, that women are particularly at risk at the time of their first childbirth, and the risk of mortality is high for men between 40 and 50 years old. The overall average age is 25, and the average age of those surviving the period of infant mortality is 37. Individuals over 50 represent more than a fifth of the total population. Such a picture is comparable with that of numerous farming populations up to the end of the nineteenth century.

Very few personal objects accompanied the deceased to the grave: two flint blades (knives) contained in a small bag attached to the belt, sometimes also a quiver containing a dozen arrows, and a few ornaments. With their arms laid on their chests, the bodies lay in winding-sheets with the heads protruding. The first were placed at the sides of the chamber, in an extended position, the head resting on the side-benches. Collective equipment such as axes and quivers had been carefully placed along the side-walls, to the left mostly, and in the antechamber. Soon space ran out, and bones had to be pushed to one side to make space for new arrivals. After the rapid introduction of a new body into the grave, the opening between chamber and ante-chamber was closed by a bung, held in place by large wooden bolts. Perhaps some funeral rite took place in the antechamber.

At Les Mournouards, archaeologists discovered the remains of a partially burned body. This could have been an accidental death by fire, but we should recall that the same observation has been made in several monuments of this type, and we have seen cremation at the *allée couverte* of Marolles-sur-Seine, which belongs to this same Seine-Oise-Marne culture.

Collective burial under slabs at Éteauville

The monument at Éteauville (Eure-et-Loir) is not the perfect example of burial under slabs insofar as it is a partially buried monument, where study of the relative positions of the bones has not been carried out completely. It seems that there was a large slab entirely or partially covering an oval chamber bounded by dry-stone walls and a few upright slabs; the whole was covered by a low tumulus. Raymond Riquet's anthropological study identified the remains of 90 people, among them 16 children of less than 12 years old, belonging to two genetic families who intermarried. A trepanation – the cutting-out of a circle of bone in the skull (a surgical practice relatively frequent among the populations at this period) – was observed on one cranium. The bodies were placed in the chamber as they died, and here also the exiguity of the chamber necessitated pushing aside the bones of those previously buried, leading to the disorganised appearance which often puts this type of monument into the 'ossuary' category. Since the bodies were placed whole into the grave and the bones later pushed to the back of the same grave, it is better not to speak of an ossuary in this case. The term 'ossuary' should be reserved for places which only received a few bones as a secondary burial, since it implies the intention of re-burying all or part of the skeleton, removed from its original burial-place. (This is obviously a question of clarity of language.) The archaeological material which accompanied the burials is in the general style of the Seine-Oise-Marne culture, but there are arrow-heads of a kind more closely linked with central Atlantic France, and a particular type of pottery which has affinities with Brittany. These details characterise a group centred on the middle of the Loire, midway, in anthropological aspects and in material goods, between the inhabitants of the Paris Basin and those of Poitou at the same period.

One other fact should also be noted, the existence of a relatively abundant fauna among the human bone remains – a few cattle bones, those of four pigs, three dogs, a deer, three boars, a horse, and a beaver. If these bones are really in a primary context, we can say that offerings accompanied some of the dead, which could not be demonstrated in the recently excavated monuments of the Paris Basin region. Obser-vations made in other regions, however, seem to support this thesis.

Collective burials under slabs of the Éteauville type, which belong to the late Neolithic, need to be distinguished from comparable monu-ments recently revealed by G. Richard and J. Vintrou in the north of Loiret. These are also burials under slabs, not covered by a mound, but which were used only once for the burial of one or two bodies. They seem to be very early, if we can judge by the radiocarbon date which would make the burial at La Chaise the oldest megalith on French soil. But we must await confirmation of this date. Besides, although the fact of using a large slab of sandstone to cover the burial relates these monuments to chamber-tombs, their non-collective character dis-tances them.

Art in the collective burial-chambers of the Paris Basin

The commonest wall decoration in the *allées couvertes* and *hypogées* of the Paris Basin is the sculpted relief of two breasts surmounted by a necklace of one or two strands (Figure 24:11), which is often interpreted as the symbol of a funerary divinity. These low-relief figures are usually in the antechamber, and always on the left-hand side of the *hypogées*. They are probably connected with a funerary rite which could have taken place in the antechamber.

In Aubergenville *allée couverte*, one slab in the antechamber bears, according to Peek, 'two breasts surmounted by a necklace of three rows of beads and some features of a head, with on the back of the same slab the drawn outline of a hafted axe, a pot and another axe'.

The hafted axe is also a symbol commonly found in collective graves of the area, but with a less restricted distribution in the grave (antechamber or funerary chamber). The breasts with necklace and the axes are symbols known in Brittany, and it is with that region also, and more especially with the *allée couverte* of Prajou-Menhir, that parallels must be established for the motif of a square with dots at Marly-le-Roi (Figure 24:10).

In La Cave-aux-Fées *allée couverte* at Breuil-en-Vexin (Yvelines), outlines pecked on to a side-orthostat of the chamber show an axe, a quadrangular figure and a spearhead, for which Prajou-Menhir *allée couverte* at Trébeurden (Côtes-du-Nord) offers an interesting parallel once again.

Other motifs, grids or groups of lines, are difficult to interpret.

Chamber-tombs of Franche-Comté

In Franche-Comté (Figure 26:1 and 2), the region of central-eastern France bordering on Switzerland, Pierre Pétrequin and Jean-François Piningre (1976) divided the megalithic monuments into three groups: *dolmens simples*, chamber-tombs with horns, and simple cists without a surviving roof. The *dolmens simples* have a square chamber and are characterised by a porthole-slab. These are of the Schwörstadt type, whose geographic extent is strictly limited to either side of the Belfort gap. The 11 monuments known, dated to the first half of the late Neolithic, form the link between the Seine-Oise-Marne culture to the west, where the type originates, and the Horgen culture to the east.

Figure 26   Megalithic monuments in eastern France and Switzerland.
1. Chamber-tomb, Santoche (Franche-Comté). (After P. Pétrequin and J.-F. Piningre)
2. Chamber-tomb, Aillevans 1 (Franche-Comté), with its wooden superstructure. (After P. Pétrequin and J.-F. Piningre)
3. Finds from chamber-tomb, Aillevans 2 (Franche-Comté). (After P. Pétrequin and J.-F. Piningre)
4. Chamber-tomb in the Vosges.
5. Chamber-tomb in the Côte-d'Or.
6. Chamber-tomb of the Aillevans type in Haute-Saône.
7. Chamber-tomb of the Schwörstadt type in Haute-Saône.
8. Pottery from chamber-tombs in Franche-Comté.
9. Chamber-tomb VI at Le Petit Chasseur, Sion, Switzerland. (After O. J. Bocksberger, 1976)

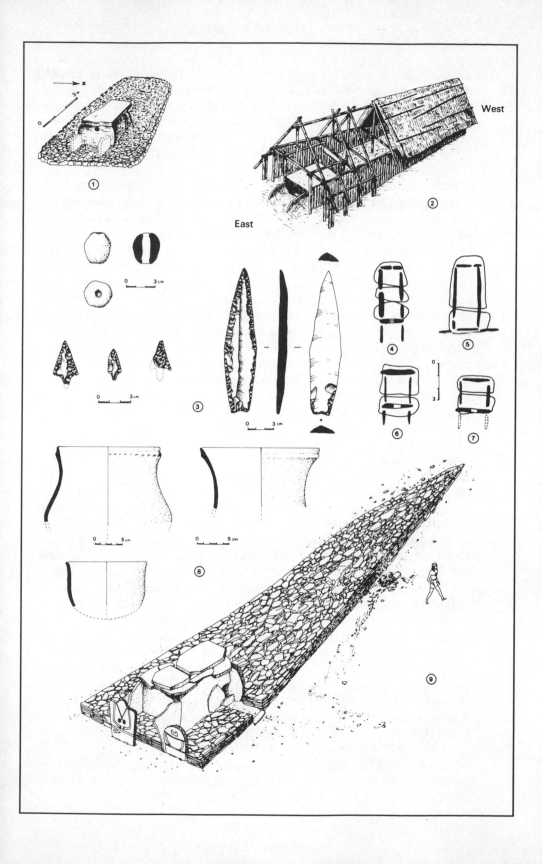

West

East

① ② ③ ④ ⑤ ⑥ ⑦ ⑧ ⑨

0   3 m

0   3 cm

0   3 cm

0   3 cm

0
3

0   5 cm

0   5 cm

Simple horned chamber-tombs (of Aillevans type) are more recent, dated to the second half of the late Neolithic. They are 'single monuments with a square or slightly rectangular chamber, with a notched slab for an entrance, and a short vestibule bounded by two vertical horns'. The surround of the tomb is made by a simple circular mound or a trapezoid of stonework: the Aillevans type derives from the Schwörstadt type.

Aillevans cemetery (Haute-Saône) deserves our stopping there for a while, given the amount of information it adds to knowledge of megalith-building in the Franche-Comté; but we should also pause in south-east Germany and Switzerland. At Aillevans, three horned chamber-tombs are from 300 m (984 ft) to 600 m (1968 ft) apart. Each chamber is four-sided in form, sometimes close to a square with 2 m ($6\frac{1}{2}$ ft) sides. All of them are perfectly oriented west-east with a slab, notched at the top, giving on to an eastern vestibule, as wide as the chamber and bounded by two upright slabs (the horns) which can be up to 1.2 m (4 ft) long. The horn-slabs reach the edge of the mound, which was circular in the first phase of chamber-tomb I. In a second phase the mound becomes a trapezoid of stonework, almost 20 m ($65\frac{1}{2}$ ft) long. Furthermore, chamber-tomb I was covered at this time by a wooden superstructure (Figure 26:2). In general the chamber of the tomb was hollowed 30 cm (12 in) to 60 cm (24 in) into the ground; it was sometimes paved with slabs. Numerous fragments of human bone, often very broken, lay in these chambers: at least 23 individuals in chamber-tomb I and 100 in chamber-tomb II. There were several phases of use separated by silt deposits. The bodies were deposited entire and in an extended position, with the head to the western wall. Collective material was placed in the corners of the monument, either side of the entrance to the chamber. These customs are singularly reminiscent of those observed in *hypogée* II at Les Mournouards. However, at Aillevans, food offerings from pigs, sheep, and cattle, and the remains of dogs were found. According to Pétrequin and Piningre, the builders of the Aillevans chamber-tombs must have been a sedentary population who developed without any great change in their customs from the late Neolithic into the early Bronze Age.

The earliest variety of Franche-Comté chamber-tomb, the Schwörstadt type, appeared in the west with the influence of the *allées couvertes* and the *dolmens simples* of the Haute-Marne. In the Aillevans type, which developed from this last, the circular or oval perforation of the entrance is replaced by a notch in the top of the slab. A particular development appeared in Switzerland (where the horned type exists) in the Basel area. Another local independent development will be seen towards the Haute-Marne and the Côte-d'Or.

As well as the chamber-tombs, single cists were used for collective burials, as at Lavans-les-Dôle (Jura), near Moulin Rouge camp. In a cist 4 m (13 ft) by 2 m (6½ ft) buried within a circular mound 14 m (46 ft) in diameter were found many skeletons, disposed in four successive layers separated by paving. Seven transverse arrowheads were found there. They indicate that the grave belongs to the late Neolithic/Chalcolithic.

Chamber-tombs of Switzerland and the Alps

We have already had occasion to mention the chamber-tombs of the Basel area, which are linked to the Franche-Comté group. More to the south, on the banks of the Rhône at Sion in the Swiss Valais, is the megalithic group of Le Petit Chasseur, studied since 1961 by Bocksberger, then by Gallay and the anthropology department of Geneva University; it is of great importance, both for the archaeological material recovered and for the way in which the excavations there were undertaken.

The lower level at Le Petit Chasseur, dated to the middle Neolithic at the end of the fourth millennium BC, comprises a village, a cist cemetery of the Chamblandes type, and an alignment of standing stones. The upper level, which interests us more particularly here, contains a dozen chests and chamber-tombs; the earliest of them, chamber-tomb VI, which was built in the late Neolithic, rises at the end of a triangular flagged area 16 m (52½ ft) long (Figure 26:9). No engraved stelae were re-used in its construction, but there must have been one or more at the southern end of the monument. It is a horned chamber-tomb, comparable to the Franche-Comté ones, apart from the access to the chamber which, instead of being through a notch in the eastern slab between the horns, was via an arc-shaped aperture at the base of the eastern lateral slab. Although the general orientation of the monument changed, access to the chamber was still in the eastern part. Among the implements of the megalith-builders, we note flint daggers from Le Grand-Pressigny (Indre-et-Loire), a sign of probable trade with western France. After a period of abandonment, chamber-tomb VI was re-used by Beaker people.

Le Petit Chasseur chamber-tomb XI (Figure 27) was entirely constructed of re-utilised anthropomorphic slabs; it was covered by a stone cairn. Its single capstone has an opening to the north-east due to its being violated by people of the early Bronze Age. The end of the chamber was divided into three parts by low slabs. Originally, access to the chamber was, as with VI, by a lateral notch. The earliest artefacts recovered in the chamber among the human bones belonged to the culture of the Beaker people. Between the horns of the mound, the opportunity had been taken to make a cist; its date of building is indicated by the presence on its flagstones of several early Bronze Age jars; it was also at this period that a small cist was built on the west side.

Finally, numerous post-holes indicate that the monument was surrounded, and perhaps roofed, by a wooden structure.

While chamber-tomb VI was built in the recent Neolithic, chamber-tomb XI, which is identical in plan, was probably the work of the Beaker people; both were re-used during the early Bronze Age.

The particular importance of Le Petit Chasseur derives from the decorated anthropomorphic stelae at the site. We cannot dissociate them from the chamber-tombs they accompany (chamber-tomb VI) or into whose walls they were built (chamber-tomb XI) in a subsequent re-use. The archaic character of these stelae, which appear in the local neolithic culture (that of the Saône-Rhône, result of the development of an old Mediterranean neolithic tradition), shows sparse decoration with engravings of daggers of the Remedello type of northern Italy. Gallay thinks this relationship extends as far as certain stelae in Corsica and Sardinia, but Gimbutas looks for the origin of this phenomenon to the Kurgan culture of the northern Caucasus. The later type of stele is characterised by profuse geometric decoration and the representation of the bow. These stelae are related to the Beaker culture, more as the result of trade than by a migrating population. They could be the work of a group from central Europe, of a distinct physical type, which would have been responsible for the disturbance of the second phase of Le Petit Chasseur.

On the other side of the Great St Bernard, in the Val d'Aosta on the Italian slopes of the Alps, the cemetery of Saint-Martin-de-Corléans is absolutely comparable in its architecture and its stelae with Le Petit Chasseur at Sion.

Along the Rhône in the Bas-Dauphiné is the megalithic burial at Verna, a cist which was altered several times (Figure 28). It was used by the Beaker people, as is shown by a copper dagger and decorated ceramics, but Aimé Bocquet thinks that it could be a little earlier in date. Like Le Petit Chasseur at Sion, the site was re-used in the early Bronze Age.

South of Geneva, several megalithic monuments existed in the Chablais of Savoy. Four remain – Reignier, Saint-Cergues, Cranves-Sales, and Pers-Jussy. Their architecture is too little studied to allow their certain assignment to any of the known groups, whether *dolmens simples*, or horned chamber-tomb, even megalithic cists.

Another group of megalithic Alpine monuments is in the *département* of Hautes-Alpes near Gap. The Tallard chamber-tomb is the one that has attracted most attention, by the extent to which its closing slab on the south was covered by cup-marks and engravings, such that it is interpreted by Bocquet as a statue-stele.

Figure 27   Cemetery of Le Petit Chasseur at Sion, Switzerland: plan of chamber-tomb XI. (After A. Gallay)

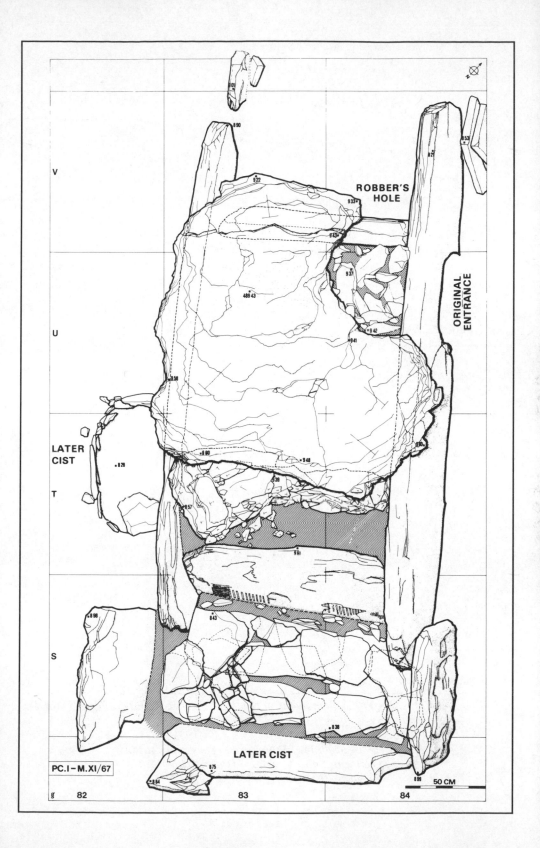

ROBBER'S
HOLE

ORIGINAL
ENTRANCE

LATER
CIST

LATER CIST

PC.I – M.XI/67

50 CM

g   82   83   84

V

U

T

S

Figure 28   Megalithic monuments in the Alps, Franche-Comté, Burgundy, and Switzerland.
1. Distribution map.
2. Three phases in the evolution of the Verna (Isère) megalith.
3. Megalithic monument, Saint-Cergues (Haute-Savoie).
4. Megalithic monument, Tallard (Hautes-Alpes).

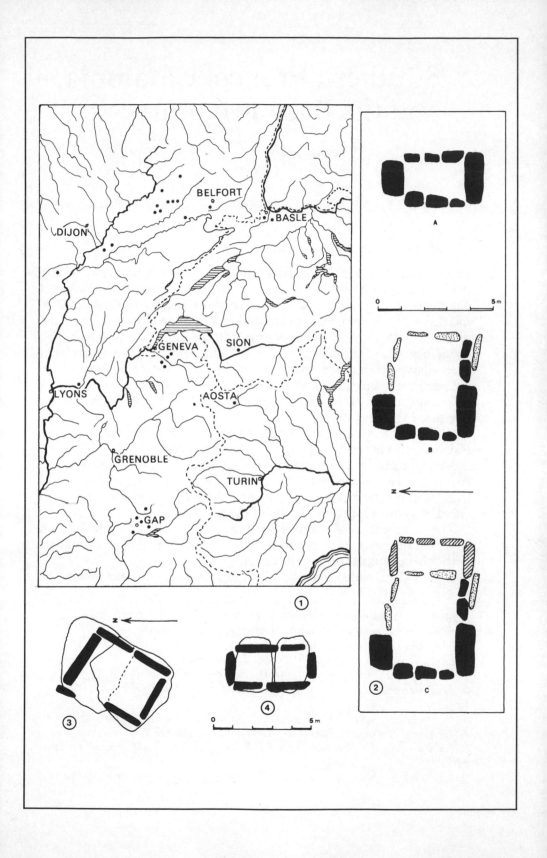

① ② ③ ④

5. Southern France, Catalonia, and the Basque country

Chamber-tombs in Aquitaine and Quercy

In Aquitaine, Mme Julia Roussot-Larroque attributes to a late neolithic culture an *ensemble* of megalithic monuments with elongated chambers, like the *allées couvertes* of Brittany and the Paris Basin. She has defined the monuments as an Isle-Dordogne group which has some affinities with the Seine-Oise-Marne culture of the Paris Basin. The monuments are considered to be close to the Breton *allées couvertes* in their above-ground construction and in the frequent absence of an antechamber; but unless they were linked by sea-routes, always a possibility at this period, no communication between Brittany and the Gironde can be envisaged.

While some monuments like Roquefort (Figure 29:1) at Lugasson (Gironde), 14 m (46 ft) long by 1.5 m (5 ft) wide and 1 m (3 ft) high, can indeed be compared to a typical *allée couverte*, in general the *allées* of Aquitaine decrease in height from the back towards the entrance, and thus cannot typologically be put into the *allées couvertes* group. In effect, they are a local adaptation of the passage-grave.

The monument of Curton at Jugazan in the Gironde has an engraved decoration on its end slab. It is difficult to establish parallels with other examples of megalithic art.

It should be added that the Blanc chamber-tomb, near Beaumont

---

Figure 29   Megalithic monuments in south-west France.
1. Roquefort, Lugasson (Gironde). (After J. Roussot-Larroque)
2. Marsalès (Dordogne). (After M. Secondat)
3. La Courrège (Dordogne). (After Dr. L'Honneur)
4. L'Étang de Dignac (Charente). (After C. Burnez)
5. La Pierre aux Fées, Le Peu de la Tache, Maillac (Haute-Vienne). (After P. Imbert)
6. Pierre Levée, Saint-Jory-de-Chalais (Dordogne). (After C. Burnez)
7. La Pierre Tournante, Puyrenier (Dordogne). (After G. Chauvet)
8. La Pierre Levée, Saint-Georges-La-Pouge (Creuse). (After C. Gautrand-Moser)
9. La Pierre Soupèse, Saint-Chabrais (Creuse). (After C. Gautrand-Moser)

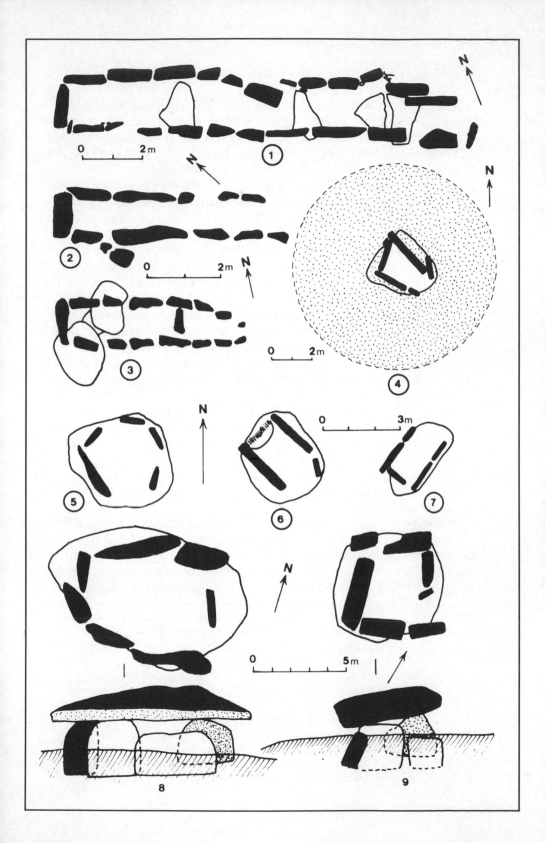

(Dordogne), in plan seems to relate to the 'Angevin' passage-graves, which can only be coincidence.

Thanks to a brilliant study by Jean Clottes, published in 1977, megalith-building is beginning to be better understood in Quercy (an area centred on Montauban and Cahors, north of Toulouse), and hence in a good part of the southern fringes of the Massif Central (Figure 30).

There are about 2000 to 3000 chamber-tombs occupying the *causses*, the high limestone plateaux which are the richest area of France for megalithic monuments. Les Grands Causses, where the average height above sea-level is around 1200 m (3940 ft), is separated from Les Petits Causses of Quercy by 40 km (25 miles). In Quercy, the recognised chamber-tombs number 750, but unhappily they are often in a bad state, emptied long ago, and studied thoroughly far too rarely. So the mounds are mostly represented on the ground by a circle or perhaps a slightly elongated oval, without any excavation having been under-taken. Now, we know from experience that an apparently round mound can certainly hide a cairn that was originally round, but it may also conceal a four-sided one (Benon, Charente-Maritime); and on an oval mound, which can represent a trapezoidal or quadrangular monument, may also be the result of two monuments set next to one another. So it is only with caution that we can say that a monument is a round barrow simply because it is dome-shaped, or talk of *dolmens simples* when the passage has not been sought in the mound. A dolmen is as simple as it is badly excavated.

These strictures apart, we can follow Clottes in his typology of Quercy monuments, which, as always in France, starts with the chamber.

While a cist is closed on all four sides and access must have been from above, the *dolmen simple* is open on one of its sides, giving lateral access. This finicking distinction in terminology is impossible to apply, most of the time. *Dolmens simples* can have their entrance closed by a movable slab obscuring the whole of one side of the monument. A part

---

Figure 30   Chamber-tombs in Quercy, France. (After J. Clottes)
1. Chamber-tombs, Le Pech du Grammont, Gramat (Lot), and their three phases: (1) dolmen simple *in a circular mound; (2)* dolmen simple *with port-hole in rectangular mound; (3) in its final form with an oval structure round the chamber-tombs.*
Diagram A gives a detailed plan of the chambers of Le Pech du Grammont.
2. Dolmen simple, *Verdier, Cajarc (Lot), in trapezoidal mound with final circular structure round the chamber-tomb.*
3. Chamber-tomb with side entrance, Les Cloups, Génouillac (Lot).
4. Chamber-tomb with vestibule, Le Pech de Rousille, Béduer (Lot).
5. Chamber-tomb, Le Pech de la Barre, Cabreret (Lot), in long mound.
6. Different types of beads and buttons found in Quercy chamber-tombs.

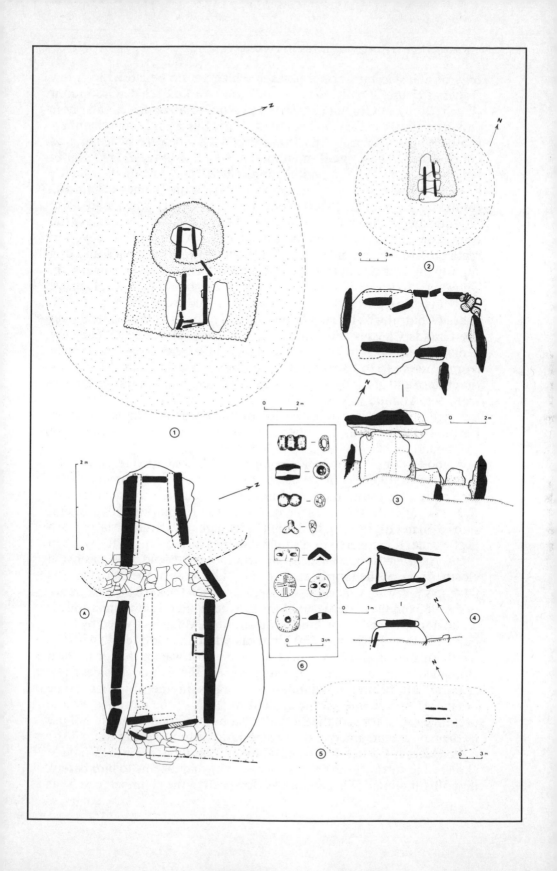

only of one side can form a passage which would be closed by a few stones after use. Finally, the chamber-tomb of Le Pech de Grammont (Figure 30:1), at Gramat (Lot) has a porthole-slab with a circular hole which recalls the *allées couvertes* of the Paris Basin, and some chamber-tombs of the Caucasus and India (but let us beware of leaping to conclusions). These small monuments, which average 2.5 m (8 ft) in length by 1.2 m (4 ft) in width, represent 82 per cent of the Quercy monuments. Obviously we are some way from the Bagneux chamber-tomb, which is 20 m (65½ ft) long and 8 m (26 ft) wide, and from Atlantic megalith-building in general. The 'giants' in this area are the ones which reach a length of 5 m (16½ ft). A single slab covers a rectangular or trapezoidal chamber, wider towards the back and dug slightly into the ground; its sides are each formed from a single slab. They open to the east, a sign they have undergone Atlantic influences, probably through the *dolmens simples* on the western fringe of the Massif Central which reach into Poitou. To the east, they extend over the Grands Causses and into the *département* of Ardèche. They are generally buried in a mound of stones, which appears to be circular and from 14 m (46 ft) to 16 m (52½ ft) in diameter, but they can also occupy the eastern end of a long mound. This arrangement probably originates from the Atlantic west where long mounds are fairly common. But, through lack of excavations, we do not know whether this is a primary position or whether the chamber-tomb is a secondary introduction into the mound.

A good example of a Quercy *dolmen simple* excavated recently is Le Rat at Saint-Sulpice (Lot), explored by Clottes. The monument was at the centre of a round mound 13 m (43 ft) in diameter. Oriented east-west and open to the east, the chamber-tomb comprises two lateral slabs 3.30 m (10¾ ft) long by 1.1 m (3¼ ft) high, and an end slab 1.15 m (3¾ ft) wide. It is covered by a single slab measuring 4 m (13 ft) by 2.8 m (9 ft). Another slab, which lay on the mound, could have been the closing stone of the fourth, eastern side. The floor of the chamber was paved. A low wall, which must earlier have been the kerb of the mound, takes off from the eastern end of the northern lateral slab; unhappily it could not be traced in the bulk of the mound, which is covered by large oak trees. A stele 80 cm (31 in) high was set up in front, in line with the southern side, wedged by blocks at its base. It was in the form of an elongated triangle, with its point sticking into the ground. Besides a few remains left behind by clandestine diggers in the chamber, some potsherds were found on the ground in front of the entrance. So the present circular form of the mound must be later than the period of use of the monument, and could correspond to its final closing-off.

In Quercy, Clottes has listed about 40 monuments which have a short, wide entrance structure, not roofed, which seems to him barely, if at all, functional. This 'vestibule', lower than the chamber, can be as wide, and even wider. It is normally made up of a small upright slab at each side, a little like the 'horns' of the Franche-Comté chamber-tombs. The side-slabs of the vestibule, not covered, do not reach the edge of the mound in its present state. Perhaps the vestibule served as an access to the funerary chamber, and was itself entered from above; but it could be that the tumbled mound now occupies a larger area than it did originally, and that the vestibule was at the edge of the mound when it was built. It is possible also that a dry-stone passage, not found through lack of excavation, linked the vestibule with the outside of the monument. According to Clottes, this was a 'degenerate structure whose use has outlived its function'.

This architectural type does not exist on the Grands Causses, and there is very probably no link with the Languedoc monuments. In contrast, the type does have several formal resemblances to the 'Angevin' chamber-tombs (and would then be a *really* degenerate type!).

In Quercy there exist small numbers of other architectural types: half a dozen chamber-tombs with side-entrances, of which the prototypes can be sought in the Grands Causses; a dozen double chamber-tombs; and even, at Souillac (Lot), a monument with a four-sided chamber built in dry-stone, which extends without perceptible narrowing as far as the edge of the mound. A transverse slab separates an antechamber, now emptied of all remains, from a chamber with archaeological material dated to the end of the third millennium BC.

Very few of the chamber-tombs of Quercy have been excavated in a thorough manner, so it is difficult to be precise about the early form of a mound, when all that can be seen is a pile of stones, hemispherical or oblong. Three relatively recent excavations have shown that sometimes there were low walls in the body of the mound. The first was at Le Verdier, Cajarc (Lot), where the chamber is at the end of an elongated trapezoidal mass, with a good kerb. The second was at Le Pech du Grammont (Figure 30:1), at Gramat (Lot); and at Le Rat, Saint-Sulpice (Lot), a low wall sprang from one of the edges of the chamber, as has been mentioned.

Le Pech du Grammont was first built as a four-sided chamber enclosed in a round mound with a low dry-stone kerb. In a second phase, another four-sided chamber was built, in front of the first and on the same axis, inside a mound with square corners, which must have hidden the first structure. This group is not unreminiscent of mound B of Champ-Châlon at Benon (Charente-Maritime); there, an original passage-grave, with four-sided chamber and passage, and surrounded by a circular cairn, was during a second phase taken into a four-sided mound built for a second passage-grave with four-sided chamber, parallel to the first. But while at Champ-Châlon we are dealing with chamber-tombs with off-centre passages of the 'Angoumoisin' type, at

Grammont no passage has been found, and the perimeter wall of the mound comes in at the level of the entrance. The finding of sherds of pottery in front of the low wall before the entrance of the second Le Pech chamber-tomb, as well as objects of chalcolithic age placed on this same wall, indicate that this did serve as the outer edge of the monument for a while. Offerings were made on the walls close to the entrance, as they were at the passage-graves of the Atlantic coast (Les Cous, Benon, Pornic, Sainte-Soline, and so on). The tradition is identical, and it is Atlantic in origin. But why this circular mass of stones around the chamber-tomb of Le Pech du Grammont? Two possibilities must be faced: either the four-sided monument was covered by a capping of stones, which has fallen down over the years and given the cairn a circular appearance (as happened at Chenon B, for example); or maybe the monument was deliberately buried in a round mound, after its use. This would be a closing-off structure, as in the *allée couverte* of La Chaussée-Tirancourt, or at a group at l'Île Carn (Finistère), which would date from at least 1000 years after the monument's first use. It is this second explanation which would be the more acceptable for the rounded phase of Le Verdier chamber-tomb at Cajarc.

All these architectural elements point towards an Atlantic origin for megalith-building in Quercy. We can imagine similar origins for the long mounds in Aveyron. Besides, Clottes arrives at identical conclusions through a study of the orientation of the chamber-tombs: the Quercy chamber-tombs are indeed open to the east, as are those in the Atlantic world, and in contrast to those of the Mediterranean Midi in Languedoc and Provence.

Perhaps it was the last men of the Neolithic, those of the Cros group, who built the first Quercy chamber-tombs; but the majority of the monuments, whatever their architectural type, are attributable to a population of the late Neolithic (often considered as an early period of the Chalcolithic) originating from the west, where they form the Artenac group.

The chamber-tombs essentially occupy the limestone areas (by '*la loi du calcaire*', the limestone law) and may often be grouped into cemeteries on the tops of hills. The bodies were placed in a flexed position in the chamber, which eventually contained several dozen skeletons. Of course, successive inhumation disturbed the previous burials. The deceased was accompanied by several objects – ornaments and arms – and offerings. By contrast with the practice of contemporaneous populations further to the east, trepanation is not known on skulls from Quercy chamber-tombs. A few unengraved stelae were found at the entrance to chamber-tombs of different types: Le Rat at Saint-Sulpice, Le Pech d'Arson at Corn, Cajarc, Roucadour (Lot). Questions should be asked about these small stelae found close to chamber-tombs (in Brittany, Quercy, Almería, north Africa, Ethiopia), which often seem to pass unobserved.

Chamber-tombs in Languedoc

In a masterly thesis published in 1963, Dr Jean Arnal examined megalith-building in the *département* of Hérault against its wider Mediterranean setting.

As a typical example of a Languedoc chamber-tomb, we shall describe Feuilles at Rouet (Hérault), recently restored in 1973–4. Situated not far from Lamalou chamber-tomb (Figure 31:3) on the Causse de l'Hortus, 20 km (12 miles) north of Montpellier, it belongs to a group of about 30 chamber-tombs which are scattered over the plateau. Villages of dry-stone huts of the Conquette type, or the type of the famous Cambous at Viols-en-Laval (Hérault), also exist on the Hortus plateau; but the majority of Languedoc chamber-tombs, even if they were used by people of the Fontbouisse Chalcolithic, the builders of villages like Cambous, had been erected several centuries before, during the late Neolithic. Three parts make up Feuilles chamber-tomb: an access passage, an antechamber, and a chamber. The whole is 12 m (39 ft) long, which makes it one of the longest chamber-tombs of the Petits Causses of Hérault, along with Ferrières-les-Verreries chamber-tomb and Pouget, which may be even bigger. The dry-stone passage is 6.8 m (22$\frac{1}{4}$ ft) long, and has a small projecting upright slab, 4 m (13 ft) from the antechamber and on the left. This disposition is unexplained, but is not a unique occurrence. The antechamber is lined on its long sides by low dry-stone walls. Where the passage meets the antechamber there is a narrowing, with two slightly scooped slabs which must have met at their top ends and left an ogival opening. The chamber is made up of two lateral supports placed edgewise and obliquely, such that their upper parts lean on the tops of the end slab and the doorway. This slanting setting is fairly common in the Languedoc chamber-tombs; in the best examples, the end slab and sometimes the portal are in the shape of an isosceles trapezoid, allowing the side-walls to make a good seal with the chest thus constructed. This is not the case at Feuilles, where dry-stone walls fill the space at either side of the end slab. The decreasing height, from the end slab to the entrance of the passage, is a peculiarity seen in other chamber-tombs with passage and antechamber in this area.

Le Capucin chamber-tomb (Figure 31:1) at Claret (Hérault) corresponds fairly well to the example given, with chamber, antechamber and passage built in dry-stone. On either side of the entrance to the passage stand small slabs such as are found by the 'Angoumoisin' chamber-tombs of Chenon B and Chenon C in Charente-Maritime. We note the trapezoidal shape of the chamber, a characteristic of the south of France – although it is also found up into Armorica. Grand-Juyan chamber-tomb (Figure 31:2) at Roubiac (Hérault), is also in three sections, but, as at Lamalou, Rouet (Hérault), the antechamber is lined with dry-stone walls. At Lamalou, a single slab covers the vaguely trapezoidal chamber; four other slabs cover a large part of the passage and antechamber at a lower level than that of the chamber. At Lamalou, as at Feuilles in the same *commune* of Rouet, two cut-away slabs are set edgewise together to form an 'oven-door' at the junction of passage with antechamber and antechamber with chamber. Grammont I chamber-tomb at Soumont (Hérault) has a slab shaped into an 'oven-door'.

While retaining the three elements of the Languedoc chamber-tomb, the monument of Viols-le-Fort (Hérault) has a peculiarity: the side-walls of the antechamber are a prolongation of those of the chamber, closing in towards the passage.

But many Languedoc chamber-tombs consist of a passage and a chamber only. The chamber, in the form of a long rectangle or a trapezoid, is usually bounded by two long lateral slabs which overlap the end slab and the portal between the chamber and the passage (examples are Coste Rouge de Grammont (Figure 31:7) and Roubiac II). The passage can be axial, or it can make a 'p' or 'q' shape with the chamber, a form well-known among 'Angoumoisin' chamber-tombs; but in the west, the chamber rather extends perpendicular to the passage's axis, and not as an extension of it, as is the case in Languedoc. The passage is usually straight, but it can be curved (Roubiac II), even sinuous (La Caumette (Figure 31:4), at Notre-Dame-de-Londres (Hérault); it is most often built of dry-stone (La Liquisse [Figure 31:5], Le Capucin, Grand Juyan, Lamalou, Grammont), occasionally with some more megalithic elements (Mas Reinart II, Roubiac II, La Caumette); or – much more rarely – it can even be entirely megalithic (Frouzet chamber-tomb at Saint-Martin-de-Londres – Figure 31:6). All these characteristics mean that the Languedoc monuments have many formal affinities with 'Angoumoisin' chamber-tombs.

The mounds of the Languedoc chamber-tombs are generally circular

Figure 31   Chamber-tombs in Languedoc (Hérault), France. (After J. Arnal)
1. Le Capucin, Claret.
2. Le Grand Jouryan de Roubiac.
3. Lamalou, Rouet.
4. La Caumette, Notre-Dame-de-Londres.
5. La Liquisse, Rouet.
6. Frouzet, Saint-Martin-de-Londres.
7. Les Fées de Coste Rouge de Grammont, Soumont.
8. Viols-le-Fort.
9. Mas Reinart II, Vailhauques.
10. Roubiac II.

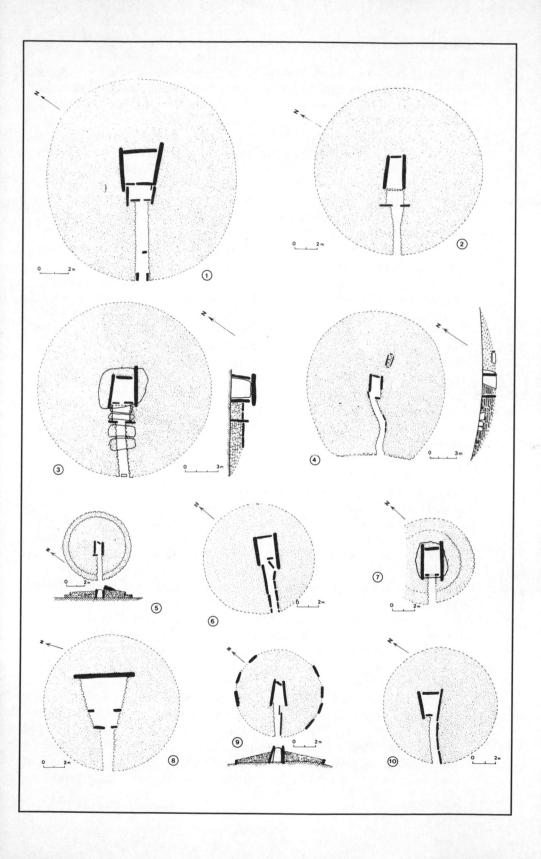

in shape, but, as always, few of them have been studied in depth. However, sometimes the facing wall has been found: so, for example, La Liquisse chamber-tomb, Les Fées at Coste Rouge de Grammont at Saumont, and Cambous, are buried in a circular mound with double concentric walls in dry-stone. This is probably very often the case.

At Le Mas Reinart II chamber-tomb (Figure 31:9) at Vailhauques (Hérault), the stone cairn is bounded by upright slabs. Finally, the passage of La Caumète chamber-tomb at Notre-Dame-de-Londres ends at a well-built rectilinear façade.

It seems that much research remains to be done before we can have some clear idea of the original appearance of the Languedoc chamber-tombs in their mounds. But it should be noted that the monuments are always built singly within a stone cairn.

The majority of the Languedoc chamber-tombs occupy a triangular area across five *départements*: Hérault, Gard, Aveyron, Lozère, and Ardéche, bounded by a line starting south of Montpellier, going up to Rodez, and back down to Privas. Dr Arnal has two sub-divisions: the one called Les Petits Causses includes Ardèche and parts of Hérault and Gard; the other, Les Grands Causses, takes in Aveyron, Lozère, and other parts of Hérault and Gard. The two *départements* of Lozère and Aveyron alone account for some 800 monuments between them.

The passages of Languedoc chamber-tombs open in the south-west sector, contrary to the general Atlantic custom of opening to the east (though this is not a constant factor). In Hérault, nearly all the chamber-tombs are oriented south-west, but as soon as the Aveyron plateau is reached, orientation becomes more anarchic; the usual orientation in Quercy is definitely to the east.

G.-B. Arnal and the Archaeological Group of the Lodévois have listed 85 megalith monuments in the mountainous region of the Lodévois (Hérault). At Saint-Pierre-de-la-Fage (Hérault), 63 monuments are scattered over the southern and south-eastern flank of one hill, across an area 1600 m (5250 ft) wide, at an altitude of between 700 m (2296 ft) and 725 m (2378 ft). These are small monuments whose capstones vary from 1.1 m ($3\frac{1}{2}$ ft) to 2.85 m ($9\frac{1}{4}$ ft) in length. Arnal notes that the smaller monuments are more closely grouped than the larger. The chambers are rectangular, with parallel sides, occasionally converging towards the entrance. The lack of serious excavation is cruelly felt, and we cannot yet talk of the existence of a passage through circular mounds bounded by a wall or upright slabs.

The builders of the Languedoc chamber-tombs are populations of the late neolithic Ferrières group, from the very beginning of the third millennium BC. They are thus contemporary with the last chamber-tombs of the Atlantic façade of France, and more particularly with the 'Angoumoisin' chamber-tombs, with which they have more than one point in common. We might be tempted to see possible links between

1   Chamber-tomb at Knebel, north-east Jutland, Denmark.
(National Museum, Copenhagen)

2   Chamber-tomb in its mound at Groenhoej, east Jutland, Denmark.
(National Museum, Copenhagen)

3 Façade of the cairn at Barnenez, Plouézoc'h (Finistère), France.
(Laboratoire de Préhistoire de Rennes)

4 'Angevin' chamber-tomb, La Roche aux Fées, Essé (Ille-et-Vilaine), France.
(Jean-Marc Briard)

5 Passage-grave with double transept at Crugellic, Ploemeur (Morbihan), France, after restoration.
(C. T. Le Roux)

6

6–7 Decorated stones from Gavrinis (Morbihan), France.
(Laboratoire de Préhistoire de Rennes)

8 Polished-stone axe and
pottery of Funnel-beaker culture,
early and middle Neolithic of
Denmark.
(National Museum, Copenhagen)

9 Portal-tomb, Pentre Ifan, Wales.
(R. Joussaume)

10 Mound C, Champ-Châlon, Benon (Charente-Maritime), France.
(Groupe Vendéen d'Études Préhistoriques)

11 Bougon (Deux-Sèvres), France: experimental transport of a 32-tonne block in 1979.
(J.-P. Mohen)

12 General view of the chamber-tomb at Lamalou. Rouet (Hérault), France, and its cairn.
(A. Colomer)

13 Chamber-tomb, Roubiac Cazevieille (Hérault), France.
(A. Colomer)

14   Rouet (Hérault) France: interior view.
(A. Colomer)

15   Rock-cut tomb at Roaïx (Vaucluse), France: upper level with its 'war layer'.
(J. Courtin)

16 Chamber-tomb, Zambujeiro, near Evoral, Alentejo, Portugal. *(V. O. Jorge)*

17 Fontanaccia chamber-tomb on Caunà plateau at Sartène, in Corsica. *(R. Joussaume)*

19   Finds from Sourré-Kabanawa 1, Ethiopia, monument with circular chamber and cella: glass beads, iron arrowhead, wood pendant comb.

18   Stele at Soddo, Ethiopia.
(R. Joussaume)

20   Dolmenic cist in the Harar, Ethiopia.
(R. Joussaume)

21-4   Megalithic monuments at San Agustín, Colombia.
(S. Cassen)

25   Megaliths at Satotabaru, Nagasaki, Japan.
(M. Komoto)

26   Dolmen at Chou-Chou Che, north-east China.

the Charentes and Languedoc via Quercy. Unfortunately, it seems that passage-graves bow out on the Causses, in favour of *dolmens simples*. However, this should be properly ascertained by systematic excavation of chamber-tombs and their mounds, especially since this west-to-east route to the south of the Massif Central does seem to have been the path for the diffusion of long mounds into Aveyron.

As for the orientation, so often the excuse for making a fundamental distinction between megalith-building in Atlantic Europe and in the Mediterranean world, the position needs re-thinking somewhat. At La Hogue and La Hoguette in Normandy, the chambers open in all directions; at Le Montiou at Sainte-Soline (Deux-Sèvres), the five chamber-tombs are oriented towards the south-west; the same is true of Bougon A, B and C, as well as the two chamber-tombs of Benon B. However, it is true, nonetheless, that on the Atlantic façade the majority of passage-graves open into the south-east quadrant of the compass, but greater anarchy reigns in the orientation of chamber-tombs in west-central France. In Quercy, the majority of monuments have their entrance in the eastern sector, with the average azimuth at 103 degrees from true north, while in the *garrigues*, the stony scrub-lands of Languedoc, the average is at 216 degrees from magnetic north, an orientation identical to that found in Provence.

Megalithic monuments in Provence

Research has recently been undertaken on the megalithic monuments of Provence; the major publications are by Jean Courtin (1974–76), Odile Roudil and Gérard Bérard (1981), and Gérard Sauzade (1983). Compared with Languedoc just next door, this area is fairly poor in chamber-tombs: 70 monuments have been listed, essentially centred on the *département* of the Var (in its central part and eastern edge) and to the west of the Alpes-Maritimes. The monuments were mostly built on limestone.

'Provençal chamber-tombs are of the passage-grave type, with square, rectangular or trapezoidal chambers, with an access passage, under a round or oval mound,' wrote Jean Courtin in 1976. The passage follows the axis of the chamber and 'p'- or 'q'-shaped chamber-tombs, so frequent in Languedoc, do not exist in Provence.

La Boussière chamber-tomb, built on top of a hill, is in the territory of the *commune* of Cabasse (Var). It was excavated by Bérard in 1950. Its rectangular chamber has side-walls made of dry-stone walling, an end slab and two upright slabs which form a neck at the entrance. It is paved, as is the passage, which is lined with large stones. The chamber-tomb is enclosed in a round mound 6 m (20 ft) in diameter, bounded by upright slabs, 70 cm (27½ in) high, which do not touch each other. The upper level of deposit in the chamber, 25 cm (10 in) thick, contained bones from three or four individuals, on a paved floor, which covered a second level, 14 cm (5½ in) thick. In this second level were found many very broken bones which had also been burnt, with a few archaeological remains, among them an arrow-head. The third layer was also separated from the second by paving. It was only 12 cm (5 in) thick. The very fragmented bones came for the most part from skulls and jaws, and were accompanied by archaeological material – eight arrowheads, a dagger, a large lamp, and 49 beads. More paving separated the third layer from the fourth, which was only 8 cm (3 in) thick and yielded very broken human bones, along with a large flint blade, an arrowhead, and 32 beads. Lastly, in the south-west corner of the chamber, a pit had been dug through the two last layers and contained the skeleton of a child: 'All the bones of the lower limbs were piled against the south wall, while the bones of the upper limbs were placed against the western slab,' wrote Roudil. Amongst the fairly rich accompanying archaeological material, we should note the presence of nine arrowheads.

A radiocarbon determination on a sample of carbonised pine from the base of the monument gives two uncalibrated dates (2035 and 2020 ± 260 years b.c.), which means towards 2500 BC in calendar years.

About 50 m (164 ft) east of the chamber-tomb, a layer of black, carbonised earth covering an area of about 100 m² (120 sq. yd) and about 50 cm (20 in) thick contained numerous fragments of carbonised human bone, as well as some archaeological remains of the chalcolithic period. This *ustrium* could therefore be associated with the chamber-tomb.

Along with these monuments with square chambers there exist in Provence a few chamber-tombs, not many, with long chambers, of the type of Gaoutobry (Figure 32:2), which is set on an eminence to the north of the Londe (Var). It comprises a chamber, an antechamber and a passage which narrows towards the entrance.

The short Provençal chamber-tombs are typologically close to the Languedoc chamber-tombs from which they seem to derive; this is borne out by the archaeological material they yield, for many elements in the Provençal monuments, such as winged beads and notched beads, different kinds of pendants, and so on originate in Languedoc. The long chamber-tombs, which have a different distribution to that of the

---

Figure 32   Chamber-tombs in Provence (Var), France.
1. Arrowhead from the chamber-tomb at La Boissière, Cabasse.
2. Gaoutobry, La Londe. (After O. Roudi)
3. 'Tholos', La Lauve, Salernes. (After J. Courtin)
4. La Verrerie Vieil, Saint-Paul-en-Forêt. (After O. Roudil)
5. Finds from the chamber-tomb at Piecervier. (After G. Sauzade)
6. Pont Neuf, Cabasse.

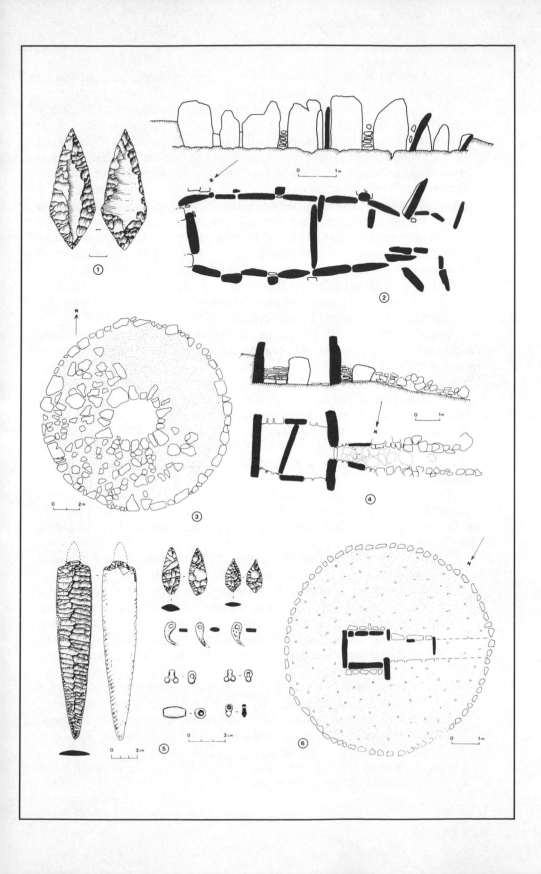

short chamber-tombs, are inspired by the Fontvieille rock-cut tombs (*hypogées*), which we will discuss presently.

As a general rule, the passage of a Provençal chamber-tomb is clearly higher than the floor of the chamber, and a threshold (or a step) separates the two levels; but not all researchers agree on what length the passage was, as it may not have reached the edge of the mound. According to Sauzade, access to the chamber was from above, through the residual uncovered passage. In 1976 he wrote: 'The presence of a passage in the Provençal chamber-tombs is due to a ritual, not a technical, necessity, since the *dromos*, always envisaged or marked in the architecture, remained closed during successive inhumations, and was thus not used to penetrate the *cella*.' Perhaps a greater number of more precise excavations would resolve this question.

Porthole slabs and 'oven-doors' do not appear in the chamber-tombs of Provence, while only the chamber-tombs of Saint-Pierre-de-Mons has a door formed by two cut-away slabs.

Funerary customs in Provençal chamber-tombs seem to be fairly complex. In some cases, the bodies were deposited entire, but their positioning has been wildly disarranged by successive inhumations. Very often the bodies were burnt, and the bones recovered from the fire were then placed inside the chamber-tomb in layers separated by paving, accompanied by the grave-goods which have been found there. It seems that there were also two-stage burials, and Roudil notes the case of Les Muraires chamber-tomb (Var), where the bodies were first put into the antechamber and then the bones gathered up and placed in the chamber.

The human remains collected from the Provençal chamber-tombs indicate a long period of use for the monument; at Peyraoutes (Alpes-Maritimes), Claude Bouville calculated a minimum of 172 individuals in the chamber-tomb.

Finally, let us recall that chamber-tombs in Provence are oriented towards the setting sun, just as they are in Languedoc.

A few Provençal monuments, not many, are grouped under the title of '*tholos*'. They consist of a chamber, most often round, but sometimes four-sided, built in dry-stone and roofed by corbelling; into it leads a passage which is often higher than the chamber. However, the *tholos* chamber is sometimes roofed by a single slab; it is at the centre of a circular mound. In the La Lauve monument (Figure 32:3) at Salernes (Var), the lower layer contained the very fragmented inhumations of a dozen individuals, accompanied by a few beads and some leaf-shaped arrowheads. The upper level contained the cremated remains of about 15 individuals, one arrowhead, and a few flakes and blades.

Figure 33   Chamber-tombs in Provence, France: La Grotte aux Fées (Bouche-du-Rhône). (After Cazalis de Fondouce, 1873)

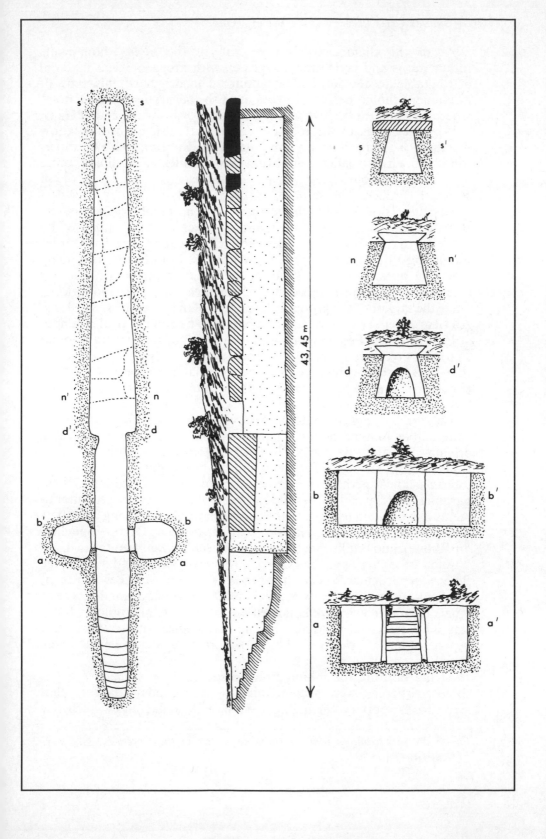

43,45 m

As in the chamber-tombs, we find in the *tholos* monuments inhumations and cremations, together with archaeological material attributable to the local Chalcolithic. The origin of this type of monument should perhaps be sought in the *départements* of Hérault, where there are the beehive tombs defined by Jean Arnal, and of Gard.

When it comes to the rock-cut *hypogée* tombs, we do not know whether we are dealing with monuments which belong with chamber-tombs or with an independent funerary manifestation, linked more closely with the burial caves which are widespread over the whole of southern France. The famous *hypogées*, rock-cut tombs at Arles-Fontvieille (Bouches-du-Rhône), are five in number: La Source, Bounias, Arnaud-Yvaren and Coutignargues on the plateau of Le Castellet, and lastly La Grotte des Fées or L'Épée de Roland on Cordes mountain. Four of them are entirely hollowed out of the rock. Only Coutignargues, although cut out of the Miocene sandstone, also has sidewalls of dry-stone; this last monument is only 14 m (46 ft) long, while the largest of the group, L'Épée de Roland, is 42 m (138 ft) long. All were covered by large slabs and buried in a round or oval mound.

La Grotte des Fées (Figure 33) has a 25 m (82 ft) long trapezoidal chamber, preceded by an antechamber on to which give two side-cells. A staircase passage gives access to the antechamber. The way from the passage to the antechamber and from the antechamber to the chamber is through an 'oven-door' cut in the rock.

The archaeological material recovered in these monuments is comparable to that of the chamber-tombs (which have the same orientation) and the *tholoi*. It links the *hypogées* with the local Chalcolithic. An origin for them should be sought in the Mediterranean islands, perhaps the Balearics, according to Bailloud, or in Sardinia. But Sauzade notes the formal resemblances between monuments like Coutignargues and the chamber-tombs with long chambers of Provence, such as Les Gavots chamber-tomb at Orgon (Bouches-du-Rhône), and thinks that there are connections between the two.

A few other *hypogées* are known in the lower valley and delta of the Rhône, in particular Perpétairi at Mollans (Drôme) and Les Crottes at Roaïx (Vaucluse), which was excavated by Jean Courtin. The site at Roaïx is an artificial cave hollowed out of the side of a hillock, but it was already half-destroyed when archaeological excavations were begun in 1965–6. Two levels of burial separated by sterile deposits were found.

At the bottom, the inhumations, disordered by successive depositions of bodies, were accompanied by rich goods – daggers, flint arrowheads, pottery (including a vase with a flat base which has

Figure 34   Distribution map of chamber-tombs in the Pyrenees. (After L. Pericot-Garcia, 1950)

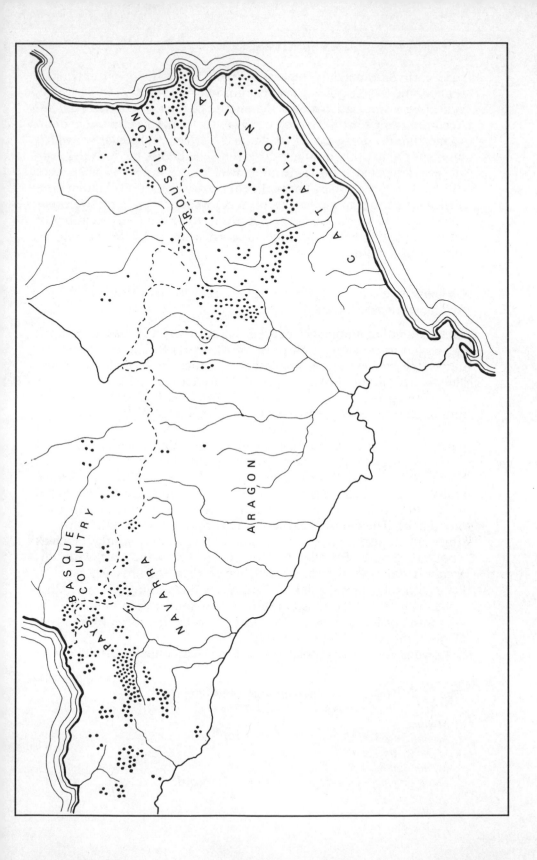

parallels in Sardinia) and numerous beads, among them one of copper. Radiocarbon dating gives an uncalibrated figure of 2150 ± 140 b.c. indicating a true date towards the middle of the third millennium BC. According to Courtin (writing in 1974) the upper level presented 'an extraordinary piling-up of skeletons, perfectly articulated, which supports the hypothesis of a "war layer", the bodies having obviously all been deposited at the same time'. Besides, several arrowheads were still stuck into the bones. The bodies of men, women and children were intermingled, accompanied by pottery, weapons and, rarely, ornaments. The 30 small pots recovered recall the Fontbouisse culture of the Chalcolithic in Languedoc, a correlation fully borne out by radiocarbon dating.

Chamber-tombs in the Pyrenean region: Aude, eastern Pyrenees, Ariège, and Spanish Catalonia

This group of monuments (Figure 34) is indivisible. Just as the Belgian *allées couvertes* belong with those of the Paris Basin, so we cannot, under the pretext of a man-made frontier, independently study chamber-tombs on the two slopes of the Pyrenees.

Following the major work of Professor Luis Pericot-Garcia, who published a study of the Pyrenean chamber-tombs in 1950, it was not until the coming of a younger wave of Catalan scholars, more particularly Miguel Cura-Morera and Joseph Castells, that we had a more up-to-date view of the megalithic phenomenon in north-eastern Spain. Over the last 25 years a great survey has been undertaken by the archaeology and prehistory institute of the University of Barcelona, which has culminated in the establishment of entries for each monument. The oldest chamber-tombs are the passage-graves with a single subcircular or polygonal chamber in a round tumulus (such as Font del Roure, Espolla; Figure 36:2). As is the rule with this architectural type, the chamber is higher than the passage, which is lined with small upright slabs or with dry-stone walling. Situated close to the frontier, on the coast, these chamber-tombs seem to have a link with those of Roussillon, as, for example, with chamber-tomb 8 at La Clape in the Aude (Figure 35:1–4).

Nowadays, we are completely at sea in researching the origins of this

---

Figure 35   Megalithic monuments in the Aude, France.
1–4. Megalithic cemetery, La Clape, La Roque de Fa. (After J. Guilaine)
1. Monument 1.
2. Monuments 3 and 5.
3. Monuments 6 and 7.
4. Monument 8.
5. Saint-Eugène, Laure-Minervois. (After G. Sicard)

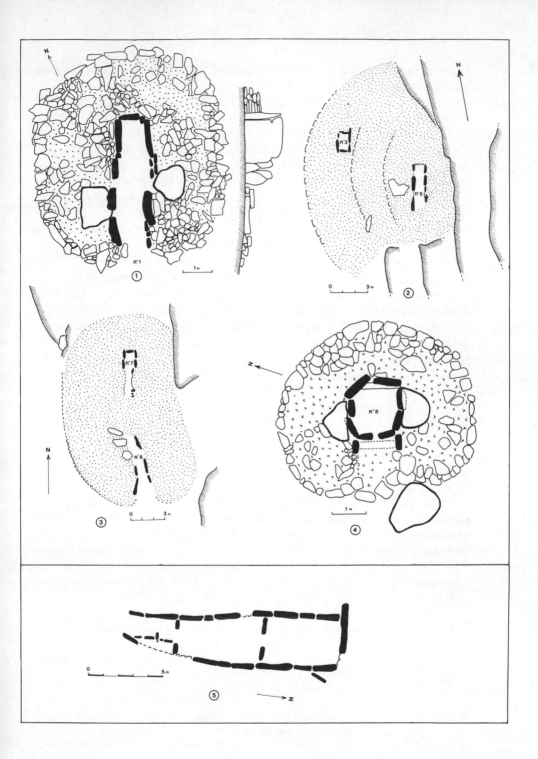

type of passage-grave with round chamber. It is a fact that this style of architecture belongs to the Atlantic world, stretching from southern Spain up to Denmark and Sweden, via Portugal, Brittany, and the British Isles. It is also certain that these chamber-tombs are very early in Portugal, as they are in Armorica and Poitou, where they are dated to the middle of the fifth millennium BC. However, we do not know for how long a period they were used. Should these Catalonian passage-graves be linked with those of the Alava at the other end of the Pyrenean chain, since no monument of this type is known in Aragon? This theory is difficult to maintain. So where do they come from, if the west is too far? There is, of course, southern Spain, Almería, which was early to adopt the passage-grave with circular chamber. But again, there is a gap between Almería and Catalonia in which there are no passage-graves at all. This leaves the sea and marine contact. Why not? The Mediterranean had boats ploughing across it long before the first Catalan chamber-tombs were built at the beginning of the third millennium BC. The fact is, we still have no idea where they came from. Jean Guilaine's hypothesis of spontaneous local generation is as acceptable as any other, but, it must be said, has as little proof. Thus we would have, at the eastern end of the Pyrenees, another centre of diffusion, comparable to those of Almería, Portugal or Brittany, If this idea could be proved, it would have great implications for explaining megalith-building in the French Midi. Unfortunately, we have not yet arrived at that point, although a connection could be envisaged with pit-burials and buried cists; these could later have been built above ground in mounds, before becoming true passage-graves. But why tombs with round chambers, when the cists are four-sided?

If we follow the chronologies established in other regions, particularly on the Atlantic façade of France, monuments with a single rectangular chamber and a passage, which occupy the same territory as passage-graves with round chambers, would belong to the early phase, like the monuments with triangular chambers. Of the Catalan chamber-tombs with four-sided chambers, three have off-set passages, a feature which links up with the Languedoc world.

Rectangular chamber-tombs with wide passages, otherwise called 'pseudo-*allées couvertes*' of the Aude type, form a spectacular group in

Figure 36   Megalithic monuments in Catalonia, Spain.
1. *Cementiri dels Moros, Puig Roig, Torrent.*
2. *Font del Roure, Espolla. (After M. Cura-Morera and J. Castells)*
3. *Cova d'En Daïna, Romanya de la Selva. (After E. Cruañas, 1970)*
4. *Mas Bousarenys, Santa Cristina de Aro.*
5. *Vinyes Mortes I, Pan. (After M. Cura-Morera and A. M. Ferran Eamis, 1970)*
6. *Coll de Creus, Gavarra. (After M. Cura-Morera and J. Castells, 1977)*

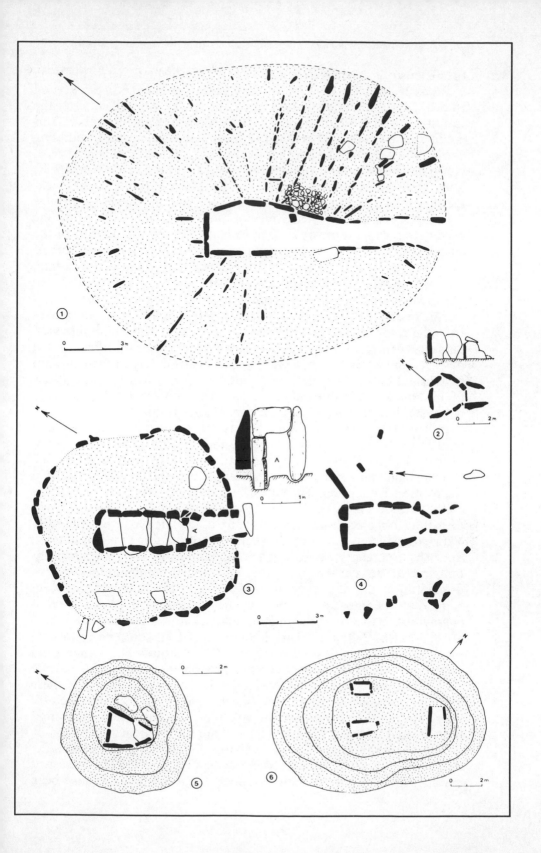

the dimensions reached by some of them, such as La Cova d'En Daïna at Romanya de la Selva (Figure 36:3). This monument is characterised by a doorway made of two uprights and a well-worked lintel at the transition, otherwise unmarked, between passage and chamber. This architectural type would belong to a second phase of megalith-building in north-east Spain, like another kind of *allée*, called the Catalan type, which has more modest dimensions – only 3 m to 5 m (10 ft to $16\frac{1}{2}$ ft) long. In a third phase, considered by most authors to be post-megalithic and occupying the late Chalcolithic and the early Bronze Age, single chamber-tombs formed of four lateral slabs and a capstone occupy the whole territory of Catalonia. Access to the interior of the chamber in one of these Pyrenean chamber-tombs was by a sort of 'window' produced by one of the four lateral slabs being set lower than the three others. Also during this post-megalithic phase there developed cist-burials, in mounds of different shapes (Figure 36:6).

This evolving schema of Catalan megalith-building, which moves from the round chamber with passage to the four-sided chamber with passage, then to the large rectangular chamber with undifferentiated passage, and lastly to the *dolmen simple*, is absolutely in the tradition established in the Atlantic world. Besides, Cura-Morera and Castells try to show several more particular parallels with Armorica. However, we must admit that all this remains very conjectural.

In Roussillon, Jean Abélanet, basing his researches on place-names (which may incorporate references to monuments which have disappeared), has listed over 100 monuments which he compares with the Catalan chamber-tombs. He notes that there are no chamber-tombs in the plain of Roussillon. They are all sited in mountainous areas, on a col or a crest. As in the Aude, he attributes the first appearance of megaliths in Roussillon to a local group of the late Neolithic, the early Vérazian, which is dated to the beginning of the third millennium BC. Spanish researchers would put the beginnings of Catalan megalith-building at an earlier date, the mid fourth millennium BC, yet originating from the French Midi. These two suggestions seem somewhat incompatible. Abélanet has noted a large number of engravings on the capstones of Roussillon chamber-tombs. Often these are cup-marks 3–8 cm (2–3 in) in diameter, which could be connected by a system of channels allowing the flow of liquids (here the Druid myth rears its head); there are also cruciform engravings which evoke human shapes, spirals, etc. Unfortunately, no reliable dating of these symbols is possible at the present time, but we can assume that they are later than the chamber-tombs on which they appear; it has sometimes been posited that they are much later, from the full Iron Age.

The megalithic ensemble of La Clape (Figure 35:1–4) at Laroque-de-Fa (Aude), recently studied by Jean Guilaine (1972), has shed considerable light in this southern area. Eight monuments have been recorded on a chalk bluff visible for many miles. Tomb 1 is a wide passage-grave, a type recognised in Corbières. It is an elongated monument, with a lowered passage whose width is constant, enclosed in a round mound. Jean Lavergne's study of the human teeth has identified 15 persons buried in tomb 1. Tomb 2 is a rectangular cist closed on three sides. Tomb 3 is a rectangular box closed on four sides, enclosed in the same mound as tomb 5. In it were found the skeletal remains of two people, aged 6–7 years and 20–30 years, together with a flint knife. Tomb 4 (like tombs 1, 5 and 6) is a wide passage-grave of the Aude type. In tomb 5 were the remains of 24 individuals, only one of them adult, a male. Beaker material – a Bell-beaker of the kind with 'international' decoration and an arrowhead with squared-off barbs (of which prototypes are found as far away as Holland) – indicates re-use of the tomb. A leaf-shaped arrowhead was found in tomb 6. Tomb 7 may belong to the same mound as tomb 6. It is a 'p'-shaped passage-grave in dry-stone, which is therefore close in form to the Languedoc types of the Gard and Hérault. In the chamber, which is higher and wider than the passage, lay the remains of 24 people, nine of them over 10 years old, and archaeological material from the recent Vérazian Neolithic, datable to the beginning of the third millennium BC. The last tomb, number 8, is a polygonal (almost circular) chamber, with the beginnings of a wide passage, enclosed in a circular mound 5 m ($16\frac{1}{2}$ ft) in diameter. We noted tomb 8 in the context of the first phase of Catalan megalith-building; this architectural type is probably the earliest in the region.

Four of the eight La Clape monuments have connections with the great monuments of the Aude, about which we must now say a few words. On the left bank of the Aude river, in the Minervois, several megalithic monuments have become famous: Saint-Eugène (Figure 35:5), Jappeloup, Pépieux and Boun-Marcou.

Les Fades monument at Pépieux (Aude), also known as Palet de Roland (Roland's Quoit), rises on a hillside at a place called Moural de las Fados (the Fairies' Hill). It was restored in 1972. It is a rectangular *allée*, 24 m (79 ft) long, enclosed in a long mound whose longest axis extends 36 m (118 ft) long. Three sections make up the whole. A passage was made from alternating opposed upright slabs and dry-stone walls. A central part, with higher slabs, was excavated a long time ago; the transition from the passage to the central part of the monument was through a large porthole made by juxtaposing two notched slabs. An identical porthole gave access to the third part, the end-cell. The first users of the monument seem to go back to the late Neolithic, but it was re-used in the Chalcolithic, the Bronze Age and even later.

Saint-Eugéne monument (Figure 35:5) is at Laure-Minervois (Aude). It is also in three sections: an access passage 4 m (13 ft) long by

1.2 m (4 ft) average width, an antechamber 5.6 m (18½ ft) long by 2.5 m (8 ft) wide, and a rectangular chamber 5 m (16½ ft) long and 3.2 m (10½ ft) wide, so the whole is close to 15 m (49 ft) long. A notched slab marks the transition from antechamber to chamber. The monument was restored in 1975. A list of the principal artefacts found in it comprises: 20 leaf-shaped arrowheads, 13 barbed and tanged arrow-heads, a lozenge-shaped arrowhead, 5 long flint knives, 2 scrapers, 17 funerary plaques in green schist, 2 pieces of talc whose purpose is unknown, a copper dagger, a spiral ring in copper or bronze, 2 lozenge-shaped awls in bronze, an olive-shaped gold bead, 40 perforated *Dentalium* shells, 2000 round beads made of *Petunculus* scallop-shell, 14 cut shells, numerous buttons, beads made of bone and *callaïs* (an imperfect form of turquoise), etc. Among the pottery sherds were fragments of Bell-beakers with 'international', 'corded' and 'Pyrenean' types of decoration.

Monuments of this Pyrenean kind were for a long time called *allées couvertes*, a name which confused them with the true *allées couvertes* of the Paris Basin and Armorica. In fact, these monuments have some features peculiar to themselves, such as the decreasing height of the sides from the end towards the entrance, which bear out Guilaine's definition of the type as 'elongated monuments, rectangular in plan, fairly lightly-built and marked by a progressive decrease in the height of the pillars from the end slab to the entrance sector'. The origin of this architectural design is difficult to find, and the idea of a link with the *allées* of the area around Agen and of Aquitaine is difficult to support. Once again, unless we find a local development out of the classic passage-graves, we should perhaps look towards southern Spain. We note with interest the affinities to be found in the Spanish province of Navarra, particularly as regards El Portillo de Eneriz monument at Artajona. All the same, the path from one form to the other is impossible to define in the current state of knowledge. Besides, if there were links between Navarra and the eastern Pyrenees, the direction of communication would be more along an east-west axis, as it is difficult to see a more westerly origin for the El Portillo monuments. However, if compelled to put forward a hypothesis, I would opt for contact with megalith-building in Portugal and megalith-building in Almeria, by way of Catalonia into Navarra and the Basque country. We should therefore take into account the monuments from the central Pyrenees

---

Figure 37   Megalithic monuments in the Pyrenees.
1. La Halliade, Bartès (Haute-Pyrénées). (After E. Piette)
2. Pouy Mayou, Bartès (Haute-Pyrénées). (After E. Piette)
3. La Romera 3, Caixas (Pyrénées-Orientales).
4. L'Arco dal Pech, Cubières (Aude).
5. Chamber-tomb d'Enveigt (Pyrénées-Orientales).

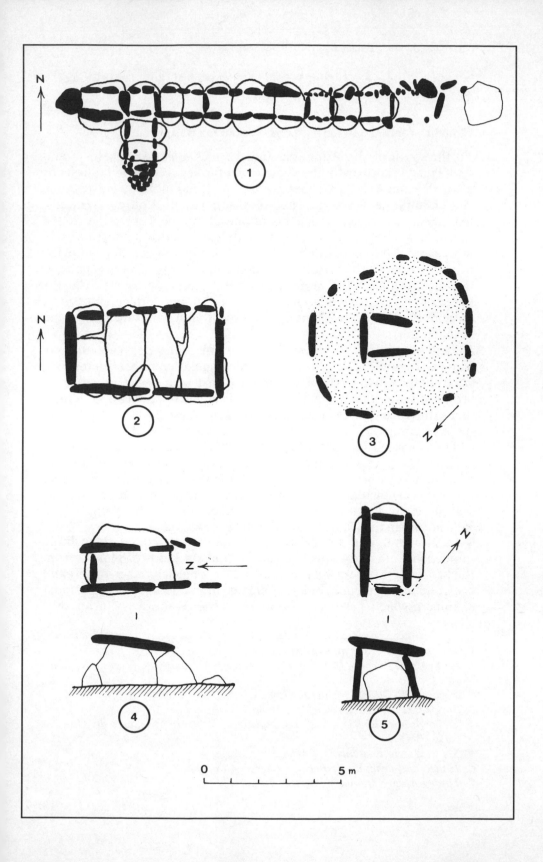

which, although few in number, may have been staging posts along the way.

Chamber-tombs from the high Pyrenees to the Basque country

To the south of the Aquitaine and Agenais *allées*, in Chalosse and Armagnac, chamber-tombs are few and far between, whether cists or *allées*. We must reach the Ger plateau, a glacial moraine between the Adour and the Gave de Pau, to the north of Lourdes (Hautes-Pyrénées), before we find a major megalithic concentration at the centre of a vast group of mounds of different periods. Most of these monuments were excavated at the end of the last century, with the rapid methods of the period which consisted of emptying the chamber in order to collect the more interesting objects. In about 1900 the Director of the Tarbes School of Artillery, Colonel Pothier, emptied 62 mounds (though not with his own hands – that was not the done thing at that time).

Piette excavated the largest chamber-tomb of the Ger plateau, Pouy Mayou (Figure 37:2). It has a huge rectangular chamber, almost 7 m (23 ft) long by 4 m (13 ft) wide, oriented east-west, which resembles a large cist more than a chamber-tomb. There were only two skeletons, in a sitting position at the centre of the long sides. The archaeological material comprised flint knives, pottery and a gold bead.

The other monument which is often referred to is La Halliade (Figure 37:1), which is like a series of cists set end-to-end in an oval mound. The whole resembles an *allée* oriented east-west, with a small cell set perpendicular to the second compartment. This excavation was also done by Piette. The pots and other objects discovered there indicate use in the Chalcolithic and the Bronze Age.

In Navarra, and in the Basque country in general, megalithic monuments are numerous and follow different kinds of plans – from the passage-grave (not very widespread) to single chamber-tombs and cists, and taking in more or less elongated monuments with trapezoidal chambers which get wider from the entrance inwards, in an oval

Figure 38 Megalithic monuments in the Basque country.
1. La Venta de Arrako, Isaba, Roncal. (After J. Maluquer de Motes y Nicolau, 1964)
2. Pagamendi, Oderiz. (After J. Altuna)
3. Sorginetxe, Arrizala. (After J. Altuna)
4. El Portillo de Eneriz, Artajona, Navarre. (After J. Maluquer de Motes y Nicolau, 1964)
5. Saint-Martin, Laguardia. (After J. Altuna)
6. Haitzetako-txabala, Renteria. (After J. Altuna)
7. Farangortea, Artajona. (After J. Altuna)

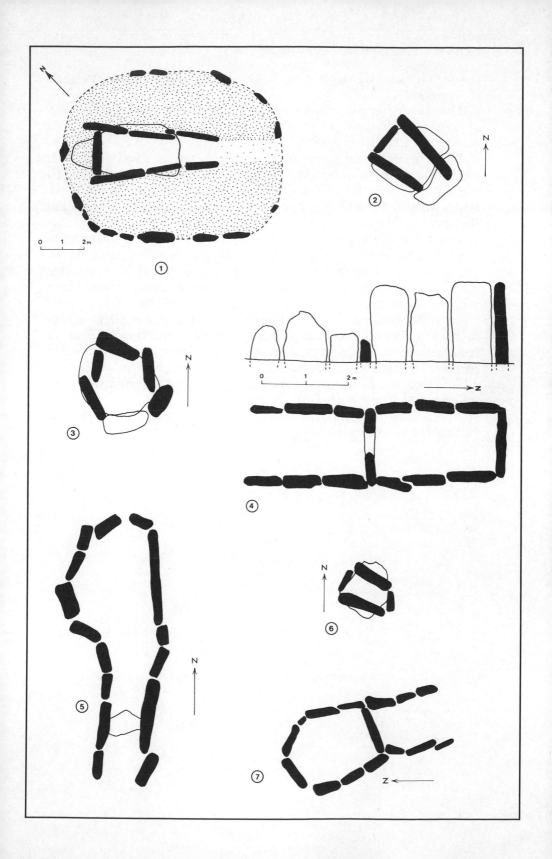

mound bounded by large stones (La Venta de Arraka, Isaba, Roncal) (Figure 38:1).

The passage-graves could have originated from Portugal, arriving via Galicia, and then developed locally afterwards, as happens in the majority of megalithic areas in western Europe.

Two particular monuments, only discovered in 1960 and 1962, deserve our stopping a moment: the chamber-tombs of La Mina and El Portillo de Eneriz at Farangortea, Artajona (Navarra) (Figure 38:4). At La Mina the chamber is an elongated rectangle, slightly bulging in the middle. The passage is practically as long and as wide as the chamber, but the height of the slabs decreases towards the entrance – a characteristic already noted in the large Aude-type monuments. At the transition from passage to chamber a perpendicular slab has an oval opening in it. Seen from the chamber side, this opening is framed by a groove, which must have allowed the fixture of a slab of stone or a wooden door as a closure. All these characteristics link these monuments with those of Aude and Catalonia, and a connection from one to the other can be considered in an east-west direction, without our being certain of the intermediate stages. So it is not impossible, as we stressed earlier, that we should find ourselves in Navarra at a crossroads of influences coming both from Portugal through Galicia and from southern Spain through Catalonia. In that case we may consider the Portuguese influences to be the earlier.

6. The Iberian Peninsula

For many megalithic specialists, the Iberian peninsula, and more precisely Portugal, seems to be an early centre of megalith-building. Some even see it as the cradle of this type of architecture along the Atlantic façade of Europe. In fact, datings made in recent years through the technique of thermoluminescence show that the first Portuguese passage-graves were built in the mid-fifth millennium BC, i.e. at exactly the same time as the earliest dated monuments of western France. However, from the very beginning a fundamental difference exists between these two megalithic phenomena. Both Barnenez (Finistère) and Bougon F0 (Deux-Sèvres) show that raising false-corbelled roofs over the chambers is an ancient art in France, contemporary with all the early, truly megalithic constructions, whereas in Portugal this method of building only appears much later, and seems to relate to influence from Almería, south-east Spain. This system of roofing, which spread right through the British Isles as far as Orkney, is an invention of Armorican populations, in the broad sense, during the fifth millennium BC. Another major difference appears from the first between these two great areas of megalith-building, for never in Portugal or in southern Spain has there been found a mound which, like Barnenez (Finistère), Saint-Soline (Deux-Sèvres), Peu-Pierroux (Charente-Maritime), La Hogue and La Hoguette (Calvados), contains several passage-graves in a primary context. This characteristic is peculiar to early megalith-building in the west of France.

These are not the only differences between megalith-building in the Iberian peninsula and in Atlantic France. To show them better we must describe the principal monuments and their contents, attempting to place them in chronological relationship each with the other. This is not an easy task, for although inventories and numerous plans are available, they are often the result of excavations much too old for us to be able to establish precise classifications. Fortunately, for some years now fresh efforts have been made in archaeological research into these countries, and no doubt in a while we shall see much more clearly.

We shall begin this exploration in southern Spain, arriving at Galicia by way of Portugal. We shall try as far as possible to give a chronological view of the monuments, based on plans and the occasionally abundant archaeological material contained in the monuments.

Megalithic monuments in Andalucia

Between the Spanish/Portuguese frontier to the west and the Mediterranean coast of Almería to the east is Andalucia, an area with a rich historic past and a great number of megalithic monuments varying greatly in both shape and size (Figure 39). The neolithic settlement of this area seems to have been due to populations using pottery decorated by impressions of the edges of cockle-shells, called 'cardial ware' after the name of the shell, which appear from the beginning of the sixth millennium BC. This early Neolithic has been brought to light for the most part in the mountainous areas of the Spanish interior and particularly in the cave of Carigüela, near Grenada, where 16 levels of occupation, studied by Pellicer, rise from the early Neolithic through to the Bronze Age. However, as Jean Guilaine stressed in 1976, 'The majority of the strata [in the cave] belong to the cardial culture and its *epiphenomenon* the "cave culture" with decorated pottery'. The lowest occupation level belongs to the early cardial, whose pots of fine ware were ornamented by using shells or combs. Polished-stone axes and schist bracelets make a timid appearance later on, in level 14, by which time the pots are decorated with smooth or impressed rims. Incised and stamped decoration on pottery dominates afterwards, while the cardial decoration disappears little by little, to vanish totally by level 9. It is not until level 3 that the first elements appear of a culture which particularly interests us in the framework of the present study, the Almerían.

The Almerían culture

The Almerían, a culture of the middle Neolithic of the Spanish southeast, is characterised by smooth ware, some of which has a conical base that could mark a legacy from the 'cave culture' of the early Neolithic. According to Jean Guilaine, the lithic tools could derive from the local Epipaleolithic, with trapezoids and triangles with abrupt retouch on the edges obtained by the 'microburin technique', a way of snapping a flint blade using two lateral notches.

In these farming communities, polished-stone axes and sickle blades with a characteristic lustre ('silica gloss', said to be from cutting cereals) are abundant. Two large villages, situated on the high ground at Três Cabezos and El Garcel, seem to have been bounded by a wall.

Figure 39   Distribution map of megalithic centres in south Spain.

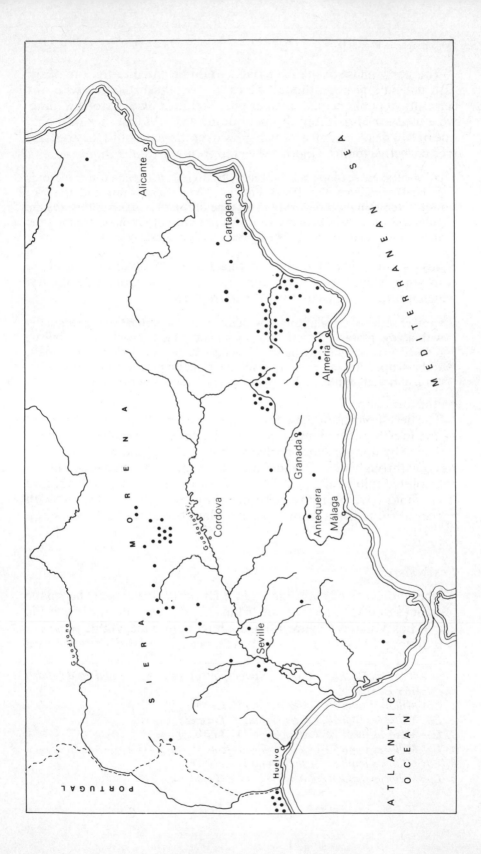

This early phase of the Almerían should be dated to the end of the fifth millennium BC; although we cannot establish the link with any certainty, it could be that circular pits, bounded by dry-stone walling, were used for burial from this period onwards. At first they held only one or two dead, a number which grew over the years until they became true collective tombs. Goods recovered from the tombs comprise

> polished axes, scallop-shell bracelets, triangles or asymmetric trapezoids with sharp retouch, flint flakes, limpets. The pottery is rare and atypical: most often round-based bowls. [This type of tomb] ... evolves towards the polygonal-plan cists also known in the province of Granada. Among the goods found in them scallop-shell bracelets figure largely.

Study of the prehistoric past in this region of Spain is still at an embryonic stage; so we will continue to follow Guilaine's theory, which would place in a middle Almerían phase

> another series of circular tombs with low walls or vertical slabs, eventually with access-passage, among the goods from which new elements appear: pointed arrowheads, triangular, lozenge-shaped or with a short shaft, violin-shaped Aegean-type idols, small terracotta plaques, and a diversification of pottery types marked by the accentuation of some shoulders

on the form of pots.

The development of these tombs leads on, in a late phase at the end of the fourth millennium BC in Almería, towards circular chambers, bounded by upright slabs, roofed with corbelling, and with an access-passage through a circular mound. These tombs are numerous in the chalcolithic culture of Los Millares. According to this thesis, the region itself could have been the place of origin of the round tombs, with corbelled roofs rising from a circular chamber of the early Almerían period.

Los Millares

At the confluence of the Andarax and Huechar rivers, near the village of Santa Fé de Mondújar about 20 km (12½ miles) from Almería, is the site of Los Millares (Figure 40). On a huge spur a megalithic cemetery was discovered. Associated with it is an occupation site, bounded by a

---

Figure 40   Los Millares, Almería, Spain: plan of the cemetery and the defended site. (After L. Siret)
1. *Los Millares tomb 36. (After G. and V. Leisner)*
2. *Los Millares tomb 28. (After G. and V. Leisner)*
3. *Los Millares tomb 26. (After G. and V. Leisner)*
4. *Los Millares tomb 63, and arrowheads from it. (After G. and V. Leisner)*
5. *Los Millares tomb 8. (After G. and V. Leisner)*
6. *Los Millares tholos 17. (After G. and V. Leisner)*

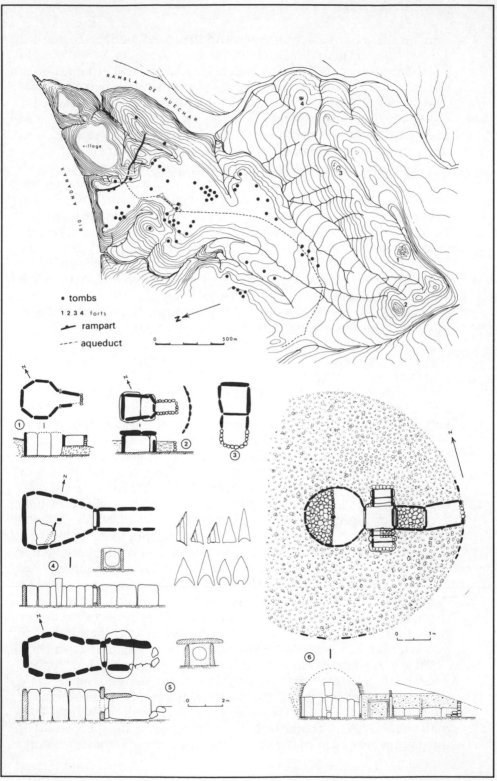

RAMBLA DE HUECHAR

RIO ANDARAX

village

- tombs
1 2 3 4 forts
▬ rampart
--- aqueduct

0   500m

N

0   1m

0   2m

wall forming a barrier across the neck of the spur. Small forts – marked 1, 2, 3, 4 on the map in Figure 40 – and an aqueduct which brought water into the enclosed area complete this remarkable group. But the site has a long history, and not all the elements which make it up are contemporary. Radiocarbon dates for one tomb (Los Millares 19: 2430 ± 120 b.c. uncalibrated) and for the wall (2345 ± 85 b.c. uncalibrated) show that the funerary chambers are of the same date as occupation in the defended area. But the monuments are not all of the same character and could belong to different periods.

At Los Millares the most common type of tomb, of which there are more than 50 examples, has a round chamber about 3 m (10 ft) in diameter. It is entered by a segmented passage through a circular mound, whose average diameter is 12 m (39 ft) or so. Various archaeologists have excavated in the cemetery, and they have used different numbers for each monument, which leads to some confusion. The numbering on our figure is Leisner's; Almagro and Arribas use another system but give equivalents where they can.

Tomb 17 (Figure 40:6) is one of the best known, because of all the rebuilding it has undergone. The chamber is circular. Lined by vertical slabs, it was roofed by corbelling, which seems also to have been supported by a central pillar set in a hole. The internal space is divided into two parts across the diameter. To the east an access-passage opens, made up of three equal sections; the way from one section to another and from the last to the chamber is through a porthole-slab pierced by a large, almost circular orifice. We have already noted this type of porthole-slab in Atlantic megalith-building, especially in west-central France, where corbelled roofs are also numerous but earlier in date. We may assume there was a system of closing the holes, with planks or stone slabs. But the peculiarity of tomb 17 is in the existence of side-cells leading off the third compartment of the passage, giving the whole a cruciform aspect which is familiar in other areas of the Atlantic world. This grave is inside the fortified enclosure, not far from the wall; it appears to be the only one in this situation. Can we deduce that it is earlier in date than the building of the wall? The mound of tomb 17 has a kerb of slabs and dry-stone walling, but the excavations conducted by Almagro and Arribas in 1953–55 revealed a second wall at the level of the first porthole-slab in the passage. Tomb 47 has a single chamber leading off the passage, in the second compartment to the south. One porthole-slab was erected between the passage and the side-chamber.

Other Los Millares monuments have a cell leading off the chamber. Thus tomb XXI in Almagro and Arribas numbering scheme has a polygonal cell at the end of the chamber, but it does not continue in alignment with the axis of the passage. Another small cell is at the level of the second part of the passage. It seems that generally the forepart of the passage was open to the sky, so the name '*dromos*' has sometimes been given to these Los Millares structures, by analogy with the monuments of a later period shaped like a Mycenean *tholos*. Chamber 47 yielded a fair number of human skeletal remains, especially to the left on entering, where the excavators' plans show a score of skulls and scattered bones. However, some articulations of bones were detectable, and could indicate that bodies were placed whole inside the tomb, to be displaced when a new body was deposited in the chamber. Abundant archaeological material was recovered during the 1955–6 excavation, notably pots with a rounded base and somewhat narrowed openings, and a pot decorated with parallel grooves juxtaposed in chevrons and forming a row of upward-pointing triangles filled with dots. Circles with radiating lines coming from them are like so many suns distributed over the centre and base of the pot. This is a typical Millarian decoration, found again in many other monuments of the cemetery (Figure 41:2–4) and in other monuments nearby. Among the worked stone we note a few large blades and arrowheads with concave bases. All these elements are relatively late in the development of the local neolithic and chalcolithic cultures.

The excavation of tomb 47 revealed many human remains lying in front of the entrance to the monument, but they could have resulted from emptying the chamber on several occasions. However, there are also deposits which appear to be much more deliberate, at the perimeter on either side of the entrance to the passage, as in the case of tomb 5 (Almagro and Arribas number IX), where sherds were collected to the north of the entrance and several pots were grouped to the south.

Among the exterior elements deserving mention we must note the ten small stelae or *betyls* at tomb 7. Each is shaped like a conical shaft about 30 cm (12 in) high. They were set in a group on a section of the south side a little over 1 m (3 ft) long, in front of the entrance to the monument. Many areas of megalith-building in the world have produced such stelae; we recall not only those in France but also those from monuments in north Africa and Ethiopia, which are morphologically much closer to Los Millares, without its being possible to establish any kind of link with them.

Generally, several concentric rows of revetment walls surround the chamber; tomb XII and tomb XVIII, in Almagro and Arribas' numbering, have three or four lines of these kerb-stones.

During the first excavations of the cemetery, Siret noted the existence of a coating painted on the internal walls of the *tholos* monuments. Unfortunately, it all very quickly disintegrated, and nothing remains of this decorative art.

As we have said, absolute datings make it certain that the false-corbelled monuments of Los Millares were built after the beginning of the third millennium BC and throughout that millennium. They could be the result of a local development of the circular dry-stone pit funerary-chambers, under the influence of an 'Atlantic current' coming from Portugal. They could also be local in origin without any external influence. For a long time they were considered to be the product of colonisation by people from the eastern Mediterranean, and linked with the *tholos* tombs found in Crete and continental Greece as well as in Asia Minor, the Cyclades, Euboea and the Ionian islands. The earliest of these monuments are those of Crete and the Aegean islands.

The *tholoi* of the Mesara plain, in Crete, were erected after the early Minoan II period, that is, between 2400 and 2200 BC. They were collective tombs reserved for one clan in the village; for that reason there are several monuments near the village forming a cemetery. Some of these tombs are even earlier. Lebena tomb at Lentar, built at the beginning of the third millennium BC and used until the Middle Minoan Ia period, might be the oldest tomb of this kind in the Aegean world. So there is some degree of contemporaneity between the Aegean tombs and those of Los Millares; it is perhaps too violent a reaction to the old idea of 'enlightenment from the East' to reject out of hand the possibility of any contact between the two regions at this time. However, the first Aegean tombs had no passage; access to the chamber was through an antechamber where rites for the dead took place and where early bones brought back out of the sepulchral chamber were placed in a secondary burial. The Greek *tholoi*, although much more elaborate, are morphologically much closer to the corbelled chambers of Los Millares, but they are also much more recent. While contacts may have existed from the beginning of the third millennium BC between south-eastern Spain and the Aegean, as some elements of material culture suggest, such as the small idols from the Millarian tombs, the antiquity of the corbelled tombs shows they could have been local in origin – especially as it is often forgotten that at Los Millares itself there exist many other forms of funerary monument. Tomb 36 (Figure 40:1) presents features that are more Portuguese than Mediterranean: a short passage bounded by a slab on either side and a chamber made up of seven upright slabs, like many monuments in Portugal, particularly in Alentejo.

Tomb 63 at Los Millares, which is bottle-shaped like tomb 8 (Figure 40:4 and 5), recalls on a reduced scale Soto chamber-tomb in Huelva province, near the Portuguese frontier. The Los Millares site has a porthole-slab at the point where the passage reaches the chamber, while at Soto there is only a narrowing marked by two upright slabs.

Figure 41   Monuments in south Spain: Los Millares cemetery, Almeria. (After G. and V. Leisner)
1. Reconstruction of a tholos monument.
2–4. Evolution of decoration on three pots: (1) from tomb 15; (2) from tomb 4; (3) from tomb 7.

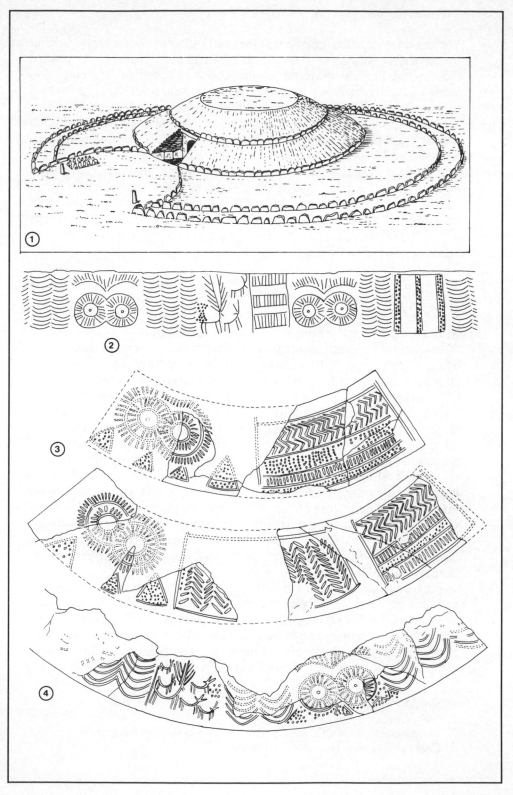

We should note that tomb 63 is somewhat outside the cemetery, behind the defensive wall and on the slope bordering the Huechar. It yielded rich archaeological material: many concave-based arrowheads and some of the barbed-and-tanged type; geometric microliths (above all trapezoids); a few flakes and scrapers, and some pottery, including round-based bowls and basins of varying depths, but also shouldered vessels with a break in profile, which can be seen in the archaeological museum in Almeria.

It is thus possible to envisage a current of megalithic diffusion flowing from the Atlantic (Alentejo, Algarve) into south-eastern Spain where, responding to local customs, it caused the early tombs to be transformed into circular chambers with corbelled roofs, designs which were to take the reverse route when chalcolithic cultures expanded towards Portugal.

The megalithic monuments of Antequera

The megalithic group of Antequera, about 40 km (25 miles) north of Malaga, is among the most impressive we know of.

In a circular mound about 50 m (164 ft) in diameter is La Cueva de la Menga, a massive bottle-shaped chamber like Soto and some other smaller monuments from the south of the Iberian peninsula. It is 6.5 m (21 ft) wide, and the ceiling height is 2.7 m (9 ft). The chamber is lined by 15 upright stones and roofed by five stone slabs, one of them weighing about 180 tonnes. We can imagine the work which building such a monument entailed, probably fairly late on in the chronology of megalith-building. With the short passage opening towards the east, the length of the whole structure exceeds 25 m (82 ft), recalling the gigantic scale of the Irish Boyne monuments, which are also relatively late in date. The ceiling of the chamber is supported by a row of three central monoliths which divide the chamber in two lengthwise. Unfortunately, by its very scale, the monument attracted attention early on, like its neighbours, and was long ago emptied of all archaeological material.

La Cueva de la Viera (Figure 42:3) is also an entirely megalithic monument, set in a circular mound about 60 m (197 ft) in diameter. There is a 25 m (82 ft) long passage made of two parallel rows of close-set orthostats supporting large capstones; its entrance is closed by a porthole-slab like those often found in the smaller monuments with rectangular chambers of Montefrio (Figure 43:6 and 8) in the province

Figure 42   Large chamber-tombs in south Spain.
1. Soto, Huelva. (After H. Obermaier)
2. Tumba de la Casilla, Gandu (Seville). (After G. and V. Leisner)
3. Cueva de la Viera, Antequera (Malaga).

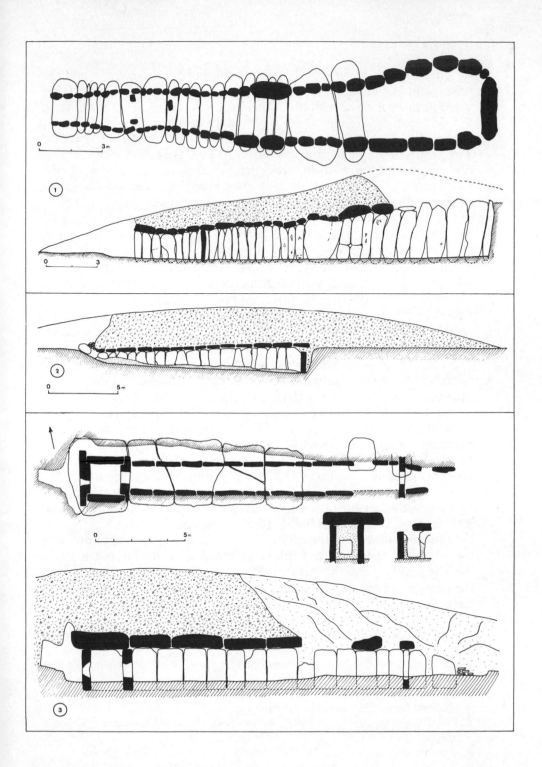

of Grenada, or in the Los Millares monuments. Access from the passage to the chamber is also through a porthole-slab whose four-sided opening measures 90 cm (35 in) by 75 cm (30 in). Another hole, in the end slab of the chamber, gives on to a space behind, a layout reminiscent of what we noticed in the *allée couverte* of La Chaussée-Tirancourt in the northern Paris Basin. At La Cueva de la Viera there is on one side a circulation area behind and to the north of the monument, and also a niche which elsewhere might be called a *muche* or secret chamber. Each side of the small, four-sided chamber, 1.8 m² (2 sq. yd) in area, is made of one upright slab which engages perfectly with the grooves of the entrance porthole-slab and the end orthostat. In this way the chamber is tightly closed.

La Cueva de Romeral (Figure 44:2) is a quite different kind of structure, which uses dry-stone construction. The mound above it is more than 90 m (295 ft) in diameter and over 9 m ($29\frac{1}{2}$ ft) high. With the two chambers and the passage, the internal structure reaches an overall length of 30.5 m (100 ft). The passage, averaging 1.5 m (5 ft) wide by 2 m ($6\frac{1}{2}$ ft) high, is lined by dry-stone walls which support juxtaposed horizontal capstones. The access-way from passage to chamber is both narrowed by upright slabs and lowered. Here again we find the general idea of a 'door' between passage and chamber. The circular chamber, about 4.5 m (15 ft) across, is built entirely of dry-stone; its corbelled vault is closed at the top by a large stone slab. At the end of the chamber, on the same axis as the passage, is another small passage lined with dry-stone and giving access to another small circular chamber; this, like the first, is built in dry-stone with a large slab at the apex of the corbelling. Here also the entrance to the chamber is marked by two parallel orthostats, which narrow the passage, and the ground level is some 50 cm (20 in) higher than in the main chamber.

Other monuments of the type of La Cueva de Romeral are known in the south of the Iberian peninsula; we shall mention particularly Alcalar number 7, in the Algarve, Portugal (Figure 43:1). Here again, the passage is built of dry-stone, but three pairs of upright stones have been set symmetrically on either side of the passage, each time

---

Figure 43 Megalithic monuments in the west and south of the Iberian peninsula.
1. Chamber-tomb built of dry-stone walling and with corbelled chamber (tholos), Alcalar 7, Algarve, Portugal.
2. Passage-grave of the tholos type, Salamanca, Spain.
3. Tholos, Barre, Extramadura, Portugal.
4. Passage-grave with corbelled chamber, Seno do Gataó, Ourique, Alentejo, Portugal.
5. Passage-grave, El Minguillo, Villanova de Cordoba, Cordova, Spain.
6–8. Chamber-tombs with rectangular chambers and entrance holes, Montefrio, Granada, Spain.

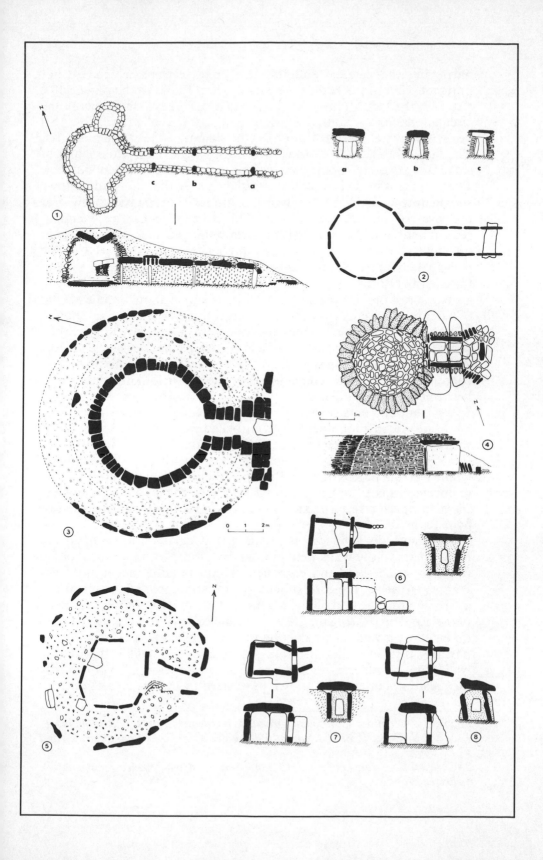

narrowing the passage and forming three sections which are not unreminiscent of the triple divisions so often found in the passages of tombs in the Los Millares cemetery. As at La Cueva de Romeral, the circular chamber is built of dry-stone, and the corbelled roof rises to a heavy slab which has broken under the weight of the earthen mound. The end of the chamber is paved with a large stone slab, while a floor of small stone slabs paves the passage and the entrance to the monument. The passage is roofed by juxtaposed slabs set on the side-walls, but we should note a somewhat strange disposition of slabs placed edgewise at the level of the second division. Off either side of the chamber, perpendicular to the main axis of the monument, there opens a small cell built of dry-stone, placed at a higher level than the end of the principal chamber. Similar cells appear at Los Millares, giving on to the chamber or the passage.

If descriptions of the mound of Peu-Pierroux on the Île de Ré (Charente-Maritime, France) are correct, there was, in a long mound containing several passage-graves, one with a circular, false-corbel-roofed chamber which supported a large slab as the 'key-stone'. At the end, a small passage gave access to another circular chamber, also corbelled. Is this simple coincidence, or should we look for direct links between these monuments?

While monuments such as La Cueva de Romeral and Alcalar 7 are not firmly dated, monuments with corbelled chambers are known from the middle Neolithic in Atlantic France. If there were a link between the French monuments and those of Iberia the direction of influence would be from north to south. But no corbelled chambers are recorded in northern Spain, and archaeologists tend to consider the Portuguese *tholoi* more as a western extension of megalith-building from the Los Millares area.

La Cueva de Romeral in Spain and Alcalar 7 in Portugal are monuments whose walls were built in dry-stone, with passages roofed by large stone slabs and corbelled chambers with megalithic 'key-stones'. However, there are other types of monument whose chambers are roofed by false corbelling. Monte do Outeiro (Figure 44:1) at Beja, in the Alentejo (Portugal), is a good example. Within a circular mound bounded by a wall; a circular chamber is reached by a relatively long passage; it is lined, like the passage, by close-set slabs rather than a wall. The chamber is entirely roofed by corbelling. Typologically identical monuments are known in western France, such as Les Cous

---

Figure 44   Chamber-tombs with corbelled chambers in Portugal and Spain.
1. Monte de Outeiro, Beja, Alentejo, Portugal. (After O. da Veiga Ferreira and V. Leisner)
2. Casa del Romeral, Antequera, Malaga, Spain. (After C. de Mergelina and R. Vélasquez Bosca)

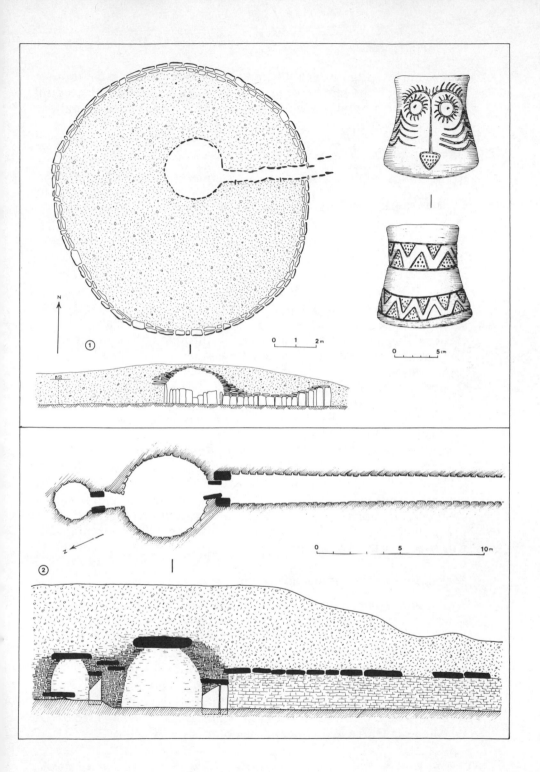

passage-grave (Figure 15) at Bazoges-en-Pareds (Vendée), but those in Portugal seem the more recent; and if we can judge from the typical Almerían decoration of the pot found in Monte do Outeiro, relations with south-east Spain are very obvious.

Other monuments in southern Spain

Apart from the famous cemetery of Antequera, southern Spain is rich in megalithic monuments; we shall give a few examples, some already quoted elsewhere.

Among the large monuments we may note La Tumba de la Casilla, at Gandul in the province of Seville, which forms a fine megalithic *allée*. Soto dolmen, at Trigueros (Huelva), is important both for its huge size and the abundant decoration on 21 of its orthostats (Figure 42:1).

In the Granada area, the Montefrio monuments (Figure 43:6–8) are characterised by a rectangular chamber usually made up of a single end slab, two side-walls each of two juxtaposed upright slabs, and an entrance through a wide porthole-slab or through two cut-away slabs. The chamber is reached by a short passage on the same level, and sometimes has an extension set at a lower level.

El Minguillo, at Villanova de Cordoba, in the province of Cordova, is a typical passage-grave with a polygonal chamber and a passage of orthostats, open to the east, in a subcircular mound with a kerb of upright slabs (Figure 43:6).

The province of Huelva holds several unusual monuments, including El Pozuelo 7 with a cruciform plan (Figure 46:5). Open to the east, it has a passage giving on to an elongated chamber, on either side of which extend two large side-cells. In the centre of the southern chamber, an upright block holds the capstones in position. It is probably quite useless to seek any origin elsewhere for this monument, which seems a local adaptation quite independent of external influence.

Megalithic monuments in southern Portugal

Although incomplete in its coverage, Georg and Vera Leisner's 1956 distribution map (Figure 45) shows perfectly the megalithic concentrations in the west of the Iberian peninsula. Two broad areas can be distinguished; one in the middle, the Alto Alentejo, is not coastal in its position; the other in the north is formed from the regions of Beira, Douro, Minho and Trás-os-Montes in Portugal and Galicia in Spain. Add to these a small centre on the coast in Estremadoura (a place not to be confused with Extremadura in Spain, from which it is separated by Alto Alentejo) and another at the point of the Algarve.

Figure 45   Distribution map of chamber-tombs in the west of the Iberian peninsula. (After G. and V. Leisner, 1956)

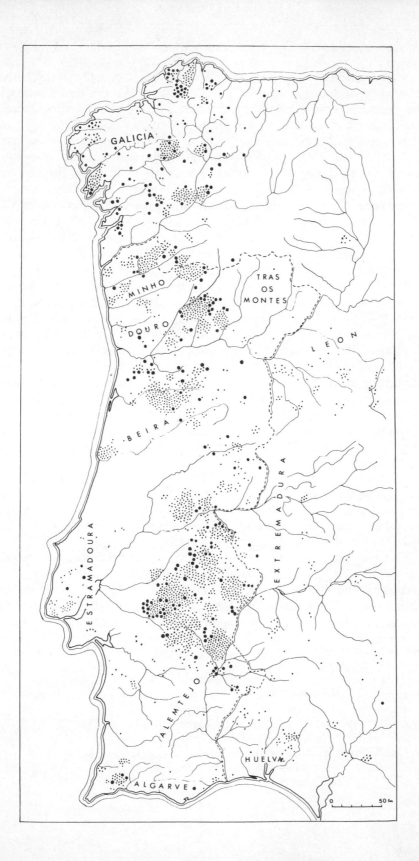

GALICIA

MINHO

TRAS
OS
MONTES

DOURO

LEON

BEIRA

EXTREMADURA

ESTRAMADOURA

ALEMTEJO

HUELVA

ALGARVE

0   50 km

Many archaeologists see Alto Alentejo as a centre of megalithic creativity, and some would like to see in it the cradle of Atlantic megalith-building, taking local cists as a point of departure. Buried cist-tombs, rectangular in plan, are considered to be individual graves, and have yielded sparse archaeological material: polished-stone axes and adzes, microlithic trapezes and triangles, with occasionally some round-based, undecorated pottery. Another birth-place for the tradition is proposed in the Algarve, where buried megalithic cists are also found, containing individual burials and funerary material comparable to that of the Alto Alentejo cists (Figure 46:1). Next, we get a prolongation of the chamber, which becomes a true *allée*; finally a passage appears at the eastern end (Figure 46:2 and 4). By then the inhumations are collective, and the chamber, up to 6 m (20 ft) long, is generally oriented east-west. This is the process by which the rite evolved from individual burial in a stone cist to collective burial in a passage-grave. The idea of this progression from cist to passage-grave and from individual to collective burial could have arisen independently in different places. In the west of France collective burials under slabs, covered by a small mound, on the islet of Téviec (Morbihan), would represent the point of departure; subsequently it was thought necessary to create a structured entrance to the funerary chamber. Perhaps the pit-burials of Catalonia and circular dry-stone tombs of Almería are themselves each the beginnings of an independent origin of megalith-building. This is an attractive hypothesis which we shall discuss later.

Like Euan Mackie, we can consider that the peoples of the Algarve, using stone cists for individual burials, one day adopted the style of megalith coming from the interior of the country – or elsewhere. But it would be especially important to know whether or not these first cists were false-corbelled and topped by a circular mound.

The fact remains that the great antiquity of Portuguese megalith-building has been demonstrated, in particular with dates obtained by the technique of thermoluminescence for two Alto Alentejo monuments excavated in 1948 and 1949 by the Leisners (both monuments are called '*antas*', from the Portuguese word for chamber-tomb). *Anta 1*

Figure 46 Megalithic monuments in the west of the Iberian peninsula. (After G. and V. Leisner)

1. *Arca de la Pissa, La Coruña, Galicia, Spain.*
2. *Palmeira 4, Monchique, Algarve, Portugal.*
3. *Palmeira 3, Monchique, Algarve, Portugal.*
4. *Buço Preto mound 7, Monchique, Algarve, Portugal.*
5. *El Pozuelo 7, Huelva, Spain.*
6. *Cas de Orca, Malhada de Cambrunho, Vouzela, Spain.*
7, *Castillejo, Vila Nova de Paiva, Beira Alta, Portugal.*
8. *Châ de Mezio, Spain.*

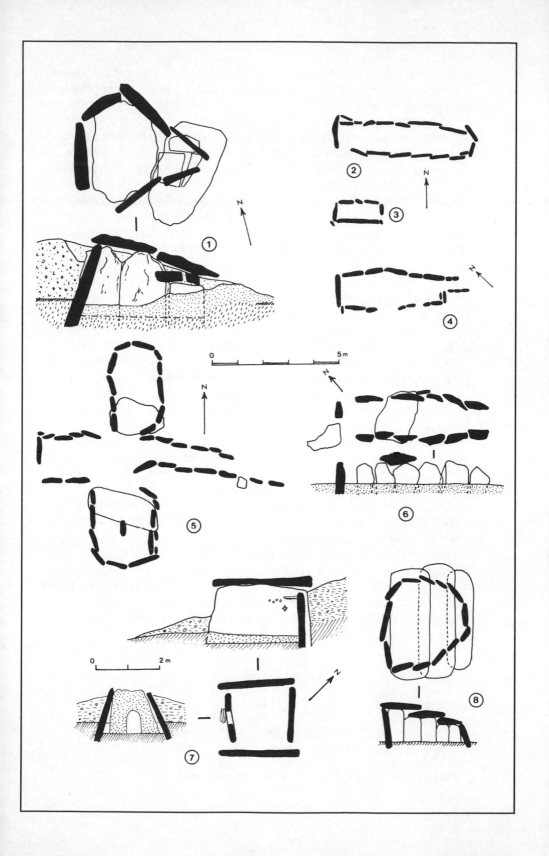

from Poço da Gateira is dated to 4510 ± 360 BC, and Anta 2 from Gorginos to 4440 ± 360 BC in calendar years, placing them well back into the fifth millennium BC.

Monument (*anta*) 1 at Poço da Gateira (Figure 48:1) is a megalithic structure whose sub-circular chamber, 3 m (10 ft) by 2 m ($6\frac{1}{2}$ ft), is reached by a short passage bounded by an upright slab on either side in a circular mound about 12 m (39 ft) in diameter. As in many Portuguese chamber-tombs, the passage is low and the tall pillars of the chamber lean inwards towards the interior, allowing the use of a closing slab much smaller than the ground area of the chamber. Very often also in Lusitanian megaliths the wall of the chamber is made of seven upright slabs which overlap slightly. In chamber-tomb 1 of Poço da Gateira human bones have not been preserved in the acid soil, but the Leisners say there would have been 12 burials, if one allocates a pot to each of the deceased. There were indeed 12 pots found, 11 of them placed in a single line down the chamber. They are round-based, fairly deep, sometimes with an out-turned lip. They have no handles and no decoration. Polished-stone axes, oval in section, and adzes were also brought to light in the tomb. Flintwork comprised rough flakes and geometrically-shaped microliths, mostly trapezoidal. This archaeological grouping belongs to the earliest phase of the Alentejo passage-graves, a fact amply confirmed by thermoluminescence dating of the ceramics.

In *anta* 2 at Gorginos, the archaeological material is much more sparse: two pots in the passage and a few sherds in the chamber with one axe and one adze, a microlith and one flint point. Was there only one inhumation in this early monument?

Anta 1 at Gorginos has a chamber, more polygonal in plan, made of slanting upright slabs. After a narrowed exit from the chamber, the passage is short and low, made of two long slabs set edgewise. The *anta* is enclosed in a vaguely circular mound, 12 m (39 ft) in diameter, which seems to have been modified on the eastern side. The passage does not seem to reach the edge of the mound with its kerb of stones, but might have been continued by an unroofed section.

Anta 1 of Vidigueiras at Reguengos de Monsaraz is a sub-circular megalithic chamber, measuring 3.5 m ($11\frac{1}{2}$ ft) by 2.75 m (9 ft), with a

---

Figure 47   Megalithic monuments in Portugal.
1. *Prado Lácara, Cáceres. (After G. and V. Leisner)*
2. *Barrosa, Caminha. (After G. and V. Leisner)*
3. *Almo da Cegonha 1, Evora (Alentejo). (After G. and V. Leisner)*
4. *Paço das Vinhas 1, Evora (Alentejo). (After G. and V. Leisner)*
5. *Cha de Parada. (After V. O. Jorge)*
6. *Cabeças, Araiolo. (After G. and V. Leisner)*
7. *Aldeia da Mata, Crato (Alenteja). (After G. and V. Leisner)*

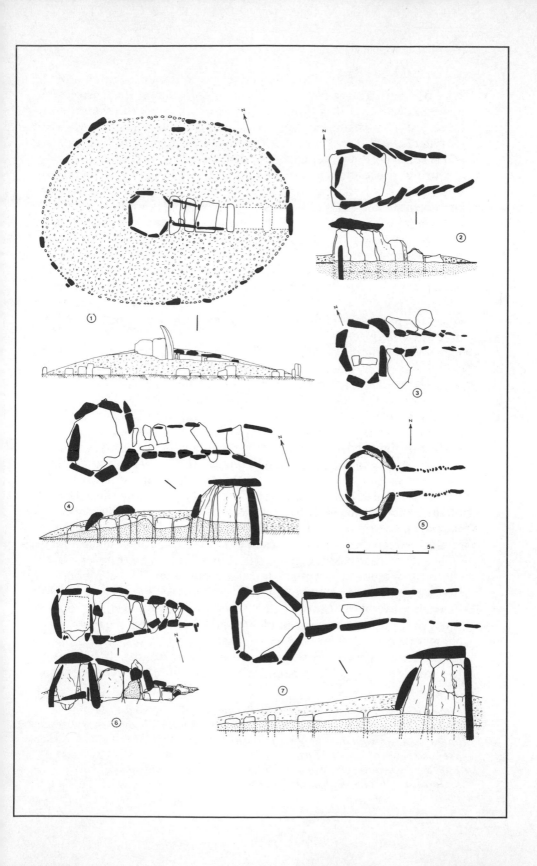

1

2

3

4

5

6

7

0   5m

short passage (scarcely 3 m [10 ft] long) which is made, like that of the Poço da Gateira *anta*, of a single slab at either side. The archaeological material recovered is comparable to that from Poço da Gateira, but there are also carinated pots with curved bodies, flat bases, and carrying lugs; this makes us think perhaps of two periods of use, or of a transitional period where early elements mix with later ones.

During a secondary phase, the passages of *antas* were lengthened. Figure 47 gives some examples of these. Certain of them are very characteristic of the type, such as *anta* 1 of Poço das Vinhas at Evora in the Alentejo (Figure 47:4), whose long low corridor ends in a chamber lined by seven leaning slabs which support a single roofing-slab. The space between the top of the passage and the single roofing-slab is blocked by a leaning slab. This same plan recurs at Aldeia da Mata *anta*, at Crato (Figure 47:4) and in many other monuments in Alentejo, notably *anta* 1 of Almo da Cegonha at Évora (Figure 47:3), where the passage, still open in the eastern section, is slightly off-centre in relation to the chamber.

Identical structures are known in other areas. There is Prado Lácara passage-grave at Cáceres, Spain, set in an oval mound, with a long passage which is closed by a heavy slab at its entrance. Two upright slabs narrow the passage two-thirds of the way along, and two more narrow it still further at the chamber entrance. The chamber, as is customary, is lined by seven leaning upright slabs. The mound had a kerb of upright slabs. Another example in the north of Portugal is Chã de Parada *anta* in the Serra de Aboboreira (Figure 47:5). It should be remembered that a very similar plan is known in the cemetery of Los Millares in south-eastern Spain (Figure 40:1), but in this case the slabs of the chamber are vertical and the roof could have been corbelled. Similarly, the monument of Font del Roure at Espolla in Catalonia could be much more than the result of a fortunate coincidence.

The Cabeças passage-grave (Figure 47:6) at Arraiolos in the environs of Évora is a rather unusual monument. The chamber is in two parts. The four-sided end-cell resembles the chamber of a classic passage-grave, with its oblique orthostats supporting a single roofing-slab 2 m ($6\frac{1}{2}$ ft) above the ground. One large slab forms the floor of this chamber. A space in the north-east corner gives access to an antechamber whose side-walls, each made of three uprights, converge towards the passage. The height of this antechamber decreases from

Figure 48   Megalithic monuments in Portugal. (After G. and V. Leisner)
1. Poço da Gateira 1, set in a circular mound with some boundary stones, and finds recovered from the chamber: burnished pottery, flint blades, polished-stone axes and geometric microliths.
2. Primary passage-grave and secondary tholos *in a round mound, Farisoa, and finds recovered from each of the chambers.*

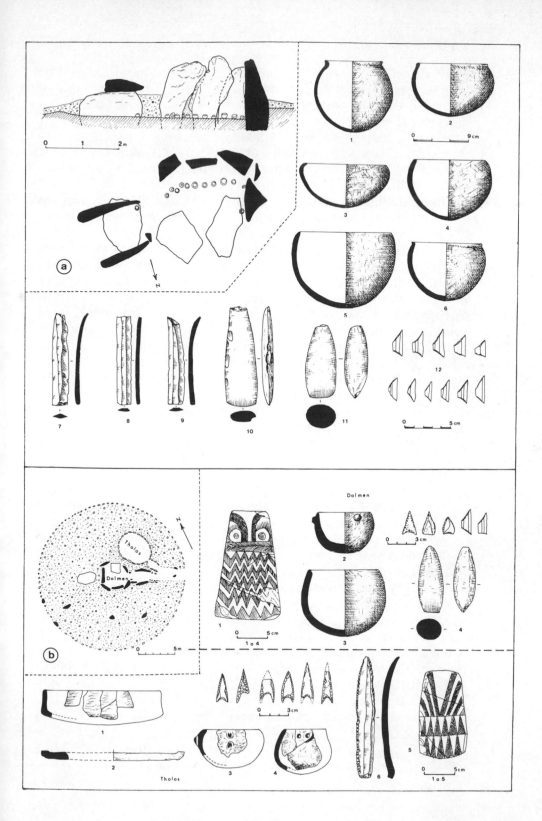

2 m ($6\frac{1}{2}$ ft) to 1.5 m (5 ft) towards the low passage, which is 2.5 m (8 ft) long and only 50 cm (20 in) to 70 cm (28 in) high. The meagre height of the passage is a constant feature of the Alentejo dolmens. The difference in level between passage and chamber leaves a space which is closed by a leaning slab. We also note a narrowing at the entrance to the passage. The whole structure is about 8.5 m (28 ft) long. Inside these monuments were found geometric microliths (essentially trapezoids), retouched blades, and lozenge-shaped arrowheads.

The megalithic monuments of Farisoa and Comenda, at Reguengos de Monsaraz, are of special value for chronology, since each contains two monuments.

Farisoa (Figure 48 : 2) is a circular mound which contains at its centre a classic megalithic monument with a sub-circular chamber about 3 m (10 ft) in diameter, bounded by seven slabs, and an access-passage which is relatively short in its megalithic part but which extends, perhaps in dry-stone, to the edge of the mound. Onto this passage gives another passage on the northern side, which leads to a false-corbel-roofed chamber usually called a '*tholos*'. From its lateral position in relation to the megalithic chamber, the *tholos* must be a secondary addition to the mound. The *tholos* has an oval shape; it is 4.5 m (15 ft) long and is hollowed into the ground to a depth of 70 cm (28 in) or 80 cm (31 in). So a gentle slope links this chamber with the outside, at the level of the passage. Narrow, well-fitting slabs, 1.25 m (4 ft) to 1.3 m ($4\frac{1}{4}$ ft) high, line the chamber, which must have had a false-corbelled roof.

At Comenda, two monuments were built in a similar circular mound. One is a megalithic passage-grave. It has a sub-circular chamber and a lower passage. The passage is built of two slabs, set edgewise and supporting a roofing-slab; a vertical slab blocks the gap between the top of the passage and the high point of the chamber. This part of the passage is comparable with those of Poço da Gateira and Vidigueiras. A second, even lower section prolongs the passage eastwards by another metre. Lined by two upright stones on either side, this part of the passage, whose entrance is closed by a slab set on end, is less than 50 cm (20 in) high, while the first part is 1 m (3 ft) high and the chamber twice that. To the south of this first structure a *tholos* was built in a secondary position, with its passage running alongside that of the dolmen. The oval *tholos* chamber is 3.5 m ($11\frac{1}{2}$ ft) long by 2.75 m (9 ft) wide, with an axial passage 2 m ($6\frac{1}{2}$ ft) long. The whole is lined with narrow juxtaposed slabs about 1 m (3 ft) high. The roof was corbelled.

Farisoa and Comenda are examples of *tholoi* introduced as secondary

Figure 49　Megalithic monuments in Portugal: artefacts from Anta Grande de Olival da Pega, Concelho de Reguengos de Monsaraz. (G. and V. Leisner, 1951)

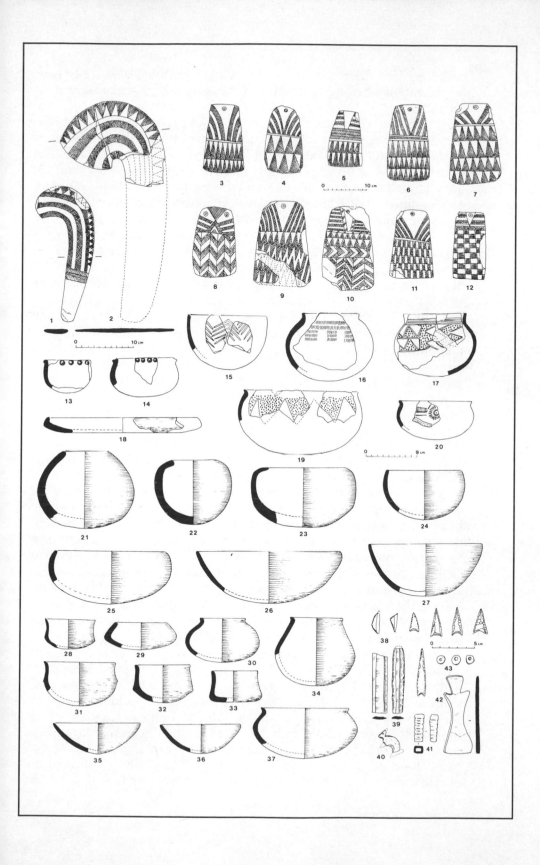

additions into the mounds of fairly long megalithic passage-graves. So these *tholoi* belong to a developed phase of Portuguese megalith-building.

At Farisoa, the chamber of the passage-grave yielded geometric microliths (trapezoids), some rough blades, polished-stone axes of thick-oval and of four-sided sections, arrowheads with concave bases (a type which first appears during this phase), smooth pottery (one pot has a large lug close to the rim), and decorated schist plaques (Figure 48:2 dolmen) which mark, as does the extension of the passage, a secondary phase in the evolution of Lusitanian passage-graves. There are no microliths in the *tholos*. All the other artefactual elements appear, but amongst the pottery types are also low, round-bottomed plates, flat bases, curved and carinated profiles, circular dishes, decorative motifs made of double 'cup-marks' and a few incised lines parallel to the rim, handles with vertical perforations, and knobs. Retouched blades are frequent in the worked-stone artefacts of this late phase of megalith-building. The *tholos* of Farisoa has been dated by thermoluminescence to 2675 ± 270 BC, while the monument of Anta Grande da Comenda de Igreja (where the pillars of the chamber rise to more than 2.4 m [8 ft] above the ground, and the access-passage is 10.5 m [$34\frac{1}{2}$ ft] long) has been dated to 3235 ± 310 BC. All this confirms the chronological evolution which study of the material suggested: from short passage-grave to long passage-grave to *tholos*.

Some Portuguese passage-graves have yielded hyper-abundant grave-goods. Anta Grande (Figure 49) at Olival da Pêga, Reguengos de Monsaraz, is a sub-circular megalithic chamber with a relatively long passage where the very rich goods belong to several chronological phases and indicate a prolonged use of the grave. We find geometric microliths, arrowheads with concave bases, blades retouched in varying degrees, bone pins with segmented heads, a small model of a hare or rabbit (Figure 49:40), polished-stone axes of a thickened oval cross-section, and the characteristic Almerían idol (Figure 49:42) whose origin has so often been sought in the eastern Mediterranean. Fifty-eight plaques of decorated schist were drawn in the Leisners' 1951 publication: they are thought to be a representation of the funerary divinity. They are found in the south of the country, and a few towards the north as far as Mondego. Associated with these plaques in Alentejo are '*báculos*', crooks (Figure 49:1 and 2), but these have a less widespread distribution. The crook appears engraved on the standing stone of Abelhoa at Reguengos de Monsaraz, and should be related to the many megalithic-art symbols in Atlantic France. They are often thought to be symbols of authority. At Olival da Pêga there were the remains of perhaps 150 pots in the chamber of smooth globular forms: plates both deep and shallow, in-curving shapes with a rolled, out-turned rim, some carinated forms and some with a well-marked break in profile, globular pots with a series of knobs in a line around the edge, circular dishes with a more or less raised rim, and some decorated pots showing Almerían influence, where we once more find upward-pointing triangles, superposed chevrons, and 'suns'.

In 1969, Leisner, Zbyszewski, and Veiga Ferreira published the results of the excavation of Praia da Maçãs, a monument 6 km ($3\frac{3}{4}$ miles) from Sintra in Estremadura. There are in fact two structures, one later than the other and built as a prolongation of the first (Figure 50). One small circular western chamber is hollowed out of the rock; it is reached by a short passage off which lead two lateral cells, the whole recalling the plan of *tholos* tomb 17 at Los Millares. Two radiocarbon dates, at 2300 and 2210 b.c. uncalibrated, from the western chamber, which was blocked with a fallen slab, indicate a date of about 2800 BC in calendar years. The archaeological material in this chamber comprised numerous arrowheads with triangular bases, large flint blades retouched to varying degrees, decorated schist plaques, bone pins with heads either smooth or decorated with horizontal grooves, and discoid beads – but only two pots. From the passage and the side-cells came smooth pottery comparable with that from the western chamber. In front of this first monument was built a *tholos* with access-passage; it is radiocarbon-dated to 1700 and 1690 b.c. on the uncalibrated scale, i.e to slightly earlier than 2000 BC in calendar years. It is a large, practically circular chamber, whose corbelled roof seems to have been held up by the central post whose post-hole was discovered at the centre of the room. After a narrowing, it is reached by a passage which was blocked by a mass of stones. This second chamber yielded a very few arrowheads, but some smooth-faced pottery and an abundance of material from the chalcolithic period, including copper '*palmela*' points and a dagger of the 'occidental' variety.

We can see that the construction of megalithic monuments in the south of the Iberian peninsula spreads over some 2500 years. It begins about 4500 BC – the period of construction of the first Alentejo passage-graves – and continues down towards 3000 BC when the building of *tholoi* began, which carried on until around 2000 BC.

However, the monuments morphologically closest to the Aegean *tholoi* (at least in plan) seem to have been built even later in the west of Portugal. We can take as an example the corbelled monument of Roça do Casal do Meio, at Calhariz, 30 or so kilometres (17 miles) from Lisbon. A circular kerb, 11 m (36 ft) in diameter and made of upright stones up to 1.5 m (5 ft) high, stands against the outer face of a wall, 2.5 m (8 ft) thick and built of stones of different sizes which are placed in no fixed order. At the centre a chamber almost 3 m (10 ft) in diameter is lined with a stone wall, not very thick and covered with a clay rendering which has survived well. The space between the external wall and that of the chamber, about 1.5 m (5 ft) to 2 m ($6\frac{1}{2}$ ft) wide, contains only earth. A passage, 4.5 m (15 ft) long and also lined with clay-rendered walls, gives access to the chamber. Since no stone was found within the chamber, which was filled with earth, it must be assumed that the roof was built of perishable material – a dome of clay or wood. The skeletons of two adult men of a robust Mediterranean type were found in the grave. The first was laid out on his back; the other was lying on his side, occupying a slightly raised area bordered with a clay rim. They were accompanied by late Bronze Age material: the first had an ivory comb, bronze tweezers and a ring; the second, a fibula (used to hold clothing at the shoulder), tweezers, and a belt buckle, also in bronze. Animal bones, from sheep and goats, probably represent food-offerings placed at the feet of the deceased. Fragments from three pots were found during the excavation. The excavators' observations show the two bodies could have been placed in the chamber simultaneously, and that they were covered at the same time by a layer of earth. (Both bodies lay on a layer of dust resulting from the disintegration of the walls.) So the monument had been built some time before – not necessarily for disposal of the dead. The passage was later closed by stones, and a slab was set upright at its end. The authors compare the monument of Roça do Casal do Meio to the archaic forms of the Sardinian *nuraghi*, although those are built only in dry-stone.

Megalithic monuments in northern Portugal and Spanish Galicia

The megalithic monuments of the north of Portugal – the provinces of Minho, the coastal Douro and Trás-os-Montes – and of Spanish Galicia (Figure 51) form a coherent group which should not be divided by an artificial frontier. The mounds are very numerous; Oliveira Jorge puts at more than 1000 the number of those situated in the northern zone of Portugal, the region north of the river Douro. Most often they form fairly large cemeteries, perched on high places. This dominant position is also that most commonly adopted in other megalithic areas of Atlantic Europe for passage-graves. The mounds fall in a band along the coast, from 200 km (124 miles) to 250 km (155 miles) wide.

The chamber-tombs are situated inside a breast-shaped, circular mound, called a '*mamoa*' locally. These mounds, whose diameter varies from 6 m (20 ft) to 30 m (98 ft), are made of earth and small stones. The commonest chamber-tomb in north Portugal and Galicia is a small monument with a polygonal chamber and no access passage, placed in an earthen mound which is covered by stones. These single, polygonal- or rectangular-chambered tombs may be open and have a side-entrance. Some are completely closed, forming a perfect polygon

Figure 50. Burial monument of Praïa das Maças, Portugal. (After V. Leisner, G. Zbyszewski, and O. da Veiga Ferreira)

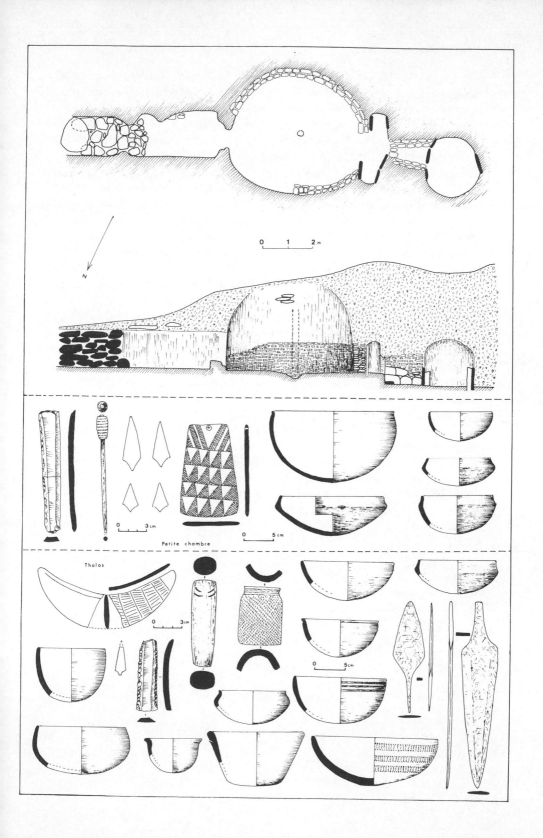

0   1   2m

N

Petite chambre

0   3 cm

0   5 cm

Tholos

0   3 cm

0   5 cm

or a rectangular megalithic cist called an '*antela*'. But alongside these single chambers exist true passage-graves, in which the polygonal chamber is distinct from the passage, which, however, always remains short. The chamber-tombs with long passages which develop in the south of Iberia do not reappear in the north-west. Some chamber-tombs have a chamber and passage not much differentiated from each other. The variety of forms of megalith-building in north Portugal and Galicia is therefore large, and examples of different types often appear in a single cemetery.

The grave-goods found in the chamber-tombs of this region are extremely poor, especially when contrasted with the richness of the southern monuments of Beira and Alto Alentejo. There are a few polished-stone axes, some triangular, semi-circular or trapezoidal geometric microliths, arrowheads with triangular bases, sometimes tanged, and pottery which is mostly undecorated and fairly rough in its modelling. Occupation sites related to this area of megalith-building are practically unknown, and Oliveira Jorge considers that 'everything points to the picture of rather poor populations, perhaps practising shifting agriculture and transhumant stock-rearing, living in homes built of perishable materials and using a small, hardly varying stock of tools'.

Few monuments have yet been dated in the north of Portugal and Galicia, but two dates obtained for the single chamber-tomb of mound 3 at Outeiro de Ante in Serra da Aboboreira (Baião) indicate occupation from the mid fifth millennium BC. These dates are comparable with those known for the short passage-graves of Alto Alentejo (Anta 1 of Poço da Gateira and Anta 2 of Gorginos), or those for some passage-graves in Brittany and west-central France.

Figure 51   Different types of chamber-tombs ('antas') *in Galicia, Spain. (After A. Rodriguez Casal, 1979)*
1. *Mourela, anta 6.*
2. *Mourela, anta 7.*
3. *Chao da Arqueta.*
4. *Dombate.*
5. *Argalo.*
6. *Capilla dos Mouros.*
7. *Chan de Arquiña.*
8. *Arca da Piosa.*
9. *Casa dos Mouros.*
10. *Berdoias.*
11. *Saa de Parga.*
12. *Ortigueira,* anta da mámoa *39.*
13. *Valavella,* anta da mámoa *229.*

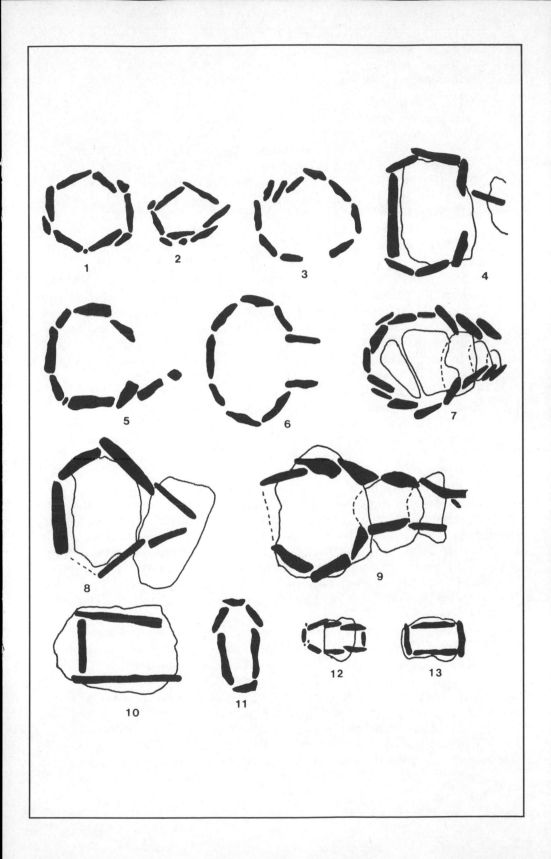

Megalithic art in Iberia

An essential trait of megalith-building in northern Portugal and Galicia is the engraved and painted decoration of the uprights of the chamber-tombs, a decoration we shall now look at more closely.

The engraved art, we have already seen, is found essentially on passage-graves – 42 sites in the Iberian peninsula, 39 in western France, 39 in Ireland, and six in Great Britain – and on the *allées couvertes* of Brittany (seven monuments) and the Paris Basin (eight monuments), and to this list must be added 11 *hypogées* from the eastern Paris Basin.

Some engravings are also known on standing stones, in both Brittany and Portugal, but only the chamber-tombs of the Iberian peninsula, and more particularly of central Portugal, still bear the traces, sometimes still clearly visible, of painted decoration. Painted decoration might once have existed also on monuments of other regions where conditions for its survival are much less favourable.

We have already remarked that engraved schist plaques barely crossed the Tagus. To the north of Mondego a single decorated monument, Vale de Fachas, yielded a perforated plaque, and we might ask, with Elizabeth Shee Twohig, whether the ritual of painting and engraving the monuments of the north did not serve the same purpose as the plaques and other engraved objects of the south.

The principal concentration of painted sites is in the Viséu region, in Beira Alta. The colour red is the most common, but there are also some drawings in black. Sometimes engraving and painting appear on the same stone.

The principal motifs of Iberian megalithic art are: human shapes; a sort of spread-out animal-skin shape; triangles; chevrons making divers motifs; snake-like shapes; disks, some with radiating lines which could be a representation of the sun; single or concentric circles; 'U' signs; and a strange symbol, specific to Iberia, which resembles a cup like a truncated cone with a foot and a handle. A stag-hunting scene with men shooting arrows and accompanied by dogs seems to be represented on a slab of the long passage-grave at Juncais, Queiriga (Viseu).

Shee Twohig states that one series of figures in the passage-graves north of the Douro originated in the Irish passage-graves. In particular, La Granja de Toniñuelo has drawings similar to those of the Loughcrew style of Ireland, as regards both motif and technique.

Her very interesting comparative table of the decorations found on the passage-graves of the Iberian peninsula, Atlantic France and the British Isles underlines both the specific nature of each group and the features they hold in common. Snake-like shapes, radiating circles, 'U'-shapes, cup-marks and coronaded circles appear in all three groups, confirming the hypothesis of inter-regional contacts.

7. The west Mediterranean islands and south Italy

Megalithic monuments in Corsica

The island of Corsica is 160 km (100 miles) from continental France, and 80 km (50 miles) from Tuscany in Italy. It has a mountainous 'backbone' running north-south, whose 'ribs' divide the territory into well-defined micro-regions. Although megalithic monuments were noted there during the last century, it was not until Roger Grosjean's first work in 1954 that prehistoric research in Corsica really began.

In fact, there are still unclear areas in the development of prehistoric populations in Corsica. It seems that the island was populated from the eighth millennium BC by 'protoneolithic' groups, perhaps from the Italian peninsula, at a time when the sea-level was at least 20 m ($65\frac{1}{2}$ ft) lower than it is today. The coastlines were nearer, and navigation by sight was possible, especially if the settlers came via the island of Elba. Besides, navigation in the Mediterranean is known to have started earlier, if we can judge from the discovery of obsidian from an offshore island in an archaeological level dated to the tenth millennium BC at Franchthi cave in Greece. These protoneolithic people were predators – hunters, fishermen and gatherers all at once. From the seventh millennium BC (as is shown by a radiocarbon date, uncalibrated, of 5750 ± 150 b.c.), neolithic groups whose pottery has affinities with 'cardial' ware occupied rock shelters all over Corsica, knapping flint and living by stock-rearing and agriculture. Alongside these is another early neolithic group, which used pottery with punched decoration, and seems to have been more conservative in retaining a predilection for fishing and hunting, while also raising goats and sheep. Their taste for agriculture was little developed. Perhaps these were people who reacted more slowly to innovation. Using obsidian for some of their tools, they mostly occupied the south of Corsica. They are given the name of 'Curasian'; according to some scholars their culture succeeded the cardial. These early neolithic groups develop through the import of external influences into an ill-defined middle Neolithic, of which the 'Basian' is one of the more important elements, from the beginning of the fourth millennium BC (a figure deriving from the uncalibrated radiocarbon date of 3300 ± 120 b.c.). Some affinities seem to exist between this Corsican culture and that of Ozieri in Sardinia. Several cultures occupy the late Neolithic, according to region and altitude. One of the best-dated, studied by Gabriel Camps in 1979, is the Terrinian, which probably began during the second half of the fourth millennium BC (the uncalibrated radiocarbon dates are between 2700 and 2300 b.c.).

It was during the course of the fourth millennium that the first megalithic structures appeared in Corsica. These are small and large cists, buried in the ground. This tradition could have come from the east coast of Italy or from Sardinia, where identical forms are found – or they could be a completely independent phenomenon. Numerous peoples throughout the world have buried their dead in stone cists put into the ground: they are known in the European Neolithic, on the Atlantic coast as well as in Catalonia and Switzerland; but they are also found in Korea and Japan, to give but a few examples.

We owe to Roger Grosjean the study of megalith-building in Corsica; little new evidence has been added since his death, but since general knowledge of the subject has developed, it has given rise to different ideas about the origins of megalithic monuments, in particular. Unfortunately in Corsica, as in most other places, many cists and chamber-tombs have long since been emptied of their contents. Anyway, the acidity of the soil has prevented the survival of bone in the majority of cases. So the traces recovered are very scanty, and dates are difficult to obtain.

The earliest phase is characterised by cists which can be buried up to 2 m (6½ ft) deep. Their greatest concentrations are in the south of the island, in the region of Porto Vecchio. Some are as much as 3 m (10 ft) long, made with monolithic granite side-walls and often placed at the summit of a slight natural eminence. Others were only half-buried; and

---

Figure 52   Megalithic monuments in the western Mediterranean.
1. Map of the western Mediterranean, showing: (1) cists in Corsica and Sardinia; (2) chamber-tombs in Corsica and Sardinia; (3) 'Giants' tombs' in Sardinia; (4) Algerian-Tunisian chamber-tombs; (5) Bari-Taranto chamber-tombs; (6) chamber-tombs of Otranto and Malta. (After R. Whitehouse)
2. Plan of stone circles with cists, Li-Muri, Arzachema, Sardinia.
3. Megalithic grave, Settiva, Corsica. (After R. Grosjean)
4. Megalithic tomb, Sa Perda'e s'Altare, Biori, Sardinia. (After G. Lilliu)
5. Megalithic tomb, Maone, Sardinia. (After M. Guido)
6. Megalithic tomb, Perta Longa, Sardinia. (After M. Guido)
7. Evolution of Corsican megaliths. (After R. Grosjean)
8. Megalithic tomb, Corato, Italy. (After M. Gervasia)
9. Megalithic tomb, Bisceglie, Italy. (After M. Gervasio)
10. Megalithic tomb, Quattromacine, Italy. (After R. Whitehouse)
11. Megalithic tomb, Scusi, Italy. (After R. Whitehouse)
12. Megalithic tomb, Ggantija, Gozo, Malta. (After J. D. Evans)

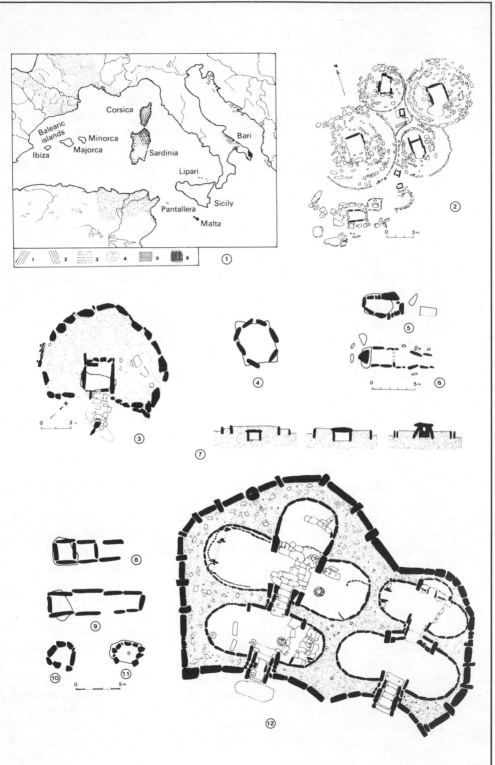

some were built at ground level. It seems that the cist emerged gradually from the ground, to become the chamber-tomb in a later phase. Upright stones are found fairly near the funerary monument, which is generally at the centre of a stone circle, the outer kerb of a terrace whose original height is unknown (Figure 52:3). These cists contained flint and obsidian blades; fine burnished pottery, attributable with difficulty to a defined cultural horizon; perforated spheroids considered by Grosjean to be 'maceheads', but which were possibly just the weights of digging-sticks, as are found still in some populations, especially in East Africa; different-shaped beads, of serpentine and schist, sometimes with V-perforations; polished-diorite axes. Such cists, which are spread all over Corsica, are to be compared with those which exist in the north of Sardinia, and particularly those of Li-Muri in Arzachena and in granitic Gallura (Figure 52:2).

This period, Grosjean's Megalithic I, is succeeded by a phase of above-ground construction of cists and chamber-tombs with the appearance of alignments of standing stones. The cist of Poggiarella at Petralonga-Filippi, half-buried, marks the transition. Oriented north-south, the chamber, with its capstone, measures 1.6 m ($5\frac{1}{4}$ ft) long by 1.6 m ($5\frac{1}{4}$ ft) wide and 1.2 m (4 ft) high. It contained a few pieces of obsidian and flint pieces, as well as sherds.

There are probably around 100 chamber-tombs in Corsica, concentrated mostly in the south. The finest, Fontanaccia on Cauria plateau at Sartène, has a funerary chamber 2.6 m ($8\frac{1}{2}$ ft) long by 1.6 m ($5\frac{1}{4}$ ft) wide and 1.0 m (3 ft) high. A standing stone, now broken, seems to be associated with the monument. Some chamber-tombs have a notch, a sort of porthole at the upper part of the entrance to the chamber, as at Cardiccia and Tavau.

While Grosjean said in 1966 that 'rarely, passages lead to the funerary chamber, with worked side slabs, sometimes polished', in 1976 the same author decided there were 'no constructions with passages nor *allées* analogous to the Giants' Tombs in Sardinia'. We do not know what to make of this, but those monuments which I have visited personally do not seem to include passages. It would be interesting to know more about this architectural characteristic.

During the same period, Megalithic II, numerous standing stones and alignments of up to 100 upright stones were erected, especially in the *canton* of Sartène, in the south of the island. These lines are generally oriented north-south, and the main façade of the monuments is to the east.

The third Corsican megalithic period dates from the middle Bronze Age. It is marked by a considerable development in monumental sculpture, whose beginnings can be recognised in the anthropomorphic character of some standing stones of the preceding phase. At this time in the south of the island there were built monuments both ritual and funerary, the work of a war-like, invading people who, according to Grosjean, must have destroyed the older granite statues.

The '*torri*' are circular monuments built of dry-stone, with a wide, tall entrance, an access passage, and a chamber roofed with false corbelling. Adjoining small cells were hollowed-out within the walls of the chamber. A terraced or sloping platform surrounds the monument, whose diameter varies between 10 m (33 ft) and 15 m (49 ft); the height is up to 7 m (23 ft). Sometimes galleries replace the chamber; in other cases 'a timber framework forms the skeleton of a roof made of stones and earth'. Inside were found thick layers of ash; it is not known precisely what these represent. According to Grosjean, 'the statues of the Corsican megalithic culture represent chiefs and enemy warriors killed in battle'. These enemies, the builders of the *torres*, would have been one of the 'Sea Peoples', the same 'Sherdana' who terrorised Egypt between the fourteenth and twelfth centuries BC.

Megalithic monuments in Sardinia

Megalith-building was common in Sardinia. Three essential forms dominate: cists or dolmen-like cists inside stone circles, which can be compared with those of Corsica, close by; monuments of chamber-tomb type; and the 'Giants' Tombs', which seem to derive from chamber-tombs. Besides these funerary structures built of large stones, Sardinia is rich in burial caves cut into bed-rock; these kind of *hypogées* are very numerous in the Mediterranean world, but their study deserves a separate book. Here we will have to be content with a brief reference to the rock-cut tombs, remembering, nonetheless, that their use begins before that of the chamber-tombs.

The dolmenic cist is a four-sided coffer which can be up to 2 m (6½ ft) by 2 m (6½ ft) in dimensions; usually it is found set in the middle of a circular area bounded by stones, set edgewise, among which are true stelae. The circular areas vary between 5 m (16½ ft) and 8 m (26 ft) in diameter and are grouped into cemeteries; at Li-Muri, for example, were found five circles with cists, which yielded human bone as well as flint knives, polished-stone axes, stone beads, and pottery (Figure 52:2).

The chamber-tombs are found in the northern half of the island: 41 monuments were listed by Lilliu in 1975, and he divided them into two groups according to whether or not the mound has a stone kerb. The chamber-tombs may have a four-sided chamber, fairly elongated, like the chamber-tomb of Elcomis at Buddusò, which is surrounded by an elliptical kerb. The passage of the chamber-tomb of Perta Longa (Figure 52:6) at Aristis widens to give access to a long chamber divided in two by an upright slab. It seems that these may be prototypes for these monuments in Catalonia and in the Aude, and that affinities exist with the Bari-Taranto group of chamber-tombs in southern Italy. Other Sardinian chamber-tombs have a polygonal chamber covered by a capstone and are built with undressed stones. They are morphologically close to the Taranto group of southern Italy and Malta, but they differ in that their capstones are not engraved and the supports are never made of several piled-up blocks. Some monuments, such as Sa Coveccada at Morels, have a porthole-slab at the entrance; here, the opening is four-sided and a groove goes round the edge of it. A similar system is to be found on the entrance stele of the 'Giants' Tombs'.

While dolmenic cists in their circular enclosures are dated in Sardinia to the fourth millennium BC, the chamber-tombs, as in Corsica, seem slightly more recent and must have begun to appear at the very beginning of the third millennium BC.

Lilliu thinks that not all the circular structures in northern Sardinia were funerary monuments; some of them could have been ritual sites.

One of the best-studied groups, Li-Muri, yielded a single skeleton in one of the large cists. It was the same at Li-Muracci, while the remains of an adult and a child were found at San Pantaleo. The archaeological material found in the cist of Li-Muri – flint, obsidian, pottery, perforated spheres, beads, and a cup of steatite – has been compared (as far as the vessel is concerned) with that of Egypt and Crete of the third millennium, but the form is close to that of a neolithic group from the Lipari islands north of Sicily, called the Diana culture. The Diana culture dates from the beginning of the fourth millennium BC, which pushes back the date of the cists in Sardinia and Corsica.

As always, most of the Sardinian chamber-tombs were emptied long ago, and only a few remains have been recovered by careful excavations, so that it is impossible to know with any certainty if these monuments were collective burials or not.

Motarra chamber-tomb at Dorgali contained several sherds of a ceramic for which affinities have been sought in the chalcolithic Ferrières-Fontbouisse groups of French Languedoc. If this relationship were certain, it would be extremely important in helping us to understand the diffusion of the megalithic phenomenon in the Mediterranean, and would at the same time allow us to date the Sardinian chamber-tombs to the beginning of the third millennium BC.

So, in the present state of knowledge, scholars like Ruth Whitehouse tend to look to southern France and Catalonia for the origin of megalith-building in the Mediterranean islands and the southern Italian peninsula. The megalithic idea would have reached the islands of Corsica and Sardinia in the first instance, then Malta, the southern tip of Italy, and the coast of North Africa (which is visible from the slopes of Sardinia in fine weather).

Of the megalithic funerary monuments of the western Mediterranean, the 'Giants' Tombs' in Sardinia are far and away the most spectacular (Figure 53). They have a gallery up to 15 m (49 ft) long, lined with upright slabs and dry-stone walling. This burial chamber stands inside a stone cairn or earthmound, which has a well-constructed kerb. The rear part of the mound is usually rounded, while two 'antennae' or 'horns', the shape of cattle horns, protrude from the front part to form a semicircular forecourt. Large upright slabs line the horns on the courtyard side, and this forecourt is often considered to be a place of worship. Access to the chamber is through an orifice hollowed out of the base of a shaped slab; this is a stele with a rounded top, of which the face was slightly hollowed out to leave the edge and a transverse bar standing in low relief. Identical arrangements can be seen at the entrances to many rock-cut tombs ('hypogées'), for example those of Ittiari at Osilo-Sassari (Figure 53:6). The upper part of those is surmounted by three protuberances from which Editta Castaldi thinks cattle-heads would have hung. So there is a definite link between the Giants' Tombs and the rock-cut tombs. And some of the rock-cut tombs, for example Las Puntas, Mesu e Montes, even have a rounded forecourt let into the rock. So the stele-entrance of the 'Giants' Tombs' is a replica of the entrances to rock-cut tombs.

The tomb cut out of the rock at Oridda is of a shape identical to the chamber of a 'Giant's Tomb'. It has two 'horns' made of stones which outline a semicircular forecourt and an entrance stele with its hole at the base.

The chamber of the 'Giant's Tomb' of Li-Lolghi (Figure 53:5) at Arzachena is a gallery almost 15 m (49 ft) long and about 1.5 m (5 ft) wide, which is lined with upright slabs and dry-stone walling. At 27 m ($88\frac{1}{2}$ ft) overall length, this Giant's Tomb is the largest we know. The end-cell, 4 m (13 ft) long, is paved and raised slightly above the passage. This section is situated inside another room lined with a dry-stone wall, that is, there is a circulation area around the funerary chamber. This is not unreminiscent of the periphery of the allée couverte of La Chaussée-Tirancourt in France, where the monument was set in a pit much larger than necessary just to accommodate it. However, it is highly improbable that there was the slightest connection between the 'Giants' Tombs' of Sardinia and the allées couvertes of the Paris Basin (although the hypothesis of a link with the Mediterranean world was at one time envisaged for the Paris Basin allées couvertes).

Another morphological similarity can be noted with a recently excavated monument in Maine-et-Loire (France), where the 'Angevin' chamber-tomb of La Bajoulière has two 'horns' in front of its oval mound. We would perhaps find even closer stylistic convergences in Wales and Ireland, at least for these protruding 'horns' and the forecourts they define. However, although the distance over time for the construction of these various groups of megaliths is not very great, the geographical distance between Ireland, central France and Sardinia prevents our finding any link between these monuments, which have, in any case, more differences than points in common.

The 'Giants' Tombs' underwent many repairs in the course of use over a long period, and their final plan may be fairly complex. They have suffered ill-conducted excavations over a long period also, but some of these have recently yielded important material. They are collective tombs: there were the remains of about 50 individuals at Preganti, 60 at Las Plassas and at least 27 in the hybrid monument of Oridda. These skeletal remains were accompanied by pottery, stone and metal objects.

For a long time the 'Giants' Tombs' were considered as the burial-places of the population which raised the *nuraghi*, those large stone towers, the simplest of which are comparable to the *torri* of Corsica. The Nuraghic culture occupied the period between 1900 and 900 BC, but *nuraghi* were built up to the third century BC in the north of the island, a region which did not come under the Carthaginian thumb. However, there was a 'protonuraghic' period from 2300 BC onwards, and the hybrid tomb of Oridda yielded objects from the Copper and early Bronze Ages which confirmed its having been used from the beginning of the third millennium BC. So the first 'Giants' Tombs' could date from the second half of the third millennium BC, while they could have been used up to the end of the Iron Age; that is the case with Li-Lolghi, a monument built in the middle Bronze Age.

In order to deal with all aspects of Sardinian megalithic monuments, we should say a word about the 'polyandric tombs' – long megalithic coffers spread everywhere on the island. Built in dry-stone or of upright slabs, they reach several metres in length and served as collective tombs: there were more than 30 skeletons at Erra'e Muros (Ossi) and 54 at San Giuliano (Alghero). Some were built after the end of the third millennium BC, others during the Nuraghic period.

To recapitulate, let us recall that the Li-Muri type of cist dates from the fourth millennium and is contemporary with the first rock-cut tombs. The chamber-tombs date from the beginning of the third millennium BC, as do the majority of the rock-cut tombs. As for the 'Giants' Tombs' and the long cists, their first period of building dates

---

Figure 53   Burial monuments in Sardinia and the Balearic islands.
1. 'Giants' Tomb', Li-Mizzani, Palau, Sardinia. (After E. Castaldi)
2. 'Giants' Tomb', Coddu Vecchiu, Arzachena, Sardinia. (After E. Castaldi)
3. Reconstruction drawing of a Sardinian 'Giants' Tomb'. (After E. Contu)
4. Reconstruction drawing of the Naveta d'Es Tudons, Minorca. (After E. Contu)
5. 'Giants' Tombs, Li-Lolghi, Arzachena, Sardinia. (After E. Castaldi)
6. Reconstruction drawing of rock-cut tombs, Ittiari, Osilo-Sassari, Sardinia. (After E. Contu)

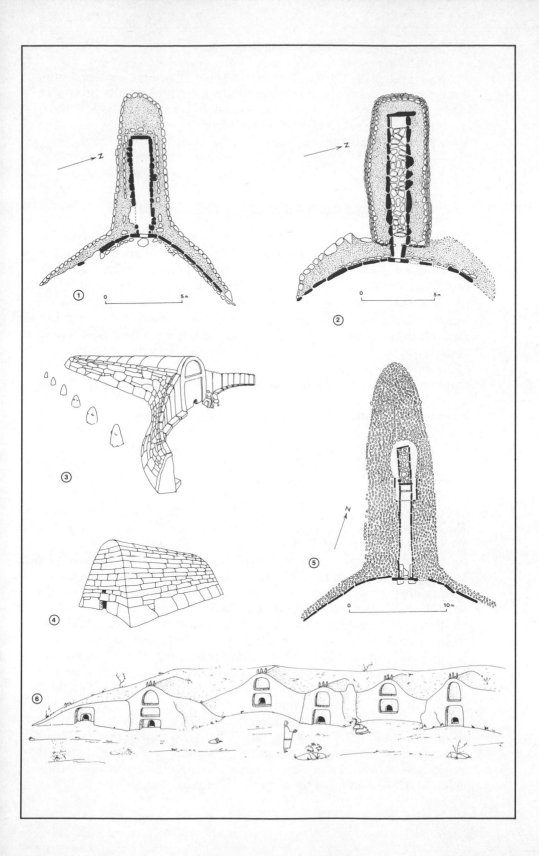

1 ⟶ Z 0 ___ 5 m

2 ⟶ Z 0 ___ 5 m

3

4

5 N 0 ___ 10 m

6

from the end of the third millennium BC, but they were used and built almost to the end of the first millennium BC. Although the Sardinian chamber-tombs could have origins in Catalonia and southern France, the 'Giants' Tombs' seem to be the result of an on-the-spot evolution from the local chamber-tombs.

Megalithic monuments in the Balearic islands

We will not linger over the megalithic monuments of the Balearic islands because their number is insignificant. One chamber-tomb has been recorded on Majorca and four on Minorca, the best example being Sa Comerca de Sa Garita at Torre d'en Goumes in the province of Alayor. No capstone survives, and the theory has been put forward that it had a wooden covering. These monuments are more like megalithic cists. Rossello-Bordoy notes the stone circle of Son Baulo, with paving at the centre of which is a coffer with a porthole-slab and a rudimentary passage, but whose roof is missing. Material recovered from it comprises a V-button, another with a double perforation, and globular or flower-pot-shaped vessels, of the kind which are already known in the artificial Majorcan caves of the Pretalayotic period.

The making of these artificial caves for funerary purposes spread to the Balearics before any megalithic construction. We are still struck by the similarity of the plans of Balearic rock-cut tombs to those in the Arles region of southern France, and more particularly to La Grotte des Fées.

The Talayotic period in the Balearics, like the Nuraghic period in Sardinia or that of the *torri* in Corsica, saw a major development in cyclopean building. *Talayots* are towers, usually round but sometimes square, built of large stones and with internal chambers. *Navetas* have an elongated apsidal plan; also built of large squared stones, the façade is rectilinear, or slightly concave, with a small entrance opening at the base. A good example is Naveta de Els Tudons on Menorca (Figure 53:4). So they are related to the 'Giants' Tombs' of Sardinia and, like them, served as funerary monuments. The religious aspect of this population comes across in particular through the 28 *taulas* of Menorca. A wall of stones encircles a ritual surface on which a kerb of upright stones surrounds a monument made of one large four-sided slab set upright in the ground. This slab, which in the case of the Trepuco *taula* is 4 m (13 ft) high, supports a parallel-sided block balanced horizontally across its top. It has been said of this T-shaped monument that it was the schematic representation of a bovid head. As in Corsica and Sardinia, this stone-working culture becomes established at the beginning of the second millennium BC.

Stone temples and chamber-tombs in Malta

The Maltese archipelago, 80 km (50 miles) south of Sicily, comprises the islands of Malta, Comino and Gozo, which together make up a surface area of 320 km² (125 sq. miles).

Although 15 or so megalithic monuments which could be related to chamber-tombs are still visible on Malta, most of them are in a wretched state. The real glory of the islands is the temples of cyclopean masonry – some blocks weigh up to 20 tonnes – that were built between 3500 and 2500 BC. Thanks to the work of John D. Evans and David Trump in particular, knowledge of the Maltese past has made great strides these last few years. At the same time that dating, origins and function of these large buildings was being defined, a new view was being taken of the development of megalith-building in general and on the role of the Near East in the construction of chamber-tombs in western Europe. The 'oriental mirage' faded, and the local origin of megalithic cultures gained importance.

Nine phases have been recognised in the development of the Maltese Neolithic between 5000 and 2300 BC – Ghar Dalam, Grey Skorba, Red Skorba, Zebbug, Mgarr, Ggantija, Saflieni, Tarxien, Tarxien cemetery – whose names derive from the representative site of each period.

Towards 5000 BC colonists from Sicily culturally related to the Stentinello group landed on the uninhabited archipelago. These were peasants who cultivated wheat, barley and lentils and reared sheep, goats and cattle. They worked stone, flint from local sources and obsidian from Lipari and Pantelleria. But trade was limited and the island self-sufficient. A second wave of immigrants at the beginning of the fourth millennium BC, also from Sicily and of the San Cono-Piano Notaro culture, started the hollowing-out of rock-cut tombs in the ground for their dead. Perhaps this fashion came from Sicily, where it is very widespread, but this is not certain. At any rate, shafts were made, at the bottom of which the funerary chamber developed, at first by widening out, then by the addition of other rooms to it. These subterranean tombs took on a multi-lobed shape; according to Evans, from 3500 BC onwards these subterranean models gave rise to above-ground structures made of large stones which, in their early phase perhaps just megalithic graves, were to become temples.

The temple first of all had a trefoil plan made of three rooms, and with time became more complex, with the construction of new oval rooms, but also with the building of a new temple in the same megalithic enclosure, or indeed the combining of two or more temples into one group (Figure 52:12). The walls were made of upright slabs or piled-up roughly-squared blocks, and the roofing of the chambers seems to have been in 'semi-corbelling' – that is, the roofing stones were laid overlapping up to a certain height and then a large slab, or more probably a wooden covering, closed the top. These monuments were places of worship, but could have several uses. They lead us to suspect the presence of a social class of priests who were more or less in control. Colin Renfrew imagines there being territorial divisions of 1000 or 2000 inhabitants around two or three temples which, as well as being religious centres, would be monuments affirming the identity of the group, symbols of ownership of the space. So we can imagine a kind of rivalry between communities, each seeking to build and have the finest, most impressive temple. It is in this manner that, during the final phase of these great stone buildings in the third millennium BC, as Jean Guilaine has it, the priest becomes a prince, the temple becomes a palace.

Alongside the monumental development of the temples, the rock-cut tombs take on considerable importance, and the one at Hal Saflieni is the best example of this. Like the temple of Tarxien, a few hundred metres away, it is surrounded by houses in a suburb of Valletta. It was discovered in 1902, during the construction of water-cisterns for new buildings, and deliberately hidden during the building work, which might otherwise have been halted. The rock-cut tomb has 20 or so chambers, in which were found the skeletal remains of almost 7000 persons. The main room is made in the image of the temples, with columns and lintels cut into the rock. Red paintings of bovids, spirals, points and lines decorated the walls of the room, a place of worship where images of the 'Great Goddess' were found, as they are in the majority of Maltese temples. This goddess of generous proportions, symbol of life and resurrection, was represented by imposing limestone statues, such as the one from Tarxien temple (which must have been 2.8 m [9 ft] tall), where there were also found sculpted spirals and a frieze of domestic animals which may have been sacrificed to the gods. The goddess appears in the form of the 'Sleeping Woman', a terracotta statuette 10 cm (4 in) high discovered at Hal Saflieni. The role of the woman in these first agrarian communities seems to have been a vital one. Among other dieties venerated we should mention the bull, symbol of power and virility – we know the respect accorded it by early societies – since the Natufian communities of Palestine in the ninth millennium BC, that is, since well before its domestication.

What exactly happened in Malta around 2500–2400 BC? No one knows for certain, but a fall in population occurred and the temples were abandoned. Towards 2300 BC arrived newcomers who knew metalwork and had bronze tools. They burned their dead, putting the ashes into urns, and the urns into the temples, which had lost all their earlier significance. From the archaeological deposits found in the chamber-tomb of Ta Hammut, on the northern coast of Malta and belonging to the period of the Tarxien cemetery, it seems that the monuments of this type could have been built in the second half of the third millennium BC and used up to 1500 BC. They are fairly similar to those of the Otranto group in the heel of Italy, where they may have originated. Each chamber-tomb has a slab of stone up 4.4 m (14½ ft) long and 3.3 m (11 ft) wide, set upon several supports.

David Trump noted that the chamber-tomb of Misrah Sinjura has a groove on its upper surface and a vertical perforation like those of the Safi and Bidni chamber-tombs – characteristics that are also found on the Otranto chamber-tombs. But he states, 'There is effectively nothing to suggest that they [the chamber-tombs of Otranto and of Malta] appeared independently in either of these areas, but hardly more to indicate how they could have reached either from further west.'

Lastly, a few standing stones have been noted, and once more it is to the Otranto group that we must turn to find any equivalent monuments.

Chamber-tombs in south-eastern Italy

Near a service-station called *Il Dolmen* on the *autostrada* between Naples and Bari in south-eastern Italy, in the middle of an olive grove, looms the Bari chamber-tomb group (Figure 52:8–11). The most imposing, at Bisceglie, has a chamber 12 m (39 ft) long with an average width of 2 m (6½ ft); it is built of two parallel rows of upright stones and a slab at either end. Its western end, which is almost 2 m (6½ ft) high, is covered by a single capstone; the rest of the monument in its present state is much lower. The trace of a mound is still visible. Altogether, the Bari-Taranto group of megaliths takes in a dozen monuments with a single, four-sided, elongated chamber whose length is between 3 m (10 ft) and 17 m (56 ft), according to Ruth Whitehouse. The most spectacular is Giovinazzo, since there the chamber-tomb grave is still inside its dry-stone cairn; this was, unhappily, damaged by the farmer who attempted to flatten the mound on his land by means of a bulldozer. The cairn, 27 m (88½ ft) long and oriented north-south, has to its south a circular forecourt, a probable place of worship and offerings. The chamber, like that at Corato, is divided into several compartments; one of the dividing slabs, probably not in its original position, shows traces of a hole and must have been a porthole-slab. The chamber-tombs of this group, all placed close to the sea, were enclosed in an oval or square mound with rounded corners, with a dry-stone kerb. Long since used for other purposes – as tool-sheds, for example – the Bari-Taranto chamber-tombs did not all yield archaeological material. However, Bisceglie contained the remains of 13 skeletons, most of them disarticulated, a few complete and in a flexed position. At Giovinazzo, disordered human bone-remains were found in only one of the compartments. According to Whitehouse they represent the bodies of at least nine adults, two adolescents and two children. We know that this same tomb also contained pottery of Mycenean I type, which proves there was a secondary use of the monument. So it appears that the Bari-Taranto monuments were collective graves, and that bones of their first occupants had to make way for the mortal remains of another deceased, put in in a flexed position.

Another group of 16 dolmens exists in the region of the port Otranto, at the extreme south-east of the heel of Italy. They are formally different from the Bari-Taranto group, and have long been empty. It is thus impossible to be certain that these monuments were graves, although that seems probable. The Otranto dolmens have a subcircular or polygonal chamber, not very high and from 2 m ($6\frac{1}{2}$ ft) to 4 m (13 ft) wide, which is covered by a single slab. Perforations, cup-marks and incised lines sometimes mark these capstones. Traces of mounds survive around the chamber-tombs, which are morphologi-cally, and even in details such as the engravings on the slabs, very close to those found on Gozo and Malta. Some link between the two groups seems certain, and traces found in a Maltese chamber-tomb attribute its use to the culture of the Tarxien cemetery, dated 2400–1600 BC.

As regards the date of the Bari-Taranto group, Ruth Whitehouse has been able to establish that the material recovered from the tombs of Leucaspide and Giovinazzo belonged to the beginning of the Bronze Age, a period known as Proto-Apennine B, between 2300 and 1750 BC.

The two megalithic groups from the south of the Italian peninsula can thus be considered to be contemporary, at the turn of the third and second millennia BC. They could represent two local adaptations of a single idea whose origin we cannot place precisely. Some people would put the origin of the Bari-Taranto group in the south of France, particularly in the group of *allée couvertes* of the Aude type, but it is difficult to see which path a diffusion would have taken from one area to the other, unless it was via the 'Giants' Tombs' of Sardinia, which is not obvious. Other workers, such as Puglisi, have seen the megalithic cists of Pian Sultano, north of Rome, as the possible link through Italy, where no other megalithic monuments are known. If the west-Mediterranean origin is the most plausible (navigation by sea provid-ing the link), it is nonetheless unproven.

Lastly, we should note the existence of standing stones up to 3 m (10 ft) high in this region of Italy. Their distribution is identical to that of the chamber-tombs, and some seem to be stelae related to them.

8. Africa, the Arabian peninsula, and Madagascar

Megalithic monuments in North Africa

Chamber-tombs

A glance at a distribution map of chamber-tombs over North Africa shows two distinct zones: one to the west, in northern Morocco, where several monuments appear; the other to the east, with its huge cemeteries and several thousand monuments. However, the Algerian-Tunisian chamber-tomb is typologically far removed from the grand architecture of the Atlantic edge of Europe: it is a fairly large cist, covered by a stone capstone rarely more than 3 m (10 ft) long. Set in huge groups in mountainous areas like Bou-Nouara, Roknia, and Gastel, they have a mode of construction comparable to that of the Ethiopian monuments. The builders often used the slope of the terrain to erect a monument. The capstone was often found on the spot and lifted onto the megalithic cist, whose uprights rarely exceed 1 m (3 ft) in height.

Gabriel Camps, who in 1962 published a magisterial study of the protohistoric funerary monuments of North Africa, said:

> the north African dolmen, of modest dimensions, [is] essentially character-ised by the monolith roofing-slab which rests, above the ground, on supports which are themselves monolithic or on dry-stone walls, can be set into a stepped plinth or a cylindrical surround, but seems never to have been covered by a mound. It cannot be dissociated, despite the chronological differences, from the small dolmens with circular enclosures and plinths which were built in the Mediterranean countries.

These pagan sepulchres, *djouala*, are attributed by the Berbers to a race of giants. Camps notes that, even when confronted with the skeleton discovered during excavation of a monument, the workers stuck to their idea of its proprietor's gigantic size, and of his riches, which could have been brought there only be magic. We find the same beliefs in most of the countries where there are dolmens; in western France the chamber-tombs are attributed to Gargantua, and, according to popular legend, often contain a calf, a bill-hook or a sickle of gold.

The first chamber-tombs were probably put up in North Africa during the second millennium BC by the Berbers, to whom anthropological studies assign an eastern and Mediterranean origin. We can even accept that some megalithic coffers of northern Morocco came from the Iberian peninsula after the end of the third millennium BC, accompanying the few Bell-beakers and the first copper work in Morocco, at the western end of the Maghreb. A small chamber-tomb in north Morocco, at El Mriès, yielded a point and an awl in copper. But most of the North African chamber-tombs, those in the Algerian-Tunisian group, have more of a double Mediterranean origin, deriving both from Sardinia and from peninsular Italy by way of Malta. At least, this is the idea of Camps, who has defined several types in the megalithic architecture of North Africa. In the region of chamber-tomb is completely buried in a mound; the roofing slab and part of the supports are always visible. Some large chamber-tombs show no trace of surrounding stuctures.

A first type comprises a dolmenic chamber, approached by an unroofed passage in a circular mound. These may be the oldest North African chamber-tombs: an example is the passage-grave of Henchir el-Hadjar (Enfida, Tunisia) (Figure 54:2 and 3). Perhaps there should be added to this group two monuments from the Tayadirt cemetery, in the Moroccan Moyen Atlas, excavated by Lambert. Burial mounds are very numerous in the area, and 35 monuments have been recognised in two groups in Tayadirt cemetery; they are single mounds, of truncated cone shape, and stone circles.

Mound T3 (Figure 54:11) concealed a lozenge-shaped structure lined with slabs of red schistose sandstone. On to the western façade opened a 3 m (10 ft) long passage, unroofed and lined with dry-stone walls, which gave access to a sepulchral chamber (2 m [$6\frac{1}{2}$ ft] by 1.5 m [5 ft]). Behind it was a four-sided structure, a sort of chest filled with

---

Figure 54   Burial monuments of the protohistoric period in North Africa.
1. Distribution map of North African chamber-tombs.
2–3. Henchir el-Hadjar, Algeria. (After E. T. Hamy)
4. Bou Nouara VIII, Algeria. (After G. Camps)
5. El-Alia, Algeria. (After D. Anziani)
6. Dougga, Tunisia. (After Dr. Carton)
7. Sigus, Algeria. (After J. Chabassière)
8. Bou Nouara, Algeria. (After L. Frobenius)
9. Bazina with cylindrical base and crater, Ain el-Hamara, Algeria. (After G. Camps)
10–11. Two monuments in the Tayadirt cemetery, Morocco. (After N. Lambert and G. Souville)
12. Mound enclosing chest, Aïn-Sefra, Algeria. (After L. Petit)
13. Choucha, Djebel Kharouba. (After S. Payen)
14. Burial within a mound, Sidi-Slimane, Morocoo. (After A. Ruhlmann)

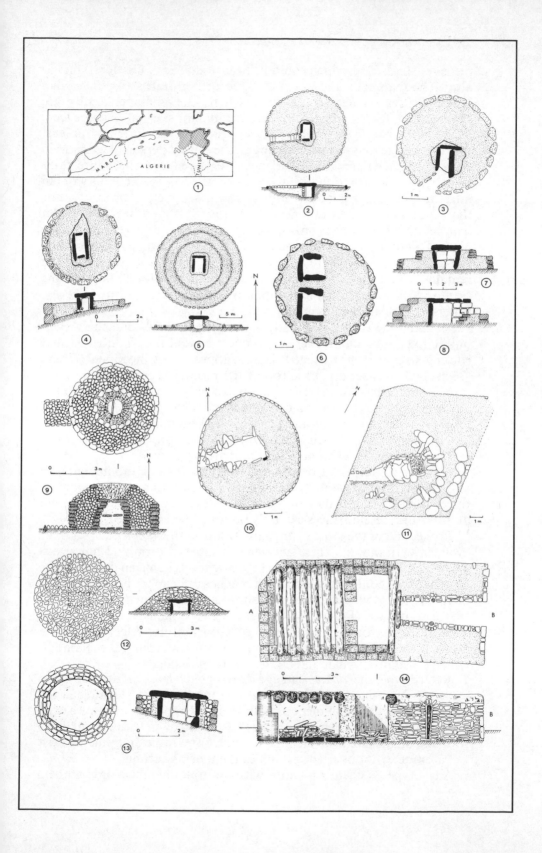

① ② ③ ④ ⑤ ⑥ ⑦ ⑧ ⑨ ⑩ ⑪ ⑫ ⑬ ⑭

MAROC   ALGERIE   TUNISIE

pieces of sandstone, which could be interpreted as a 'libation table' or altar. The chamber was covered by three large granite slabs, unusual in North African megalith-building, where the chamber-tombs are generally roofed by single slabs. Sparse human skeletal remains were found in the passage and the chamber, and pose the question, at least for the passage, of sacrifices relating to the buried person (a woman) in the chamber, whose bones had been scattered over its entire floor surface after decarnation. Rich grave-goods accompanied this woman into the after-life: a gold ear-ring, a bronze bracelet, 10 bronze spirals (hair ornaments, or from a necklace), a large ring, a bronze crescent (ear pendant?), a large bronze ear-ring, an amulet representing a male head of a unique type, numerous beads of metal, cornelian and ostrich egg-shell, and a few sherds of pottery. The excavators recovered the remains from a mat of vegetable fibres which was found beneath the skull and the amulet, and noted that 'this arrangement forms part of a funerary ritual of the Egyptian Eneolithic'.

Mound T4 (Figure 54:10), adjacent to the previous one, has a well-built circular surround; there is no chest behind the chamber, whose roofing-slab, if it ever existed, has disappeared. A small stele 75 cm (30 in) high was set up at the top of the mound. There were no bone remains in the passage, and the remains of only one person were found in the chamber. As in the other monument, a hearth was found above food offerings. Chambers and passages had been filled with sandy silt and pebbles after the funeral ceremony. Among the grave-goods recovered from this chamber was a flint arrowhead.

We may be surprised by the architecture of these monuments, so close in overall morphology to those of Atlantic Europe. But we note the character and late date of the archaeological material. The formal architectural resemblances can only be coincidental.

The second of the types defined by Camps is the 'dolmen sur socle' or 'dolmen with plinth'. These are very variable in form and numerous above all in the large cemeteries of the Algerian-Tunisian group. Some have a sort of conical mound which reaches only up to the roofing-slab at its highest point; a circle of stones, a kind of low kerb-wall, can surround its base (Figure 54:3). In other cases, such as chamber-tomb VIII at Bou Nouara (south-east of Constantine, Algeria) (Figure 54:4), the plinth can form a horizontal platform around the chamber, which is usually circular and occasionally four-sided.

A third type, the 'dolmen engagé dans un manchon', or 'dolmen set in a casing', has round its edges a pile of stones laid flat which reach the upper level of the monument's roofing-slab. Numerous examples exist in the Bou Nouara cemetery. The 'casing' is cylindrical, sometimes four-sided, and can be of stepped form. Comparable monuments exist in Palestine, without a generic link to them being certain.

A last type, of chamber-tombs with multiple chambers or chambers grouped in a single structure, also exists in the Algerian-Tunisian style of megalith-building.

On the coast of Grande-Kabylie, at Aït Racuna (Algeria), Camps notes a small cemetery of monuments formally related to *allées couvertes*. One *allée* at Aït Garet measures 12.5 m (41 ft) long by 1.4 m (4½ ft) wide and 2 m (6½ ft) high. It is partly covered by a mound. The walls of this collective grave are of piled-up slabs, and the roof of juxtaposed large slabs. Paving covers the floor of the monument. The origin of these last structures should perhaps be sought in the Mediterranean islands.

Other stone monuments

Graves made of dry-stone, either megalithic or 'paramegalithic' (without monolithic slabs), are found by the hundreds of thousands all over the Maghreb; and mounds made of simple piles of stones occupy vast areas of northern Africa, occasionally grouped into large cemeteries, from the Atlantic Ocean to the Red Sea – and even into the Arabian peninsula. The dimensions of the mounds vary considerably from one to another; some are bounded by a kerb of larger stones. They cover single or collective burials in more or less complex structures.

Camps excludes monuments with external features from his definition of a 'tumulus'. If we adopt his viewpoint, we have to abandon the 'term 'mound' for the mass which covers the chamber-tombs of the Atlantic coastline of Europe, chamber-tombs very often encircled by a built wall. Perhaps we could, in France at least, use the term *'chiron'* (cairn) to designate fairly conical piles of stones covering burials. In North Africa, Reygasse used the Arab term *'redjem'* to designate this type of monument, but without excluding from the definition monuments with retaining walls. Confined to piles of stones, the names *'redjem'* in North Africa and *'Daga Tuli'* in Ethiopia would have a well-defined meaning. The term 'mound' could then be reserved for the group of monuments with an external structure, whether a kerb-wall or not.

The typological classification of *redjem* includes mounds that cover a body laid directly on the ground, a frequent occurrence in the Sahara. These structures may be less funerary than commemorative, just as some funerary mounds can also be boundary markers. In Moslem countries mounds covering the tombs of sacred personages, *marabouts*, may be very recent. Among other types of *redjem*, Camps recognises: mounds with funerary cists containing skeletons in a drawn-up position with poor grave-goods; mounds with platform; mounds with hollows (which allow re-use); and mounds with pits. Burial methods include: single or collective inhumations; successive inhumations of entire bodies in a flexed position or laid on the back; and inhumation by the deposit of decarnated bones.

Alongside the stone cairns there are earth mounds, such as the monument of Mzora in north-west Morocco, which was built before the Roman era for a Moorish chief or king. This mound was between 54 m (177 ft) and 58 m (190 ft) in diameter, bounded by a low kerb-wall and flanked by a circle of 167 monoliths averaging 1.5 m (5 ft) in height. A standing stone placed to the east, called El-Outed ('the stake'), is 5 m (16½ ft) high, and another fallen stone at its base is 4.2 m (14 ft) long. At the centre of the mound were the remains of a burial chamber.

Circular, crescent- or horseshoe-shaped enclosures, made of rows of stones, are also very widespread in North Africa.

Still following Camps' classification, we come to his 'evolved forms'. The first are the *'bazinas'* (Figure 54:9), which appear over almost all the Maghreb. These monuments derive from the mound type, but are bounded by a well-built wall; their internal structures are comparable to those of other mounds. Different forms exist: with concentric surrounds; with outer shells; in steps, of which the commonest form has a plan which is circular (sometimes four-sided), as at El Fezzan, Germa and El Charaig (Libya); with cylindrical base (more common in the semi-steppe regions of the south Maghreb); and finally with multiple graves. According to Camps, these are autochthonous burials: 'they seem, more often than the other North African burials, to contain remains previously decarnated in a primary burial'. Some could have been built late, as late as the introduction of Islam.

'Chouchet' (*'choucha'* in the singular) are circular graves in the form of a tower 2.5 m (8 ft) to 3 m (10 ft) high, roofed by a visible stone slab which never overhangs the tower itself (Figure 54:13). *Chouchet* contain a small, four-sided chamber which allowed the deposition of a single body, in a drawn-up position, accompanied by poor goods. This type of monument is confined to eastern Algeria; in the Sahara, monuments which have a central chimney, but are otherwise comparable share the same name.

A whole series of later monuments are described by Camps: mounds with ritual furnishings, monuments at once funerary and sanctuary, with passages, arms or horns; monuments with niches and with chapels, whose origin should be sought in the Nile valley; mounds with skylights and sacrificial altars; monuments with ambulatories; and others in the form of a house hidden beneath a mound (a type known only from the monument of Sidi Slimane).

The funerary monument of Sidi Slimane (Morocco)

Sidi Slimane (Figure 54:14), with its Wednesday *souk* (market), is an important centre of commerce; but the market was cramped by a large knoll of earth, which hindered its much-needed expansion. It was decided to remove the 'small red hill', a mound 47 m (154 ft) across and a 6 m (20 ft) high. Excavation began in April 1937 under the direction of Armand Ruhlmann. The mound, composed of superimposed layers of earth, hid a four-sided monument, off-centre within its mass. The mound formed the capping of a funerary monument 13.25 m ($43\frac{1}{2}$ ft) long, 5.5 m (18 ft) wide and a 2 m ($6\frac{1}{2}$ ft) high. Except for the eastern façade and the passage, built of squared stones with earth, the exterior and interior walls were of unfired brick. The space between the internal and external walls was filled with earth.

The monument is in three parts: the passage; a small court; and the funerary chamber itself. The passage, opening from the eastern façade, was blocked at its entrance by several slabs set edgewise. It is 5.2 m (17 ft) long, narrowing progressively and giving access to a small four-sided court which, like the passage, has no roof. Half-way along the passage two opposed semi-circular niches had been let into the side-walls; each contained a post, whose function is unknown. Stretched along the left-hand side, directly on the floor of the passage, lay the not very well-preserved skeleton of a middle-aged man. Nearby were recovered a dozen semi-cylindrical ivory objects, which could have come from a wooden chest. The passage opens out into a rectangular antechamber 2.8 m (9 ft) long by 1.9 m ($6\frac{1}{4}$ ft) wide. In the centre of the end-wall an opening giving access to the main burial-chamber was blocked by a mass of compacted earth. In front of this, a body lying on its left side rested on a bed of plaster, protected by a pile of flat slabs. Pieces of ivory hinges found there must have belonged to another wooden chest with a movable lid, left in the south-west corner of this antechamber. The plan of the main burial chamber was a 3 m (10 ft) square, with the northern corner cut off. Its floor was flagged with three touching slabs, on which lay two skeletons. The ceiling was made of six trunks of Barbary *thuja* trees, each 60 cm (24 in) in diameter, supporting a layer of beaten earth. One of the skeletons, stretched on its left side along the western wall of the chamber, was covered by a layer of sherds of pottery. The other, oriented east-west, was in a flexed position, the head to the west, not far from the north wall. Both lay on a bed of plaster under a pile of stone slabs which must originally have been a chest for each corpse.

We can see in this tomb, which is dated by the pottery to the fourth or third century BC, the burial of an important person of the period. No anthropological study has been done of the bones, but we might envisage a couple in the main burial-chamber, with two servants (perhaps the wife also) who were immolated on the occasion of their master's death and accompanied him into the unknown. A few years before the excavation, a stele with a Libyan inscription had been found not far from the mound. The epitaph on it indicates that it refers to the tomb of a father and his son. They could well be the occupants of the funerary monument of Sidi Slimane, which Camps finds to resemble in its shape the traditional Maghreb house.

Funerary customs

In North African ritual, a pottery vessel seems to have accompanied each body in the grave. Curiously, early modelled pottery in North Africa displays a great unity from east to west, and it is identical to that made in the countryside today, both in decoration and in manufacturing technique. Berber pottery with a characteristic flat base may have come from Sicily, from Sardinia or from Spain at any time from the middle Bronze Age onwards. Rituals linked with the body itself are very numerous. The body can be placed in an extended, flexed or crouched position in a primary burial. The extended supine position is more recent than flexed on side or back, which often necessitated tying- or parcelling-up of the body.

In some monuments the bones of a person put into the grave in earlier times have been pushed aside to make room for another body. Occasionally, bodies were decarnated before the bones are placed in the grave. If the flesh of a first burial had naturally decayed, the bones were gathered up and placed in the monument as a secondary burial. A grave takes the name of 'ossuary' when the remains of several previously decarnated bodies are found there. We should note in this connection that if decarnation takes place in the open air – the body left on a platform for the vultures, for example – the collected bones when placed in a chamber-tomb constitute a primary burial (another difficulty for the archaeologist!).

Evidence of cremation, found in some monuments, is relatively rare, and seems to be a late phenomenon among the burial customs of North Africa. In the chamber-tombs, the most common practice consists of scattering the bones of the deceased around the chamber after decarnation. In these cases a pot occupies the centre of the chamber-tomb, containing slivers of bone or a stone. Sometimes, the skulls are the objects of particular attention. In the rock-cut tombs at Sila (eastern Algeria), Camps noted: 'after the primary inhumations had been left for a long period in the collective graves, sorting took place in the course of transfer: the skulls were carefully collected into the tomb to be arranged along the walls; all the other bones, particularly the long bones, were put into the middle, while the small bones and fragments which might get lost were collected into pots'. Camps continues his analysis, writing:

> At Tiddis [eastern Algeria], deposited in one primary burial, where they stayed only a short time, human remains were collected into *bazinas* serving

as ossuaries. During the transfer ceremony, large ritual pots, each containing an offering vessel, were filled with earth and a few bones, then capped with a skull to which the cervical vertebrae were still attached: the large bones, carried separately, were deposited in bulk in the pit while skull and pottery remained in close contact.

Sometimes no offering acompanies the dead person to his final resting-place, but the bones of animals (cattle, sheep, goat, birds – but never pigs, already!) have occasionally been found, along with pottery, personal ornaments, and weapons. Small stelae, of fairly cylindrical shape, can be found right inside the chamber, or just beside the monument. They are often taken to be phallic symbols. Comparable stelae have been found in the chamber-tombs of the Harar in Ethiopia, and we have already noted formal similarities with the North African chamber-tombs. In fact, stelae are very often linked with monuments of chamber-tomb type. This is the case in Spain, particularly at Los Millares, but also in the Quercy and Languedoc chamber-tombs, as in several monuments of the Atlantic façade; yet no cultural link is visible to join all these areas, where megalith-building has in any case not been contemporaneous.

Ethiopian megalithic monuments: in the land of the Queen of Sheba

In East Africa, Ethiopia is a country of megalith-building. Thousands of stelae were put up in the south, some of them very recently. Others are the work of the Axumite peoples of the north, and they are known of as far as the territory of the Republic of Djibouti, without there being any apparent cultural relationship between the three groups.

Halfway between Addis Ababa and the Somalian coast in the mountains of Tchertcher, Azaïs and Chambard in 1922 discovered a series of monuments which they called 'dolmens', in that two rows of upright stones supported a slab of undressed stone. This is indeed the popular definition of the term dolmen, the picture in all our minds. When I myself studied these 'dolmens' in 1970, I had to modify the terminology. I saw 92 of these monuments in several cemeteries, and a good number of others, still unstudied to this day, were reported to me.

The Galla people, who have occupied the region only since the sixteenth century, continue to venerate certain of the chamber-tombs, of which they are not, however, the builders. They come to bring offerings and burn incense on a sherd of pottery, which remains in place until the next ceremony. They call the chamber-tombs' 'Daga Kofiya' or 'covered stones'. Several centres of worship have been recognised at Dobba and Tchelenko (Sourré-Kabanawa and Ganda Hassan Abdi) at altitudes between 1700 m (5577 ft) and 2300 m (7545 ft). Another major grouping of the chamber-tombs is in the Ourso region, dominating the desert and the Danakil depression.

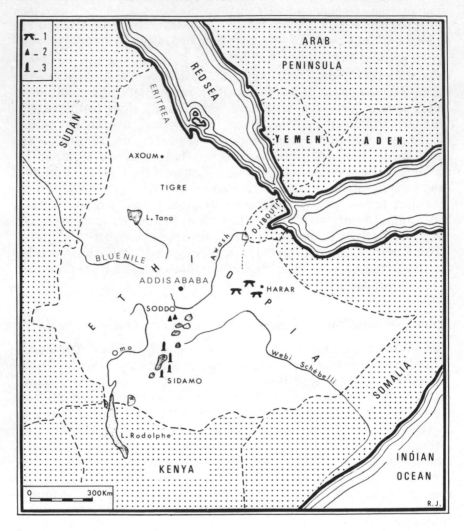

The builders of the dolmenic cists were established on the northern slopes of the Tchertcher mountains, in a fairly confined territory, and were nothing to do with the builders of the mounds which abound in this area, and whose overall distribution is much wider. Nor do they have any links with the artists of the rock-paintings which are confined to the region between Karamillé, Diré-Dawa and Harar, that is, partly covering the area occupied by the chamber-tombs of Tchelenko, but spilling over from it and not reaching the sites at Dobba. The dolmenic cists which we have visited are only very occasionally isolated; most often they are grouped into veritable cemeteries. Much destruction has taken place among these megaliths, probably in connection with the cultivation of land, but also by treasure-hunters. Nowadays, chamber-tombs are found only in uncultivated regions where stones are numerous. About two hours' walk usually separates two cemeteries. This implies a territorial unity corresponding to villages occupied by sedentary populations, doubtless comparable to what exists today.

The builders of the chamber-tombs were not too interested in the orientation of the monuments. Their over-riding concern in building the cist was ease of construction. They preferred to chose a fairly steep slope where the roofing slabs were quite easily extracted and put on top of their supports. Most frequently the slab was found free-lying on the land. There are great similarities between these monuments and those of North Africa, but this could just be a matter of coincidence.

In a place where limestone slabs occur naturally, one began by cutting a horizontal surface into the side of the mountain and setting up two rows of parallel uprights, usually squared and spaced about 50 cm (20 in) to 90 cm (35 in) apart, their height sometimes more than 1 m (3 ft). These pillars were held in place by a buttress of stones on the mountain-side which reached up as far as the roofing-slab; a retaining wall of dry-stone extended the slope at either end to keep the earth in place. Paving was laid on the floor of the chamber. Then it only remained to slide the roofing-slab, taken from higher up, into place on top of the uprights. The chamber's short sides were closed with small slabs, set edgewise. Sometimes two slabs were required to make a short side. (These are not pillars: they never support the roof.) Behind these 'doors', stones were piled up to make a complete seal of the chamber at either end. On the long side, facing the valley, stones and earth were piled up to what must have been the level of the roof. So the corpse was completely protected from attack by animals such as hyenas and other carnivores. In general, the chambers are small cells which can contain one body in a flexed position, on average 1.5 m (5 ft) long by 65 cm ($25\frac{1}{2}$ in) wide and 60 cm ($23\frac{1}{2}$ in) high. The stone roofing-slab is up to 3 m (10 ft) long by 1.2–2.8 m (4–9 ft) wide; its thickness varies from 15 cm (6 in) to 1.1 m ($3\frac{1}{2}$ ft), but this last figure is absolutely exceptional (Figure 55).

Since a skeleton was found in one of the chamber-tombs of Sourré-Kabanawa, we have reason to think that dolmenic cists were funerary monuments designed for the burial of an individual – which the very dimensions of the cist allow us to assume. We know, however, very little about the material and spiritual life of their builders; in fact, the remains recovered from them are disappointingly scarce, and most often have no archaeological value. The rare existence of lithic industry in flint or obsidian is no help, for it could be very recent in date. There are areas of Ethiopia where obsidian is still regularly used for the manufacture of scraper, and almost everywhere in the countryside blades of this material are still used to cut hair. The same is true of the potsherds, which we have already indicated can be evidence of a fairly recent offering.

Several times, we have found a small stele or *betyl*, cylindrical or polyhedral, in the chamber itself or sometimes in a sort of antechamber made at one end of the monument, beneath the overhanging roofing-slab.

In North Africa, Camps thinks, 'these stones which have been given a roughly cylindrical shape ending in a fairly pointed cone' are phallic symbols; he notes that 'the funerary megalith is often, whatever its shape, a symbol of fecundity and fertility'. It is probable that the symbolism is the same in Ethiopia, where we also find triangular stelae.

There remains much work to be done, therefore, on the chamber-tombs of the Harar, to discover who used them, and to define better their date of construction; if we can believe the two radiocarbon dates, this was during the second millennium BC.

Circular chamber and cella *monuments*

It is very difficult to consider circular-chambered and *cella* monuments as chamber-tombs. All the same, some megalithic elements occur in the structure of these collective graves which, in some aspects, recall the passage-graves of western Europe, if only in that access to the chamber is from above.

At Tchelenko, at the centre of a group of dolmenic cists, three monuments with circular chamber and *cella* were studied at the place called Ganda-Midjou. A link might exist between these funerary

---

Figure 55 Dolmenic cists of the Harar mountains, Ethiopia. (After R. Joussaume)
1. Sourré-Kabanawa C1.
2. Ganda-Midjou B2.
3. Ganda-Midjou A7.

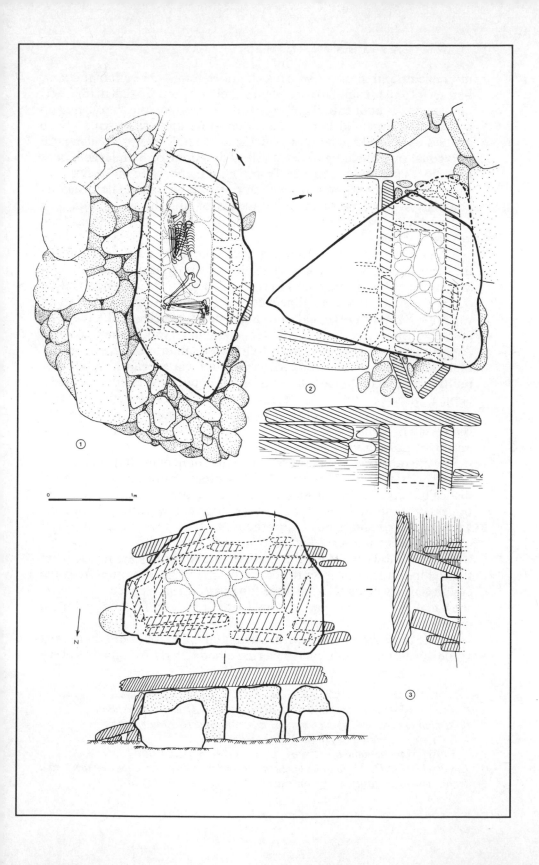

monuments and the neighbouring chamber-tombs. The circular chamber, set into the ground to a depth of 1.2 m (4 ft) and 2.7–2.8 m (8¾–9 ft) in diameter, is built entirely of dry-stone. Elsewhere, the chamber is up to twice as large and built on a much more impressive scale above ground and inside a mound. All those studied had a small lateral polygonal or circular chamber, built of dry-stone or with large blocks set into the ground. Passage from one chamber to the other was through a trilithon porch of two supports and a lintel. The principal chamber was compartmented by means of upright slabs, and each compartment was closed by other slabs laid flat. The whole was then covered by stones.

These structures are collective graves. The dead were placed inside the compartments – there must have been four to six in the chamber – in a crouching position, backs to the wall. They were accompanied by pottery, essentially spherical necked vases, cups and bowls, and vases with ring bases or polygonal onto a flat stand, which could have been incense-burners (Fig. 56:3). Their weaponry, comprising javelins, daggers and arrowheads of iron, followed them into the grave, as did their ornaments: limestone, cornelian and glass beads, smooth or multi-lobed, or of copper, silver or gold; copper ear-pendants; spiral copper or silver rings; bracelets – simple rings sometimes open, swelling at the centre, in copper or iron; pendants of wood, stone or bone; sawn shells, cowries or olive-shaped; small bottles of kohl, antimony powder used as eye-shadow.

The introduction of a new body into the compartment displaced the bones of its predecessors, so there is great confusion in the final disposition of the bones in these collective graves. Perhaps certain bones, of hand and feet in particular, together with the ornaments, were recovered and deposited in the *cella*; that is what excavation of one monument at Sourré-Kabanawa seems to indicate.

The few known dates for this architectural type indicate its use from the eighth to the twelfth centuries AD. Islam reached this area from the eighth century onwards; but these funerary customs, collective graves, the cadaver crouched against a wall, are in no way Islamic and must date back to an earlier period.

Beside these monuments with circular chamber and *cella* there exist stone cairns, fairly high, each covering a body. Perhaps some people of

---

Figure 56   Ethiopian monuments and ceramics. (After R. Joussaume)
1. Monument with circular chamber and cella, Sourré-Kabanawa
1. (a) Cross-section through the trilithon doorway.
2. Vessel from monument with circular chamber and cella, Raré.
3. Vessels from Déder mound: large, straight-necked vessel (cinerary urn), and deep cup with perforations below the rim and four-legged flat base.

high rank were permitted a different, more personalised type of burial – but this is only a hypothesis.

Fortresses with cyclopean walls

Still in the Tchertcher mountains, the heights, which have views over a wide area or which dominate the only road, are often topped by the ruins of fortresses built of dry-stone blocks which sometimes weigh several tonnes each. The enclosure walls can be over 4 cm (13 ft) thick, and the sherds of pottery which litter the ground inside are comparable to those recovered in the monuments with circular chamber and *cella* and in other mounds. No one knows exactly who built these fortresses. Legend attributes them to the Arlas, a race of giants who were said to occupy the area before the arrival of the present Gallas. These Arlas were also said to be the builders of the chamber-tombs and mounds (we note again the intervention of giants). Some consider these to be defensive sites erected in the time of the emperor Zara Yacob (1434–68), which were razed at the time of the Moslem invasion led by Emir Ahmed ben Ibrahim, better known as Gragne ('The Left-handed One'), between 1523 and 1543. It is improbable that not all these fortifications date from the same period, and the radiocarbon-dates obtained for one of them indicate that it was occupied in the eighth to ninth century AD, or at the same time as the monuments with circular chamber and *cella*.

Archaeological studies in this area have barely begun, but are extremely promising. Traffic must have been busy in the whole Horn of Africa at this period, if we can judge from the presence alone of the perfume-burner (otherwise called a *polypode à plaque*), known from the excavations of A. T. Curle, undertaken in 1927 into the mounds of the Kenyan frontier, and which was recently found in the Handoga site in the Republic of Djibouti.

However, even if we recognise megalithic characteristics in the monuments with circular chamber and *cella*, both in construction and the collective aspect of the burials, these monuments seem to have no links with the dolmenic cists which precede them.

Megalithic monuments in the Central African Republic and Cameroon

In the west of the Central African Republic, Pierre Vidal discovered in 1969 a megalithic group with stone cists surmounted by stelae. Again, it is difficult to talk about chamber-tombs with regards to these monuments, but since the term has been used to designate them, we must investigate.

The megalithic monuments of Bouar are called *'Tajunu'* by the autochthonous people, a word which describes the external aspect of the group: 'standing-stones'. They are situated along the crest which separates the Chad basin from the Congo valley. Southwards, they are found to within 20 km (12½ miles) of Bouar; northwards, they seem to go on to the other side of the Cameroon frontier, where Marliac took particular note of the mound of Yikpangma, which sprawls across 50 m (164 ft) and within which a 'chamber-tomb' (in fact a large slab resting on supports) was found.

Vidal noted that almost all the *Tajuna* are sited close to a spring, as is also the case in the Cameroon monuments. *Tajuna* are oval mounds 2 m (6½ ft) to 3 m (10 ft) high, of varying size: some are not more than 25 m² (30 sq. yd) in area, while others are up to 2000 m² (2392 sq. yd). They are topped by crudely prepared upright stones, which measure up to 3.5 m (11½ ft) or 4 m (13 ft) in height, and which are variable in number also. The *Tajunu* of Tuakolo, 35 m (115 ft) long by 25 m (82 ft) wide, supports around 100 upright stones.

Vidal excavated three mounds in the environs of Bouar (Tajuna Beforo I, Tajunu Gam, and Tajunu Tia I) and established the internal structure of these monuments. A layer of earth about 1 m (3 ft) thick was spread over the laterite or granite ground-surface. It was topped with a layer of approximately even-sized rubble into which were set the megalithic structures. These are chests of stone made of three slabs placed edgewise, the fourth side being closed by a dry-stone wall. A dry-stone wall also edges the mound. A thin slab provides the cover for the chests, whose volume varies between 0.25 and 1 m² (9 and 35 cu. ft). Unfortunately all were found empty. The acidity of the soil must be blamed; it will have dissolved any bones. Into the mass of rubble are also fixed stones; some do not protrude, some rise to almost 4 m (13 ft) above the mound. Archaeological remains found during the excavations are very scarce: a few sherds, sometimes decorated with impressions are scratches, very occasionally a complete bowl (except at Beforo I and Tajuna Gam, where a pipe-bowl was found), struck pieces of quartz, and iron objects, among them iron lanceheads which seem to have been a relatively recent introduction into one of the chambers of Beforo I. Several hearths were also discovered in the mounds and gave radiocarbon dates. Among the six dates thus obtained, the two earliest are 5490 and 4750 b.c. on the uncalibrated scale. Taking the calibration into consideration, we would have the earliest dated megalithic structures in the world. But this assessment should probably be modified. Charcoal recovered on the early ground-surface beneath a mound can come from a period well before the construction of the monument itself. The other three dates, at 610, 450, and 250 b.c. in uncorrected years, seem much more plausible and agree better with what we know of megalith-building on the African continent; but this is only an idea which requires confirmation. Nothing is known of the authors of these monuments, built probably with a funerary purpose.

Megalith-building, but not chamber-tombs, elsewhere in Central and West Africa

The African continent, especially in its central part, is a land of standing stones. We have just described the Bouar group, which relate somewhat to chamber-tombs in that upright stones surmount stone coffers, but there are many other groups of stelae which deserve a whole book to themselves; we can only describe them briefly here.

One of the best-studied groups is the Senegambian in West Africa, the subject of a very important publication in 1980 by Thilmans, Descamps, and Khayat. At the moment Gallay is directing fresh excavations at Mbolob Tobé, Santhiou Kohel. The Senegambian megalithic territory, covering an area about 300 km (186 miles) long by 120–130 km (75–80 miles) wide, contains four main types of monument:

> The *megalithic circle* is made up of a circular enclosure of monoliths defining a flat or slightly domed interior space, which may or may not be scattered with laterite blocks. In the majority of cases a frontal structure, comprising one or two rows of monoliths, flanks the circle, which may be double. The *stone mound* is scattered with laterite blocks or gravel. It mostly has a frontal structure. The *stone circle* comprises a circular enclosure of laterite blocks which protrude slightly from the ground surface. This enclosure surrounds a flat or slightly convex surface, with very few or no blocks. This type of monument nearly always has a frontal structure. The *mound* can be considered as a megalithic monument when it has a frontal structure.

There is nothing very 'dolmenic' about this Senegalese megalithic group.

The most important site, at Siné-Ngayène, comprises around 50 circles of upright monoliths. They form the superstructure of more or less collective graves. One circle marked the position of 10 bodies buried under 1.3–2 m ($4\frac{1}{4}$–$6\frac{1}{2}$ ft) of earth; circle number 25 rose above 28 bodies, four of them buried shallow in a sitting position, and 24 buried more deeply in two well-defined groups which seem to have been buried together. To have an idea of the archaeological material which accompanied these collective graves, let us note that from circle 25 were recovered: eight complete or fragmented annular necklaces, two rings, two cornelian beads, a glass bead, 26 iron spearheads and an iron knife, and a fair number of sherds of pottery. Besides these, 14 pots were found to the east of the circle: 12 just to the east of the frontal monoliths, two between them and the circle. The pots had been turned upside down, and most of their bases had been deliberately perforated. In circle 28 of the same cemetery, the bones of 59 simultaneously-buried skeletons were found between 30 cm (12 in) and 2.12 m (7 ft) deep. The collective aspect of burial is less evident at Tiékène-

Boussoura, where seven monuments studied contained only one or two skeletons each. We are lost in conjecture when we try to understand why so many bodies were deposited simultaneously in the grave: were these the results of battle, or of sacrifice following the death of a high-ranking personage? This last hypothesis seems the most likely.

Radiocarbon dates for these different megalithic sites indicate a period running from the second century BC to the ninth century AD for the megalithic circles, with even a date in the sixteenth century AD from one eastern site. Thilmans, Descamps, and Khayat favour diffusion from a single centre for the megalithic phenomenon in this region:

Appearing first in the centre of the area, it was adopted by neighbouring groups having affinities with the Dioron-Boumak culture for the western group and one of the Senegal river cultures for the eastern group. Assimilation was less total in the east, where the most elaborate monuments [megalithic circles] were not taken up.

Other sites with standing stones are known in West Africa, both in Mauritania and in Mali, where the Tundidaro group in the Niafounké region comprises at least 150 upright stones. Other sites are known in Niger and Togo, and graves similar to those of Bouar have been noted in Chad. In Nigeria, Allison's 1983 study shed more light on a group of stelae with sculpted human faces. The earliest of these 'Akwanshi' have been dated to the sixteenth century AD, and the most recent date to the beginning of the present century. The largest group, amounting to more than 300 stelae, is in Ogoja province to the east of Nigeria.

But let us return to Ethiopia to say a word about the thousands of stelae south of Addis Ababa. Since 1974 a meticulous survey has been made of them by F. Anfray and the Mission Française d'Archéologic at Addis Ababa. Recent years have seen the beginning of excavation on some sites.

In the north of Ethiopia, the Axumite civilisation produced several fine examples of standing stones, including the tallest in the ancient world, 33 m (108 ft) high. This was erected around the third century AD; but other, smaller ones are known, dating from the fifth century BC.

The tallest stele recorded in south Ethiopia measures 8 m (26 ft). But most of the much smaller and more numerous stelae carry symbolic figures whose meaning for the most part eludes us. They fall broadly into four categories: anthropomorphic stelae with or without figures; figurative stelae whose shape is in some cases anthropomorphic; phallic-shaped stelae, occasionally figured (these are the most widespread); and simple monoliths, without human shape or any figuration.

In the Soddo area of Ethiopia, stelae with swords on them, measuring between 1 m (3 ft) and 5 m ($16\frac{1}{2}$ ft) high, have been the object of recent excavations. They mark one of the sides of a polygonal structure made of stones set edgewise in the ground. This structure was built over a pit which encloses the body of a person, generally laid on one side and in a flexed position. The head of the corpse was put at the level of a biconical perforation in the base of the stele, whose carvings face outwards. We are still perplexed as to the meaning of the 'symbolic triad' represented both in association with the swords on the stele, and alone. Excavations will have to continue in order to throw light on this problem and to establish the period of erection, which radiocarbon dates suggest to be around the tenth to fifteenth centuries AD.

We should not agonise over Central African megalith-building, which has taken us a long way from our proper subject in this book. We have said a few words only to show its formal difference from dolmens and chamber-tombs in general. The specifically African character of these stelae is noteworthy: they were put up only in a central band across the continent, and are still erected in some areas of Africa; the Arussi in the region of the Ethiopian lakes still erect stelae, as do the Konso, but this time in wood.

Megalithic monuments in the Arabian peninsula

Study of early funerary monuments has barely begun in the Arabian peninsula. Although we know that mounds of all kinds are particularly numerous in this huge area of the Middle East, it is very rarely that excavation has revealed the internal structure of any of them. It is thus practically impossible to know whether, as in Europe, any of them shelter a monument of the dolmen type.

In the islands of Bahrein in the Persian Gulf, Geoffrey Bibby and Peter Glob brought to light, from 1953 onwards, traces of the kingdom of Dilmun, a lost civilisation which, from 4000 BC onwards, was at the crossroads of trading routes between the peoples of the Indus valley and of Mesopotamia. A number of the inhabitants of Bahrein from the mid third millennium BC were buried in stone chests under mounds made of piled-up blocks, topped by one or several slabs. The mounds formed cemeteries of several hundred monuments. The royal tombs, over 12 m (39 ft) high, had a complex internal arrangement of walls and chambers. Similar arrangements inside mounds appear again on the land of the principality of Abu Dhabi, also in the Persian Gulf, where graves under complex mounds at Bouraymi, 160 km (100 miles) into the hinterland, used large slabs in their construction. They bear rock-engravings which would have been forbidden by Islamic law, and so must be earlier. Mounds with internal wall structures and complex cells were also built in very early times in the Yemen (Bayle des Hermens and Grebenart made preliminary studies of these in 1980). So it seems that there was a strong tradition of burial beneath mounds throughout the Arabian peninsula. Bibby notes immense areas of mounds 350 km

(217 miles) into Saudi Arabia, which date from the second millennium BC. They stand at the edge of the great Empty Quarter of the Arabian desert, the Rub' al-Khali.

We find more mounds in large numbers on the other side of the Gulf of Aden, in particular in the Harar Mountains of Ethiopia, but also in the Republic of Djibouti, where they have not yet been investigated, essentially in the north of the country. Here there is a whole range of protohistoric studies to be undertaken, but one comes up against local tradition which make the possibility of excavation remote.

In the Arab Republic of Yemen, Bernardelli and Parinello noted in 1970 numerous standing stones, and in particular the curious monument of Mohamdid-al-Hamli, which extends over more than 50 m (164 ft). Untrimmed stones are set up in parallel rows which increase in height towards a circular area about 10 m (33 ft) in diameter, which is itself bounded by standing stones. Obviously, this monument has nothing to do with dolmens; I simply want to point out its similarity of form with certain western European monuments, particularly the alignments at Carnac (Morbihan), France, but on a much smaller scale.

Further north in the Arabian peninsula, gigantic raised stones arranged in several circles stand between the mountainous area of Schomer and Nedjed, in the Hazim near Howarah. Two more circles are known at Rass and at Hevakia. And there are many more; these are just a few examples.

In the Yemen, however, Bayle des Hermens has noted monuments in the surroundings of the village of Al Khurays which derive from chamber-tombs, at least in their shape. Here there are stone platforms, 7–8 m (23–26 ft) in diameter, at the centre of which upright stones form an elongated chamber (3–4 m [10–13 ft] long by 1 m [3 ft] wide) roofed by large flat slabs. Unfortunately, that is all we know of them.

Recent megalith-building in Madagascar

The peopling of Madagascar, according to Verin, resulted from several migrations. The early establishment of the Indonesians, who brought with them the practice of agriculture in burnt clearings, pottery, smithing, basket-making and weaving, took place towards the end of the first millennium AD. Another wave of immigrants, this time from Africa, reached Madagascar about the same time, and the two populations must very rapidly have made contact. There may have been a second wave of Indonesian colonists in the fourteenth century, who spread over the high land in Imerina. It is not impossible that these moves from the east to the west were made in stages, passing through southern India and the Maldive Islands. Be that as it may, we find in Madagascar burial rituals whose origins must be sought partly in

Indonesia, where stones still play a large part in the customs of certain regions of the Sunda islands.

Thanks to the work of R. P. Callet, who early this century assembled a huge documentation of Malagasy customs, drawing on the still-vivid memories of the inhabitants, we can know about funerary practices which are linked to the building of megaliths of forms close to the chamber-tombs and standing stones of western Europe. The cult of the ancestors is a deeply-rooted idea with the inhabitants of Madagascar and especially with the Merina, who live in Imerina (the central part of the Malagasy plateau – an area which seems to have been colonised twice over by Indonesian populations). In central Imerina, the people established themselves in fortified sites positioned at a height so as to protect the rice-fields in the valleys. Changes in the siting and the form of these defensive positions have been studied by Mille. Before the fifteenth century AD, the village was set high up, and surrounded by a shallow, narrow ditch. The sixteenth century saw consolidation of the defences and especially reinforcement of the entrance in stone. In the seventeenth century more ditches were cut, and the inner one was augmented by a dry-stone wall. The defensive system became much more complicated in the eighteenth century, when fresh trenches, wide and deep, surrounded larger sites. By contrast, the nineteenth century saw an abundance of smaller sites set lower down, closer to the cultivated land. This descent into the valleys must correspond to a period of greater security.

Ancestral tombs in Imerina in the nineteenth century

Eleven stones were needed for tombs built in the nineteenth century: four for the walls, five for the beds, one for the door, and the last as a large roofing-slab. These stones were taken from quarries and brought to the building-place of the tomb. Before the stones were broken up, a red cock or a sheep was sacrificed, and its blood was drained on to the slab. Once the weak point of the stone had been established, a fire was lit and moved along until the stone split. To transport the stones a sort of sledge was made, and the slab tied onto wooden cross-pieces. This, the loading phase, was accompanied by a meal of cooked beef and rice.

The stone was watched overnight by the 'stone master', and early in the morning everyone, men, women and children, gathered to haul it. With ropes of vegetable fibre it was dragged by all, under the direction of one man who rode on the slab and guided manoeuvres by a chant that was taken up by the hauliers. When, at last, all the stones were ready at the site cleared for building, the stone master slaughtered two or three fine fat cattle, whose grease was smeared on the stones. The meat was distributed to all. Then began the digging of the tomb. This could only be done with the approval of the astrologer, who determined the correct day – the end of the lunar month *asorotany* – and after the exorcism of a fowl of a certain colour. It fell to the youngest man to begin digging with the 'old well-worn spade'; once the work had been started, the others carried on. The 11 stones were taken down into the cavity: the four walls, then the five beds, then the large roofing slab and finally the door, always oriented to the west. Then began the transfer of the dead from their old to their new 'ancestral tomb', or their 'temporary burial' in the tomb. Temporary burials were frequent in Imerina, for several reasons. A person who died too close in time to the feast of *Fandroana*, the anniversary feast of the three most famous kings, could not be buried in the vault of the ancestors, nor could those who died far away and who had to wait for someone to fetch them home. The same waiting period in a temporary grave was necessary for those who had no ancestral tomb. Lastly, those who died of smallpox or infectious illnesses could not enter the ancestral tomb, by an interdict which could, however, be raised by order of the king.

The temporary burial followed the same ritual of cattle sacrifice as did burial in the ancestral tomb. Other cattle were killed at the moment of transfer of the body which, on this occasion, was wrapped in new *lambas*, winding-sheets. The *lamba*, red in colour (*lamba mena*), symbolised honour, wealth and, above all, royalty. The rich instituted the use of the red shroud for their own burial, and the poor imitated them. But it was the number of coverings which distinguished the social classes (up to 20 *lambas* for a wealthy man). In modern times the shroud is of natural silk, hand-woven; although its colour can vary, its title of *lamba mena* remains.

When a new tomb, finer than the old, was completed, the people transferred the bodies from the old tomb. They were put, three or four together, in a single shroud and deposited on one end of the new tomb. The *lambas* on the bodies of rich men were renewed every four or five years. Bodies were moved around within the tomb to make more space, but it does not seem that the 'ritual of turning', often recorded by Europeans in their writings, was very strong in Imerina. The bodies were always laid on their back, never on one side or face down.

At one time, the tomb was the place where money and family valuables were kept. When hard times came, the ancestors were petitioned. The money was recovered after a family reunion, or on opening the tomb for burial of another corpse. This custom had to be abandoned because of the cupidity of some who did not hesitate to rifle tombs in spite of the death penalty which they risked. Henceforth, only a small amount of money was put into the mouth of the dead person, according to his means.

Not all people were permitted to lie in the ancestral tomb. Sorcerers, dragged at the end of a rope, were put into simple pits, the head to the south, because they had led a bad life. Those condemned to death could not generally lie in the ancestral vault without royal authorisation. Anyone who disregarded this saw his wife and children sold into slavery and had his head cut off.

Burial in the ancestral tomb was of prime importance to the Merina. Occasionally a body could not be brought back to the tomb of the ancestors; when this happened, a stone was erected close to the body, as a memorial to the dead person. The standing stone is considered to be a tomb; it is a cenotaph. During the feast of *Fandroana*, it is smeared with grease and the ancestors are invoked. But everything possible was done to bring the body back to the ancestral tomb. If a warrior died in battle in a far-off land, the slave who accompanied him was obliged to bring back the body. If a relative recovered the body, he had to pay someone to carry it back, or bury it on the spot if he could find no one. There was great sadness if no one managed to return the body of the deceased, for his bones could not then mingle with those of his family. Eight bones, those of the arms and legs, had at all costs to be returned to the family vault. If the carrier was too weak to bring back the body, he had to prepare it in such a way as to make transport possible. The flesh was scraped off and buried on the spot; then the limbs and other disarticulated bones, carefully covered with salt, were put into a more easily carried basket. The bones of the dead could then go home to join those of his ancestors.

The archaeologist is perplexed by such complicated funerary customs. Let us imagine what archaeological study would provide, in the absence of any oral history. There would be the megalithic tomb, containing some complete skeletons laid on their backs, some incomplete skeletons, their bones intermingled (the bones of those transferred from one vault to another, which have been grouped together), and bundles of long bones (brought back from far away) on which scrape-marks could be found. Elsewhere, there would be isolated skeletons in pits (the bodies of slaves and poor people), sometimes just the bundle of bones from a skeleton without its limbs, and, close to the tombs, standing stones with no remains at their feet; not forgetting the bodies deliberately abandoned, of which a few scattered bones might be found in the course of excavation. It is almost certain that the archaeologist would be absolutely unable to fathom the meaning of the standing stone, which could, for example, be thought a *menhir* indicating a burial. The ancestral tomb would be a chamber-tomb, with its collective burials as primary or secondary deposits. Doubtless the investigator would understand that at certain times the bodies were displaced and rearranged, but that could take place inside the grave itself; how could one imagine a transfer on the occasion of a new tomb being built? And what could one say about those long bones having been scraped? A forest of hypotheses would spring up. Why are some bodies in collective burials inside chamber-tombs and others isolated in pits? Which echelons of society had the right to use the chamber-tomb? Were they family graves? Why were there empty ones?

Malagasy standing stones

The habit of setting up stones in solidly rooted in Malagasy custom, as we can see from the number of 'Independence' stelae erected in 1960 all over the island. But the standing stones can have more than one meaning. Suzanne Raharijaona found that the compelling reasons the Madagascans have for raising standing stones are to be divided into two groups, one relating to the dead, the other to the commemoration of an event. The significance of a stone may be limited to the family or clan, but it may also affect the entire population. Raharijaona writes:

> Structures relating to the dead, the ancestors, are as follows: a monument commemorative of a person who died far from his land of birth and whose remains could not be returned to the family or clan tomb, or whose remains will be brought back at a later stage; a memorial of a rich or famous man; memorial of a famous warrior; a monument commemorating a drowning, a murder, or a disappearance; a stopping-place for the funerary cortège of an important man; a figurative memorial of a notable ancestor close to the tomb where he is buried; a memorial of a feast given in honour of the dead of the family, clan, or tribe.
>
> Structures relating to events can be connected with several things, on a tribal or family basis. On a tribal basis, they could be: frontier markers between neighbouring tribes; indicators of political alliance contracted by a marriage uniting the royal families and two tribes, neighbouring on distant; memorials of departure for war; of reconciliation after a short or long period of conflict; of the passage of a victorious chief, establishing his sovereignty in the country; of deliverance after a war; of recognition by the king of services rendered by the people; of the installation of a prince, or of a lord representing the king or chief; of the building of a royal residence.
>
> On the family basis the erection of the stone can mark: the foundation of a village; the adoption or rejection of a child; a memorial of living persons (kidnapped people, old men's favourite spots, the children of the rich); a memorial of an important event; a memorial of a persecution; a memorial of an unforgettable situation: the purchase of something enormous; being the victim of a stingey meal; the hundredth birth in the herd of cattle; and so on.

If we have to allow as many different reasons for the erection of *menhirs* in France, we will assuredly never know for what reasons they were put up. This is why, despite all that we can say on the subject, we are still as puzzled as ever by the neolithic standing stones, whose function often remains a mystery. And we have here counted only the stone ones, but there may well have been the equivalent in wood also.

In Madagascar, the size of the stone to be put up depended on the income of the man who ordered the ceremony; the largest known is 8 m

(26 ft) long by 1 m (3 ft) wide. After its extraction and trimming by the specialist quarryman and his assistants, the stone was transported on a sledge of logs. In former times it must have been taken in a dug-out canoe made from the trunk of a tree, but in some areas the stone could only be moved by manpower; up to 300 people took part in its transport. Sometimes several days were required to bring the stone to a conspicuous place by the side of a track, or on a high place. There, a pit was dug beneath the base of the stone laid on the ground. The stone was raised by means of levers, timber and ropes, swung into the hole, and held in place by a packing of stones and earth. All this was accompanied by very elaborate ceremony with distinction of the meat of sacrificed cattle, and sprinkling of the stone with fat. Renel reported in 1921 that when the King of Ambohimanga married the Queen of Ambohidratrima, his neighbour and cousin, in 1797, he decided to commemorate the event by erecting a *menhir*. The stone, taken from a mountain 30 km (19 miles) or so to the west of Tananarive, and roughly shaped, measured more than 5 m (16$\frac{1}{2}$ ft) in length by 80 cm (31 in) wide and 15–20 cm (6–8 in) thick. Its cutting and transport took two months, during which time 100 cattle were slaughtered.

Stones commemorating collective events were inviolable; their meaning could never disappear unless there was a change of population. By contrast, a stone put up to commemorate a death very quickly became a resting-place for the spirit of the dead person. While the ancestral tomb preserved the bodies, and hence family unity, the standing stone was the home of the dead spirit. The living could have access to that spirit by speaking to the stone.

Sometimes standing stones no longer claimed as anyone's property become the object of a phallic cult, particularly for women who wish to conceive. This custom has developed in many areas of the world where there are standing stones, and the number of *menhirs* used to this end in Brittany is quite large. In Betsileo country, Raharijaona says:

> a woman desiring to have a child goes alone to a standing stone dedicated to this use by all the women in this situation. Although considered to be a stone of fertility, the standing stone is used in the manner of a stone of fortune and of chance. The women seeks pebbles and throws one towards the top of the standing stone. The pebble must lodge on the top. Success at the first throw is a favourable omen, and she can continue to make other attempts in a determined number of throws, usually twice seven. Finally the woman makes a vow, expecting her prayer to be answered.

Identical practices are known in France, for example at the Menhir de la Gamerie at Avrillé (Vendée), which is always topped by a small pile of pebbles. It is probable that this stone was never put up with this intention and there has been some sort of change of use from its forgotten primary function, just as in Madagascar, 10,000 km (6215 miles) away.

9. The Near East: Syria, Lebanon, Israel, and Jordan

More than 15,000 years ago the exploitation of wild cereals began between Sinaï and Syria. It was at the same time that upper palaeolithic people in western Europe created their finest works of art in the depths of caves and hunted reindeer in the cold. In time, the troglodyte Natufians of Judaea, who had the benefit of fields of wild cereals, gathered together in villages of circular huts and buried their dead in a communal cemetery.

Nearly 350 m (1148 ft) below sea-level, in a torrid desert, is the verdant oasis of Jericho, north of the Dead Sea and west of the Jordan. By 8000 BC it was already an agglomeration of 2000 to 3000 inhabitants, covering a surface area of 4 hectares (10 acres) and surrounded by a wall almost 3 m (10 ft) thick and 6–7 m (20–23 ft) high, according to estimates by Kathleen Kenyon, who directed excavation there from 1952 onwards. This impressive wall was reinforced on the outside by a ditch 8 m (26 ft) wide and 2.7 m (9 ft) deep. Also at Jericho was found a round tower from the same period, 10 m (33 ft) in diameter and still standing 9 m ($29\frac{1}{2}$ ft) high. During this time the inhabitants cultivated the alluvium, growing cereals (bread-wheat and two-row barley) and legumes (lentils and peas); they hunted gazelle, which provided their meat. They did not yet use pots of fired clay, so the name 'Pre-Pottery Neolithic A' is given to this period. They lived in round houses built with bricks shaped like 'asses' backs', and some archaeologists think that a system of irrigation for the cultivated areas could have existed as far back as the eighth millennium BC. It is difficult to imagine the rampart being built, the ditch being dug, and an irrigation system being organised without a minimum of social hierarchy and division of labour. This would have been the first organised society known.

A new population occupied Jericho from the seventh millennium BC, living in four-sided houses, still built of brick, but from now on bonded by mortar. Goat-rearing gradually replaced gazelle-hunting. A second wall of larger stones was built towards 6000 BC. From this period date the famous human skulls with plaster masks found inside the walls of

Jericho, a sort of ancestor-worship and family portrait-gallery. However, the town was abandoned from the beginning of the sixth millennium, and no other people settled there for almost 1000 years. Although they were familiar with pottery, these later occupants were not great architects and are not known to have built any walls. It was not until later on, at 3000 BC and with a knowledge of bronze, that another group occupy Jericho. These people buried their dead in chambers let into the ground at the bottom of shafts. During the next 1800 years the walls of Jericho were rebuilt a score of times, showing the insecurity of the period, with occupation of the site by different peoples, interspersed by periods of abandonment. Then came Joshua, and the biblical battle of Jericho, which felled the walls around 1500 BC with the sound of trumpets.

The megalithic cemetery of Ala-Safat, Jordan

A pupil of the Abbé Breuil, Moshe Stékélis was probably the archaeologist who worked hardest towards a knowledge of megalith-building in the Near East. We owe to him especially the 1933 excavation of the El-Adeimeh cemetery some 15 km (9 miles) south-east of Jericho. In his publication, the author gives a list of all the sites known in Palestine about 1930. But Stékélis' excavations at El-Adeimeh essentially concern more or less megalithic cists, built with rude stone blocks, and often covered by a mound. Oriented east-west, they all contained a single body in a flexed position and were accompanied by hearths close by. This vast cemetery covering 25 km² (10 sq. miles) comprises 'a hundred great chamber-tombs, numerous cists, mounds, stone enclosures and other rude stone structures'. There is nothing to indicate that these monuments are all of the same period. Stékélis attributed this cemetery to the town of Teleilat-Ghassul, and more precisely to its lowest level which is dated to the Bronze Age (the third millennium BC, perhaps the second half of the fourth), which seems plausible with regard to what we know about funerary customs of the inhabitants of Jericho at the period.

Figure 57   Megalithic monuments in the Near East. (After M. Stékélis)
Distribution map. Megalithic monuments occur in the hatched area.
1. Two-storey chamber-tomb in the Ala-Safat cemetery, Jordan, chamber-tomb 84.
2–3. Megalithic monuments between Khirbert Haufa and Ham, Jordan.
4. Ala-Safat monument 11.
5. Ala-Safat monument 23.
6. Ala-Safat monument 19.
7. Ala-Safat monument 13
8. Ala-Safat monument 146, carved out of a monolithic block.

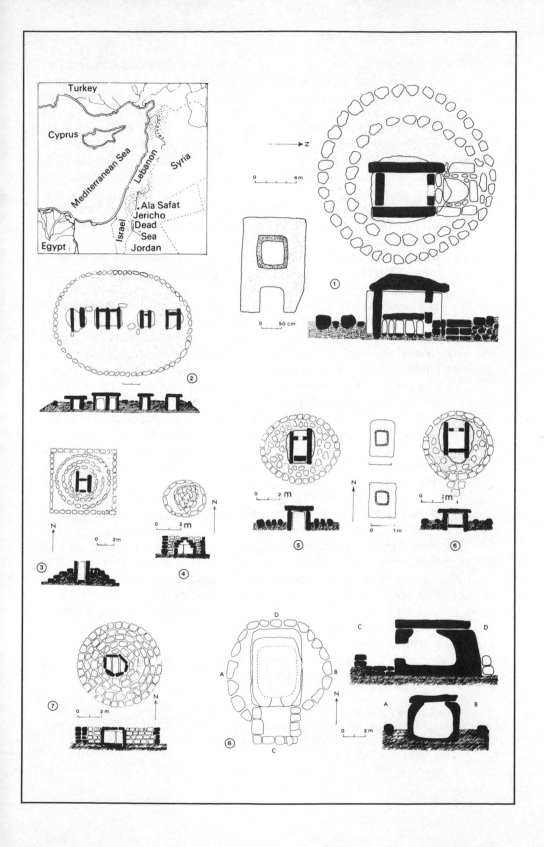

Turkey

Cyprus

Mediterranean Sea

Lebanon

Syria

Israel

Egypt

Ala Safat

Jericho

Dead

Sea

Jordan

0   4m

0   50 cm

0   2m

N

0   2m

N

0   2m

N

0   2m

0   1m

5

6

3

4

7

8

1

2

Z

N

N

C   D

A   B

C

D

A   B

0   2m

More important for the present purpose is the 1961 publication by Stékélis of his excavation work at Ala-Safat (Figures 57 and 58), a huge cemetery 4 km ($2\frac{1}{2}$ miles) long by 2 km ($1\frac{1}{4}$ miles) wide, set on the eastern foothills overlooking the Jordan to the north-west of Jericho. These monuments had first been noted by Irby and Mangles during their *Journey through Egypt and Nubia, Syria and Asia Minor in 1816–17*. According to Stékélis' inventory, this group comprises almost 200 monuments, divided as follows: 164 chamber-tombs, 14 cists, two circular tombs, three chamber-tombs cut from a monolithic block, one tomb followed into a monolithic block, 12 stone circles, and two mounds. But the circular tombs in particular seem to be of a more recent date and might belong to the Iron Age. Built from blocks of local limestone, the Jordan Valley chamber-tombs are usually made up of five stone slabs; the side-walls are the longest and overlap the end slab and the entrance slab. The whole defines a four-sided space, the chamber; and the gaps left between the standing stones are filled with smaller stones, to close off the funerary space. In most of the monuments, whose roof is made of a single slab sometimes more than 3 m (10 ft) long and 25–70 cm (10–28 in) thick, the entrance-slab has a rectangular opening permitting successive deposits into the chamber. The edges of the hole are grooved, indicating that a movable section, perhaps wooden, closed the access. Often the floor of the chamber is covered by a large limestone slab. At Ala-Safat, some chamber-tombs have two-storey chambers. The entrance-slab then has two holes, one above the other, corresponding to the two superimposed cells; these are separated by a slab supported half way up by two lateral rows of small juxtaposed slabs. This is particularly clear with chamber-tomb 84 of the cemetery (Figure 57:1). In front of the porthole-slab opens a passage just the same width as the chamber. Its side-walls are normally built of superimposed stones set flat, and the entrance to the passage is itself closed in the same way, giving the whole more the appearance of an antechamber than that of a true access-passage. It seems that numerous offerings were made in this four-sided paved area. The chamber-antechamber ensemble is enclosed inside a circular space bounded by large rocks; they must have served as foundations for a mound, mostly now disappeared.

Sometimes several chamber-tombs are covered by a single mound, but this does not seem to occur at Ala-Safat. Again, the monument may be inside a four-sided enclosure.

Figure 58   Megalithic monuments in the Near East: Ala-Safat, Jordan. (Drawn by R. Joussaume after photographs by M. Stékélis)
1. *Chamber-tomb 103.*
2. *Chamber-tomb 26.*

1

2

At Ala-Safat, three monuments of the chamber-tomb type have been made from single monolithic blocks. The block was hollowed out from the top and the chamber established inside it. The fore-part was shaped to make the four-sided aperture, and a roofing slab closed the hole through which the chamber had been hollowed out of the mass (Figure 57:8). The chamber made this way was surrounded by a stone circle, whose uselessness as a practical means of retaining a mound we note. The stone circle surrounding the chamber-tomb must have had a symbolic value. Like the chamber-tombs made of slabs set edgewise, these monolithic chamber-tombs are preceded by a four-sided ante-chamber, a place for offerings in front of the entrance hole. Most often the chamber-tombs have their opening to the north, but in some cases they are oriented east-west with the hole facing the rising sun. There seems a desire for orientation among the Palestinian chamber-tombs. Alongside the chamber-tombs of Ala-Safat there exist completely closed monuments, made of upright stones defining a more or less polygonal chamber, roofed by small slabs which may even form corbelling. The whole is supported by a 'collar' of stones, bounded by a built wall. These monuments are morphologically very close to those found in North Africa, and also in the Arabian peninsula as far as the Yemen (Figure 57:7).

Stékélis noted two types of inhumation in the cemetery. In the first the bodies are deposited in a drawn-up position, surrounded by small stones and covered by a slab. There are several skeletons in one chamber. However, cremation seems to have been the more common practice, and several bundles of burnt bones were found in the tombs' chambers, which were therefore collective graves, or ossuaries. Numerous calcined human remains were found inside the large stone circles of the cemetery, and we can wonder whether these surfaces were areas dedicated to the practice of burning the bodies, whose remains were later deposited in the megalithic monuments. The two types of structure would therefore be complementary. Offerings were left in the chambers, but the greatest number were found in the antechamber at the foot of the hole cut into the entrance slab. They consisted mainly of pots, which must have contained some product, perhaps resins or aromatic herbs, or food for the journey into the beyond. The monuments were in use for a long time, but the antechambers, made of dry-stone, rapidly fell down, effectively protecting the remains inside them, which are well preserved. This is the earliest archaeological material in the cemetery; according to researchers, it belonged to a farming population, living in tells and cultivating the fertile soil of the Jordan Valley, probably in the fourth millennium BC at the earliest. This early megalithic culture of the Jordan Valley is called Ghassulian. Later on, the monuments were re-utilised several times, after emptying the funerary chamber, over perhaps 1000 years.

Other megalithic monuments of the Near East

The largest Near Eastern concentration of monuments of chamber-tomb type is in Jordan, east of the river. Often there are very large cemeteries grouping together several dozen chamber-tombs. However, megaliths are also known to the west of the river Jordan, but seemingly more dispersed. According to Moshe Stékélis, 'megalithic monuments are always found on plateaux or on the valley-slopes. They are often associated with springs, or close by them.' We note that chamber-tombs are relatively rare west of the Jordan, in Judaea and Samaria, where there are more often found dry-stone monuments with particular characteristics, such as the one called 'Oobour bene Israil' (Tomb of the children of Israel), to the north of Jerusalem. These are long structures, sometimes over 50 m (164 ft) long by 5–6 m (16½–20 ft) wide and 2 m (6½ ft) high, bounded by stone walls and containing a more or less megalithic chamber. There seems to be little established dating for all these monuments. They could be later than the crude stone monuments described as dolmens. Chamber-tombs are also noted in Galilee, around Lake Tiberias (the Sea of Galilee, Yam Kinneret), where thousands of megalithic structures are known in Djolan: 'Dolmens, sometimes still under tumuli, rude stone structures of different types, standing stones, single or set into alignments, and stone enclosures.'

Schumacher, in 1896, discovered in Adjloun 15 or so vast cemeteries with simple-shaped chamber-tombs, their relatively small rectangular chambers, covered by roofing slabs up to 4 m (13 ft) long.

The *Naoumi* of Sinai are not exactly dolmens. They are round, oval, rectangular or square monuments, built of dry-stone, which measure from 2 m (6½ ft) to 3.5 m (11½ ft) in diameter and up to 3 m (10 ft) in height. They have a false-corbelled roof and are entered by a square door. Comparable monuments are known as far as the south Arabian peninsula, but their dating is not established, although they appear more recent than the chamber-tombs in general.

In Syria and Lebanon, the work of Tallon in particular has made known a number of megalithic groups. The Freiké group, in the Ghâb plain of the Orontes valley, comprises 'single dolmenic chambers, square or rectangular in shape, with a very short entrance passage or a simple door marked by two long stones lying on edge, perpendicular to the east wall of the monument'. All the entrances open to the east, which is a notable difference from the monuments of Ala-Safat, more usually oriented to the north. The chambers measure around 2 m (6½ ft) wide by 2–3 m (6½–10 ft) long, and the passage is not more than 1.2 m (4 ft) long. They would have been covered by an earthen mound and the hypothesis has been put forward that several chamber-tombs may have lain under the same mound. According to Tallon, the existence of this cemetery, which presupposes occupation of the surrounding land, was linked to the fertility of the Orontes valley.

Other groups have been recognised by the same author in the Tleil-Moungez (Akkar) region, where seven types have been distinguished in the environs of Tleil. We note, among others, circular paved chambers, whose diameter can be more than 2 m (6½ ft). Near Moungez, certain chambers are roofed by stone slabs, and others have corbelled roofs. One of the monuments has a square chamber 2 m (6½ ft) by 2.15 m (7 ft), edged by orthostats up to 90 cm (35 in) high; a door to the south opens on to a 2.2 m (7 ft) long passage, 70 cm (27 in) wide. In general 'the square or rectangular chambers are of more modest proportions than round or oval cells'.

The Syria-Lebanon cemeteries are sited on the high plateaux at the foot of the mountains. Writing in 1958, Tallon, like most researchers who have studied the Near Eastern megaliths, said the Syria-Lebanon chamber-tombs were built at the beginning of the third millennium BC. Unfortunately, I do not know whether more recent publications have modified this date.

Megalith-building and the Bible

We cannot leave the Near East without a word about the standing stones mentioned in the Bible.

> And Jacob went out from Beer-sheba, and went toward Haran. And he lighted upon a certain place, and tarried there all night, because the sun was set; and took of the stones of that place, and put them for his pillows, and lay down in that place to sleep. . . . And Jacob rose up early in the morning, and took the stone that he had put for his pillows, and set it up for a pillar, and poured oil upon the top of it. And he called the name of that place Beth-el. . . . And this stone, which I have set for a pillar, shall be God's house . . .
>
> *Genesis 28, verses 10–11, 18–19, 22*

This tradition, of pouring oil on stones set upright, is found in many countries, on some *menhirs* of the Atlantic west, in India and in some African countries. This custom, and many others related to the stones, brought down the anger of the Church, which was the instigator of the destruction of large numbers of megalithic monuments. Allusions to building stone altars, mounds and standing stones are fairly frequent in the Bible. After receiving the Ten Commandments on Sinai, Moses 'rose up early in the morning, and builded an altar under the hill, and twelve pillars, according to the twelve tribes of Israel'. (*Exodus 24, verse 4*). In fact, most of the time these were simply commemorative or symbolic stones – as are many standing stones in the world – but nowhere is there a biblical mention of a chamber-tomb, a burial monument in rude stone and not to be confused with altars, which may be stone slabs resting on several supports.

10. The Caucasus

Between the Black Sea and the Caspian Sea, the Caucasus occupied a dominant position all through the third millennium BC, which was due, above all, to its great mineral resources.

A 'royal' burial: the *kurgan* of Maïkop

The *kurgan* or mound of Maïkop was studied in 1897 by the Russian archaeologist N. I. Vesselovsky. The town of Maikop is on the south side of the river Kuban, on the lower northern slopes of the Caucasus mountains. The mound, whose sides had been partly destroyed, stood almost 11 m (36 ft) high; it concealed a pit with rounded corners, lined with wooden logs and planks, that was 5.33 m ($17\frac{1}{2}$ ft) long by 3.73 m ($12\frac{1}{4}$ ft) wide. Its base was cobbled, and its roof was made of a double ceiling of logs between which a layer of earth had been spread. Its long axis was north-south. The burial pit was divided into two parts, north and south, by a wooden partition, and the northern part was subdivided in two along the north-south axis. Each of the three divisions held one skeleton, laid on its back with legs folded. In the southern, largest cell, the deceased occupied the central position along the axis of the pit and had been covered with red ochre, a very ancient custom which we meet in numerous sites of the ancient world. It was accompanied by very rich goods. By contrast, the two bodies in the northern cells, similarly deposited in the middle of their cells, had been only lightly powdered with ochre and had only a few objects to accompany them on their journey: a few gold and cornelian beads, ear-rings of gold and silver, fired-clay pots. Some would see these as the wives of the 'royal' deceased, others as slaves – in either case two sacrifices.

It seems that the chief personage had been buried beneath a sort of canopy of fabric or leather, scattered with small golden beads and stamped shapes of the same metal, of which 70 represented lions, 23 bulls and 40 were ring-shaped. This canopy seems to have been supported on six silver tubes almost 1 m (3 ft) long, of which four were set into statuettes of bulls. Perhaps the man wore a tiara made of two golden diadems decorated with double rosettes and temple-rings in solid gold. At the level of the neck was a collar of beads of gold, lapis lazuli, turquoise, and cornelian. At the level of the knees lozenge-shaped arrowheads were found, as well as flint knife-blades.

In the south-eastern corner lay 10 copper objects – axes, picks, scissors, daggers. Analysis of the copper shows that it contains nickel, non-existent in the Caucasus, which proves their importation from Iran, Near Asia or Anatolia. Along the east wall, 14 silver vases, two of gold and the golden ferrule of a ritual club had been placed. The decorated vases represented animals and a landscape which could correspond to the Caucasus mountains. Specialists see in 'the theme of the animals walking in a circle its very ancient roots in the east, in Sumerian symbolism'. On the other side, near the western wall, was a row of eight clay pots. According to Zavitoukhina and Piotrovsky, 'among the great diversity of forms of Near Eastern pottery, it is among Syrian ceramic of the second half of the fourth millennium BC that we find the closest analogies with the clay and metal pots of Maïkop'. Also in this sepulchral chamber were exceptional funerary goods: a great clay pot with a conical base in the north-west corner, and copper utensils in the south-west corner, comprising a flat cup, a small bucket with a handle, and a large jug, as well as a large and a small cauldron.

The *kurgan* of Maïkop, by its richness, seems to be that of a tribal chief, perhaps even the head of a federation of tribes.

Burials of the Maïkop culture

Based on this exceptional discovery and 40 or so other sites, essentially *kurgans* but also some of settlements, a 'Maïkop culture' was defined; according to Tadeuz Sulimirski, it was formed under the impact of the Kura-Araxes and Sachkhere cultures of Transcaucasus. Two sub-groups have been recognised: the first to the west, south of the river Kuban, and the other to the east, in the region of Pyatigorsk-Nalchik. This culture occupies the second half of the third millennium BC.

South of Maïkop, in the Belaya valley, excavation of the site of Meshoko has revealed two levels in this culture. Usually, settlements are sited in naturally protected places, by the edge of a ravine or on a spur, and provided with a defensive system in the weakest parts of this natural protection – a ditch backed up by a palisade or even a wall. At Meshoko the houses established on the periphery, backing on to the palisade, are rectangular in plan and reach an average of 12 m (39 ft) long by 4 m (13 ft) wide. The central part of the site served as an enclosure for livestock. This is a method of habitation very widespread in eastern Europe, where it is already the plan adopted by the chalcolithic farmers of the Tripolye culture north of the Black Sea from the fourth millennium BC. At Tripolye, as later in the Maïkop culture, bull-worship occurred, and we recall the four magnificent statuettes of bulls from the canopy of the Maïkop *kurgan*.

Burials in the Maïkop culture were in pits beneath mounds (*kurgan*), a mode of burial which occupies the third and second millennia BC, in a huge area of steppe extending from southern Siberia to the Caucasus. But in the villages themselves, flat tombs existed. The tomb itself can be a coffer of stone slabs or be bounded by rows of wooden logs. These individual burials are accompanied by a few offerings – one or two vases and sometimes a small copper knife. Three 'royal' mounds have been found, two at Novovosbodnaya, and the one at Maïkop, of which we have seen the richness of the funerary deposit.

Two phases have been identified in the Maïkop culture. While metal was imported during the first phase, the objects from the second were produced from local wrought metal. But the first period saw greater development in the west, while the eastern areas, Pyatigorsk and Nalchik, belong rather to the second phase, as if there had been a displacement from west to east.

One hundred and twenty burials were found in the Nalchik *kurgan*, which consisted of 120 small close-set mounds covered over by one barrow. As at Maïkop, the skeletons were laid on their back with their legs drawn up. They were in a shallow pit. Later, the crouching position prevailed. Usually these are the poor burials from a whole population over a long period; one of the latest dates from the middle of the second millennium BC.

The origin of the Maïkop culture is hard to establish. Some authors favour the development from some local neolithic substratum, unfortunately so far unknown. Others think the local substratum of mesolithic hunters evolved under the influence of Transcaucasian groups. Finally there are some who recognise in certain tombs of the Maïkop culture area, south of the river Kuban, burials proper to the Yamnaya culture from the steppes north of the Kuban. These people also used to bury their dead laid on their back with their legs bent. Whatever the origin of the culture, it certainly acquired great wealth, at least at the level of its ruling class. But we can ponder the origin of this material richness and the reasons for it. Researchers have established that some of the metal objects and semi-precious stones in Maïkop *kurgan* came from Anatolia and Syria, others from Iran and India. We should remember these links with India and the Indus culture, as well as with Syria, two areas with megalithic monuments. The Maïkop culture indicates that objects and ideas travelled from Syria and India into the Caucasus, and we know that the inhabitants of Mohenjo Daro had had contacts with the Mesopotamians, all at the end of the third millennium BC. Other connections have been established between the Maïkop culture and Sumerian art, as well as with Troy II in Anatolia, the town which was destroyed towards 2300 BC. Eastern prospectors seeking mineral ore disembarked at the mouth of the Kuban, the easiest way to reach the metalliferous sites still unexplored in the Caucasus mountains. We may consider that these prospectors paid tribute to the inhabitants of the place for a safe passage, which would augment the riches of the local chiefs. The destruction of Troy II is perhaps the origin of change in the Maïkop culture, and of the transition into its second phase, called Novovosbodnaya, when the people produced their own metal objects and imported produce from different regions. The destruction of Troy II is attributed to a first wave of Indo-European invasion, arriving from the north (the Balkans and Romania). In the second millennium, the North Caucasian culture succeeded Maïkop. The influence of Near Asia disappeared.

Chamber-tombs of the western Caucasus

In the western Caucasus, edged by the Kuban river and on the territory of the Abhasy, chamber-tombs (Figure 59) occupy a huge surface; they were first noted by P. S. Pallas in 1794. The megalithic territory partly overlaps that of the Maïkop culture, which we have therefore been obliged to present here. The chamber-tombs are concentrated in the metalliferous zone where the first copper-mining in the Caucasus took place. L. I. Lavrov produced a typological classification of the Caucasus chamber-tombs in 1960 (Figure 59:5). He had then recognised 1139 monuments, but it seems there used to be many more, with concentrations of 200 chamber-tombs, and even 500, if we are to believe Sulimirski, at sites between the Laba and Belaya rivers.

The first type, the most widespread, is a 'rectangular cist, whose vertical sections as well as the roof and, often, the base seem each to be made of one monolithic slab'. V. I. Markovin, from whom we have taken a good part of this information, adds that the shape of the chamber is often trapezoidal, the slabs being carefully adjusted, often with grooves and projections on the roofing slabs and the uprights. In

Figure 59   Chamber-tombs in the Caucasus.
Distribution map. Megalithic monuments occur in the hatched area.
1. Saint-Nicolas, on the river Atakhoum. (After Dubois de Montpéreux in E. Chantre, Recherches anthropologiques dans le Caucase)
2. Pchada valley. (After photograph by A. M. Tallgren in T. Sulimirski, Prehistoric Russia)
3. Pchada valley. (After Bayern in E. Chantre, Recherches anthropologiques dans le Caucase)
4. Pchada valley. (After Bayern in E. Chantre, Recherches anthropologiques dans le Caucase)
5. The different types of megalithic monuments in the Caucasus. (After V. I. Markovin)

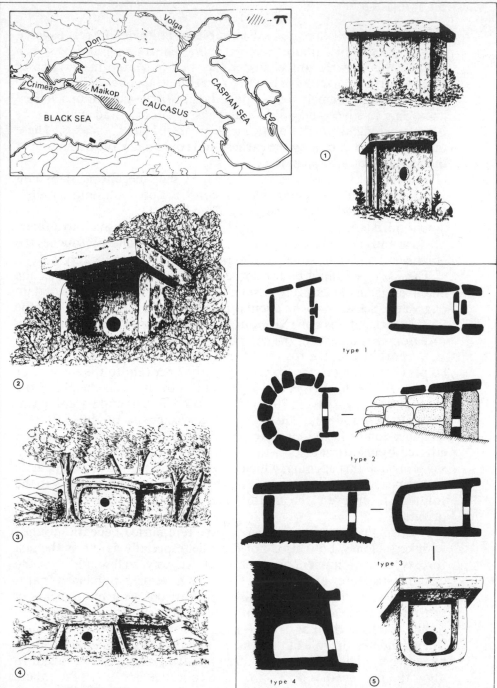

BLACK SEA

Crimea

Maikop

Don

Volga

CAUCASUS

CASPIAN SEA

① ② ③ ④

type 1

type 2

type 3

type 4

⑤

the Novovosbodnaya region exist double megalithic chambers covered by a single slab or a double-pitched roof, beneath a mound. Between the chamber and the antechamber the transverse slab has a circular perforation – a porthole-slab. The archaeological material inside these monuments is extremely rich: copper daggers, pick-axes, hooks, hafted axes, pins in silver and gold, cauldrons of bronze, and many more objects belonging to the early metal phase of the Caucasus. These monuments are probably the earliest and could mark the beginning of the megalithic tradition in the Caucasus.

The second type is a mixed model, in that megalithic slabs and superimposed blocks enter into its construction, outlining circular, horseshoe-shaped, or even polyhedral surfaces.

Our third type is a trough-shaped monument, hollowed into a block of stone and covered by a slab usually shaped to fit where it touches the chamber. This is a relatively rare type and limited as to locality.

The last type cannot be considered to be a chamber-tomb, since the chamber is made entirely inside a monolithic block. But certain characteristics, such as the circular perforation of the entrance and the fact that it contains collective burials, cannot dissociate the architecture from monuments of the chamber-tomb type.

A report by L. I. Lavrov establishes that out of 400 chamber-tombs, 80 per cent belong to the first type, nearly 7 per cent to the second, 11 per cent to the third type, and 2 per cent to the last. The height of the monument can vary from 70 cm (28 in) to 2.4 m (8 ft) and its length can be up to 5.4 m (18 ft). The essential characteristic of the Caucasus chamber-tombs is the circular perforation, occasionally four-sided, effected by the front slab of the monument. A groove has often been made around this opening, which was closed by a stone plug. The hole never opens to the north; usually it is to the east, but occasionally to the south-east, or even the south. The monuments are deliberately oriented.

It seems that certain chamber-tombs were buried beneath mounds with kerb-stones, but this is not the rule, especially as far as the last three types of monument are concerned. Anyway, so few studies of the external structures of the chamber-tombs have been published that it would be very difficult to establish comparisons with monuments in other countries, such as those of India or Palestine, where chamber-tombs also have circular or four-sided perforations. Researchers have often pondered the role of these holes in the Caucasus chamber-tombs, as elsewhere. Their diameter is often relatively small, but sufficient to allow the passage of a body into these collective graves. In fact, there would have been no question of removing the roofing-slab to put a new body in, especially when it weighed more than 20 tonnes; nor would it have been possible to re-enter the rock-cut tombs.

The Caucasian chamber-tombs were collective graves. The first burials seem to have been placed in the corners in a sitting position, with the legs stretched out. We note the difference in funerary ritual from the *kurgans* of the Maïkop culture; indeed the position recalls that of the mother-goddess figures in terracotta of the neolithic populations of eastern Europe. But the Caucasian chamber-tombs also received bones as secondary burials, after decarnation in another place. To explain these different burial rites, Markovin recalls observations recorded in the seventeenth century by Archangelo Lamberti and Giovanni da Duca about the western Caucasus: the Colchidians put male bodies into trees, while the female were buried in the ground. This sexual differentiation may not apply to the people of the chamber-tombs, whose anthropological characteristics do not seem to have been studied closely. We note that there are both primary and secondary inhumations in the Caucasian chamber-tombs, without our really knowing whether the two rituals are contemporaneous or whether there was re-use of the chamber-tombs, which we know to have been used over a long period. In fact, the first monuments date from the first age of metal-working, in the second half of the third millennium BC, but we also find them in the middle Bronze Age Eshery culture, and at the beginning of the Iron Age, up to nearly 1000 BC. The three stages of occupation may exist in one and the same monument.

There is some confusion in the writings of different researchers, and it is not always easy to orientate oneself. In the latest of Markovin's studies that we have read, he considers that the earliest chamber-tombs served for individual burials; that during the period of expansion of Caucasian megalith-building several bodies were put in a seated position in the corners and along the walls; and that the latest chamber-tombs served as ossuaries. Tomb furnishings can be divided into chronological groups occupying a slice of time from 2400 to 1400 BC.

Engraved symbols have been found on the interior and exterior sides of the tomb uprights: zigzags, broken lines, tooth shapes, dashes, runnels, and cup-marks. Leschenko finds several links between these signs and the art of the Maïkop *kurgan*, and he would connect the engravings on the chamber-tombs with a water cult. All this is not very convincing. In fact, the links which exist between the Maïkop culture and the populations who made the chamber-tombs, of whom unhappily no village-site has been found, are very difficult to establish.

'The earliest monuments of the chamber-tomb culture of the Kuban basin are the chamber-tombs beneath mounds of the Novovosbodnaya.' These would be individual burials, which would bring them closer to the *kurgans* and flat tombs of the Maïkop culture. They have a slab perforated by a circular hole, which would link them with the Caucasian chamber-tombs of the Abhasy region. They would be a sort of junction between the two cultures, and could indicate a local origin for Caucasian megalith-building.

Of course, there have already been suggestions of links between the Caucasus and India at the end of the third millennium BC, and the (more recent) Indian monuments could have a Caucasian origin. As for links between the Caucasus and Syria at the same period, they could explain possible relations between the Palestinian chamber-tombs, built from the fourth millennium BC onwards, and those of the Caucasus. But all this remains very conjectural, in that a local origin for Caucasian megaliths is distinctly possible.

However, there are other chamber-tombs on the edge of the Black Sea, also in the southern Crimea, where they are noted in the Gaspra and Aloutcha areas and in the Baydar Valley. Many were covered by an earthen mound and surrounded by a stone circle. But we have no information regarding them, nor for those on the shores of Bulgaria, where 60 or so were listed to the north of Andrinopolis at the beginning of this century. But we do know that chamber-tomb structures with pierced slabs have been noted in Thrace. There could be a link between all these monuments around the Black Sea, but that deserves deeper study than we have yet been able to achieve.

We will end this chapter by recalling a legend, reported by Chantre in his 1885 book *Recherches anthropologiques dans le Caucase*, regarding the chamber-tombs of this land:

> To the Bagovski, the dolmens, which they considered to be very old, were the dwellings of a race of dwarves which once occupied the area, and the work of a race of giants, their neighbours, who, pitying their weakness, built these solid shelters for them. The hole pierced in one of the slabs was the entrance of the dwelling. According to this legend, the giants had such strength that they could carry on their shoulders all the stones needed for the buildings.

11. India

Megalithic monuments are numerous, especially in southern peninsular India, although some groups appear in the north, into Kashmir
and not far from the Nepalese frontier. The most western group is in
Pakistan, north of Karachi, and the most eastern on the frontier
between Assam and Bangladesh, where there persist degenerate forms
of megalith-building at the present day (Figure 60).

Modern megalith-builders in India

We must record here what James Fergusson tells us in a book of 1872
about a population living in the Khassia mountains, an area between
the Assam valley and the plains of Sylhet:

> Throughout the whole of the portion of the hilly region, inhabited by tribes
> bearing the generic name of Khassias, rude-stone monuments exist in
> greater numbers than perhaps in any other portions of the globe. . . .
>   The Khassias burn their dead . . . during three months in the year, it is
> impossible, from the rain, to light a fire out of doors and consequently, if
> anyone dies during that period, the body is placed in a coffin, formed from
> the hollowed trunk of a tree, and pickled in honey, until a fine day admits of
> his obsequies being properly performed. . . . The urns containing the ashes
> are placed in little circular cells, with flat tops like stools, which exist in the
> immediate proximity of all the villages, and are used as seats by the villagers
> on all state occasions of assembly. . . .
>   The origin of the menhirs is a little different. If any of the members of the
> Khassia tribe falls ill or gets into difficulties, he prays to some one of his
> deceased ancestors, whose spirit he fancies may be able and willing to assist
> him . . . to strengthen his prayer, he vows that, if it is granted, he will erect a
> stone in honour of the deceased. This he never fails to perform, and if the
> cure has been rapid, or the change in luck so sudden as to be striking, others
> address their prayers to the same person, and more stones are vowed. It thus
> sometimes happens that a person, man or woman, who was by no means
> remarkable in life, may have five, or seven, or ten – two fives, for the number
> must always be unequal – erected in their honour. The centre stone
> generally is crowned by a capital, or turban-like ornament, and sometimes
> two stones are joined together, forming a trilithon. . . .

The origin of the stone tables or dolmens is not so clearly made out. Like the tomb stools, they frequently at least seem to be places of assembly. One ... measured 30 feet 10 inches [about 9 m] by 10 feet [about 3 m] in breadth, and had an average thickness of 1 foot [30 cm]; it had steps to ascend it; and certainly it looks like a place from which it would be convenient to address an audience. The great stone of this monument weighed more than 23 tons 18 cwt, and another is described as measuring 30 feet [about 9 m] by 13 feet [about 4 m], and 1 foot 4 inches [40 cm] in thickness; and they are frequently raised some height from the ground, and supported on massive monoliths or pillars.

If the term '*menhir*' could at a pinch be applied to the stones set up by the Khassias, there is no question of calling these stone tables dolmens or chamber-tombs, as they have only a distant relationship with the funerary monuments of other countries. Fergusson thinks that any rude stone slab laid flat constitutes a dolmen. This almost-contemporary tradition of megalith-building in Assam is comparable to that found in many of the south-east Asian islands of Indonesia, Malaysia, and the Philippines, but it seems that it should be clearly dissociated from the megalith-building of peninsular India, which seems to be much earlier.

In the course of a mission in 1925 to the heart of Tibet, N. Roerich discovered, near the lake of Pang-gong at Do-ring, alignments of standing stones in 18 parallel rows, which ended in two concentric semi-circles of standing stones. At their centre rose an altar made of three blocks. We can make formal comparisons with the Carnac alignments in the Morbihan (France), but also with those at Mohamdid-al-Hamli in the Arab Republic of Yemen. It is very difficult to see anything other than coincidence between these three sites, so geographically distant one from another. Many other standing stones are known in Tibet and Bhutan.

In 1984 Michel Peissel recounted his meeting with the Minaro people, whose rituals he studied in Kashmir. This white population, pre-Aryan according to the author, lived in a matriarchal system where the women often had several husbands. Set apart from many currents of civilization, this people, now only a few hundred individuals, retained a deep memory of their prehistoric past; when the men had been ibex-hunters, they drew pictures of it on the rocks as a sign of thanks to the gods. The Minaro buried their dead, laid on the right side, with legs bent, and hands beneath the head. This is not a custom among the Himalayan Buddhists, who usually burn their dead on pyres, sometimes cutting them into pieces which they leave for the vultures or throw into the rivers.

The Minaro erect stones on several occasions, but most often to mark the seasons. Thus near the village of Gyagam, six standing stones on the skyline indicate different days in the year, such as solstices and equinoxes. But they also build altars of stone, formed of one slab resting on three uprights, which sometimes have two storeys. Set up at the foot of the mountain, these tables served as altars to the divinities who lived among the peaks. As always when a slab is laid flat on top of several stones, these monuments have been called dolmens by those who come across them, though incorrectly, as a dolmen is first and foremost a closed monument with a funerary purpose.

A little Indian history

Like an enormous spearhead burying itself deep in the Indian Ocean, bordered to the east by the Gulf of Bengal and to the west by the Sea of Oman, bounded to the north by the Himalayan mountain barrier and to the north-west by that of the Hindu Kush and Beluchistan, the Indian subcontinent seems to be impenetrable territory. The northern Indus-Ganges plain is divided from the Deccan plateau by the Thar Desert and the Vindhya mountains. The Deccan, a huge area with a harsh climate, where cultivation is difficult, forms a triangular plateau, higher to the west (with the chain of the Western Ghats) than to the east. To the south, the coastal plain with its temperate climate is still occupied by the dark-skinned Dravidians who were the first immigrants. It was during the fifth millennium BC that the first farming communities appeared on the edges of the Iranian plateau and the slopes of Beluchistan. They were the beginnings of the brilliant Harappan or Indus civilisation, which flourished between 2500 and 1500 BC. With ports on the Oman Sea, and the two capitals of Mohenjo Daro and Harappa, they occupied a huge territory drained by the Indus. They traded far afield, as far as Mesopotamia, where the famous seals carved with a bestiary were discovered. But the pictograms which accompany these animal representations are still undeciphered. The towns of brick houses, opening on an interior court, were quadrangular in plan; they were dominated by a citadel, which was both an administrative and a religious focus. The Harappans are known to have had the best sanitary arrangements of the ancient world. Their pottery was made on a wheel, and they were the first producers of cotton.

But what exactly happened around 1500 BC? No one knows precisely. The fact is that at Mohenjo Daro we see a period of decline, and the upper level of the city is strewn with bodies which seem to have been abandoned after a particularly violent attack. The same abandonment occurred at the city of Harappa, at the same time, but before decline had set in. Like a volcano erupting, central Asia was bubbling over and torrents of human lava flowed in all directions during this second millennium BC. Thus the Dorians settled in Greece, the Hittites in Anatolia, and the Aryans, the people who interest us here, filtering through the northern and eastern passes of Khyber, Karakoram, and Bolam, gradually occupied the Indus-Ganges plain. These nomadic barbarians, cattle-breeders, bearers of iron weapons, riding in light horse-drawn chariots, mark the end for the already-declining Harappans.

There was, practically speaking, a cultural void for 1000 years, from 1500 to 500 BC, a period often called the Vedic Age. It was the time when Brahminism was conceived and produced its four books, the *Vedas*, which concern the beliefs and practices of the religion, with their commentaries. The unconquered populations took refuge in the Deccan. It was these Dravidians who were the builders of megalithic monuments during the Vedic Age of the Indus-Ganges plain. They were gradually submerged by the Aryans, although these never reached the south of the peninsula. But the Dravidians had themselves already come up against the autochthonous people, considered to be troglodytes with negroid characteristics. Elsewhere isolated groups subsisted, characterised by the co-existence of matriarchal and of patriarchal societies.

The Vedic Age was succeeded by the Mauryan Empire, which was established progressively from 320 BC onwards by a young warrior-king, the Indian Chandragupta Maurya. His grandson Ashoka is the most famous of the dynasty, due to his generosity, gentleness and non-violence, qualities to which he became adherent after the massacre of hundreds of thousands of people. A convert to Buddhism, he succeeded in preaching it to almost the whole of the Indian peninsula. It is from the beginning of the present era that Buddhism began its decline in India.

Chamber-tombs in India

The Indian megalithic group is particularly large. It essentially occupies the Deccan peninsula, as we have said, with a few northern groups in Râjasthân, central India, Uttar Pradesh, Kashmir and towards the mouth of the Indus in Pakistan, in the Karachi area. Unfortunately studies are still few in number and not always very accessible.

Researchers are more or less in agreement that there are two types of chamber-tomb, according to whether they are built with trimmed flat slabs or, conversely, with untrimmed blocks.

Chamber-tombs of the first type are often called 'cists'. One of the best examples was excavated at Brahmagiri (Chitaldrug district, State of Mysore) in 1947 (Figure 61:1). The base of the chamber is formed by

Figure 60   Distribution map of megalithic monuments in the Indian subcontinent. Megalithic monuments occur in the hatched areas.

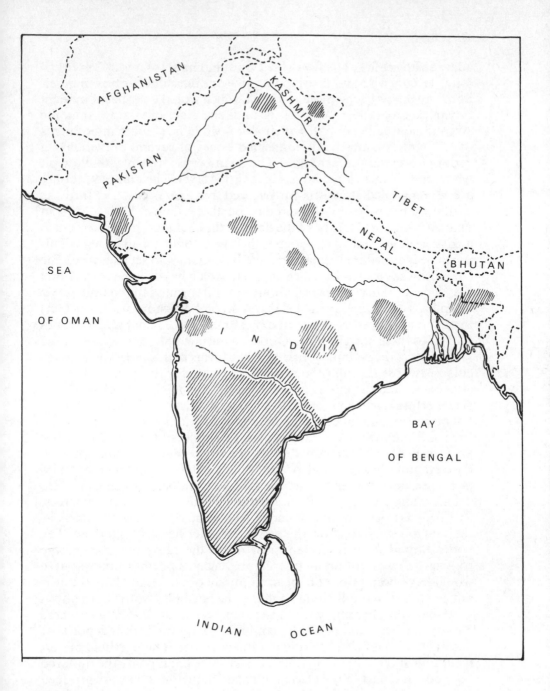

AFGHANISTAN

KASHMIR

PAKISTAN

TIBET

NEPAL

BHUTAN

SEA

OF OMAN

I N D I A

BAY

OF BENGAL

INDIAN   OCEAN

a large slab set flat. The four sides are standing slabs about 2 m (6½ ft) long, set edgewise and overlapping one another in a curious manner. Some see this as a schematic swastika, which would give the monument Aryan connotations; but this is unlikely, since we know that the Aryans habitually cremated their dead, while megalithic monuments of this type contain the disconnected bones of several individuals, a proof of previous decarnation. The chamber is let into a shallow pit which cuts through a neolithic-chalcolithic layer. The numerous bones are accompanied by wheel-thrown red and black pottery. Into the eastern slab has been cut a circular porthole almost 50 cm (20 in) in diameter, set 1 m (3 ft) above the floor of the chamber. It gives access to a passage at ground level, which is therefore about 1 m (3 ft) high. This porthole is closed on the passage side by a small slab set edgewise. The chamber was covered by a large flat slab which has disappeared. A first circular wall of drystone is set about 1 m (3 ft) around the chamber; it is bounded by a row of upright slabs. A second dry-stone wall, 1 m (3 ft) further out, is likewise supported by stone slabs. A final line of stones buttresses these upright slabs. Opposite the porthole, and so not on the same axis as the chamber with which it forms a 'q' shape, the passage cuts eastwards through the mound. It is lined with upright slabs on either side, and the end is closed by a relatively large block of stone. Architectural coincidences with features of Atlantic megalith-building are numerous and, of course, perturbing. Certain dolmenic chambers, such as Sittanaval, near Pudukkotai, in Tamilnad district (Madurai), are formed of a chamber divided into two by a transverse slab, which in that example has an oval perforation. So this monument has two portholes, one between the two parts of the chamber, the other between chamber and passage. N. R. Bannerjee considers that these portholes, and the passages, are not intended to give access to the chamber, as they are too small to allow the bones and offerings through them. The bodies would have been deposited all at the same time before the roofing-slab was put on, and structures such as porthole and passage would have been symbolic, or even purely ornamental. This thesis is difficult to maintain. It could be that some portholes would have only a symbolic value, but many could be functional, as at Brahmagiri, where passage as well as porthole could have allowed the deposit of decarnated bones and offerings in the chamber. The porthole monuments, most often opening to the east, can be counted by the hundred on the central part of the Deccan plateau. Sometimes they are grouped into vast cemeteries, like those at Rajankolur and Hire, and can have uprights more than 2 m (6½ ft) tall. B. Subbarao has noted the presence of 2000 megalithic tombs within a radius of 8 km (5 miles) around Brahmagiri.

The second type of chamber-tomb is made up of crude blocks; plans of a few are given in Figure 61. The mound often reaches the level of the roofing-slab or slabs. At Halingali (Figure 61:2) there is a transepted monument inside a circular mound faced with blocks of untrimmed stone, itself enclosed in a four-sided platform, also bordered by large blocks. The ensemble has an overall length of around 15 m (49 ft) and an average width of 12 m (39 ft). Such transepted monuments appear again at Terdal, where three transepted chamber-tombs may be enclosed in the same rectangular mound with double kerb. Still at Halingali are chamber-tombs with four-sided, fairly elongated chambers, with an axial passage, in mounds of various forms but most often circular. Square megalithic coffers are also enclosed in circular mounds with kerbs made of large blocks; sometimes other coffers develop around the periphery of a first round structure (Figure 61:5). Finally, there exist sub-circular chambers with access passage inside a mound which is also circular, with large kerb-stones. A chamber-tomb of this kind at Terdal is itself situated inside a polygonal enclosure (Figure 61:3). At the centre of these megalithic groups are wide, deep pits, covered by a cairn, often a low one, which is circled by a row of large stones. According to Sir Mortimer Wheeler, who was Director General of Archaeology in India, and to whom we owe a careful district-by-district survey of southern India, these pits were places of decarnation. The bones recovered from them would then have been deposited in the tombs' chambers.

Monuments of a rather special kind were erected in Kerala (South Western districts). These are, first, the *topikallus* or stone hats, monuments made of a cap-shaped hemispherical slab whose flat side rests on the tips of four uprights which join at the top. The bases of the four uprights are set into the ground, and define a four-sided area (Figure 61:7). Next are the *kudakallus* which, like the *topikallus*, are hemispherical blocks cut from laterite, but resting directly on the ground and concealing a pit. These *kudaïs* can be in groups and encircled by upright slabs leaning inwards. Also in Kerala, and at Hyderabad, authors note standing stones, *menhirs* which can be related to a grave, although that is not the general rule. In fact, few monuments have been studied here. Some of the standing stones form alignments. In this same Kerala district, researchers tend to associate with the megalithic monuments artificial caves cut into the soft laterite. These rock-cut tombs are made of a vertical, four-sided shaft; at its bottom a narrow passage leads from one side into a larger room, semi-circular and vaulted. These were also tombs, and the accompanying pottery, black or red, show that they were used at the same period as the megalithic monuments. Sundara Rajan attempts to relate these artificial grottoes to the rock-cut tombs of Palestine and Cyprus – but why not also to the graves of the Axumite civilisation which flourished from 500 BC in Ethiopia, close to the Red Sea? There is nothing very convincing in this argument.

As far as the megalithic monuments of the northern zone are concerned, we have very little information, despite a few recent excavations. However, we do know that one chamber-tomb in Pakistan has a porthole slab, which shows an affinity with the Deccan monuments. But in which direction does the relationship go? From Karachi to the Deccan, or from the Deccan to Karachi?

In the east of the Indian peninsula, around Madras, funerary deposits were made in sarcophagi of baked clay set on small feet. These sarcophagi were deposited, singly or severally, inside dolmenic chambers, even in simple pits beneath a cairn. Thus in a chamber-tomb of rough stone blocks at Sanur in the Chingleput district (Madras), three sarcophagi, each containing the bones of several individuals, filled the chamber; in a gap between two sarcophagi, numerous pots had been placed. It seems that the custom of leaving offerings beside the sarcophagus is usual in this type of burial.

Lastly, in the extreme south of the peninsula, which was not affected by the tide of Aryans, the dead were buried in large urns of baked clay.

So four large funerary areas can be recognised in the Deccan, with zones of overlap, of course (Figure 61:a): the largest and central part, where chamber-tombs contain the skeletal remains of several decarnated individuals; the western part, with the *topikallus* and *kudakallus* and also with rock-cut tombs; the east, where there are sarcophagi in baked earth which contained the dead; and the south, where the dead were put into funerary urns.

Funerary offerings and the antiquity of the Indian megalithic monuments

Indian megalithic monuments have yielded a great number of archaeological remains. There is a plethora of iron artefacts: hoes, adzes,

---

Figure 61   Megalithic monuments in India. (After A. K. Sundara and N. R. Banerjee)

(a) Distribution map of megalithic monuments in the Deccan peninsula: (1) topikallus *and rock-cut tombs; (2) chamber-tombs built of flat slabs with porthole entrances; (3) baked-clay coffins placed in chamber-tombs built of rough stone or of slabs, or in pits: (4) funerary urns, alone or placed in chamber-tombs or in cists.*

1. Chamber-tomb, of the type called a 'cist', Brahmigiri, Chitaldrug district, Mysore.

2. Transepted chamber-tomb, Halingali.

3. Chamber-tomb with subcircular chamber, Terdal.

4. Chamber-tomb with rectangular chamber and axial corridor, Halingali.

5. Megalithic chests in a circular mound, Halingali.

6. Chamber-tomb in a quadrilateral mound, Kaladji.

7. Topikallu, *Cheramangad, Trichna, Kerala.*

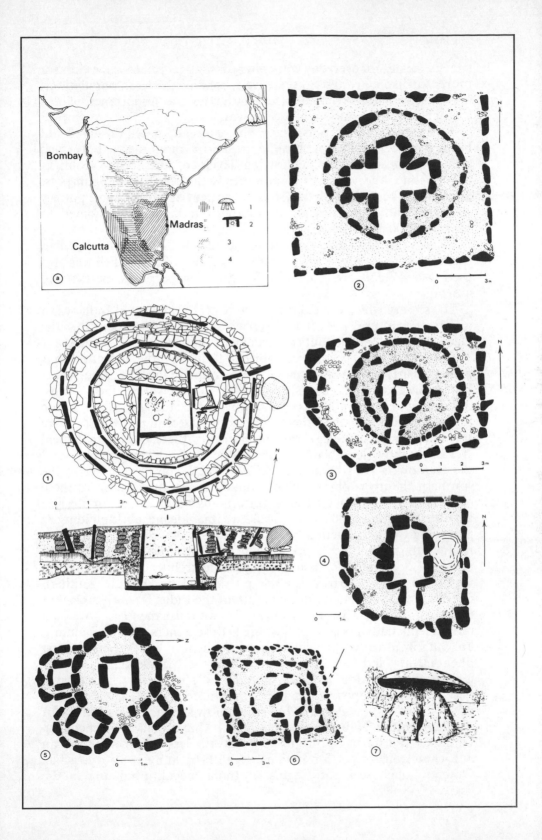

Bombay

Madras

Calcutta

1

2

3

4

(a)

N

0   1   2   3m
②

(1)

(2)

N

N

(3)

N

(4)

(5)

(6)

(7)

0   3m
②

0   1   2   3m
③

0   1m
④

0   1m
⑤

0   3m
⑥

0   1   3m
①

N

spades, sickles for everyday work; swords, daggers and arrowheads for more war-like activities. So there were conflicts between populations, and the presence of horses' teeth indicates the importance of this animal, which doubtless was used in war.

There are numerous pots, and we have already noted those red and black ceramics so abundant in the megalithic monuments, but which are also known in the underlying levels of the local Neolithic-Chalcolithic, and which show affinities with certain Harappan pots. Sundara makes links with the Group C pottery of Nubia. Some pottery from megalithic monuments in southern India has been dated to between 2000 and 1000 BC.

Beads of all kinds are abundant in the burials. Some are of carnelian (the red agate variety), others – rare, it is true – of gold. Shell was also used. Stone items are essentially for grinding purposes: pestles and mortars.

The society which erected the megalithic monuments of India was a purely agricultural one. It had replaced the pastoral society of the Neolithic-Chalcolithic. But the settlement sites are still little-known.

The great number of iron objects found in the megaliths has provoked attribution of the monuments to the Indian Iron Age, which began towards 1300 or 1200 BC, with the arrival of the Aryans. According to some authors, these Aryans chased the Dravidians before them, and the Dravidians then occupied the Deccan plateau and were the builders of the megalithic monuments there. Anthropological studies do show resemblances between the megalithic populations and the Harappans. Furthermore, graffiti collected on the pottery of the southern chamber-tombs are not unlike the seal inscriptions of these same Harappans from the Indus, Harappans who lived, we emphasise, between 2500 and 1500 BC. So should we imagine megalith-building as preceding the introduction of iron to India? We may be tempted to reply in the affirmative, especially since in Harappan territory, in the region of Karachi in Pakistan, a megalithic architecture developed in which we note in particular the porthole-slab. Did the southern chamber-tombs originate at the mouth of the Indus? It is possible, but this would not resolve the problem, for we must then ask how such monuments had appeared in that area. Researchers such as Sundara, an author already extensively quoted, believe in the diffusionist phenomenon and seek an explanation in the Middle East, with the monuments of Palestine. They underline the relations which existed between the Harappans and the Mesopotamians: the sarcophagus-urns of Iran and the Persian Gulf (they show similarities with those of southern India), Nubian pottery (which we have already touched on). Of course, all this is disturbing, but nevertheless convincing; and an autochthonous origin for Indian megalith-building is also possible. Other scholars seek the origins of India megalith-building in the

Caucasus, where chamber-tombs exist which are comparable particularly as regards the porthole-slab. Since the Caucasus is not exactly next door to India, however, staging-posts would have to be found in Iran, and none have been!

We summarise from this tour through India that two principal types rub along together, particularly in the south of India: monuments made of flat slabs with porthole-slab and passage within a circular mound (they contain the bones of several bodies as secondary burial); and monuments made of large slabs where the bodies have been buried in terracotta coffins. The earliest could have been built at the end of the second millennium BC, and their fullest flowering was during the second half of the first millennium BC. We are still lost in speculation as to their origin.

12. The Far East: China, Korea, and Japan

Chamber-tombs in China, Korea, and Japan

It was right at the end of the nineteenth century that learned European society became aware of the existence of megalithic monuments, comparable to our own chamber-tombs, in the Far East. But, curiously, the royal burials which William Gowland presented to the respected Japan Society in London in 1897 are not recognised today by Japanese and Korean prehistorians as chamber-tombs. However, there does exist a megalithic group (Figure 62) which extends over all Korea, spilling over some distance to the north, in China (especially Manchuria) and to the south, as far as Japan, especially in the island of Kyushu.

Unhappily, in those countries the state of research is not far advanced, and it is particularly difficult to get access to Chinese publications. To cap it all, acid soil has usually meant that no bones have survived in the monuments. To this must be added the recent cultivation of the hills and alluvial plains which has led to the destruction of many monuments. Thus in the north-west of the island of Kyushu (Japan), there are now no more than 200 chamber-tomb sites, as against 500 at the beginning of this century. How many Japanese gardens are now the richer by blocks of stone and small bridges!

Figure 62 Chamber-tombs in the Far East.
Distribution map. Megalithic monuments occur in the dotted areas.
1. Chamber-tomb of the Jéju type, South Korea.
2. Chamber-tomb with simple chamber and external blocking, Bukchang 5, P'yongyang, North Korea.
3. Chamber-tomb with unblocked chamber, Fing-Sei, Liaoning, north-eastern China.
4. Chamber-tomb with unblocked chamber, Chou-Chou-Che 2, Liaoning, north-eastern China.
5. Chamber-tomb with unblocked chamber, Songshin-Dong 4, Hwanghae, North Korea.
6. Evolution of Japanese chamber-tombs. (After M. Kômoto)

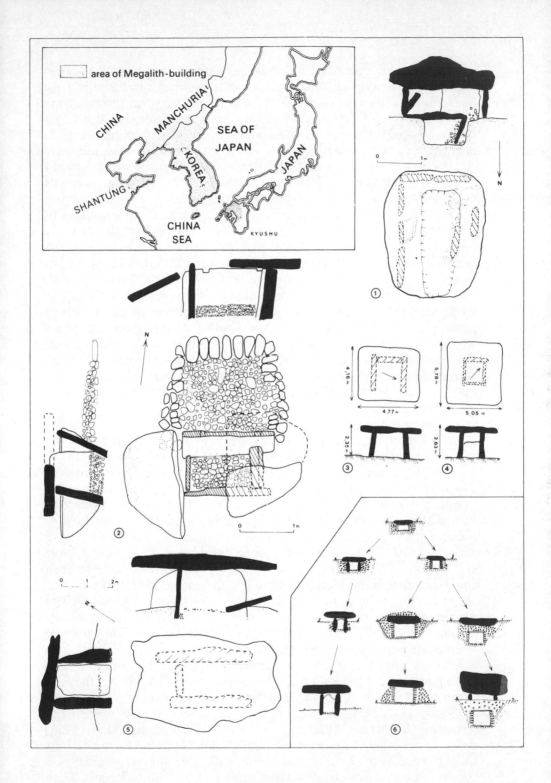

area of Megalith-building

CHINA
MANCHURIA
SEA OF JAPAN
KOREA
JAPAN
SHANTUNG
CHINA SEA
KYUSHU

① ② ③ ④ ⑤ ⑥

N

0   1m

0   1m

0   1   2m

4.16 m   4.77 m   2.35 m

5.78 m   5.05 m   2.63 m

In Korea, the French or English word 'dolmen' is translated as *ko-in-dol*, that is, 'supported stone'. Imagine the joy of the diffusionist who hears this: on the one hand the *dol*men of Brittany, on the other the Korean ko-in-*dol*! There could be no doubt in his mind that a single race produced these constructions which carry such a 'similar' name. It is a shame that in Brittany the word was brought into use only relatively recently; it derives from the Celtic, a language which was not introduced until some 1500 years after the last chamber-tomb was erected. Shame, too, that so much time elapsed before the construction of the first Korean chamber-tombs which, besides, have nothing in common morphologically with those of Atlantic Europe. It is by leaning on such ridiculous relationships that we can learn that the Gallas of the Harar (Ethiopia) must have been the Gauls, because both lots built chamber-tombs. ... And of course 'Gallas', 'Gaels', 'Gauls', and so on, all come to the same thing. We repeat this if only to emphasise the misconceptions so easily passed on to us in history lessons: chamber-tombs had not been built for more than 1500 years when the Gauls appeared on the Atlantic coast; and as for the Gallas of Ethiopia, they occupied the area from the sixteenth century AD, their skin is unremittingly coloured – which is not a Gaulish characteristic – and they could not have built the Harar chamber-tombs because those are much earlier.

But let us return to our chamber-tombs of the Far East. In north-eastern China, chamber-tombs are called *che-pin* which means 'stone tables', and the expression sums up quite well what archaeologists of these regions mean by 'chamber-tomb'. Several typological classifications have been given for these monuments, but we will follow most carefully the thesis of Gon-Gil Ji, Curator of the National Museum of Korea at Seoul, published in 1981. He distinguishes two types: those of the north (four-sided chamber with a megalithic roof, built above ground); and those of the south (stone chest or pit covered by a large slab). Although the borderline of the two groups is about the level of the Northern Han river, the two groups interpenetrate in places. Several tens of thousands of chamber-tombs have been identified in Korea, but they are more numerous to the west, a less mountainous region which is still today the more densely populated. They may be isolated or grouped into cemeteries.

Chamber-tombs, all of this northern type, are less numerous in Manchuria and in the Shantung peninsula than in Korea, but they are often much bigger. In North Korea, one of the two great chamber-tombs of Gwanson-ni, on high ground overlooking the Yellow Sea, has a roofing-slab 8.7 m ($28\frac{1}{2}$ ft) long by 4.5 m (15 ft) wide and 30 cm (12 in) thick. Its four-sided chamber measures 3.3 m (11 ft) by 1.2 m (4 ft), its height being 2.2 m ($7\frac{1}{4}$ ft). But there are still more impressive chamber-tombs. Thus the slab of chamber-tomb I of Songshin-dong is 8.3 m

(27¼ ft) long, 6.3 m (20½ ft) wide and 50 cm (20 in) thick, which gives it a weight of around 65 tonnes. In Manchuria, it is estimated that the gneiss slab of the Che-pin-shan chamber-tomb weighs 70 tonnes. Usually, the slabs come from quarries closeby. Among the chamber-tombs of the northern type, Gon-Gil Ji distinguishes: chamber-tombs with external buttressing with a single chamber, such as chamber-tomb V at Bukchang (Figure 62:2), or with multiple chambers, such as Kindong chamber-tomb (Figure 63:1), and chamber-tombs without external structure, which appear often to be more carefully made and larger. Those are the ones we have just discussed (Figure 62:3–5). The external buttressing of some chambers can be assumed to be the remains of a mound which closed off the chamber; but it does not seem that the large monuments of North Korea and of north-east China had this arrangement. The chamber in these cases was closed off by a system of uprights, which sometimes slotted into one another.

The typology of the southern type of chamber-tomb is a little more complex. They occupy the south of Korea and the island of Kyushu in Japan, as well as part of north-west Korea. Usually, the funerary area is underground and the chamber-tomb, if we may so call it, is made up of a slab or block of stone held off the ground by uprights or by a simple pile of stones. If it is simply laid on the ground, which is often the case (Figure 63:2), we should speak of 'burial beneath a slab'. Archaeologists of the Far East consider as a dolmen or chamber-tomb any funerary architecture which is covered by a more or less crude megalithic slab. At the extreme, is this slab called a dolmen in that it covers a burial. Beneath the covering slab is the cist; its walls are slabs of stone, or dry-stone, or, occasionally, composite construction. There may be one or several cists, with or without external structures. Pit burials beneath slabs are numerous, especially in Japan. Sometimes one or several funerary urns of terracotta have been deposited in the pit. The monument of Asada (Fukucka) is made of a slab laid on the ground and retained by rubble, above an urn which is 1.3 m (4¼ ft) long.

In the southern type of monument, the roofing-slab is generally thicker than in the northern variety. At Sanggap-ni one of the blocks measures 6.5 m (21 ft) long by 5 m (16½ ft) wide and 2 m (6½ ft) thick, with a weight reaching 170 tonnes.

The site of Harayama, in Nagasaki province in Japan, at the foot of Mount Unzen in the Shimabara peninsula, is very famous for its group of chamber-tombs. It was discovered after the Second World War in a plain recently put under cultivation. Most of the monuments were destroyed, but a systematic study has been going on since 1953.

At Harayama there exist three groups of monuments. The first comprised a dozen monuments, all destroyed before excavation began. They were formed of buried stone cists or funerary pits, each beneath a stone slab which was held up by three or four supports. The pottery recovered from them belongs to the final stage of a cultural phase, the Jomon, which precedes the Yayoi period. The second group, at the centre of the site, was composed of 30 or so monuments, of which three were excavated. Beneath the roofing-slab, the small rectangular coffer contained tubular beads, arrowheads and fragments of pottery. The third group, of over 100 monuments, was studied in its entirety. There were discovered urns, stone cists, and funerary pits beneath slabs with or without supporting uprights. According to Masayuki Kômoto, these tombs contained pottery from the late Jomon and the beginning of the Yayoi.

All along the coast of the Sea of Japan, chamber-tombs coexist with other types of burial in urns, stone cists, simple pits, pits lined with stone, and pits with wooden coffins – structures which all become 'chamber-tombs' as soon as they are covered over with a stone slab.

In the Far East, as elsewhere in the world, study of funerary furnishings has permitted the establishment of a chronology and a grasp of some aspects of custom and social belief. Usually, the furnishings are more abundant in monuments of the southern type than in the northern type, but less varied. Although architectural similarities between South Korean monuments and those of Japan are incontestable, it is not so for the archaeological material. There are no polished daggers in the Japanese chamber-tombs, but there are shaped arrowheads of chipped stone, non-existent in Korea. Study of these polished-stone daggers, which could be copies of native or Chinese daggers in bronze, is of great importance for the chronological classification of the monuments. There exist three principal types (Figure 63:5), and cross-checking against other dated archaeological elements has shown that in South Korea the 'chamber-tombs' without uprights, simple blocks of stone set directly on the ground, precede the construction of monuments whose megalithic covering is supported by upright slabs (Figure 62:6). The earliest bronze daggers, prototypes of

---

Figure 63   Chamber-tombs in the Far East.
1. Chamber-tomb with multiple cists, externally blocked by megalithic slabs, Kindong, Hwanghae, North Korea.
2. Chamber-tomb with unblocked cist, Tanikiyama, Nagasaki, Japan.
3. Different types of polished-stone arrowheads found in Far Eastern chamber-tombs.
4. Pottery from Bukchang 5 chamber-tomb, North Korea.
5. Different types of polished-stone daggers from Far Eastern chamber-tombs: (Ab) tongue-shaped dagger with undecorated blade, Kindong 3, Hwanghae, North Korea; (BIb) dagger with central narrowing of the handle and undecorated blade, Sangjapo-ni 4, Gyongki, South Korea; (BIIb) dagger with concave outline to the handle and undecorated blade.
6. Ceramic types from Japanese chamber-tombs, Yayoï period. (After J. Gon Gy)

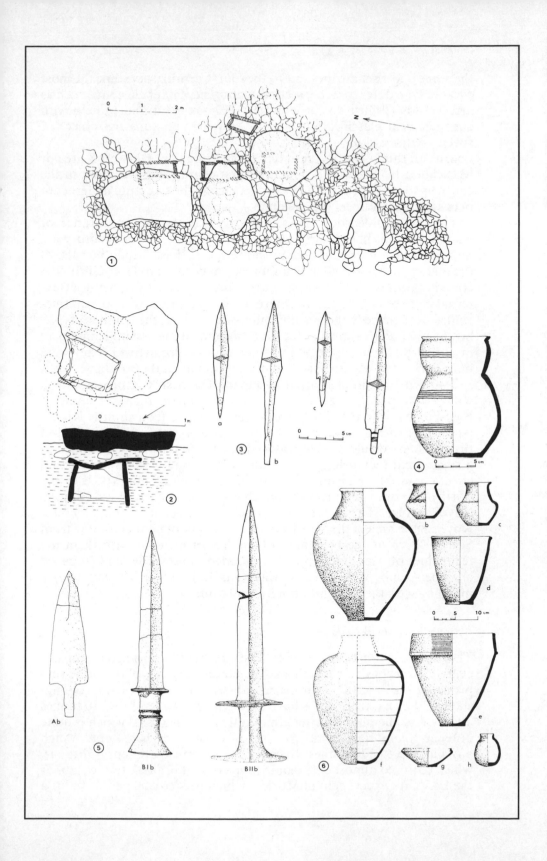

the stone ones, are attributable to the fourth century BC, while the most evolved type dates from the second century BC. Other elements, such as arrowheads (Figure 63:3) or pottery (Figure 63:4 and 6) help with chronological classification, which, however, remains the object of specialist discussion.

Migami thinks the northern type, appearing in north-west Korea or Manchuria between the second and first century BC, was built in the south up to the fourth century AD; then, while the structure underneath persisted, the 'dolmen' disappeared.

The few radiocarbon dates seem to indicate the appearance of chamber-tombs in the north during the eighth or seventh century BC, and some authors would even push the age of these megaliths back to the middle of the second millennium BC. According to Gon-Gil Ji, 'the chamber-tombs with external buttressing precede those without external buttressing in the northern type and those with megalithic-walled cists precede those with composite walls in the southern type'. So chamber-tombs appeared at the beginning of the first millennium BC in northern Korea, at the period when bronze also arrived. They were built during the whole of the first millennium BC in that country.

Two types of dolmen occur in Japan. The first, comprising a slab without supporting uprights, was introduced on the west coast of Kyushu towards the third century BC, coming from South Korea. According to Komoto, these monuments contained cremations, and their builders would have introduced dry-terrain farming. Confined to a small area, they belong to the late Jomon, and would have had no effect on Japanese history. The second type, with supports, is in the north of Kyushu and marks social changes which correspond with the Yayoi culture. They were built under the direct influence of South Korea in the area of the Sea of Japan. A tall race of people coming from South Korea at the beginning of the Yayoi brought with them the technique of rice-cultivation on flooded land. The new type of chamber-tomb, with pillows, was thus built by a Korean people mingling with the autochthonous population.

Chamber-tombs for whom?

The chamber-tombs of the Far East are individual graves, but not everyone was buried beneath a slab, and the very size of the stone slab probably indicates a social order, a hierarchy. Most of the roofing-slabs of the chamber-tombs have a weight of between 1 and 10 tonnes and require the physical strength of only a few persons, which is quite different from slabs which, as we have seen earlier, could weigh anything up to 170 tonnes. Recall the Bougon experiment in France, which required almost 200 people to move and lift a 32-tonne slab, or the La Venta experiment in Mexico, which needed 500 people to lift a

50-tonne stele. Besides, the sometimes very small dimensions of the funerary chest imply two phases in the funerary ritual: either cremation followed by the deposit of the ashes in the monument, as Komoto thinks in respect of several Japanese monuments; or, most importantly, the deposit of bones gathered together after decarnation in the open air or in the ground. This was a frequent custom up to recent times, especially in maritime areas of the Far East such as Taiwan, Okinawa, and the South Korean islands. In Korea and north-east China, offerings accompany the dead into the grave, while they are left outside in Japan. Alongside the two-stage burial rite, there also exist many primary burials, but the acidity of the soil mostly prevents precise study of funerary customs.

No orientation has been recognised in the Far Eastern chamber-tombs, where several ceremonies occasionally take place for the granting of a vow – a birth, for example – for better production, or for the safety of the village.

In popular tradition, as in most countries where chamber-tombs are found, their construction is attributed to a race of giants.

Megalithic tombs of the first Japanese emperors

We cannot leave the Far East without saying a word about the megalithic funerary structures which were built in Japan from the year AD 250 until about the seventh century. They are formally much closer to the passage-graves of Atlantic megalith-building than to the 'chamber-tombs' of Korea, Manchuria and the island of Kyushu which we have just described. Although Japanese and Korean archaeologists refuse to consider them as belonging to Far Eastern dolmen architecture, there is no valid reason for excluding them.

The 'Yayoi' period in Japan began in the second century BC, and went on until the third century AD. Its culture comes from an amalgamation of the autochthonous populations of Kyushu with the invaders who, having crossed the Korean Strait in great numbers, brought with them a knowledge of rice-cultivation, weaving, and the use of iron. Before this date, Japan knew no metal. These immigrants also introduced the use of megalithic slabs in funerary customs, which is why, as we have just seen, burial customs are more or less similar on either side of the Strait.

In the middle of the third century AD a second wave of invaders, fierce Mongolian riders with metal armour, came to Japan, also from the other side of the Korean Strait, established themselves, and rapidly formed an aristocracy; from it there emerged after a few generations the imperial family which reigns to this day over the whole country. This Japanese state developed outwards from Kyushu into the northern provinces. The emperor, a religious symbol rather than a temporal chief, had very limited power over the rather turbulent clan chiefs. The Shinto beliefs of the period are entirely directed to a cult of nature. But from AD 552 the influence of Buddhism – the religion founded by the Indian prince Gautama in the sixth century BC – gradually came to dominate, to the extent that 100 years later several dozen Buddhist temples had already been built in the country. No towns existed, and men lived in thatched cabins, grouped into villages. On the death of the emperor, the imperial village had to be moved to avoid the ritual soiling which, according to the Shinto beliefs of the period, the emperor's death had caused. But often, the body of the emperor like those of several personages of high rank was put into wooden or stone sarcophagi, or even directly on the ground, in a megalithic chamber reached by a passage through a mound. This custom lost its power at the time when a decree of the emperor Kotoku, in 646, fixed the dimensions of burial mounds and their chamber for different ranks of the hierarchy, determining that the chambers would be built of small stones (and no longer of large slabs or blocks), and that no precious objects would be laid beside the deceased in his honour. The introduction of cremation at the end of the seventh century marked the end, or almost the end, of this funerary custom.

Perhaps the idea of the construction of a dolmenic chamber beneath a mound had its origins in the burials beneath slabs of the Yayoi culture which preceded the formation of the first dynasties. Nothing is less certain, and spontaneous generation of this type of burial can also easily be imagined. What is less plausible is that one could find in the west – where the latest monuments of this type were abandoned in the third millennium BC – the model for Japanese structures which date from the beginning of the Christian era.

We owe to William Gowland a well-documented study, which appeared in England in 1897, of what he called Japanese 'dolmens'. These he defined as 'a stone burial chamber, usually of rude megalithic structure larger than a cist and whether covered by a mound or not'. He himself recognised a great number (more than 400) which he classified in four large groups according to their shape (Figure 64): chamber-tombs of the *allée couverte* type with undifferentiated chambers; chamber-tombs whose passage forms with the chamber a 'p' or a 'q';

Figure 64   Royal tombs of the period of the first emperors, Japan. (After W. Gowland)
I–IV. Different types of 'dolmens'.
1. Shiba, Kawachi.
2. Imaichi, Izumo, with a stone sarcophagus in one of its chambers.
3. Koshi, Yamato, built of shaped stone.
4. Abe-mura, Yamato, holding a stone sarcophagus.
5. Principal types of pottery found in the chamber-tombs.

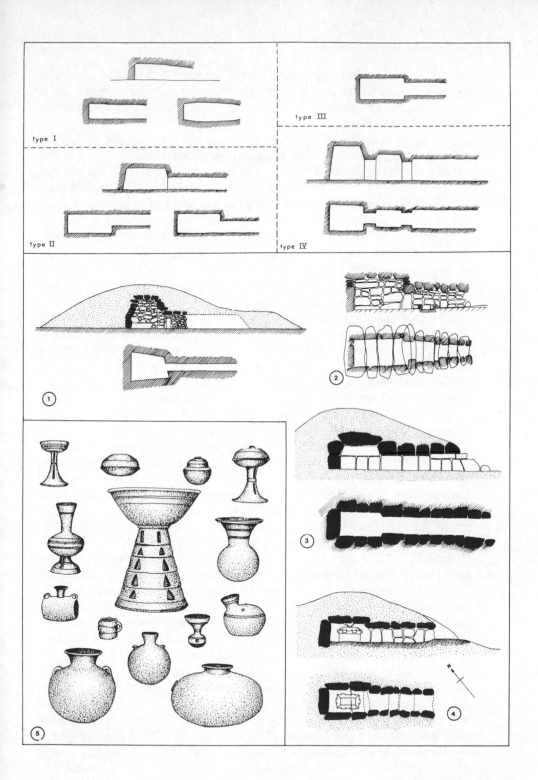

type I

type III

type II

type IV

① ② ③ ④ ⑤

chamber-tombs whose passage is on the same axis as the chamber (the most widespread type); and finally chamber-tombs which, while having a passage on the same axis as the chamber, have an ante-chamber between the two.

The Japanese chamber-tombs are enclosed in a mound, usually circular. The chambers are always four-sided and usually extend lengthwise along the same axis as the passage. The size of the mound varies from 5 m (16½ ft) in diameter for some of the Mino monuments to 30 m (98 ft) for some large examples at Kawachi and elsewhere. They are made of earth which, with time, has often partly disappeared, revealing the internal megalithic structure. Gowland notes the exceptional case of a stone cairn 32 m (105 ft) in diameter and 7 m (23 ft) high at Matsushiro (Shinano). In this type of simple mound, the floor of the chamber-tomb is at the same level as the natural surface of the ground. The chambers are made of undressed stones, with no mortar. The side-walls are of blocks, sometimes very large, piled one upon another and without any drawings or inscriptions. In rare cases, the slabs used in the construction are well squared and fit perfectly one with another (this is how the Koshi-Yamato monument was built); but most often the blocks used were taken from the nearest hillside, and it was the nature of the rock which determined the elegance of the building. We note that, as in the European chamber-tombs, the chamber is taller than the passage. This chamber is normally rectangular, occasionally trap-ezoidal, and received one or two bodies, put onto the ground or placed in a wooden or stone coffin. The bones do not survive in these soils. However, there is the exceptional case of the *allée couverte* tomb of Shimotsuke, which contained the mingled bones of 14 individuals. Usually, however, this type of funerary monument was not a collective grave, and the body in the few observable cases had the head to the south, the section off which the passage opened.

Thanks to Gowland, the chamber-tomb of Shiba (Kawachi) (Figure 64:1) was perhaps the first chamber-tomb in the world to be excavated with proper method. The surface of the ground was divided into 20 compartments with aid of a bamboo structure, and each square of this grid carried a number. Double sieving of the earth permitted recovery of all the archaeological remains, which were placed in baskets corresponding to the compartments. The precise distribution of the remains could be seen; it showed that the body had been placed in a wooden coffin accompanied by personal objects (weapons), while the offerings were placed around it. The harness and bit of the dead warrior's horse had been placed on top of the coffin, and a woman may have been buried close to him. The mound of the Shiba passage-grave measures 30 m (98 ft) across by almost 5 m (16½ ft) high. A passage about 1 m (3 ft) wide by 7.3 m (24 ft) long and 1.6 m (5 ft) high led to a trapezoidal chamber whose average dimensions are 4 m (13 ft) long by

2.6 m (8½ ft) wide and more than 3 m (10 ft) high. The ceiling is corbelled. The passage was closed by a wall 1.5 m (5 ft) thick, a custom frequent in Japan and which we know was similarly practised 3000 years earlier on the Atlantic coast of France. Offerings had been placed in this passage, and sherds of pottery found outside the mound prove that certain religious practices took place well after the complete closure of the monument.

As well as the simple mounds, there exist great terraced monuments, up to 60 m (197 ft) in diameter and 7 m (23 ft) high, and often surrounded by a ditch. But even more prodigious are the 'imperial mounds' which reach a considerable size. One of them, near Nara, is more than 200 m (656 ft) long by 20 m (65½ ft) high. These mounds, *misasagi*, are imperial tombs; they only rarely contain a chamber-tomb as we have described it, but do have a wooden or stone sarcophagus. If they enclose a chamber-tomb, it is at the level of the first terrace.

It would not occur to anyone to seek a link between the Japanese 'chamber-tombs' of the beginning of the present era and Atlantic megalith-building in the fourth and third millennia BC. Here we have one of the finest examples of architectural coincidence. It can happen that, thousands of kilometres distant and at very different times, men arrive at identical responses to similar questions. We will have further proof of this in the monuments of South America.

13. South America: the *huila* at San Agustín, Colombia

Although the notoriety of the San Agustín 'temples' crossed the Atlantic many years ago now, these monuments remain shrouded in mystery in the mind of many Old World scholars. It is thus with real interest that we have followed the results of work undertaken several years ago in Colombia by Serge Cassen; and it is from his own memory that I draw the essentials of what follows. The photographs and drawings here are also by him (Figure 65; Plates 21–4).

On either side of the deep valley of Rio Magdalena, whose old name, Rio Guacallo, means 'river of the tombs', 60 or so sites are attributable to the San Agustín culture. At an altitude of almost 2000 m (6560 ft), this fertile region in the south Colombian Andes has lush vegetation, thanks to a humid and relatively warm climate. The two major archaeological sites at Alto de los Idolos and San Agustín are separated by the river; and although they are only 3 km (2 miles) apart as the crow flies, it takes two hours on horseback to get from one to the other. Each site shows much evidence for modification of the terrain; the tops of the hills were flattened, and artificial causeways of earth and stone built between the different platforms, which hold abundant and diverse archaeological remains. Although the stone statues are so remarkable that archaeology seems to have been interested in them alone for nearly 100 years, the most surprising monuments are those which seem to be dolmens, so like are some of them to those of western Europe.

Two types of megalithic structure have been revealed. First are the great rude-stone cists, like the one in mound IV of Mesita B at San Agustín, which measures 4 m (13 ft) long by 2 m (6½ ft) wide. Its side-walls are made of four upright slabs, the two ends being closed by one and two slabs respectively. The cover of the chest was made with three juxtaposed slabs (Figure 65:9). Serge Cassen has noticed engravings on the upright slabs of these coffers (lines of dashes, snaking shapes, and anthropomorphic figures), as well as yellow, red or black paintings of circular or linear motifs on the internal walls. Sometimes there is a paved floor to the chamber. The coffer was enclosed inside a circular earth and stone mound, bounded by a row of standing slabs or a retaining wall.

The second architectural type is a typical passage-grave by the European definition; that is, it has an elongated four-sided chamber preceded by a narrow passage, often lowered, the whole being built with upright slabs which support several stone capstones. Sometimes side-cells have been added to the chamber. Like the coffers, a circular mound with a well-built outer face covers the monument, whose walls also had engravings and paintings (Figure 65:7 and 8).

Beside these megalithic structures beneath mounds, the plateaux are strewn with individual tombs in many guises: small stone coffers set into the red clay; long pits covered by slabs; shafts for vertical inhumation; shafts at the bottom of which a vaulted lateral chamber has been hollowed out, with a burial or a funerary urn.

The acidity of the soil prevents preservation of the bones. 'Although there is no doubt about the individual character of the coffers, pits and funerary shafts, one can conclude absolutely nothing, despite the interpretations of Colombian scholars, about the collective or non-collective nature of the large monuments,' is Cassen's conclusion. However, the many excavations effected since the beginning of this century on the megalithic structures have yielded a great amount of material – obsidian artefacts, pottery, ornamental objects, and monolithic statuettes.

In the current state of knowledge, that is, after sometimes ill-considered restoration, we can say that the stone statues were placed on either side of the entrance to the passage and supported a flat slab, where they formed a kind of portico in front of the monument. Under this entrance portico, if it is not in the very centre of the chamber, another large statue stands. But what was really the primary position of these statues? It is not at all certain that they all stand today in their original positions, and the interpretation of Colombian archaeologists who take the megalithic constructions to be 'temples' poses a question. They could, in fact, be none other than the tombs of important personages, even collective tombs dedicated to an entire population, to a social class, or to a family.

This remarkable statuary art, in which can be recognised gods, priests, warriors and great dignitaries, the portrait of the deceased or the representation of animals (felines, monkeys, crocodilians), seems to belong to two major phases of development. The first phase is characterised by cylindrical statues: one arm brought across the chest joins the other, downward-pointing arm at the level of the elbow. The second phase, with its monumental statues, is called classical.

Thanks to the work of Reichel-Dolmatoff (1972), a stratigraphic study has been undertaken which reveals five ceramic groups: Horqueta, Primavera, Isnos, Potrero, and Sombrerillos:

Very roughly, the Horqueta complex is characterised by round based carinated pots, Primavera by globular pots, painted decoration appears for Isnos and tripod pots for Sombrerillos, but with a continuity of shape and decoration (Figure 65:3–5).

Radiocarbon dates place Horqueta and Primavera before the Christian era; Isnos dates from the first four centuries AD, and Potrero and Sombrerillos follow on.

Few studies have been done of the lithic material of these populations. Cassen has seen large scrapers and retouched blades in obsidian, polished axes, scissors and picks of hard rock, as well as grindstones and small pestles.

The San Agustín culture occupied more than 2000 years, from the sixth century BC to the fifteenth AD. It is almost certain that in the course of this long period changes took place, not only in the pottery, as we have seen, but very probably also in statuary art and funerary customs.

Not all the megalithic monuments can have been erected at the same period. Cassen has evolved a chronology which seems coherent:

Towards the sixth century BC, in the San Agustín area, a human group established itself. They buried their dead in individual graves, or collective ones, making cists out of stone slabs. Monolithic cylindrical statuettes, wearing a cap on top of the head and whose technique of shaping and the schematic outline recalls woodworking, accompany the deceased who sometimes lies in a wooden sarcophagus.

A 'classical' period follows, where the architectural types develop, for example with the addition of an access-passage to the grave. The monumental statues seem still to be associated with the burials and denote a perfect mastery of stone-working.

Finally, modes of burial diversify under the influence of neighbouring small tribes, and funerary shafts take over from megalithic structures. The bodies are finally cremated and the ashes deposited in urns.

As for their ultimate origins, one of the most plausible would be the Amazon Basin.

Despite the originality of their mode of sculpture, the San Agustín group is culturally close to the neighbouring pre-Columbian clans – in the jaguar myth, plumed serpent, sarcophagi, statues, shapes of pots – such as that of

---

Figure 65   Megalithic monuments in Colombia.
1. Location of San Agustín, Colombia.
2. Different groups of megaliths in the San Agustín region.
3. Pottery of the Horqueta period, of the pre-Christian era.
4. Pottery of the Isnos period, of the first four centuries AD.
5. Pottery of the Sombrerillos period, of recent date.
6. Section through Mesita A mound. (After S. Cassen, 1979)
7. Arto de Los Idolos. (After S. Cassen, 1979)
8. Mesita B, San Agustín.
9. Large chest in mound 4, Mesita B, San Agustín. (After S. Cassen, 1979)

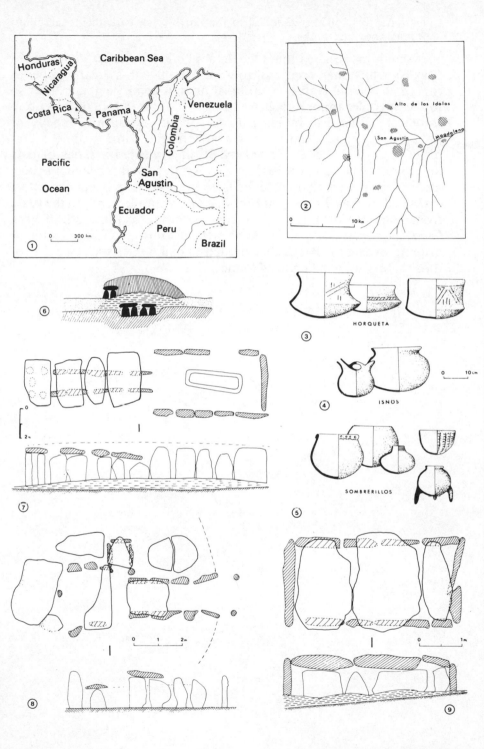

① Caribbean Sea · Honduras · Nicaragua · Costa Rica · Panama · Venezuela · Colombia · Pacific Ocean · San Agustin · Ecuador · Peru · Brazil · 0 300 km

② Alto de los Idolos · San Agustin · Magdalena · 0 10 km

③ HORQUETA

④ ISNOS · 0 10 cm

⑤ SOMBRERILLOS

⑥

⑦ 0 2m

⑧ 0 1 2m

⑨ 0 1m

Tierradentro, 150 km [93 miles] to the north-west, with their marvellous painted rock-cut tombs.

It should be recalled that the Olmecs built, on the La Venta site in Mexico, which they occupied from 1100 to 600 BC, a great number of carved altars and statues: a colossal human head weighing 20 or so tonnes, people, animals (jaguar, monkey). At the centre of this group stands a four-sided building made of sub-cylindrical blocks of juxtaposed stones. The roof is made in the same manner. This megalithic structure, excavated by Stirling, yielded a series of jade objects and was considered as having possibly served as a jaguar's cage. Here is a special kind of 'dolmen'! We note in passing the effort expended by the Olmecs: while they occupied San Lorenzo in the years from 1300 BC, 80 km (50 miles) from the coast, to the south of Vera Cruz, they went 60 km (37 miles) north-east into the Tuxtla region in order to obtain the basalt they needed to make their statues. Some of those blocks weighed up to 34 tonnes.

Conclusion

Diffusionism: a paradigm lost?

This journey through the world of dolmens has led us to consider monuments in many countries: Atlantic Europe (from Denmark to Spain, taking in the British Isles and France), the Mediterranean islands and southern Italy, North Africa, Ethiopia and the Central African Republic, Palestine, the Caucasus, India, the Far East, and Colombia, not forgetting Madagascar and its modern megaliths. We have been able to see how monuments which differ, as much in their architecture as in the funerary customs which produced them, are known by the name of dolmens, to the point where the term has been abandoned by a great number of specialists. Most often, these days, dolmens are known as 'chamber-tombs' or 'megalithic graves', equally general expressions but ones which have the merit of emphasising the funerary character of these structures.* However, not all dolmens or chamber-tombs are megalithic in the sense that certain of them were built of small stones and only their bulk is imposing.

By Jean Arnal's definition, a dolmen is an 'open sepulchral chamber, usually megalithic, covered by a mound and intended to house several burials'. Notice that it should be possible to gain access to the structure and that, in principle, it contains the remains of several individuals. We would have to reject all monuments with single individual burials, even if the chamber is built of large stones. This is the case, it seems, with the Ethiopian and central African monuments, also most of those in the Far East, which are burials under slabs or in more or less megalithic chests.

So we are dealing above all with collective burial. The funerary deposit may be primary (a body or cremation installed in the grave at the time of death) or secondary (bones brought into the sepulchral chamber after a period in another tomb; in which case the structure is an ossuary). The collective character of the tomb may result from: the accumulation of successive individual burials; the accumulation of successive collective burials; or a simultaneous collective inhumation (after an act of war or an epidemic, for example). Normally the chamber-tomb contains a fairly high number of successive individual inhumations, not of successive collective inhumations (as has some-

---

* [Translators' note: it is for this reason that we have generally used the phrase 'chamber-tombs' in this edition, as explained in our preface.]

times been written). Indeed, in many cases, an access structure allowed the deposit of a new body when a member of the clan or family died. The body was placed in the chamber, often in a flexed posture, hands in front of the face; but occasionally lack of space compelled the stacking-up of bones already contained in the grave. Perhaps some of them were even removed. Then the chamber-tomb became a place of transit. However, these funerary customs are not universal; in Ireland, it is cremation which prevails.

So we can retain only the collective character as defining the dolmenic burial. But can one compare the huge cemeteries made up of thousands of monuments in North Africa with the smaller groups of megalithic monuments along the Atlantic coastline of Europe? This is very difficult, and touches a sensitive point about dolmens and chamber-tombs throughout the world: are they the result of sponta-neous generation in different parts of the globe, or the result of diffusion from one centre of origin? These two ideas are fiercely defended, while the monuments are, largely, very little studied. The finding of comparable morphological characteristics – such as the porthole-slab that is found in France as well as in Spain, Palestine, the Caucasus and as far east as India – led to the invention of a 'megalithic civilisation' as an idea. So why do we find archaeological material differing from one area to another, and from structures so separated by time? There cannot be one 'megalithic race'. Perhaps it is a 'megalithic religion' with missionaries ploughing through the world and bringing their gospel of collective burial in stone chambers into all parts of it? The idea would have sprung from some part of western Europe (Brittany or Portugal) and been transmitted by sea. So how do we explain those vast lapses of time between the Breton monuments which date back to the fifth millennium BC, and the present-day Malagasy tombs!

For the opposition, anti-diffusionists find almost as many creative centres of megalith-building as there are areas of megaliths. Thus Colin Renfrew, after stating what P.-R. Giot had revealed many years before – that western European megalith-building had a local origin inde-pendent of any Near Eastern influence – would like to have four or five autonomous centres of megalithic production along the 'Atlantic façade': the Iberian peninsula, Brittany, southern England, Ireland, Denmark. The cists of the Algarve and Alentejo would be the origin of the Iberian chamber-tombs; collective burials such as Téviec (Mor-bihan) would be the origin of megaliths in western France; megalithic chambers in the English long barrows would be stone copies of earlier wooden monuments; and so on. It is obvious under these conditions that we need seek no relationship between African, Palestinian, Caucasian, and Indian schools of megalith-building. The difficulty with this reasoning is that we have never, in any region, found any proof of the transition from closed to open collective grave.

If it is not good form nowadays to hold a diffusionist position, it must also be remarked that megalith-building in Madagascar was not a production of local origin. It came from Indonesia at the time of the first colonists and evolved into the forms which we know there now.

But let us recognise that in the current state of our knowledge, no one is in any position to define the origins of megalith-building. To date, two areas of the world share the earliest dating: Portugal and western France, both towards 4500 BC. The neolithic transformation in western France seems to have been the result of colonisation from the Mediterranean Midi, passing around the edge of the Iberian peninsula at the end of the sixth millennium BC. There must, therefore, have been contacts between these diverse regions, and one of them could have led the other in the building of these first structures. Later, identical contacts could have been made with Great Britain and the Nordic countries, introducing passage-graves into the locally originating long barrows. Thus we would have a northern area where long mounds developed with cists and mortuary-houses, and an Atlantic zone with passage-graves, the two currents crossing over ... not a very original idea.

This Atlantic megalith-building, one way or another, could be the origin of the dolmens of the Mediterranean Midi which, in their turn, as has been proposed, could have influenced the productions of the Mediterranean islands, and from there North Africa (Algeria, Tunisia), although this is less certain. However, it is practically impossible to link Palestinian megalith-building with that of western Europe, and we will have to imagine another, independent centre of creation in that area.

Besides, we have seen that the chamber-tombs of the Caucasus and those of India might have a tenuous connection, but a large space without megaliths makes this improbable; there, too, different creative centres can be envisaged. What can we say about the Colombian monuments, if not that they can only be the result of a happy coincidence? So why not the others?

So it is practically impossible to hold a world-wide diffusionist position as far as dolmens are concerned. We must imagine a number of independent creative centres, separated by long distances and far apart in time. But must we hold to such a definite position as regards Atlantic megalith-building, about which we know that it is original and that it is the earliest in the world? It is still difficult to answer.

Whatever megalithic phenomena and their origins may be, they left across the world a series of monuments, sometimes, grandiose, which are often the first buildings in a country. This is certainly true for western Europe, where monuments such as Barnenez in France, New Grange in Ireland, or Antequera in Spain bear witness to the creative genius of these ancient European peoples, whom we have too often been happy to think of as mentally retarded, just capable of slavishly copying the masters of the near East. The 'oriental mirage' has evaporated in the clearer light of radiocarbon dating.

We would have to enquire far more than I have done into the societies who built these structures, and into the reasons which caused them to do so. In this regard the model suggested by Renfrew for the British Isles is particularly important. However, as we have seen in the Nordic countries, it does not seem possible to generalise about 'megalithic societies' in western Europe as a whole. We are hampered by the current state of research.

Thus in western France, where several good excavations of megalithic monuments have taken place during the last 20 years, we have found not a single habitation-site which can be linked with any certainty to these neolithic builders.

From the very positioning of passage-graves on high ground, from the (relatively limited) studies made of bones from them, from the size and displacement of the stones used, from the discovery of offerings on the façades of monuments and in the chambers, from concentrations of megaliths, from environmental studies which are coming to light, etc., we can begin to put forward some hypotheses about the designers of these buildings. But can we really say that the megalithic phenomenon marks 'the expression of particular social and economic preoccupations, reflecting the management of materials, information and energy; a specific relationship with time and space'?

We are well aware that in order to shift blocks of considerable weight, a large number of people had to be brought together, several villages teaming up, impelled by a single purpose, but for whom, or what? Are we right in thinking that the social structure of the period was necessarily hierarchical? It is possible, even probable, that there do exist ethnographic instances where large numbers assembled to work to a common end without there being a central authority.

We can envisage many social systems, but on what can we base our reasoning, when this population is known to us only from a few monuments, often in a ruinous state of preservation; while anthropological studies of skeletal remains have barely begun, and no precise territorial study for any given period has yet come to any successful conclusion?

It would be irresponsible to pronounce on this, and I have not wished to pursue the argument in these pages.

From our acknowledgement of the existence of 'dolmens' to an understanding of the societies which built them remains a huge step to take, on the level both of social organisation and of any metaphysical ideas of the people they contained. This will doubtless provide fascinating research for years to come.

Bibliography

Sources are subdivided geographically; section numbers do not refer to chapter numbers

1. General studies of megaliths

R. W. Chapman, 'Archaeological theory and communal burial in prehistoric Europe', in I. Hodder, G. Isaac, N. Hammond (ed.), *Pattern of the past: studies in honour of David Clarke*, pp. 389–411. Cambridge: Cambridge University Press, 1981

G. E. Daniel, *The megalith builders of western Europe*. London: Hutchinson, 1958

J. Fergusson, *Rude stone monuments in all countries*. London: John Murray, 1872

A. Fleming, 'The myth of the mother goddess', *World Archaeology*, vol. 1 (1969), pp. 247–61

A. Fleming, 'Tombs for the living', *Man*, vol. 8 (1971), pp. 177–93

P.-R. Giot, 'Le rituel funéraire, les mégalithes, et la religion néolithique', in *Colloque du 150ᵉ anniversaire de la Société Polymathique du Morbihan: L'architecture mégalithique*, pp. 7 14. Vannes: Société Polymathique du Morbihan, 1977

J. Guilaine, *Premiers bergers et paysans de l'Occident méditerranéen*. Paris: Mouton, 1976

R. von Heine Geldern, *Das Megalith Problem*. Wenner Gren Foundation, 1958

V. O. Jorge, 'Em torno de alguns problemas do megalitismo europeu', *Arqueologia*, vol. 8 (1983), pp. 12–22

F. Lynch, 'The use of the passage in certain passage graves as a means of communication rather than access', in G. E. Daniel and P. Kjaerum (ed.), *Megalithic graves and ritual: papers presented at the III Atlantic Colloquium, Moesgârd, 1969*, pp. 147–61. Copenhagen: Jutland Archaeological Society, 1973. (Jutland Archaeological Society Publications 11)

E. MacKie, *The megalith builders*. Oxford: Phaidon, 1977

S. Piggott, 'Problems in the interpretation of chambered tombs', in G. E. Daniel and P. Kjaerum (ed.), *Megalithic graves and ritual: papers presented at the III Atlantic Colloquium, Moesgârd, 1969*, pp. 9–15. Copenhagen: Jutland Archaeological Society, 1973. (Jutland Archaeological Society Publications 11)

G. Raclet, *Les mégalithes mystérieux*. Paris: R. Laffont, 1981

S. von Reden, *Die Megalithkulturen*. Berlin: Dumont Buchverlag, 1979

C. Renfrew, *Before civilization: the radiocarbon revolution and prehistoric Europe*. London: Jonathan Cape, 1973

C. Renfrew (ed.), *The explanation of culture change: models in prehistory*. London: Duckworth, 1973.

H. de Saint-Blanquat, 'Les mégalithes', *Sciences et Avenir*, no. 342 (1975), pp. 754–69

J.-P. Savary, 'Étude théorique et statistique sur l'orientation des monuments funéraires à structure d'accès rectiligne', *Bulletin de la Société Préhistorique Française*, vol. 63 (1966), pp. 365–94

A. Service and J. Bradbery, *A guide to the megaliths of Europe*. London: Weidenfeld & Nicolson, 1979
R. Wernick, *The monument Builders*. London: Time-Life, 1974

2. Northern and eastern Europe: Belgium, Denmark, East Germany, Holland, Poland, Sweden, West Germany

E. Aner, 'Die Stellung der Dolmen Schleswig-Holsteins in der nordischen Megalithkultur', *Offa*, vol. 20 (1973), pp. 9–38
C. J. Becker, 'Problems of the megalithic "mortuary houses" in Denmark', in G. E. Daniel and P. Kjaerum (ed.), *Megalithic graves and ritual: papers presented at the III Atlantic Colloquium, Moesgård, 1969*, pp. 75–9. Copenhagen: Jutland Archaeological Society, 1973. (Jutland Archaeological Society Publications 11)
P. Bonenfant, *Civilisations préhistoriqes en Wallonie: des premiers cultivateurs aux premières villes*. Brussels: Fondation Charles Plisnier, 1969. (Études d'Histoire Wallonne no. 2)
J. Broendsted, *Danmarks Oldtid*. Copenhagen: Nordisk forlag, 1938
J. G. D. Clark, 'The economic context of dolmens and passage graves in Sweden', in V. Markotic (ed.), *Ancient Europe and the Mediterranean*, pp. 35–49. Warminster: Aris and Phillips, 1977
S. de Laet, 'Megalithic graves in Belgium – a *Status Questionis*', in J. D. Evans, B. Cunliffe and C. Renfrew (ed.), *Antiquity and man: essays in honour of Glyn Daniel*, pp. 155–61. London: Thames & Hudson, 1981
S. de Laet, *La Belgique d'avant les Romains*. Brussels: Éditions Universa, 1982.
K. Ebbesen, *Die jüngere Trichterbecherkultur auf der dänischen inseln*. Copenhagen: Akademisk Forlag, 1975
V. Fischer, 'Os túmulos megalíticos da Baixa Saxónia e suas relações com o resto da Europa', *Arqueologia*, no. 3 (1981), pp. 19–28
P. V. Glob, *Danish prehistoric monuments: Denmark from the Stone Age to the Vikings*. London: Faber & Faber, 1971
P. V. Glob, *Danske oldtidsminder*. Copenhagen: Gyldendal, 1967
A. Hyenstrand, *Ancient monuments and prehistoric society*. Stockholm: 1979
K. Jazdzewski, 'The relations between Kujavian barrows in Poland and megalithic tombs in northern Germany, Denmark and western European countries', in G. E. Daniel and P. Kjaerum (ed.), *Megalithic graves and ritual: papers presented at the III Atlantic Colloquium, Moesgård, 1969*, pp. 63–74. Copenhagen: Jutland Archaeological Society, 1973. (Jutland Archaeological Society Publications 11)
J. Jensen, *The prehistory of Denmark*. London: Methuen, 1982
L. Kaelas, 'Dolmen und ganggräber in Schweden', *Offa*, vol. 15 (1956), pp. 5–24
L. Kaelas, 'The megalithic tombs in south Scandinavia – migration or cultural influence?', *Palaeohistoria*, vol. 12 (1966–7), pp. 287–321
L. Kaelas, 'Megaliths of the Funnel Beaker culture in Germany and Scandinavia', in J. D. Evans, B. Cunliffe and C. Renfrew (ed.), *Antiquity and man: essays in honour of Glyn Daniel*, pp. 141–54. London: Thames & Hudson, 1981
P. Kjaerum, 'The chronology of the passage graves in Jutland', *Palaeohistoria*, vol. 12 (1966), pp. 323–34
P. Kjaerum, 'Mortuary houses and funerary rites in Denmark', *Antiquity*, vol. 41 (1967), pp. 190–6.
O. Klindt-Jensen, *Denmark before the Vikings*. London: Thames and Hudson, 1960
R. H. J. Klok, *Hunebedden in Nederland*. Haarlem: Fibula-Van Dishoeck, 1979
T. Madsen, 'Earthen long barrows and timber structures: aspects of early neolithic mortuary practice in Denmark', *Proceedings of the Prehistoric Society*, vol. 45 (1979), pp. 301–20

P. J. R. Modderman, 'The neolithic burial vault at Stein', *Analecta Praehistorica Leidensia* (1964)

M. Muller-Wille, 'Allées couvertes françaises et Steinkisten allemandes', *Congrès préhistorique de France, 16th session, Monaco, 1959*, pp. 904–19

E. Schuldt, *Die Mecklenburgischen Megalithgräber: Untersuchungen zu ihrer Architektur und Funktion*. Berlin: Deutscher Verlag der Wissenschaften, 1972. (Beiträge zur Ur- und Frühgeschichte der Bezirke Rostock, Schwerin und Neubrandenburg, no. 6)

E. Sprockhoff, *Die nordische Megalithkultur*. Berlin: W. de Gruyter, 1938

E. Sprockhoff, *Atlas der Megalithgräber Deutschlands*. Bonn: Römisch-germanische Kommission der Deutschen Archäologischen Institut, 1965–7

M. Strömberg, *Der Dolmen Trollasten in St. Köpinge, Schonen*. Lund: C. W. K. Gleerups Förlag (*Acta Archaeologia Lundensia*, vol. 7)

M. Strömberg, *Die Megalithgräber von Hagestad: zur Problematik von Grabbauten und Grabriten*. Lund: C. W. K. Gleerups Förlag (*Acta Archaeologia Lundensia*, vol. 8)

M. Strömberg, 'Megalithgräber bei Hagestad', in G. E. Daniel and P. Kjaerum (ed.), *Megalithic graves and ritual: papers presented at the III Atlantic Colloquium, Moesgård, 1969*, pp. 81–92. Copenhagen: Jutland Archaeological Society, 1973. (Jutland Archaeological Society Publications 11)

3. The British Isles: Channel Islands, England, Ireland, Scotland, Wales

V. A. Aleskin, 'Burial customs as an archaeological source', *Current Anthropology*, vol. 24 (1983), no. 2, pp. 137–50

A. ApSimon, 'L'architecture du dolmen de Tregiffian à Saint-Burgan (Cornwall) et la question des relations mégalithiques entre l'ouest de la France et la Grande-Bretagne', in *L'architecture mégalithique*, pp. 15–29. Vannes: Société Polymathique du Morbihan, 1977

P. Ashbee, 'The Fussell's Lodge long barrow', *Archaeologia*, vol. 100 (1966), pp. 1–80

P. Ashbee, *The earthen long barrow in Britain*. London: Dent, 1970. (Second edition, Norwich: Geo Books, 1984)

P. Ashbee, *Ancient Scilly: from the first farmers to the early Christians*. Newton Abbott: David & Charles, 1974

P. Ashbee, *The ancient British: a social-archaeological narrative*. Norwich: Geo Abstracts, 1978

P. J. Hartnett, *The excavation of two tumuli at Fourknocks (sites II and III)*. Dublin: Royal Irish Academy, 1971

J. Hawkes, *The archaeology of the Channel Islands*, vol. 2, *The bailiwick of Jersey*. Jersey: Société Jersiaise, 1937

A. S. Henshall, *The chambered tombs of Scotland*. Edinburgh: Edinburgh University Press, 1963–72

A. S. Henshall, 'Scottish chambered tombs and long mounds', in C. Renfrew (ed.), *British prehistory: a new outline*, pp. 137–64. London: Duckworth, 1974

M. Herity, 'Irish Sea and Scandinavian passage graves', in G. E. Daniel and P. Kjaerum (ed.), *Megalithic graves and ritual: papers presented at the III Atlantic Colloquium, Moesgård, 1969*, pp. 129–35. Copenhagen: Jutland Archaeological Society, 1973. (Jutland Archaeological Society Publications 11)

M. Herity, *Irish passage graves*. Dublin: Irish Universities Press, 1974

M. Herity and G. Eogan, *Ireland in Prehistory*. London: Routledge & Kegan Paul, 1977

T. D. Kendrick, *The archaeology of the Channel Islands*, vol. 1, *The bailiwick of*

Guernsey. London: Methuen, 1928

I. Kinnes, 'Monumental function in British burial practices', *World Archaeology*, vol. 7 (1975), pp. 16–29

I. Kinnes, 'Les Fouillages and megalithic origins', *Antiquity*, vol. 56 (1982), pp. 24–30

I. Kinnes, *Les Fouillages and the megalithic monuments of Guernsey*. 1983

I. Kinnes and R. Burns, 'The Channel islands: archaeology and early history', in P. M. Eadie, *Blue Guide to the Channel islands*, pp. 9–26. London: Ernest Benn, 1981

F. Lynch, 'The megalithic tombs of north Wales', in T. G. E. Powell (ed.), *Megalithic enquiries in the west of Britain*, pp. 107–48. Liverpool: Liverpool University Press, 1969

F. Lynch, *Prehistoric Anglesey*. Llangefai: Anglesey Antiquarian Society, 1970

F. Lynch, 'Portal dolmens in the Nevern valley, Pembrokeshire', in F. Lynch and C. Burgess (ed.), *Prehistoric man in Wales and the west*, pp. 67–84. Bath: Adams and Dart, 1972

F. Lynch, 'Towards a chronology of megalithic tombs in Wales', in G. C. Boon and J. M. Lewis (ed.), *Welsh antiquity: essays presented to H. N. Savory*, pp. 63–79. Cardiff, 1976

T. G. Manby, 'Excavation of the Kilham long barrow, East Riding of Yorkshire', *Proceedings of the Prehistoric Society*, vol. 42 (1976), pp. 111–59

L. Masters, 'The chambered tombs of Scotland', *Antiquity*, vol. 48 (1974), pp. 34–9

L. Masters, 'Chambered tombs and non-megalithic barrows in Britain', in J. D. Evans, B. Cunliffe and A. C. Renfrew (ed.), *Antiquity and man: essays in honour of Glyn Daniel*, pp. 161–76. London: Thames and Hudson, 1981

J. V. S. Megaw and D. D. A. Simpson, *Introduction to British prehistory*. Leicester: Leicester University Press, 1979

J.-P. Mohen, 'Les mégalithes d'Irlande', *Archéologia*, no. 173 (December 1982), pp. 14–18

F. de M. Morgan, 'The excavation of a long barrow at Nutbane, Hants.', *Proceedings of the Prehistoric Society*, vol. 25 (1959), pp. 15–51

C. O'Kelly, 'Passage grave art in the Boyne valley', *Proceedings of the Prehistoric Society*, vol. 39 (1973), pp. 354–82

C. O'Kelly, *Illustrated guide to Newgrange and the other Boyne monuments*. Cork, 1978

M. J. O'Kelly, 'Bryn Celli Ddu, Anglesey: a reinterpretation', *Archaeologia Cambrensis*, vol. 118 (1969), pp. 17–48

M. J. O'Kelly, 'Current excavations at Newgrange, Ireland', in G. E. Daniel and P. Kjaerum (ed.), *Megalithic graves and ritual: papers presented at the III Atlantic Colloquium, Moesgård, 1969*, pp. 137–46. Copenhagen: Jutland Archaeological Society, 1973. (Jutland Archaeological Society Publications 11)

M. J. O'Kelly, 'The megalithic tombs of Ireland', in J. D. Evans, B. Cunliffe and A. C. Renfrew (ed.), *Antiquity and man: essays in honour of Glyn Daniel*, pp. 177–90. London: Thames & Hudson, 1981

M. J. O'Kelly, *Newgrange: archaeology, art and legend*. London: Thames & Hudson, 1982

M. J. O'Kelly, F. Lynch, and C. O'Kelly, 'Three passage graves at Newgrange', *Proceedings of the Royal Irish Academy*, section C, vol. 78 (1978), pp. 249–352

S. Ó Nuallain, 'Boulder burials', *Proceedings of the Royal Irish Academy*, section C, vol. 78 (1978), pp. 75–114

S. Ó Nuallain, 'The megalithic tombs of Ireland', *Expedition*, vol. 21, pp. 6–15

S. Piggott, *The West Kennet long barrow*. London: Her Majesty's Stationery Office, 1962

S. Piggott, 'Unchambered long barrows in Britain', *Palaeohistoria*, vol. 12 (1967), pp. 381–93

S. Piggott, 'Problems in the interpretation of chambered tombs', in G. E. Daniel and P. Kjaerum (ed.), *Megalithic graves and ritual: papers presented at the III Atlantic Colloquium, Moesgård, 1969*, pp. 9–15. Copenhagen: Jutland Archaeological Society, 1973. (Jutland Archaeological Society Publications 11)

T. G. E. Powell (ed.), *Megalithic enquiries in the west of Britain*. Liverpool: Liverpool University Press, 1969

T. G. E. Powell, 'Excavation of the megalithic chambered cairn at Dyffryn Ardudwy, Merioneth, Wales', *Archaeologia*, vol. 104 (1973), pp. 1–49

T. G. E. Powell and G. Daniel, *Barclodiad y Gawres*. Liverpool: Liverpool University Press, 1956

R. C. Reed, 'Earthen long barrows: a new perspective', *Archaeological Journal*, vol. 131 (1974), pp. 33–57

C. Renfrew, *Investigations in Orkney*. London: Society of Antiquaries, 1979. (Research Report no. 38)

J. N. G. Ritchie, 'Excavation of the chambered cairn at Achnacreebeag', *Proceedings of the Society of Antiquaries of Scotland*, vol. 102 (1973), pp. 31–55

M. Ryan, 'Survol historique de la culture irlandaise', in *Catalogue de l'exposition 'Trésors d'Irlande' au Grand-Palais, Paris*, pp. 17–76. Paris, 1982

A. Saville, 'Hazleton', *Current Archaeology*, vol. 87, no. 4 (1983), pp. 107–12

J. G. Scott, 'The Clyde cairns of Scotland', in T. G. E. Powell (ed.), *Megalithic enquiries in the west of Britain*, pp. 175–222. Liverpool: Liverpool University Press, 1969

J. G. Scott, 'The Clyde cairns of Scotland', in G. E. Daniel and P. Kjaerum (ed.), *Megalithic graves and ritual: papers presented at the III Atlantic Colloquium, Moesgård, 1969*, pp. 117–28. Copenhagen: Jutland Archaeological Society, 1973. (Jutland Archaeological Society Publications 11)

M. Shanks and C. Tilley, 'Ideology, symbolic power and ritual communication: a reinterpretation of neolithic mortuary practices', in I. Hodder (ed.), *Symbolic and structural archaeology*, pp. 129 54. Cambridge: Cambridge University Press.

D. Simpson, 'Timber mortuary houses and earthen long barrows', *Antiquity*, vol. 42 (1968), pp. 142–4

4. France and Switzerland

J. Abelanet, 'Les dolmens du Roussillon', in J. Guilaine (ed.), *Les civilisations néolithiques du Midi de la France*, pp. 74–9. Carcassone: Gabelle, 1970

J. Abelanet, 'Roussillon, province méconnue du mégalithisme', *Archéologia*, no. 83 (1975), pp. 16–21

G.-B. Arnal, *Les mégalithes du Lodevois (Hérault). I, Groupe archéologique. II, L'ensemble mégalithique de Saint-Pierre-de-la-Fage*. Lodève: Imprimerie des Beaux Arts, 1961–79. (Mémoire du Centre de Recherche Archéologique du Haut-Languedoc, no. 11)

J. Arnal, *Les dolmens du département de l'Hérault*. Paris: Presses Universitaires de la France, 1963. (*Préhistoire*, vol. 15)

J. Arnal and L. Balsan, 'Les longs tumulus à dolmen décentré du département de l'Aveyron', *Gallia-Préhistoire*, vol. 23 (1980), no. 1, pp. 183–207

J. Arnal and C. Burnez, 'Les longs tumulus en France', in *Congrès International de Hambourg*, p. 27, 1958

S. Arnette, 'Allées couvertes Seine-Oise-Marne dans la région d'Esbly', *Gallia-Préhistoire*, vol. 4 (1961), pp. 17–89

P. Ayroles, J. Della Libera, and G. Taupenas, 'Coup d'oeil sur la mégalithisme de la Haute-Ardèche', *Études préhistoriques*, no. 12 (1975), pp. 41–7

G. Bailloud, *Le Néolithique dans le bassin parisien*. 2nd supplement to *Gallia-Préhistoire*. Paris: CNRS, 1964

F. Bauman, J. Tarrette, Y. Taborin, E. Patte, A. Roblain-Jouve, and M. Girard, 'La sépulture collective des Maillets à Germiny-L'Évêque (Seine-et-Marne)', *Gallia-Préhistoire*, vol. 22 (1979), no. 1, pp. 143–204

O. S. Bocksberger (edited by A. Gallay), 'Le dolmen MVI: le site préhistorique du Petit-Chasseur (Sion-Valais) 1 et 2', *Cahiers d'Archéologie Romande*, vols. 6–7 (1976)

A. Bocquet, 'La tombe de Verna (Isère) et les mégalithes alpins', *Études préhistoriques*, vol. 13 (1976), pp. 23–32

M. Brézillon and J. Tarrete, 'Deux sculptures inédités de l'allée couverte de la Pierre-Turquaise à Saint-Martin-du-Tertre (Val-d'Oise)', *Gallia-Préhistoire*, vol. 14 (1971), no. 2, pp. 263–5

J. Briard, 'Mégalithes et tumulus de l'Age du Bronze: La "Dame de Kersandy", Plouhinec, Finistère', in *L'Architecture mégalithique*, pp. 31–47. Vannes: Société Polymathique de Morbihan, 1977

C. Burnez, *Le Néolithique et la Chalcolithique dans le Centre-Ouest de la France. Mémoires de la Société Préhistorique Française*, vol. 12 (1976). Paris: Klincksieck

C. Burnez and C. Gabet, 'Destruction du tumulus géant de la Grosse-Motte á Bouhet (Charente-Maritime)', *Bulletin de la Société Préhistorique Française*, vol. 64 (1967), pp. 633–8

R. Caillaud and E. Lagnel, 'Le cairn et la crématoire néolithiques de la Hoguette à Fontenay-la-Marmion (Calvados)', *Gallia-Préhistoire*, vol. 15 (1972), pp. 137–85

M. Carrière and J. Clottes, 'Le dolmen du Pech numéro 1 à Alvignac (Lot)', *Gallia-Préhistoire*, vol. 13 (1970), no. 1, pp. 109–49

M.-C. Cauvin, *Les industries postglaciaires du Périgord*. Paris: Maisonneuve, 1971

P.-R. Chaigneau, 'Les dolmens vendéens', *Société d'Émulation de la Vendée* (1966–7), pp. 17–31

C. Chauchat, *Sept dolmens nouveaux dans le massif de Xoldokogaña (Urrugne). Bulletin du Musée Basque*, vol. 33 (1966)

G. Chauvet and E. Lièvre, 'Les tumulus de la Boixe (Charente)', *Bulletin de la Société Archéologique de la Charente* (1877), pp. 35–78

J. Clottes, 'Les dolmens du Rat (Saint-Sulpice, Lot) et du Pech d'Arsou (Corn, Lot) et leurs stèles aniconiques', *Gallia-Préhistoire*, vol. 9 (1966), no. 2, pp. 387–404

J. Clottes, *Inventaire des mégalithes de la France*, vol. 5, *Lot*. 1st supplement to *Gallia-Préhistoire. Paris:* CNRS, 1977

J. Clottes, 'Le mégalithisme en Quercy', in *L'Architecture mégalithique*, pp. 49–70. Vannes: Société Polymathique du Morbihan, 1977

J. Clottes and M. Lorblanchet, 'Le dolmen du Verdier, Carjac (Lot)', *Bulletin de la Société Préhistorique Française*, vol. 65 (1968), pp. 559–74

J.-R. Colle, 'Inventaire des mégalithes de la Charente-Maritime', *Les Cahiers de l'Ouest*, no. 27 (1959), pp. 40–7

G. Cordier, *Inventaire des mégalithes de la France*, vol. 1, *Indre-et-Loire*. 1st supplement to *Gallia-Préhistoire*. Paris: CNRS, 1963

G. Cordier, 'Le "dolmen" des Marais de Villerable (Loir-et-Cher)', *Bulletin de la Société Archéologique, Scientifique et Littéraire du Vendômois* (1968), pp. 45–64

G. Cordier, Riquet, H. Brabant, and T. Poulain, 'Le site archéologique du dolmen de Villaine à Sublaines (Indre-et-Loire)', *Gallia-Préhistoire*, vol. 15 (1972), no. 1, pp. 1–135

J. Courtin, *Le Néolithique de la Provence. Mémoires de la Société Préhistorique Française*, vol. 11. Paris: Klincksieck, 1974

J. Courtin, 'Les dolmens de Provence', in *UISPP IX Congrès, Livret-guide de l'excursion B2*, pp. 11–18. Nice: UISPP, 1976

L. Coutil, 'Les monuments mégalithiques de la Normandie (dolmens, allées couvertes, menhirs, polissoirs)', in *Congrés préhistorique de France*, pp. 654–7. Paris, 1907

L. Coutil, *Les tumulus de la Hogue à Fontenay-la-Marmion, Calvados: étude des tumulus néolithiques du Calvados et de l'Orne*. Le Mans: Société Préhistorique Française, 1918

G. E. Daniel, *The prehistoric chamber tombs of France: a geographical, morphological and chronological survey*. London: Thames & Hudson, 1960

J. Degros, J. Tarrete, C. Girard, C. Monmignaut, F. Poplin, and M. Girard, 'Observations sur l'allée couverte du Bois-Couturier à Guiry-en-Vexin (Val-d'Oise)', *Gallia-Préhistoire*, vol. 18 (1975), no. 2, pp. 423–51

J. Despriée and C. Leymarios, *Inventaire des mégalithes de la France*, vol. 3, *Loire-et-Cher*. 1st supplement to *Gallia-Préhistoire*. Paris: CNRS, 1974

H. Duday and J. Guilaine, 'Les rites funéraires en Languedoc et Roussillon du Néolithique au Premier Age du Fer', *Cahiers Ligures*, vol. 24 (1975), pp. 141–51

G. Fabre, *La civilisation protohistorique de l'Aquitaine: suivi du répertoire des découvertes protohistoriques faites dans las départements des Landes, Basses et Hautes-Pyréneés, Gers, Lot-et-Garonne*. Paris: Picard, 1952

C. Gabet, 'Les dolmens de la région de Rochefort', *Bulletin de la Société de Géographie de Rochefort*, 2nd series, vol. 1, nos. 7/8/10/11 (1961–4)

A. Gallay, 'Recherches préhistoriques au Petit-Chasseur à Sion', *Helvetica Archeologia*, vols. 10–11 (1972), pp. 35–61

A. Gallay, 'Constitution et analyse des données archéologiques dans un site mégalithique', in *UISPP IX Congrès: Colloque IV*, pp. 107–32. Nice: UISPP, 1976

A. Gallay, 'Stèles néolithiques et problématique archéologique', *Archives Suisses d'Anthropologie Générale*, vol. 42 (1978), no. 2, pp. 75–103

A. Galley, L. Chaix, and R. Menk, *Sion, Petit-Chasseur (Valais-Suisse), Dolmen M XI: problèmes d'élaboration, stage d'étude 1974*. Geneva: Département d'Anthropologie de l'Université, 1974

A. Gallay and K. Spindler, 'Le Petit-Chasseur, problèmes chronologiques et culturels', *Helvetia Archeologia*, vols. 10–11 (1972), pp. 62–89

G. Gaucher, C. Girard, J. Leclerc, T. Poulain, A. Roblain-Jouve, F. Guillon, D. Jagu, 'La sépulture Seine-Oise-Marne de Pincevent (La Grande Paroisse, Seine-et-Marne)', *Gallia-Préhistoire*, vol. 23 (1980), no. 1, pp. 115–51

E. Gauron and J. Massaud, *Nécropole de Chenon (Charente)*. 18th supplement to *Gallia-Préhistoire*. Paris: CNRS, 1983

G. Germond, *Inventaire des mégalithes de la France*, vol. 6, *Deux-Sèvres*. 1st supplement to *Gallia-Préhistoire*. Paris: CNRS, 1980

G. Germond and R. Joussaume, 'Le tumulus du Montiou à Sainte-Soline (Deux-Sèvres)', *Bulletin de la Société Historique et Scientifique des Deux-Sèvres*, vol. 11 (1978), nos. 2–3, pp. 129–88

P.-R. Giot, 'Le tumulus de Kermené en Guidel (Morbihan)', *Annales de Bretagne*, vol. 66 (1959), pp. 5–30

P.-R. Giot, *Barnenez*. Rennes: Direction des Antiquités Préhistoriques de Bretagne, 1970

P.-R. Giot, 'Réflexions sur la signification symbolique des mégalithes', in *Mélanges offerts à A. Varagnac*, pp. 333–9. 1971

P.-R. Giot, 'Les leçons finales du cairn de Barnenez', in G. E. Daniel and P. Kjaerum (ed.), *Megalithic graves and ritual: papers presented at the III Atlantic Colloquium, Moesgård, 1969*, pp. 197–201. Copenhagen: Jutland Archaeological Society, 1973. (Jutland Archaeological Society Publications 11)

P.-R. Giot, 'Dolmens et menhirs, le phénomène mégalithique en France', in J. Guilaine (ed.), *La préhistoire française*, vol. 2, *Les civilisations néolithiques et protohistoriques de la France*, pp. 202–10. Paris: CNRS, 1976

P.-R. Giot *et al.*, *UISPP IX Congrès, livret-guide de l'excursion A3: Bretagne*. Nice: UISPP, 1976

P.-R. Giot, 'Le rituel funéraire, les mégalithes et la religion néolithique', in

L'Architecture mégalithique, pp. 7–14. Vannes, 1977

P.-R. Giot, J. Briard and J. L'Helgouach, 'Fouilles de l'allée couverte de Men-Ar-Rompet à Kerbors', *Bulletin de la Société Préhistorique Française*, vol. 54 (1957), no. 9, pp. 493–502

P.-R. Giot, J. Briard and J. L'Helgouach, 'L'allée couverte de Men-Art-Rompet à Kerbors', *Gallia-Préhistoire*, vol. 1 (1958), pp. 67–77

P.-R. Giot and J. L'Helgouach, 'Le tertre tumulaire de la Croix-Saint-Pierre en Saint-Just (Ille-et-Vilaine)', *Annales de Bretagne*, vol. 62 (1955), no. 2, pp. 282–92

P.-R. Giot and J. L'Helgouach, 'Fouille du tertre tumulaire de Notre-dame de Lorette au Quillio (Côtes-du-Nord)', *Annales de Bretagne*, vol. 63 (1956), pp. 22–8

P.-R. Giot, J. L'Helgouach, and J.-L. Monnier, *Préhistoire de la Bretagne*. Rennes: Ouest-France, 1979

M. Gruet, *Inventaire des mégalithes de la France*, vol. 2, *Maine-et-Loire*. 1st supplement to *Gallia-Préhistoire*. Paris: CNRS, 1967

M. Gruet, 'L'ossuaire semi-mégalithique de Chacé (Maine-et-Loire)', *Bulletin de la Société Préhistorique Française*, vol. 70 (1973), pp. 385–400

M. Gruet and J.-B. Glotin, 'L'allée couverte de Pontpiau en Champtocé (Maine-et-Loire)', *Bulletin de la Société Préhistorique Française*, vol. 69 (1969), no. 2, pp. 585–98

J. Guilaine, *Premiers bergers et paysans de l'Occident méditerranéen*. Paris: Mouton, 1976

J. Guilaine, 'Dolmen des Fades (Pépieux-Aude)', in *UISPP IX Congrès, livret-guide de l'excursion C2*, pp. 267–8. Nice: UISPP, 1976

J. Guilaine, 'Les civilisations néolithiques dans les Pyrénées', in J. Guilaine (ed.), *La préhistoire française*, vol. 2, *Les civilisations néolithiques et protohistoriques de la France*, pp. 326–7. Paris: CNRS, 1976

J. Guilaine with H. Duday and J. Lavergne, *La nécropole mégalithique de la Clape, Laroque-de-Fa, Aude*. Carcassone: Laboratoire de Préhistoire et de Palethnologie, 1972

J. Guilaine and J. Vaquer, 'Dolmen de Saint-Eugène (Laure-Minervois, Aude)', in *UISPP IX Congrès, livret-guide de l'excursion C2*, pp. 269–71. Nice: UISPP, 1976

X. Gutherz, 'Dolmen de Feuilles (Rouet, Hérault)', in *UISPP IX Congrès, livret-guide de l'excursion C2*, pp. 213–16. Nice: UISPP, 1976

C. Hebras, 'Fouille d'un dolmen du groupe de Monpalais, commune de Taizé (Deux-Sèvres)', *Bulletin de la Société Préhistorique Française*, vol. 57 (1960), nos. 11–12, pp. 666–71

C. Hebras, 'Le dolmen E136 du groupe de Monpalais, commune de Taizé (Deux-Sèvres)', *Bulletin de la Société Préhistorique Française*, vol. 62 (1965), no. 1, pp. 139–58

J. Joly, 'Les tombes mégalithiques du département de la Côte-d'Or', *Revue Archéologique de l'Est et du Centre-Est*, vol. 16 (1965), pp. 57–74

R. Joussaume, 'Le dolmen à couloir dit "La Ciste des Cous" à Bazoges-en-Pareds (Vendée)', *Bulletin de la Société Préhistorique Française*, vol. 75 (1978), nos. 11–12, pp. 579–96

R. Joussaume, *Le Néolithique de l'Aunis et du Poitou occidental dans son cadre atlantique*. Rennes: Université de Rennes I, 1981

R. Joussaume with M. Gruet, 'Dolmen de Pierre Levée à Nieul-sur-L'Autize (Vendée)', *Bulletin de la Société Préhistorique Française*, vol. 73 (1976), pp. 398–421

R. Joussaume with M. Gruet, 'Le mégalithe de la Pierre Virante à Xanton-Chassenon (Vendée)', *L'Anthropologie*, vol. 81 (1977), no. 1, pp. 5–66

R. Joussaume with J. L'Helgouach, J.-P. Mohen, M. Gruet, A. Arnaud, M. Brabant, and T. Poulain, 'Le dolmen angevin de la Pierre Folle à Thiré (Vendée)', *Gallia-Préhistoire*, vol. 19 (1976), no. 1, pp. 1–67

J. Leclerc and C. Masset, 'Construction, remaniements et condamnation d'une sépulture collective néolithique: la Chaussée-Tirancourt (Somme)', *Bulletin de la Société Préhistorique Française*, vol. 71 (1980), no. 2, pp. 57–64

A. Leroi-Gourhan, G. Bailloud, M Brézillon, and C. Monmignaut, 'L'hypogée II des Mournouards (Mesnil-sur-Oger, Marne)', *Gallia-Préhistoire*, vol. 5 (1962), no. 1, pp. 23–133

C. T. Le Roux and Y. Lecerf, 'Le dolmen de Gruguellic en Ploemeur et les sépultures transeptées armoricaines', in *L'Architecture mégalithique*, pp. 143–60. Vannes: Société Polymathique du Morbihan, 1977

C. T. Le Roux and J. L'Helgouach, 'Le cairn mégalithique avec sépultures à chambres compartimentées de Kerleven, commune de la Forêt-Fouesnant (Finistère)', *Annales de Bretagne*, vol. 74 (1967), pp. 7–52

Z. Le Rouzic, *Tumulus de Mont-Saint-Michel (1900–1906)*. Vannes 1932

J. L'Helgouach, 'Le dolmen de Conguel à Quiberon (Morbihan)', *Bulletin de la Société Préhistorique Française*, vol. 59 (1962), nos. 5–6, pp. 371–81

J. L'Helgouach, *Les sépultures mégalithiques en Armorique (dolmens à couloirs et allées couvertes)*. Rennes: Laboratoire d'Anthropologie Préhistorique, 1965

J. L'Helgouach, 'Fouilles de l'allée couverte de Prajou-Menhir en Trébeurden (Côtes-du-Nord)', *Bulletin de la Société Préhistorique Française*, vol. 63 (1966), pp. 311–42

J. L'Helgouach, 'Les sépultures mégalithiques à entrée latérale', in J. D. van der Waals (ed.), *Neolithic studies in Atlantic Europe: proceedings of the second Atlantic colloquium, Groningen, 1964, pp. 259–81*. Groningen, 1967 (*Palaeohistoria* vol. 12)

J. L'Helgouach, 'Le monument mégalithique à entrée latérale de Crec'h Quillé en Saint-Quay-Perros (Côtes-du-Nord)', *Bulletin de la Société Préhistorique Française*, vol. 64 (1970), pp. 659–98

J. L'Helgouach, 'Le monument mégalithique de Goerem à Gâvres (Morbihan)', *Gallia-Préhistoire*, vol. 13 (1970), no. 2, p. 217

J. L'Helgouach, 'Les mégalithes de l'ouest de la France: évolution et chronologie', in G. E. Daniel and P. Kjaerum (ed.), *Megalithic graves and ritual: papers presented at the III Atlantic Colloquium, Moesgård, 1969*, pp. 203–19. Copenhagen: Jutland Archaeological Society, 1973. (Jutland Archaeological Society Publications 11)

J. L'Helgouach, 'Le tumulus de Dissignac à Saint-Nazaire (Loire-Atlantique) et les problèmes du contact entre le phénomène mégalithique et les sociétés à industrie microlithique', in S. J. de Laet (ed.), *Acculturation and continuity in Atlantic Europe mainly during the Neolithic period and the Bronze Age: papers presented at the IV Atlantic Colloquium, Gant, 1975*, pp. 142–9. Bruges, 1976. (*Archaeologicae Gandanses*, vol. 16)

J. L'Helgouach, 'Le cairn des Mousseaux à Pornic (Loire-Atlantique), nouvelles fouilles et restaurations', in *L'Architecture mégalithique*, pp. 143–60. Vannes: Société Polymathique du Morbihan, 1977

J. L'Helgouach, 'Le site mégalithique de "Min Goh Re" près de Larcuste à Colpo (Morbihan)', *Bulletin de la Société Préhistorique Française*, vol. 73 (1976), pp. 370–97

C. Masset, D. Mordant, C. Mordant, T. Poulain, R. Baron, J.-L. Demetz, C. Monmignaut, P. Horemans, F. Poplin, and I. L. Roux, 'Les sépultures collectives de Marolles-sur-Seine (Seine-et-Marne)', *Gallia-Préhistoire*, vol. 10 (1967), no. 1, pp. 75–167

J.-P. Mohen, 'Les tumulus de Bougon', *Bulletin de la Société Historique et Scientifique des Deux-Sèvres*, nos. 2–3 (1973) and nos. 2–3 (1977)

J.-P. Mohen, 'La construction des dolmens et menhirs au Néolithique', *Dossiers d'Archéologie*, no. 46 (1980), pp. 58–67

A. Nouel, M. Dauvois, G. Bailloud, R. Riquet, T. Poulain, N. Planchais, and P. Horemans, 'L'ossuaire néolithique d'Éteauville, commune de Lutz-en-Dunois (Eure-et-Loire)', *Bulletin de la Société Préhistorique Française*, vol. 62 (1966), no. 3, pp. 576–648

B. Pajot and J. Clottes with C. Bouville and F. Delpech, 'Le dolmen Q du Frau à Cazals (Tarn-et-Garonne)', *Bulletin de la Société Préhistorique Française*, vol. 72 (1975), pp. 382–414

É. Patte, 'Quelques sépultures du Poitou du Mésolithique au Bronze moyen', *Gallia-Préhistoire*, vol. 14 (1971), no. 1, pp. 139–244

J. Peek, *Inventaire des mégalithes de la France*, vol. 4, *Région parisienne*. 1st supplement to *Gallia-Préhistoire*. Paris: CNRS, 1975

P. Pétrequin and J.-F. Piningre, 'Les sépultures collectives mégalithiques de Franche-Comté', *Gallia-Préhistoire*, vol. 19 (1976), no. 2, pp. 287–394

É. Pothier, *Les tumulus du plateau de Ger*. Paris, 1900

G. Richard and J. Vintrou, 'Les sépultures néolithiques sous dalles des "Marsaules" et de "La Chaise" à Malesherbes (Loiret)', in *Préhistoire et protohistoire en Champagne-Ardennes: colloque interrégional sur la Néolithique de l'est de la France, pp. 175–81*. Chalons-sur-Marne: Association d'Etudes Prehistoriques et Protohistoriques de Champagne-Ardenne, special number, 1980

O. Roudil and G. Bérard, *Les sépultures mégalithiques du Var*. Paris: CNRS, 1981

J. Roussot-Larroque, 'Les civilisations néolithiques en Aquitaine', in J. Guilaine (ed.), *La préhistoire française*, vol. 2, *Les civilisations néolithiques et protohistoriques de la France*, pp. 338–50. Paris: CNRS, 1976

H. de Saint-Blanquat, 'Une nécropole mégalithique', *Sciences at Avenir*, no. 369 (1977), pp. 60–5

M.-R. Sauter and J.-C. Spanni, 'Révision des dolmens de la Haute-Savoie (France)', *Archives Suisses d'Anthropologie Générale*, vol. 14 (1949), pp. 152–68

G. Sauzade, 'Le dolmen de Peicervier à Lorgues (Var) et les poignards à soie courte en silex poli du Midi de la France', *Bulletin du Muséum d'Histoire Naturelle de Marseille*, vol. 35 (1975), pp. 241–57

G. Sauzade, 'Le dolmen de Coutignargues, commune de Fontvieille (Bouches-du-Rhône)', *Congrès préhistorique de France, 20ème session, Provence, 1974*, pp. 567–80. Paris: Société Préhistorique Française, 1977

G. Sauzade, 'Monuments mégalithiques de Fontvieille (Bouches-du-Rhône)', in *UISPP IX Congrès, livret-guide de l'excursion C2*, pp. 189–91. Nice: UISPP, 1976

G. Sauzade, *Les sépultures du Vaucluse du Néolithique à l'Age du Bronze*. Aix: Université de Provence, 1983

J. Tarrete, 'Les gravures de l'allée couverte de la Cave-aux-Fées à Brueil-en-Vexin (Yvelines)', *Bulletin de la Société Préhistorique Française*, vol. 75 (1978), no. 8, pp. 241–9

J.-P. Thevenot and H. Carré, 'Les civilisations néolithiques de la Bourgogne', in J. Guilaine (ed.), *La préhistoire française*, vol. 2, *Les civilisations néolithiques et protohistoriques de la France*, p. 413. Paris: CNRS, 1976

G. Verron, 'L'ensemble mégalithique de La Butte à Vierville (Manche)', in *UISPP IX Congrès, livret-guide de l'excursion A3: Bretagne*, pp. 17–23. Nice: UISPP, 1976

G. Verron, 'Un type de monuments funéraires classique dans le Néolithique de Normandie: les cairns en pierre sèche contenant des chambres sépulcrales de plan circulaire, montées en encorbellement et reliées à l'éxtérieur par un couloir d'accès', in *L'Architecture mégalithique*, pp. 188–219. Vannes: Société Polymathique du Morbihan, 1977

5. *The Iberian peninsula: Spain and Portugal*

M. J. Almagro Gorbea, *Las tres tumbas megalíticas de Almizaraque*. Madrid, 1965 (*Trabajos de prehistoria*, vol. 18)

M. J. Almagro Gorbea, *El poblado y la necrópolis de El Barranquete (Almería)*. Madrid, 1973. (*Acta arquelogica hispánica*, vol. 6)

M. J. Almagro Gorbea and A. Arribas, *El poblado y la necropólis megalíticos de Los Millares (Santa Fe de Mondújar, Almería)*. Madrid, 1963. (*Bibliografia Praehistorica Hispana*, vol. 3.)

M. J. Almagro Gorbea and M. Fernandez Miranda, *C14 y la Prehistoria de la Peninsula Ibérica*. Madrid, 1978

J. Altuna, *Guide illustré de préhistoire basque*. 1975

J.-M. Apellániz Castroviejo, *Monumentos megalíticos de Vizcaya y Alava*. *Munibe*, vol. 17 (1965)

J.-M. Apellániz Castrovijo and J. Altuna Echave, 'Excavaciones en dolmenes de Guipúzcoa', *Munibe*, vol. 18 (1966), nos. 1–4, pp. 167–84

T. de Aranzadi and F. de Ansoleaga, *Exploración de cinco dólmenes del Aralar*. Pamplona, 1915

J. M. Arnaud, 'O megalitismo en Portugal: problemas e perspectivas', in *Actas das III Jornadas Arqueológicas*, pp. 91–112. Lisbon: Associacâo dos Arqueólogos Portugueses, 1978

A. Arribas, 'El sepulcro megalítico del Cabecico de Aguilar de Cuartillas (Mojácar, Almería)', *Ampurias*, vols. 17–18 (1955–6), pp. 210–14

A. Arribas, 'Megalitismo peninsular', in *Primer Symposium de prehistoria de la Peninsula iberica, Pamplona, 1959*, pp. 69–102. 1960

A. Arribas and J. M. Sanchez del Corral, 'La necrópolis megalitica del Pantano de los Bermejalas (Arenas del Rey, Granada)', in *XIe Congreso nacional de Arqueologia*, pp. 284–91. 1970

J. M. de Barandiaràn, *El hombre prehistorico en el Pais Vasco*. Buenos Aires, 1953

J. M. de Barandiaràn, 'En el Pirineo Vasco: prospecciones y excavaciones prehistoricas', *Munibe* (1962), nos. 3–4

P. Bosch-Gimpera, 'Civilisation mégalithique portugaise et civilisations espagnoles', *L'Anthropologie*, vol. 71 (1967), nos. 1–2, pp. 1–48

R. W. Chapman, 'Transhumance and megalithic tombs in Iberia', *Antiquity*, vol. 53 (1979), pp. 150–2

R. W. Chapman, 'The megalithic tombs of Iberia', in J. D. Evans, B. Cunliffe and C. Renfrew (ed.), *Antiquity and man: essays in honour of Glyn Daniel*, pp. 93–106. London: Thames & Hudson, 1981

A. Cipres, F. Galilea and L. Lopes, 'Dolmenes y tumulos de las Sierras de Guibijo y Badaya: plantamiento para su estudio a la vista de los ultimos decubrimientos', *Estudios de Arqueologia Alavesa*, vol. 9 (1978), pp. 65–125

F. Colantes de Teran, 'El dolmen de Matarrubilla', in *Tartessos y sus problemas: V symposium internacional de prehistoria peninsular*. Barcelona

V. Correia, *El Neolítico de Pavia (Alentejo-Portugal)*. Madrid: Musco Nacional de Ciencias Naturales, 1921

M. Cura-Moréra and J. Castells, 'Évolution et typologie des mégalithes de Catalogne', in *L'Architecture mégalithique*, pp. 71–97. Vannes: Société Polymathique du Morbihan, 1977

M. Cura-Moréra and A. M. Ferran Ramis, *Sepulcros megaliticos de la Sierra de Roca*. Barcelona, 1970

M. Cura-Moréra. J. Guilaine and J. Thommeret, 'Une datation C14 du dolmen da Llanera (Solsona)', *Pyrenea*, vol. 2

G. E. Daniel, 'Spain and the problem of European megalithic origins', in *Estudios dedicados al Professor Dr Luis Pericot*, pp. 209–14. Barcelona: Universidad de Barcelona Instituto de Arqueología y Prehistoria, 1973. (Publicaciones Eventuales 23)

L. Esteva-Cruanas, *Sepulcros megalíticos de Las Gabarras (Gerona)* Gerona, 1964–70

M. Farinha Dos Santos, 'Dolmens et menhirs de l'Alentejo', *Dossiers d'Archéologie*, no. 4 (1974), pp. 10–19

G. Gallay, 'Étude anthropologique des restes humaines trouvés dans la sépulture de Roça do Casal do Meio', *Communicações dos Serviços Geológicos de Portugal*, vol. 57 (1973–4), pp. 183–202

M. Garcia-Sanchez and J. C. Spanhi, 'Sepulcros megalíticos de la région de Gorafe (Granada)', *Archivo de Prehistoria Levantina*, vol. 8 (1959), pp. 43–113

J. Guilaine and A.-M. Munos, 'La civilisation catalane des sepulcros de fosa et les sépultures néolithiques du sud de la France', *Cahiers d'Études Ligures*, vol. 30 (1964), pp. 1–4

V. O. Jorge, 'O megalitismo do Norte de Portugal', *Actas da Mesa Redonda sobre o Neolitico e o Calcolitico em Portugal*. Porto, 1979, pp. 83–102

V. O. Jorge, 'Escavação da mamoa 1 de Outeiro de Gregos, Serra da Aboboreira, Baião', *Portugalia*, vol. III (1980), pp. 9–28

V. O. Jorge, 'Escavação da Mamoa 3 de Outeiro de Ante (Serra da Aboboreira, Concelho de Baião', *Actas do Seminário de Arqueologia do Noroeste Peninsular*, vol. I, pp. 41–69. Guimarães, 1980

V. O. Jorge, 'Le mégalithisme du nord du Portugal: un premier bilan', *Bulletin de la Société Préhistorique Française*, vol. 79 (1982), no. 1, pp. 15–22

V. O. Jorge, 'À propos d'un travail récent sur le mégalithisme du nord du Portugal', *L'Anthropologie*, vol. 87 (1983), no. 1, pp. 145–6

V. O. Jorge, 'Tres dólmenes do distrito do Porto', *Arqueologia*, no. 8 (1983), pp. 103–9

G. Leisner, 'A cultura eneolítica do Sul da Espanha e suas relações com Portugal', *Arqueologia e Historia*, 8 série, vol. 1 (1945), pp. 11–28. Lisbon: Associação dos Arquéologos Portugueses

G. Leisner, *Antas dos Arredores de Évora*. Évora: Éd. Nazareth, 1949

G. Leisner and V. Leisner, *Die Megalithgräber der iberischen Halbinsel: der Süden*. Berlin: Romisch-Germanische Kommission, 1943

G. Leisner and V. Leisner, *Antas do Concelho de Reguengos de Monsaraz*. Lisbon: Instituto para Alta Cultura.

G. Leisner and V. Leisner, *Die Megalithgräber der iberischen Halbinsel: der Westen*, Band I. Berlin: Walter de Gruyter, 1956. (Madrider Forschungen, vol. 1)

G. Leisner and V. Leisner, *Die Megalithgräber der iberischen Halbinsel: der Westen*, Band II. Berlin, Walter de Gruyter, 1959

V. Leisner, *Die Megalithgräber der iberischen Halbinsel: der Westen*, Band III. Berlin: Walter de Gruyter, 1965

V. Leisner, 'Die Dolmen von Carapito', *Madrider Mitteilungen*, vol. 9 (1968), pp. 11–62

V. Leisner, G. Zbyszewski and O. da Veiga Ferreira, *Les grottes artificielles de Casal do Pardo (Palmela) et la culture du vase campaniforme*. Lisbon: Serviços Geológicos de Portugal, 1961. (Mémoire 8)

V. Leisner, G. Zbyszewski and O. da Veiga Ferreira, *Les monuments préhistoriqes de Praia das Maças et de Casainhos*. Lisbon: Serviços Geológicos de Portugal, 1961. (Mémoire 16)

H. Losada, 'El dolmen de Entreterminos (Madrid)', *Trabajos de Prehistoria*, vol. 33 (1976), pp. 209–26

J. Maluquer de Motes y Nicolau, *Notes sobre la cultura megalitica navarra*. Barcelona: Universidad de Barcelona Instituto de Arquaologia y Prehistoria, 1964

C. Cerdán Márquez, G. Leisner and V. Leisner, *Los sepulcros megalíticos de Huelva*. Madrid: Ministerio de Educación Nacional, 1952

A. M. Munoz, *La cultura neolítica catalana de los 'sepulcros de fosa'*. Barcelona: Universidad de Barcelona, 1965

L. Pericot-Garcia, *Los sepulcros megalíticos catalanes y la cultura pirenaïca*. Barcelona, 1950

E. Ripoll Perelló and M. Llongueras Campaña, *La cultura neolítica de los sepulcros de fosa en Cataluña*. Barcelona: Instituto de Prehistoria y Arqueologia, 1963

A. Casal Rodriguez, 'O megalitismo na Galiza: a sua problemática e o estado actual da investigación', *Actas da la Mesa Redonda sobre o Neolitico e o Calcolitico en Portugal*, Porto, 1978, pp. 103–14

J. Ruiz Solanes, 'Para el estudio estadistico de los sepulcros megalíticos', *XII Congreso Nacional de Arqueologia*, pp. 201–10. 1973

V. dos Santos Gonçalves, *A neolitização e o megalitismo da região de Alcobaça*. Lisbon, 1978

H. N. Savory, 'The role of the upper Duero and Ebro basins in megalithic diffusion', *Boletin del Seminario de Estudios de Arte et Arqueologia*, vols. 40–41 (1975), pp. 159–74

H. N. Savory, 'The role of Iberian communal tombs in Mediterranean and Atlantic prehistory', in V. Markotic (ed.), *Ancient Europe and the Mediterranean*, pp. 161–80. Warminster: Aris & Phillips, 1977

E. Shee and C. Garcia Martinez, 'Tres tumbas megalíticas decoradas en Galicia', *TP*, vol. 30

J. Soares and C. Tavares da Silva, 'Portugal: la poterie préhistorique', *Dossiers d'Archéologie*, no. 4 (May–June 1974), pp. 35–45

K. Spindler, A. de Castello Branco, G. Zbyszewski and O. da Veiga Ferreira, 'Le monument à coupole de l'Age du Bronze Final de la Roça do Casal do Meio (Calhariz)', *Communicações dos Serviços Geológicos de Portugal*, vol. 57 (1973–4), pp. 91–154

K. Spindler and A. Gallay, 'Die tholos von Pai Mogo, Portugal', *Sonderdruck aus den Madrider Mitteilungen*, vol. 13

J. L. Uribarri Angulo, *El fenomeno megalitico en la provincia de Burgos*. Burgos: Publicaciones de la Institución Fernam Gonzales, 1975

A. Viana, O. da Veiga Ferreira, and R. Freire de Andrade, 'Descoberta de dois monumentos de falsa cúpula na região de Ourique', *Revista de Guimarães*, vol. 71 (1961), pp. 5–12

A. Victor Guerra and O. da Veiga Ferreira, 'Inventário dos monumentos megalíticos dos arredores da Figueira da Foz', *Arquivo de Beja*, 25–27 (1968–70), pp. 45–56

M. J. Walker, 'Laying a mega-myth: dolmens and drovers in prehistoric Spain', *World Archaeology*, vol. 15 (1983), no. 1, pp. 37–50

G. Zbyszewski and O. da Veiga Ferreira, 'Acerca duma "tholos" encontrada en Castro Marim', *O Arqueológo Português*, 3rd series, vol. 1 (1967), pp. 11–17

G. Zbyszewski, O. da Veiga Ferreira, M. Leitão, C. T. North, and J. Norton, 'Le monument de "Pedras da Granja" ou de "Pedras altas" dans la "Várzea de Sintra"', *Ciências da Terra (UNL)*, no. 3 (1977), pp. 197–239

6. The west Mediterranean islands, south Italy, and north Africa

CORSICA

G. Camps, 'La préhistoire dans la région d'Aléria', *Archeologia Corsa*, no. 4 (1979), pp. 5–21

R. Grosjean, *La Corse avant l'histoire*. Paris: Klincksieck, 1966

R. Grosjean, 'Classification descriptive du mégalithique corse: classification typologique et morphologique des menhirs et statues-menhirs de l'île', *Bulletin de la Société Préhistorique Française*, vol. 44 (1967), pp. 707–42

R. Grosjean with J. Liégeois and G. Péretti, 'Les civilisations de l'Age du Bronze en Corse', in J. Guilaine (ed.), *La préhistoire française*, vol. 2, *Les civilisations néolithiques et protohistoriques de la France*, pp. 644–53. Paris: CNRS, 1976

F. Lanfranchi and M.-C. Weiss, *La civilisation des Corses, les origines*. 1973

J. Lewthwaite, 'The Neolithic of Corsica', in C. Scarre (ed.), *Ancient France: neolithic societies and their landscapes 6000–2000 b.c.*, pp. 146–83. Edinburgh: Edinburgh University Press, 1984

M.-C. Weiss and F. Lanfranchi, 'Les civilisations néolithiques de la Corse', in J. Guilaine (ed.), *La préhistoire française*, vol. 2, *Les civilisations néolithiques et protohìstoriques de la France*, pp. 432–42. Paris: CNRS, 1976

SARDINIA

E. Acquaro, *Sardegna: itinerari archeologici*. Rome: Newton Caupton, 1979
J. Audibert, 'Préhistoire de la Sardaigne', *Bulletin du Musée d'Anthropologie Préhistorique de Monaco*, fasc. 5
E. Castaldi, 'Tombe di Giganti nel Sassarese', *Origini*, vol. 3, pp. 119–274
E. Castaldi, *Domus nuragiche*. De Luca, 1976
E. Contu, *Il significato delle 'stele' nelle tombe di giganti*. Rome. (*Quadermi*, vol. 8)
G. Lilliu, *La civiltà dei Sardi dal Neolitico all'eta del Nuraghi*. 2nd edition. Turin: Edizioni Radiotelevisione Italiana, 1975
R. Whitehouse, 'Megaliths of the central mediterranean', in J. D. Evans, B. Cunliffe and C. Renfrew (ed.), *Antiquity and man: essays in honour of Glyn Daniel*, pp. 106–27. London: Thames & Hudson, 1981
C. Zervos, *La civilisation de la sardaigne du début de l'Énéolithique à la fin de la période nouragique*. Paris: Cahiers d'Art, 1954

BALEARIC ISLANDS

M. Doria, 'Les monuments cyclopéens des îles Baléares', *Travaux du Laboratoire d'Anthropologie, de Préhistoire et d'Ethnologie d'Aix-en-Provence* (1974)
V. Grinsell, *Barrow, pyramid and tomb: ancient burial customs in Egypt, the Mediterranean and the British Isles*. London: Thames & Hudson, 1975
R. Grosjean, 'Les Baléares et leurs rapports avec la Méditerranée occidentale', *L'Anthropologie*, vol. 65 (1961), nos. 5–6, pp. 491–501
R. Grosjean, 'Destination et utilisation primaire des nuraghi, talaiots, torre (Sardaigne, Baléares, Corse)', *Actes du VIIIe Congrès International des sciences pré- et protohistoriques, Belgrade, 1971*. 1974
G. Rossello-Bordoy, 'Majorque préhistorique et ses relations avec la Méditerranée occidentale', *Congrès Préhistorique de France, XVIIIe session, Ajaccio*, pp. 288–94. Paris: Société Préhistorique Française, 1966

MALTA

J. D. Evans, *The prehistoric antiquities of the Maltese islands*. London: Athlone
J. Guilaine, 'Les mégalithes de Malte', *La Recherche*, no. 125 (1981), pp. 962–71
D. Trump, *Malta: an archaeological guide*. London: Faber & Faber, 1972
D. Trump, 'Megalithic architecture in Malta', in J. D. Evans, B. Cunliffe and C. Renfrew (ed.), *Antiquity and man: essays in honour of Glyn Daniel*, pp. 128–40. London: Thames & Hudson, 1981

ITALY

G. Palumbo, 'Inventario dei dolmen di YTerra d'Otranto', *Rivista di Scienca Prehistorica*, vol. 11 (1956). pp. 84–108
S. M. Puglisi, 'Civiltà appenninica a sapoolcri di tipo dolmenico à Pian Sultano (San Severa)', *Rivista de Antropologia*, vol. 61 (1954), pp. 3–32
S. M. Puglisi, *La civiltà appenninica: origine delle communità pastorali in Italy*. Florence: Istituto Italiano di Preistoria e Protoistoria, 1959
R. Whitehouse, 'Megaliths of the central Mediterranean', in J. D. Evans, B. Cunliffe and C. Renfrew (ed.), *Antiquity and man: essays in honour of Glyn Daniel*, pp. 106–27. London: Thames & Hudson, 1981

NORTH AFRICA

G. Camps, *Aux origines de la Berberie: monuments et rites funéraires protohistoriques*. Paris: Délégation Générale en Algérie, 1962
G. Camps, 'Essai de classifications des monuments protohistoriques de l'Afrique du Nord', *Bulletin de la Societé Préhistorique Française*, vol. 62 (1965), pp. 476–81
N. Lambert and G. Souville, 'La nécropole de Tayadirt (Moyen Atlas Marocain): note préliminaire', in *Congrès Préhistorique de la France, XVIIIe session, Ajaccio*, pp. 217–29. Paris: Société Prehistorique Française, 1966
M. Reigasse, *Monuments funéraires préislamiques de l'Afrique du Nord*. Paris, 1950
A. Ruhlmann, 'Le tumulus de Sidi Slimane (Rharb)', *Bulletin de la Societé Préhistorique du Maroc* (1930), pp. 37–70
G. Souville, 'Principaux types de tumulus marocains', *Bulletin de la Societé Préhistorique Française*, vol. 56 (1959), pp. 394–402
G. Souville, 'Élements nouveaux sur les monuments funéraires préislamiques du Maroc', *Bulletin de la Societé Préhistorique Française*, vol. 62 (1965), pp. 482–93

7. Africa, the Arabian peninsula, and Madagascar

ETHIOPIA

F. Anfray, *Les stèles du Sud: Shoa et Sidamo. Annales d'Éthiopie*, vol. 12 (1982)
F. Anfray, R. Joussaume, and C. Bouville, 'Des milliers de stèles en Éthiopie', *Archéologie*, no. 185 (1983), pp. 34–47
M. Azais and R. Chambard, *Cinq années de recherches archéologiques en Éthiopie*. Paris, 1931
R. Joussaume, 'Le mégalithisme en Éthiopie', *Archéologia*, no. 64 (1973), pp. 20–33
R. Joussaume, *Le mégalithisme en Éthiopie: monuments funéraires protohistoriques du Harar*. Addis Ababa: Service Culturel de l'Ambassade de France, 1974

CENTRAL AFRICAN REPUBLIC, CAMEROON, AND WEST AFRICA

P. Allison, *Cross River monoliths*. Lagos: Federal Republic of Nigeria, Department of Antiquities, 1968
R. de Bayle des Hermens, *Recherches préhistoriques en République Centrafricaine*. Paris: Université de Paris X, Laboratoire d'Ethnologie et de la Sociologie Comparative, 1975
A. Marliac, 'Le mégalithisme au Cameroun', *Archéologia*, no. 93 (1976), pp. 58–60
C. Thilmans, C. Descamps, and B. Khayat, *Protohistoire du Sénégal: les sites mégalithiques*. Dakar: IFAN, 1980
P. Vidal, *La civilisation mégalithique de Bouar: prospection et fouilles 1962–1966*. Paris, 1969. (Recherches Oubanguiennes, vol. 1)

ARABIAN PENINSULA

R. de Bayle des Hermens, 'Première mission de recherches préhistoriques en République arabe du Yémen', *L'Anthropologie*, vol. 80 (1976), pp. 5–38
R. de Bayle des Hermens and D. Grebenart, 'Deuxième mission de recherches préhistoriques en République arabe du Yémen', *L'Anthropologie*, vol. 84 (1980), pp. 563–82
G. Benardelli and A. Parinello, 'Note su alcune località archeologiche del Yemen', *Istituto Orientale di Napoli*, vol. 30 (1970), fasc. 1, pp. 117–20
G. Bibby, *Looking for Dilmun*. London: Collins, 1970
C. Blanc, P. Bouvier, and A. Planes, 'Monolithes phalliformes et pierres levées en TFAI', *Pount*, no. 9 (1971), pp. 13–15

M. Palgrave, *Narrative of a year's journey through central and eastern Arabia (1862–63)*. London: Macmillan, 1865

MADAGASCAR

M. Bloch, *Placing the dead: tombs, ancestral villages and kinship organisation in Madagascar*. London: Seminar Press, 1971
R. P. Callet. *Histoire des rois (Tantaran'ny andriana)*. Tananarive: Éditions Librairie de Madagascar, 1974. (Translation by G. S. Chapus and E. Ratsimba of the original 1909 edition)
H. Descamps, *Histoire de Madagascar*. Paris, 1972
R. Joussaume and V. Raharijaona, 'Sépultures mégalithiques à Madagascar', *Bulletin de la Société Préhistorique Française*, vol. 83, 1986
A. Mille, *Contribution à l'étude des villages fortifiées de l'Imerina ancien*. Tananarive: Musée d'Art et d'Archéologie de Tananarive, 1970. (Travaux et Documents, vols. 2–3)
S. Raharijaona, 'Les pierres levées à Madagascar', *Revue de Madagascar*, no. 20 (1962), pp. 17–30
C. Renel, 'Ancêtres et dieux', *Bulletin de l'Academie Malgache*, vol. 5 (1920–21)
P. Vérin, 'Le problème des origines malgaches', *Taloha*, vol. 8 (1979), pp. 41–55. Tananarive: Musée d'Art et d'Archéologie
P. Vérin, *La Mort et l'ancêtre à Madagascar* (exhibition catalogue). Bordeaux: Musée d'Aquitaine, 1985

8. Palestine, Caucasus, India, Far East, and Colombia

PALESTINE

L. Lartet, 'Géologie de la Palestine, 2e partie: paléontologie', *Annales des Sciences Géologiques*, vol. 3 (1872). pp. 16–25
M. Stékélis, *Les monuments mégalithiques de Palestine*. Paris: Institut de Paléontologie Humaine, 1935. (Archives de l'Institut de Paléontologie Humaine, Mémoires, no. 15)
M. Stékélis, 'Las necrópolis megalitica de Ala-Safat, Transjordania', *Ampurias*, vols. 22–3 (1960–1), pp. 49–128
M. Tallon, 'Monuments mégalithiques de Syrie et du Liban', *Mélanges de l'Université Saint-Joseph*, vol. 35 (1958), pp. 21–34

CAUCASUS

E. Chantre, 'Monuments mégalithiques', in E. Chantre, *Recherches Anthropologiques dans le Caucase*. Paris, 1885–7
N. G. Gorbounova and N. K. Katchalova, 'Énéolithique: les agriculteurs du Sud', in *Avant les Scythes: préhistoire de l'art en URSS*, pp. 76–81. Paris: Éditions de la Réunion des Musées Nationaux, 1979
V. I. Markovin, 'Quelques résultats des études sur les monuments mégalithiques du Caucase occidental', *Antiquités Nationales et internationales*, nos. 14–16 (1963), pp. 42–51
E. A. Martel, 'Les dolmens taillés du Caucase occidental', in *1er Congrès Préhistorique de France, Périgueux, 1905*, pp. 31–7. Paris: SPF, 1906
T. Sulimirski, *Prehistoric Russia: an outline*. New York: Humanities Press, 1970
M. P. Zavitoukhina and Y. Y. Piotrovsky, 'Age du Bronze', in *Avant les Scythes: préhistoire de l'art en URSS*, pp. 107–26. Paris: Editions de la Réunion des Musées Nationaux, 1979

INDIA

N. R. Banerjee, 'Le problème des mégalithes aux Indes', *Antiquités Nationales*, vols.
3–4 (1960), pp. 63–77

A. K. Sundara, *The early chamber tombs of south India*. Delhi: University Publishers
(India), 1975

A. K. Sundara, *Megalithic architecture in southern India*. Columbia (Missouri):
University of Missouri, 1975

R. E. M. Wheeler, 'Brahmagiri and Chandravalli, 1947: megalithic and other cultures
in Mysore State', *Ancient India*, vol. 4 (1947–8), pp. 180–310

FAR EAST

J. Gon Gy, *Le mégalithisme d'Extrême-Orient: typologie, chronologie, originalité par
rapport au mégalithisme occidental*. Rennes: Université de Haute-Bretagne, 1981

W. Gowland, 'The dolmens and burial mounds in Japan', *Archaeologia*, vol. 55
(1897), pp. 439–524

M. Kômoto, 'Megalithic monuments in ancient Japan', *International symposium of
the comparative study of the megalithic culture in Asia*. Seoul, 1981

T. Migami, 'Dolmens et cistes en Mandchourie et en Corée', *Antiquités Nationales et
Internationales*, nos. 11–12 (1962), pp. 70–6

T. Migami, *Les dolmens et les coffres de la Mandchourie et de Corée*. Tokyo, 1977

COLOMBIA

J. Alcina Franch, *Manual de arqueologia americana*. Madrid, 1965

S. Cassen, 'Sépultures mégalithiques et stèles funéraires de Huila en Colombie',
Groupe Vendée d'Études Préhistoriques, no. 4 (1980), pp. 25–31

L. Duque-Comez, *Exploraciones arqueologicas en San Agustin*. Bogotá, 1966

K. Preuss, *Arte monumental prehistórico*. Bogotá, 1974

G. Reichel-Dolmatoff, *San Agustín: a culture of Colombia*. London, 1972

T. Stopel-Karl, *Archaeological discovery in Ecuador and southern Columbia during
1911 and the ancient stone monuments of San Agustín*. London, 1912

9. Megalithic art

M. Péquart, S. Péquart, and Z. Le Rouzic, *Corpus des signes gravés des monuments
mégalithiques du Morbihan*. 1927

T. G. E. Powell, *Prehistoric Art*. London: Thames & Hudson, 1966

E. Shee, 'Techniques of Irish passage grave art', in G. E. Daniel and P. Kjaerum (ed.),
*Megalithic graves and ritual: papers presented at the III Atlantic Colloquium,
Moesgård, 1969*, pp. 163–71. Copenhagen: Jutland Archaeological Society, 1973.
(Jutland Archaeological Society Publications 11)

E. Shee, 'L'art mégalithique de l'Europe occidentale', in *Actas de las primeras
jornadas de metodologia aplicado de las ciencias historicas, Santiago de Compostela*,
vol. 1, pp. 101–20. 1975

E. Shee Twohig, *The megalithic art of western Europe*. Oxford: Clarendon, 1981

Index